高等学校规划教材

河南省"十四五"普通高等教育规划教材

化学化工专业英语

第三版

张裕平　王丙星　龚文君　主编

化学工业出版社

·北京·

内容简介

《化学化工专业英语》(第三版)选材广泛,使用专业面宽,采用递进式写作,首先是概括性的学科描述性短文,宏观介绍化学化工学科的特点以及各二级学科、实验室工作的特点;其次是描述化工过程单元操作及基础化工知识的短文;然后是代表性精读文章,内容涉及普通化学、无机化学、有机化学、分析化学、物理化学、材料科学及制药工程等;最后为化学专业术语,并进行了简单解释,可作为选读内容。本书每篇文章后对一些重难点句型进行了分析和解释,对一些专业词汇标注了音标,对一些语法和构词规律进行了分析,以帮助读者更好地理解本书内容。

本书可作为高等院校化学、化工、材料等专业本科生的专业英语教材,也可供相关专业的从业人员参考使用。

图书在版编目(CIP)数据

化学化工专业英语/张裕平,王丙星,龚文君主编. —3版. —北京:化学工业出版社,2021.7(2024.2重印)
高等学校规划教材
ISBN 978-7-122-39066-0

Ⅰ.①化… Ⅱ.①张…②王…③龚… Ⅲ.①化学-英语-高等学校-教材②化学工业-英语-高等学校-教材 Ⅳ.①H31

中国版本图书馆CIP数据核字(2021)第080942号

责任编辑:宋林青　　　　　　　装帧设计:关　飞
责任校对:王素芹

出版发行:化学工业出版社(北京市东城区青年湖南街13号　邮政编码100011)
印　　刷:北京云浩印刷有限责任公司
装　　订:三河市振勇印装有限公司
787mm×1092mm　1/16　印张15½　字数439千字　2024年2月北京第3版第5次印刷

购书咨询:010-64518888　　　　　售后服务:010-64518899
网　　址:http://www.cip.com.cn
凡购买本书,如有缺损质量问题,本社销售中心负责调换。

定　价:39.80元　　　　　　　　　　　　　　　　　　版权所有　违者必究

前言

高等教育已逐步从过去的精英教育过渡到大众教育，目前出版的很多专业英语教材针对性太强，涉及的专业面较窄，导致某些学校二级学院具有多个化学或化工类专业的专业英语课程，学生所需购买的教材太多，同时在教师配备上也存在一定的困难，基于此，我们编写了这本对化学化工类专业普遍都适用的教材。本书第一版于2007年出版，面市之后得到了国内众多院校的认可，并提出了许多中肯的意见和建议。第二版于2013年出版，对第一版进行了一定程度的精简，但即便如此，我们在多年的讲授过程中仍然发现课本内容偏多，生词量过大，因大部分高校开设的专业英语课都在32～48学时。为使本书内容更加简洁适用，特在第二版的基础进行了一定程度的调整和修改。

本次修订整体增加了对不常见词汇的解释，修正了个别对课文的不当注释，增添了部分图例。Part A，精简了部分内容，使课文更简洁，更通俗易懂。Part B，删除了部分晦涩难懂的短文。Part C，删除了部分基本理论方面的内容，增加了相关专业的内容，比如应用化学、材料化学和制药工程的相关内容等。

本书第三版仍然保留了第二版分成四部分的结构，Part A 共 8 课，主要是宏观介绍化学、化工学科的特点，对四大基础化学（无机化学、有机化学、分析化学和物理化学）分别进行了阐述，另外还介绍了实验室安全、实验记录以及普通化学实验仪器等共性的知识。Part B 由第二版的 50 个小短文缩减为 40 个，主要描述化工过程单元操作及介绍基础化工知识。Part C 是精读部分，共 18 课，内容涉及普通化学、无机化学、有机化学、分析化学、物理化学、材料科学及制药工程等。Part D 主要是化学专业术语，对常用化学各学科专业术语进行简单解释，可作为选读部分。每篇文章后有对重难点句子的注释，很多文章中附有插图，以增加可读性。本书涉及的词汇量较大，对专业词汇均注有音标和一些构词规律，对一些语法现象也进行了解释和分析，书尾列有常用化学化工词汇的英语详细注释。该教材可作为高等院校化学、化工、材料及相关专业本科生的专业英语教学用书,也可作为化学和化工领域的教学、科研和工程技术人员的自学用书。

本书由河南科技学院张裕平、王丙星、龚文君任主编,张毅军、冯瑞(南阳医学高等专科学校)、白秀芝、陈军、陈娜、崔乘幸、杨胜凯、李永芳任副主编,另外多位老师为此书的再版提出了宝贵意见和帮助,再次深表谢意!

由于水平所限,加上时间仓促,难免有不足之处,恳请读者在使用过程中能多提宝贵意见和建议。

编者
2021 年 3 月

Contents

Part A Comprehensive Articles 1

1. Chemistry: a Science for the Twenty-First Century 1
2. What is a Chemical Engineer? 9
3. Applications of Inorganic Chemistry 15
4. The Map of Organic Chemistry 20
5. Introduction to Analytical Chemistry 24
6. What is Physical Chemistry? 30
7. Working in the Lab 34
8. Basic Laboratory Apparatus and Manipulation 38

Part B Basic Knowledge of Chemical Engineering 45

1. Chemical Engineering 45
2. The Difference Between Engineering and Science 45
3. Pipe Lines 46
4. Valve 46
5. Centrifugal Pump 47
6. Cyclone Separator 48
7. Cooling Tower 49
8. Membrane 49
9. Diffusion Process 50
10. Reverse Osmosis 50
11. Filtration 51
12. Evaporation 52
13. Crystallization 52
14. Drying 53
15. Mixing 53
16. Distillation 54
17. Adsorption 55
18. Reciprocating Compressor 55

19. Batch and Continuous Processes 56
20. Removal of Dust from Gases 57
21. Centrifugal Settling Processes 57
22. Heat Transfer 58
23. Heat Exchanger 59
24. Single and Multiple-Effect Evaporation Operation 60
25. Extraction 60
26. The Phenomenon of Fluidization 61
27. Applications of Size Reduction 62
28. Screening 63
29. Instrumentation and Control 64
30. The Material Balance 65
31. The Energy Balance 65
32. The Ideal Contact (the equilibrium stage model) 66
33. Rates of an Operation (the rate of transfer model) 66
34. Application of Computers in Chemical Engineering 66
35. Chemical Manufacturing Process 67
36. Biotechnology 69
37. Genetic Engineering 69
38. Tissue Culture 70
39. Cloning 70
40. Fermentation Technology 71

Part C General Chemistry 73

1. Introduction of General Chemistry 73
2. Chemical Bond and Bonding Theory 77
3. Brønsted Acids and Bases 81
4. Chemical Reaction and Equilibrium 86
5. Structure and Nomenclature of Hydrocarbons 91
6. Type of Organic Chemical Reactions 99
7. Briefing on Chemical Thermodynamics and Chemical Kinetics 105
8. Applied Chemistry 110
9. High Performance Liquid Chromatography and Capillary Electrophoresis 114
10. Structure Determination 120
11. Electrochemistry 131
12. How to Develop a New Pesticide 134
13. What is Materials Chemistry? 138
14. Materials Characterization 144
15. Nanotechnology 155
16. Ceramic 161
17. Biomaterials: Body Parts of the Future 166
18. The Future of Pharmaceutical Engineering 172

Part D Chemistry Glossaries 177

1. General Chemistry 177
　1.1　Atoms, Elements and Ions 177

1.2	Electrons in Atoms	180
1.3	Gases, Liquids and Solids	183
1.4	Solution	188
1.5	Reactions in Solution	191

2. Inorganic Chemistry 195
   2.1   The Periodic Table 195
   2.2   Chemical Bonds 197
   2.3   Redox Reactions 202
   2.4   Simple Compounds 204

3. Organic Chemistry 208
   3.1   Organic Chemistry 208
   3.2   Polymer 213

4. Analytical Chemistry 214
   4.1   Basic Terms 214
   4.2   Base Units 217

5. Physical Chemistry 222
   5.1   Energy and Chemical Change 222
   5.2   Reaction Rate 226
   5.3   The Quantum Theory 228

6. Other Related Chemistry 231
   6.1   Consumer Chemistry 231
   6.2   Environmental Chemistry 233
   6.3   Biochemistry 233

Appendix 235

   Appendix Ⅰ   IUPAC Names and Symbols of Elements 235
   Appendix Ⅱ   Laboratory Equipments 238

References 239

Part A

Comprehensive Articles

1. Chemistry: a Science for the Twenty-First Century

Chemistry is the study of matter and the changes it undergoes. Chemistry is often called the central science, because a basic knowledge of chemistry is essential for students majoring in biology, physics, geology, ecology, and many other subjects. Indeed, it is central to our way of life; without it, we would be living shorter lives in what we would consider primitive conditions, without automobiles, electricity, computers, and many other everyday conveniences.

Although chemistry is an ancient science, its modern foundation was laid in the nineteenth century, when intellectual and technological advances enabled scientists to break down substances into ever smaller components and consequently to explain many of their physical and chemical characteristics.[1] The rapid development of increasingly sophisticated technology throughout the twentieth century has given us even greater means to study things that cannot be seen with the naked eye. Using computers and special microscopes, for example, chemists can analyze the structure of atoms and molecules — the fundamental units on which the study of chemistry is based — and design new substances with specific properties, such as drugs and environmentally friendly consumer products.

As we enter the twenty-first century, it is fitting to ask what part the central science will have in this century. Almost certainly, chemistry will continue to play a pivotal role in all areas of science and technology. Before plunging into the study of matter and its transformation, let us consider some of the frontiers that chemists are currently exploring. Whatever your reasons for taking introductory chemistry, a good knowledge of the subject will better enable you to appreciate its impact on society and on you as an individual.[2]

Health and Medicine

Three major advances in the past century have enabled us to prevent and treat diseases. They are public health measures establishing sanitation systems to protect vast numbers of people from infectious disease; surgery with anesthesia, enabling physicians to cure potentially fatal conditions, such as an in flamed appendix; and the introduction of vaccines and antibiotics that make it possible to prevent diseases spread by microbes. Gene therapy promises to be the fourth revolution in medicine. Many other ailments, such as cancer, heart disease, and AIDS, result to an extent from impairment of one or more genes involved in the body's defenses. In gene therapy, a selected healthy gene is delivered to a patient's cell to cure or ease such disorders. To carry out such a procedure, a doctor must have a sound knowledge of the chemical properties of the molecular components involved. The decoding of the human genome, which comprises all of the genetic material in the human body and plays an essential part in gene therapy, relies largely on chemical techniques. [3]

Chemists in the pharmaceutical industry are researching potent drugs with few or no side effects to treat cancer, AIDS, and many other diseases as well as drugs to increase the number of successful organ transplants. [4] On a broader scale, improved understanding of the mechanism of aging will lead to a longer and healthier life span for the world's population.

Energy and the Environment

Energy is a by-product of many chemical processes, and as the demand for energy continues to increase, both in technologically advanced countries like the United States and in developing ones like China, chemists are actively trying to find new energy sources. Currently the major sources of energy are fossil fuels (coal, petroleum, and natural gas). The estimated reserves of these fuels will last us another 50~100 years at the present rate of consumption, so it is urgent that we find alternatives.

Solar energy promises to be a viable source of energy for the future. Every year the Earth's surface receives about 10 times as much energy from sunlight as is contained in all of the known reserves of coal, oil, natural gas, and uranium combined. [5] But much of this energy is "wasted" because it is reflected back into space. For the past 30 years, intense research efforts have shown that solar energy can be harnessed effectively in two ways. One is the conversion of sunlight directly to electricity using devices called photovoltaic cells. The other is to use sunlight to obtain hydrogen from water. The hydrogen can then be fed into a fuel cell to generate electricity. Although our understanding of the scientific process of converting solar energy to electricity has advanced, the technology has not yet improved to the point where we can produce electricity on a large scale at an economically acceptable cost. [6] By 2050, however, it has been predicted that solar energy will supply over 50 percent of our power needs.

Another potential source of energy is nuclear fission, but because of environmental concerns about the radioactive wastes from fission processes, the future of the nuclear industry in the United States is uncertain. Chemists can help to devise better ways to dispose off nuclear waste. Nuclear fusion, the process that occurs in the sun and other stars, generates huge amounts of energy without producing much dangerous radioactive waste. In another 50 years, nuclear fusion will likely be a significant source of energy.

Energy production and energy utilization are closely tied to the quality of our environment. A major disadvantage of burning fossil fuels is that they give off carbon dioxide, which is a greenhouse gas (that is, it promotes the heating of Earth's atmosphere), along with sulfur dioxide and nitrogen oxides, which result in acid rain and smog. By using fuel-efficient automobiles and more effective catalytic converters, we should be able to drastically reduce harmful auto emissions and improve the air quality in areas with heavy traffic. In addition, electric cars, powered by durable, longlasting batteries, should become more prevalent, and their use will help to minimize air pollution.

Materials and Technology

Chemical research and development in the twentieth century have provided us with new materials that have profoundly improved the quality of our lives and helped to advance technology in countless ways. A few examples are polymers (including rubber and nylon), ceramics (such as cookware), liquid crystals (like those in electronic displays), adhesives and coatings (for example, latex paint).

What is in store for the near future? One possibility is room-temperature superconductors. Electricity is carried by copper cables, which are not perfect conductors. Consequently, about 20 percent of electrical energy is lost in the form of heat between the power station and our homes. This is a tremendous waste. Superconductors are materials that have no electrical resistance and can therefore conduct electricity with no energy loss. Although the phenomenon of superconductivity at very low temperatures (more than 400 degrees Fahrenheit below the freezing point of water) has been known for over 80 years, a major breakthrough in the mid-1980s demonstrated that it is possible to make materials that act as superconductors at or near room temperature. Chemists have helped to design and synthesize new materials that show promise in this quest. The next 30 years will see high-temperature superconductors being applied on a large scale in magnetic resonance imaging (MRI), levitated trains, and nuclear fusion.

If we had to name one technological advance that has shaped our lives more than any other, it would be the computer. The "engine" that drives the ongoing computer revolution is the microprocessor—the tiny silicon chip that has inspired countless inventions, such as laptop computers and fax machines. The performance of a microprocessor is judged by the speed with which it carries out mathematical operations, such as addition. The pace of progress is such that since their introduction, microprocessors have doubled in speed every 18 months. The quality of any microprocessor depends on the purity of the silicon chip and on the ability to add the desired amount of other substances, and chemists play an important role in the research and development of silicon chips. For the future, scientists have begun to explore the prospect of "molecular computing", that is, replacing silicon with molecules. The advantages are that certain molecules can be made to respond to light, rather than to electrons, so that we would have optical computers rather than electronic computers.[7] With proper genetic engineering, scientists can synthesize such molecules using microorganisms instead of large factories. Optical computers also would have much greater storage capacity than electronic computers.

Food and Agriculture

How can the world's rapidly increasing population be fed? In poor countries, agricultural activities occupy about 80 percent of the workforce, and half of an average family budget is spent on foodstuffs. This is a tremendous drain on a nation's resources. The factors that affect agricultural production are the richness of the soil, insects and diseases that damage crops, and weeds that compete for nutrients. Besides irrigation, farmers rely on fertilizers and pesticides to increase crop yield. Since the 1950s, treatment for crops suffering from pest infestations has sometimes been the indiscriminate application of potent chemicals. Such measures have often had serious detrimental effects on the environment. Even the excessive use of fertilizers is harmful to the land, water, and air.

To meet the food demands of the twenty-first century, new and novel approaches in farming must be devised. It has already been demonstrated that, through biotechnology, it is possible to grow larger and better crops. These techniques can be applied to many different farm products, not only for improved yields, but also for better frequency, that is, more crops every year.[8] For example, it is known that a certain bacterium produces a protein molecule that is toxic to leaf-eating caterpillars. Incorporating the gene that codes for the toxin into crops enables plants to protect themselves so that pesticides are not necessary.[9] Researchers have also found a way to prevent pesky insects from reproducing. Insects communicate with one another by emitting and reacting to special molecules called pheromones. By identifying and synthesizing pheromones used in mating, it is possible to interfere with the normal reproductive cycle of common pests; for example, by inducing insects to mate too soon or tricking female insects into mating with sterile males. Moreover, chemists can devise ways to increase the production of fertilizers that are less harmful to the environment and substances that would selectively kill weeds.

The Study of Chemistry

Compared with other subjects, chemistry is commonly believed to be more difficult, at least at the introductory level. There is some justification for this perception; for one thing, chemistry has a very specialized vocabulary. However, even if this is your first course in chemistry, you already have more familiarity with the subject than you may realize. In everyday conversations we hear words that have a chemical connection, although they may not be used in the scientifically correct sense. Examples are "electronic", "equilibrium", "catalyst", "chain reaction", and "critical mass". Moreover, if you cook, then you are a practicing chemist! From experience gained in the kitchen, you know that oil and water do not mix and that boiling water left on the stove will evaporate. You apply chemical and physical principles when you use baking soda to leaven bread, choose a pressure cooker to shorten the time it takes to prepare soup, add meat tenderizer to a pot roast, squeeze lemon juice over sliced pears to prevent them from turning brown or over fish to minimize its odor, and add vinegar to the water in which you are going to poach eggs. Every day we observe such changes without thinking about their chemical nature. The purpose of this course is to make you think like a chemist, to look at the macroscopic world—the things we can see, touch, and measure directly—and visualize the particles and events of the microscopic world that we cannot experience without modern technology and our imaginations.

At first some students find it confusing that their chemistry instructor and textbook seem to be continually shifting back and forth between the macroscopic and microscopic worlds. Just keep in mind that the data for chemical investigations most often come from observations of large-scale phenomena, but the explanations frequently lie in the unseen and partially imagined microscopic world of atoms and molecules. In another words, chemists often see one thing (in the macroscopic world) and think another (in the microscopic world). Looking at the rusted car, for example, a chemist might think about the basic properties of individual atoms of iron and how these units interact with other atoms and molecules to produce the observed change.

The Scientific Method

All sciences, including the social sciences, employ variations of what is called the scientific method, a systematic approach to research. For example, a psychologist who wants to know how noise affects people's ability to learn chemistry and a chemist interested in measuring the heat given off when hydrogen gas burns in air would follow roughly the same procedure in carrying out their investigations. The first step is to carefully define the problem. The next step includes performing experiments, making careful observations, and recording information, or data, about the system—the part of the universe that is under investigation.

The data obtained in a research study may be both qualitative, consisting of general observations about the system, and quantitative, comprising numbers obtained by various measurements of the system. Chemists generally use standardized symbols and equations in recording their measurements and observations. This form of representation not only simplifies the process of keeping records, but also provides a common basis for communication with other chemists.

When the experiments have been completed and the data have been recorded, the next step in the scientific method is interpretation, meaning that the scientist attempts to explain the observed phenomenon. Based on the data that were gathered, the researcher formulates a hypothesis, a tentative explanation for a set of observations. Further experiments are devised to test the validity of the hypothesis in as many ways as possible, and the process begins anew.

After a large amount of data has been collected, it is often desirable to summarize the information in a concise way, as a law. In science, a law is a concise verbal or mathematical statement of a relationship between phenomena that is always the same under the same conditions. For example, Sir Isaac Newton's second law of motion, which you may remember from high school science, says that force equals mass times acceleration ($F=ma$). What this law means is that an increase in the mass or in the acceleration of an object will always increase its force proportionally, and a decrease in mass or acceleration will always decrease the force.

Hypotheses that survive many experimental tests of their validity may evolve into theories. A theory is a unifying principle that explains a body of facts and/or those laws that are based on them. Theories, too, are constantly being tested. [10] If a theory is disproved by experiment, then it must be discarded or modified so that it becomes consistent with experimental observations. Proving or disproving a theory can take years, even centuries, in part because the necessary technology may not be available. Atomic theory, which we will study later, is a case in point. It took more than 2000 years to work out this fundamental principle of chemistry proposed by Democritus, an ancient Greek philosopher. A more contemporary example is the Big Bang theory of the origin of the universe.

Scientific progress is seldom, if ever, made in a rigid, step-by-step fashion. Sometimes law precedes a theory; sometimes it is the other way around. Two scientists may start working on a project with exactly the same objective, but will end up taking drastically different approaches. Scientists are, after all, human beings, and their modes of thinking and working are very much influenced by their background, training, and personalities.

The development of science has been irregular and sometimes even illogical. Great discoveries are usually the result of the cumulative contributions and experience of many workers, even though the credit for formulating a theory or a law is usually given to only one individual. There is, of course, an element of luck involved in scientific discoveries, but it has been said that "chance favors the prepared mind". It takes an alert and well-trained person to recognize the significance of an accidental discovery and to take full advantage of it. More often than not, the public learns only of spectacular scientific breakthroughs. For every success story, however, there are hundreds of cases in which scientists have spent years working on projects that ultimately led to a dead end. And in which positive achievements came only after many wrong turns and at such a slow pace that they went unheralded. Yet even the dead ends contribute something to the continually growing body of knowledge about the physical universe. It is the love of the search that keeps many scientists in the laboratory.

New Words and Expressions

undergo [ˌʌndərˈgəu] v. 经历，承受
primitive [ˈprimətiv] adj. 原始的，远古的
convenience [kənˈviːniəns] n. 便利，方便
sophisticated [səˈfistikeitid] adj. 精密复杂的，高度发展的
naked [ˈneikid] adj. 肉眼的，无遮盖的
pivotal [ˈpivətl] adj. 关键的，枢轴的
frontier [ˈfrʌntiə] n. 前沿，新领域
sanitation [ˌsæniˈteiʃ(ə)n] n. 卫生，卫生设施
infectious [inˈfekʃəs] adj. 易传染的
vaccine [ˈvæksiːn] n. 疫苗
antibiotic [ˌæntibaiˈɔtik] n. 抗生素；adj. 抗生的
inheritance [inˈherit(ə)ns] n. 遗传，遗产
microbe [ˈmaikrəub] n. 微生物，细菌
microscope [ˈmaikrəskəup] n. 显微镜
inborn [inˈbɔːn] adj. 天生的，先天的
ailment [ˈeilm(ə)nt] n. 疾病，不宁，不安
impairment [imˈpeəm(ə)nt] n. 损害，损伤
decoding [ˈdiːˈkəudiŋ] n. 译码，解码
genome [ˈdʒiːnəum] n. 基因组，染色体组
pharmaceutical [ˌfɑː(r)məˈsjuːtik(ə)l] adj. 药物的
transplant [trænsˈplænt] v. 移植，移民；n. 移植，被移植物
aging [ˈeidʒiŋ] n. 老化，老龄化，衰老
fossil fuel n. 化石燃料
reserve [riˈzəːv] n. 储备，预备队员，保护区；v. 保留，预订，拥有
consumption [kənˈsʌmpʃn] n. 消费，消耗量，肺结核
alternative [ɔːlˈtəːrnətiv] n. 可供选择的事物；adj. 替代的，备选的，另类的
viable [ˈvaiəbl] adj. 能养活的，可行的

greenhouse gas 二氧化碳、甲烷等导致温室效应的气体
uranium [juˈreiniəm] n. 铀
photovoltaic [ˌfəutəuvɔlˈteiik] adj. 光电池的，光致电压的
fission [ˈfiʃən] n. 裂变；v. (使)裂变
carbon dioxide 二氧化碳
sulfur dioxide 二氧化硫
drastically [ˈdræstikəli] adv. 激烈地，彻底地
emission [iˈmiʃ(ə)n] n. 散发，发射，喷射
prevalent [ˈprev(ə)l(ə)nt] adj. 流行的
ceramics [səˈræmiks] n. 制陶术，制陶业
resistance [riˈzistəns] n. 电阻，阻力
adhesive [ədˈhiːsiv] n. 黏合剂；adj. 带黏性的，胶黏的
latex [ˈleiteks] n. 乳胶，橡胶
superconductor [ˌsuːpəkəndʌktə] n. 超导体
levitate [ˈleviteit] v. 使升空，使飘浮
microprocessor [ˌmaikrə(u)ˈprəusesə] n. 微处理器，单片机
laptop [ˈlæptɔp] n. 便携式电脑
budget [ˈbʌdʒit] n. 预算；vi. 做预算
irrigation [ˌiriˈgeiʃ(ə)n] n. 灌溉，冲洗
pesticide [ˈpestisaid] n. 杀虫剂，农药
infestation [ˌinfeˈsteiʃən] n. 感染，侵扰
indiscriminate [ˌindisˈkriminət] adj. 不加选择的，不分皂白的
detrimental [ˌdetriˈment(ə)l] adj. 有害的
caterpillar [ˈkætəpilə] n. 毛虫
incorporate [inˈkɔːpəreit] vi. 合并，混合
pesky [ˈpeski] adj. 烦恼的，讨厌的
nutrient [ˈnuːtriənt] n. 营养物，养分
pheromone [ˈferəməun] n. 信息素
sterile [ˈsterail] adj. 不育的，消过毒的

fertilizer ['fə:rtəlaizər] n. 肥料，化肥
leaven ['lev(ə)n] vt. 使发酵
tenderizer ['tendəraizə] n. 嫩肉粉
roast [rəust] n. 烤肉；v. 烤，焙
vinegar ['vinigə] n. 醋
poach [pəutʃ] vt. 水煮（荷包蛋）

rusted ['rʌstid] v. 生锈的
interpretation [intə:pri'teiʃ(ə)n] n. 解释，阐明，口译，通译
hypothesis [hai'pɔθisis] n. 假设
unify ['ju:nifai] vt. 统一，使成一体
disprove [dis'pru:v] v. 反驳，证明……为误

Phrases

plunge into   投入，跳入，开始
not only... but also...   不但……而且……
break down   分解
be delivered to   被输送到
carry out   完成，实现，贯彻，执行
in addition   另外

in store   贮藏着，保存着，准备着
interfere with   妨碍，干涉，干扰
trick sb. into   欺骗，坑人
take full advantage of   充分利用
keep in mind   谨记

Affixes

anti- 表示"反对，抵抗"；如 antibiotics, antibody, antilogarithm
in- 不，表示"否定，与……相反"，在字母 l 之前常用 il-，字母 r 之前常用 ir-，字母 b、m、p 之前常用 im-；如 indiscriminate, inability, illegal, irregular, impossible

Notes

1. Although chemistry is an ancient science, its modern foundation was laid in the nineteenth century, when intellectual and technological advances enabled scientists to break down substances into ever smaller components and consequently to explain many of their physical and chemical characteristics. "when" 引导的定语从句修饰先行词 "century"。参考译文：虽然化学是一门古老的科学，但是其现代基础却是在19世纪才建立起来的，当时知识和技术的进步使科学家们能把物质分解成更小的成分，从而能解释物质的很多物理和化学性质。

2. Whatever your reasons for taking introductory chemistry, a good knowledge of the subject will better enable you to appreciate its impact on society and on you as an individual. 参考译文：无论你学习基础化学的原因是什么，拥有丰富的化学知识将使你能更好地认识它对社会及个人的影响。

3. The decoding of the human genome, which comprises all of the genetic material in the human body and plays an essential part in gene therapy, relies largely on chemical techniques. "which" 引导的非限制性定语从句，对主句 "The decoding of the human genome" 起进一步解释和说明作用；非限制性定语从句与主句间要用逗号隔开。参考译文：破译人类基因组主要依赖于化学技术，这些基因组包括人体所有的遗传物质，这对基因疗法起重要作用。

4. Chemists in the pharmaceutical industry are researching potent drugs with few or no side effects to treat cancer, AIDS, and many other diseases as well as drugs to increase the number of successful organ transplants. "as well as" 是表示联合关系的连词，意思是"以及"。参考译文：制药行业的化学家们正在研发用于治疗癌症、艾滋病等疾病的副作用小或无副作用的特效药，以及能提高器官移植成功率的药物。

5. Solar energy promises to be a viable source of energy for the future. Every year earth's surface receives about 10 times as much energy from sunlight as is contained in all of

the known reserves of coal, oil, natural gas, and uranium combined. 参考译文：太阳能有望成为未来可能的能量来源。每年，地球表面接收到来自太阳光的能量是已知储量的煤，石油，天然气和铀中能量总和的大约10倍。

6. Although our understanding of the scientific process of converting solar energy to electricity has advanced, the technology has not yet improved to the point where we can produce electricity on a large scale at an economically acceptable cost. "although" 引导的是让步状语从句。参考译文：虽然我们对太阳能转换为电能的科学过程的认识已经有很大进步，但目前的技术还没达到能以经济合理的成本大规模发电的地步。

7. The advantages are that certain molecules can be made to respond to light, rather than to electrons, so that we would have optical computers rather than electronic computers. "rather than" 的意思是 "是……，而不是……"。参考译文：优点在于可以制备某种对光而不是对电子响应的分子，这样就可以制造出取代电子计算机的光学计算机。

8. These techniques can be applied to many different farm products, not only for improved yields, but also for better frequency, that is, more crops every year. "not only…but also…" 是表示联合关系的并列连词，其意思是 "不仅……而且……"。参考译文：生物技术可应用于多种农产品，不仅可以提高产量，而且还可提高收获次数，即每年收获更多的农作物。

9. For example, it is known that a certain bacterium produces a protein molecule that is toxic to leaf-eating caterpillars. Incorporating the gene that codes for the toxin into crops enables plants to protect themselves so that pesticides are not necessary. 参考译文：例如，已知某种细菌能合成一种对吃叶毛虫有毒的蛋白质分子。把编译这种毒素的基因转录到农作物上，将会使植物实现自我保护而不必再使用杀虫剂。

10. Hypotheses that survive many experimental tests of their validity may evolve into theories. A theory is a unifying principle that explains a body of facts and/or those laws that are based on them. Theories, too, are constantly being tested. 参考译文：经过多次实验来验证其正确性的假说可能最终会变成理论。理论是解释大量现象和/或基于这些现象得到的法则的统一原理。理论也是不断地被验证的。

2. What is a Chemical Engineer?

Chemical engineering is the study and practice of transforming substances at large scales for the tangible improvement of the human condition. Such transformations are executed to produce other useful substances or energy, and lie at the heart of vast segments of the chemical, petroleum, pharmaceutical, and electronic industries.

Chemical engineering differs from chemistry mainly in the focus on large scales. The definition of "large" is a bit arbitrary, of course, but is set mainly by the scale of useful commercial production. Typically, this scale ranges from barrels to tank cars, whereas the chemist tends to be concerned about sizes from vials to beakers.

For many years, most chemical engineers took jobs in the oil or petrochemical industry. Job functions typically involved the development or operation of processes to convert oil-based feedstocks into energy or other useful chemical products ranging from fibers for clothing to lubricants to fertilizers.[1] In recent decades, however, job descriptions have become far more diverse. Chemical engineers often develop or operate processes to create products ranging from integrated circuits to disease-fighting drugs to fuel cells. Some recent graduates use a chemical engineering Bachelor's Degree as a launching pad for careers as physicians or patent attorneys.

How do chemical engineers think?

The unique focus perspective of this discipline can be represented by an extension ladder, shown in the figure. The two uprights of this very useful tool represent the two primary physical foundations upon which all of chemical engineering rests: chemistry and transport. Here, "chemistry" refers to the rates and extents of transformation among substances. "Transport" refers to the movement of mass, energy or momentum.

The rungs of the ladder represent the mathematical balance equations that connect chemistry and transport. The balance equations can be time-dependent or steady state. Whatever their nature, however, these balance equations are rarely written in their own right; they are almost always written to optimize or control some variable within them.[2] The rungs therefore also represent the use of balance equations for the optimization and control of useful commercial processes.

Chemical engineering embraces an enormous range of size scales in a fully integrated way—commonly ranging from atoms to oil tankers. The figure represents this notion by three extension segments, representing length scales corresponding to the microscopic, the bench scale (or "unit operation" in the lingo of the discipline) and the factory. At the molecular level, the balance equations might incorporate variables like temperature or pressure. At the unit operation level, the key variables might be flow rate or controller gain. At the factory level, the variables might be operating cost or overall production rate.

In a similar way, when we want to transform chemical substances, the "ladder" of chemistry/transport, balances, and optimization offers a versatile tool (Fig. 1). The skilled chemical engineer moves continually over the span of length scales from atomic to factory-level as circumstances dictate. When designing or optimizing an overall process flow, the chemical engineer may move rapidly up and down the span of length scales. When troubleshooting a particular unit operation, however, the chemical engineer may need to stay at

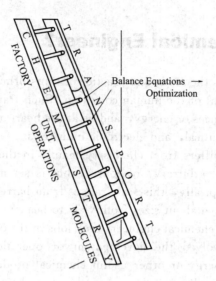

Fig. 1 An extension ladder can represent important aspects of how chemical engineers think.

that level for a long time with just a few balance equations. Good chemical engineering requires a constellation of intellectual skills integrated judiciously: knowing what kind of balance equation to write, what control volume to use, what terms to neglect, when to overlap tools from different length scales, what mathematics to use[3]. Although these skills can be described and listed, they cannot be employed algorithmically. Judicious chemical engineering requires judgment and experience, i. e., "chemical engineering wisdom". Thus, chemical engineering has been aptly called the "liberal arts of engineering."

The ability to think quantitatively and integratively about chemistry and transport over many length scales, with wise judgment born of experience, underpins the true value-added contribution of chemical engineering. This ability probably forms part of the reason chemical engineers continue to enjoy high entry-level salaries.

All engineers employ mathematics, physics, and the engineering art to overcome technical problems in a safe and economical fashion. Yet, it is the chemical engineer alone that draws upon the vast and powerful science of chemistry to solve a wide range of problems. The strong technical and social ties that bind chemistry and chemical engineering are unique in the fields of science and technology[4]. This marriage between chemists and chemical engineers has been beneficial to both sides and has rightfully brought the envy of the other engineering fields.

The breadth of scientific and technical knowledge inherent in the profession has caused some to describe the chemical engineer as the "universal engineer." Yes, you are hearing me correctly; despite a title that suggests a profession composed of narrow specialists, chemical engineers are actually extremely versatile and able to handle a wide range of technical problems.

During the past century, chemical engineers have made tremendous contributions to our standard of living. To celebrate these accomplishments, the American Institute of Chemical Engineers (AIChE) has compiled a list of the "10 Greatest Achievements of Chemical Engineering." These triumphs are summarized below:

The atom Biology, medicine, metallurgy, and power generation have all been revolutionized by our ability to split the atom and isolate isotopes. Chemical engineers played a prominent role in achieving both of these results. Early on facilities such as DuPont's Hanford Chemical Plant used these techniques to bring an abrupt conclusion to World War II with the production of the atomic bomb. Today these technologies have found uses in more peaceful applications. Medical doctors now use isotopes to monitor bodily functions; quickly identifying clogged arteries and veins. Similarly biologists gain invaluable insight into the basic mechanisms of life, and archaeologists can accurately date their historical findings.

The plastic age The 19th century saw enormous advances in polymer chemistry. However, it required the insights of chemical engineers during the 20th century to make mass produced polymers a viable economic reality. When a plastic called Bakelite was introduced in 1908 it sparked the dawn of the "Plastic Age" and quickly found uses in electric insulation, plugs & sockets, clock bases, iron cooking handles, and fashionable jewelry. Today plastic has become so common that we hardly notice it exists. Yet nearly all aspects of modern life are positively and profoundly impacted by plastic.

The human reactor Chemical engineers have long studied complex chemical processes by breaking them up into smaller "unit operations." Such operations might consist of heat exchangers, filters, chemical reactors and the like. Fortunately, this concept has also been applied to the human body. The results of such analysis have helped improve clinical care, suggested improvements in diagnostic and therapeutic devices, and led to mechanical wonders such as artificial organs. Medical doctors and chemical engineers continue to work hand in hand to help us live longer fuller lives.

Wonder drugs for the masses Chemical engineers have been able to take small amounts of antibiotics developed by people such as Sir Arthur Fleming (who discovered penicillin in 1929) and increase their yields several thousand times through mutation and special brewing techniques. Today's low price, high volume, drugs owe their existence to the work of chemical engineers. This ability to bring once scarce materials to all members of society through industrial creativity is a defining characteristic of chemical engineering[5].

Synthetic fibers From blankets and clothes to beds and pillows, synthetic fibers keep us warm, comfortable, and provide a good night's rest. Synthetic fibers also help reduce the strain on natural sources of cotton and wool, and can be tailored to specific applications. For example, nylon stockings make legs look young and attractive while bullet proof vests keep people out of harm's way.

Liquefied air When air is cooled to very low temperatures it condenses into a liquid. Chemical engineers can then separate out the different components. The purified nitrogen can be used to recover petroleum, freeze food, produce semiconductors, or prevent unwanted reactions while oxygen is used to make steel, smelt copper, weld metals together, and support the lives of patients in hospitals.

The environment Chemical engineers provide economical answers to clean up yesterday's waste and prevent tomorrow's pollution. Catalytic converters, reformulated gasoline, and smoke stack scrubbers all help keep the world clean. Additionally, chemical engineers help reduce the strain on natural materials through synthetic replacements, more efficient processing, and new recycling technologies.

Food Plants need large amounts of nitrogen, potassium, and phosphorus to grow in abundance. Chemical fertilizers can help provide these nutrients to crops, which in turn provide us with a bountiful and balanced diet. Fertilizers are especially important in certain regions of Asia and Africa where food can sometimes be scarce. Advances in biotechnology also offer the potential to further increase worldwide food production[6]. Finally, chemical engineers are at the forefront of food processing where they help create better tasting and most nutritious foods.

Petrochemicals Chemical engineers have helped develop processes like catalytic cracking to break down the complex organic molecules found in crude oil into much simpler species.[7] These building blocks are then separated and recombined to form many useful products including: gasoline, lubricating oils, plastics, synthetic rubber, and synthetic fibers. Petroleum processing is therefore recognized as an enabling technology, without which, much of modern life would cease to function.

Synthetic rubber Chemical engineers played a prominent role in developing today's synthetic rubber industry. During World War II, synthetic rubber capacity suddenly became of paramount importance. This was because modern society runs on rubber. Tires, gaskets, hoses, and conveyor belts (not to mention running shoes) are all made of rubber. Whether you drive, bike, roller-blade, or run; odds are you are running on rubber.

More typically, chemical engineers concern themselves with the chemical processes that turn raw materials into valuable products. The necessary skills encompass all aspects of design, testing, scale-up, operation, control, and optimization, and require a detailed understanding of the various "unit operations", such as distillation, mixing, and biological processes, which make these conversions possible. Chemical engineering science utilizes mass, momentum, and energy transfer along with thermodynamics and chemical kinetics to analyze and improve these "unit operations". Chemical engineering is not a profession that has to dwell on the achievements of the past for comfort, for its greatest accomplishments are yet to come.[8]

New Words and Expressions

tangible ['tændʒəbl] adj. 切实的
arbitrary ['ɑːrbitrəri] adj. 武断的，任意的
vial ['vaiəl] n. 小瓶，小玻璃瓶
beaker ['biːkə(r)] n. 烧杯，高脚杯
fiber ['faibər] n. 纤维(制品)，丝
lubricant ['lubrikənt] n. 润滑剂，润滑油

integrated circuit ['intigretid 'səːkit] 集成电路
physician [fi'ziʃn] n. 医生，内科医生
attorney [ə'təːrni] n. 律师，代理人
discipline ['disəplin] n. 学科，训练，纪律，自制力，行为准则

upright [ˈʌprait] n. 立柱；adj. 直立的
lingo [ˈliŋɡəu] n. 方言，行话
variable [ˈveriəbl] n. 可变因素，变量；adj. 变化的，可变的
constellation [ˌkɔnstəˈleiʃən] n. 星群，一系列（相关的想法、事物）
judiciously [dʒuːˈdiʃəsli] adv. 明智地
underpin [ˌʌndərˈpin] vt. 加固（墙等）的基础，加强……的基础
algorithmically [ælˈɡɔriθmikli] adv. 算法地，系统地
specialist [ˈspeʃəlist] n. 专家，专科医生
versatile [ˈvəːrsətail] adj. 多才多艺的，多用途的
triumph [ˈtraiʌmf] n. 巨大的成就，胜利；vi. 获胜，克服
isotope [ˈaisətəup] n. 同位素
clog [klɑɡ] v. 阻塞，堵塞；n. 木屐
monitor [ˈmɔnitə] v. 监控；n. 监听器，监控器
arteries [ˈʌtəriz] n. 动脉（artery 的名词复数），干线，要道
vein [vein] n. 静脉，气质，倾向
archaeologist [ˌɑːkiˈɔlədʒist] n. 考古学家

spark [spɑːk] vt. 发动，鼓舞；vi. 闪烁，发火花；n. 火花，瞬间放电
insulation [ˌinsjuˈleiʃ(ə)n] n. 隔离，绝缘，隔声
plug [plʌɡ] n. 塞子，插头，消防栓，火花塞；vt. & vi. 插上插头
socket [ˈsɔkit] n. 插口，灯座
therapeutic [ˌθerəˈpjuːtik] adj. 治疗（学）的，疗法的
pillow [ˈpiləu] n. 枕头；v. 枕着
stocking [ˈstɑkiŋ] n. 长筒袜，似长袜之物
weld [weld] vt. 焊接；n. 焊接，焊缝
bullet proof vest 防弹背心
reformulate [riːˈfɔːmjuleit] vt. 再形成
cease [siːs] v. 停止，终了
gasket [ˈɡæskit] n. 垫圈，衬垫
hose [həuz] n. 水管，软管，袜类
scale-up [ˈskeilˌʌp] n. 按比例增加，扩大
distillation [ˌdistiˈleiʃn] n. 蒸馏，蒸馏物
thermodynamics [ˌθəːrməudaiˈnæmiks] n. 热力学
kinetics [kaiˈnetiks] n. 动力学

Phrases

conveyor belt 传送带
differ from... 有别于……
refer to... 涉及
convert sth. into sth. 把……转变为……

Affixes

petro- [ˈpetrəu] 表示"石，岩石"；如 petroleum 石油，petrology 岩石学，petrologist 岩石学家
syn- [sin] 表示"同，共，合"；如：synonym 同义词，synactic 共同作用的，synthesis 合成

Notes

1. Job functions typically involved the development or operation of processes to convert oil-based feedstocks into energy or other useful chemical products ranging from fibers for clothing to lubricants to fertilizers. 参考译文：（化学工程师的）工作职能主要是开发或者操作将油基原料转变为能源或者衣用纤维、润滑油、化学肥料等其他有用化工产品的工艺。

2. Whatever their nature, however, these balance equations are rarely written in their own right; they are almost always written to optimize or control some variable within them. 两个"their"都指"these balance equations"。参考译文：然而，不管这些平衡方程式的本质是什么，但很少用原本的形式写出来，几乎总是为了优化或者控制方程中的某个变量而写出。

3. Good chemical engineer requires a constellation of intellectual skills integrated judiciously: knowing what kind of balance equation to write, what control volume to use, what terms to neglect, when to overlap tools from different length scales, what mathematics to use. 参考译文：优秀的化学工程师需要一系列智慧综合的聪明技巧：知道要写什么样的平衡方程式，知道用什么方法控制容积，知道忽略什么样的条件，知道什么时候根据不同长度范围使用不同的工具，知道用什么样的数学公式。

4. The strong technical and social ties that bind chemistry and chemical engineering are unique in the fields of science and technology. 参考译文：技术和社会之间的紧密联系把化学和化学工程结合在一起，这在科技领域是独一无二的。

5. This ability to bring once scarce materials to all members of society through industrial creativity is a defining characteristic of chemical engineering. 参考译文：通过产业创新使曾经稀缺的材料可以在全体社会成员中普及是化学工程的一个明显特征。

6. Advances in biotechnology also offer the potential to further increase worldwide food production. 参考译文：在生物技术方面的进步也有望进一步增加全球食物产量。

7. Chemical engineers have helped develop processes like catalytic cracking to break down the complex organic molecules found in crude oil into much simpler species. 参考译文：化学工程师已经协助开发了许多工艺，例如将原油中复杂有机分子分解成简单小分子的催化裂解工艺。

8. Chemical engineer is not a profession that has to dwell on the achievements of the past for comfort, for its greatest accomplishments are yet to come. 参考译文：化学工程师不是一个只能坐享以往成就的职业，因为它最大的成就还没有到来。

3. Applications of Inorganic Chemistry

Inorganic chemistry is a wondrous subject in itself with every element and compound having some unique property. But more than its academic interest, inorganic chemistry is an integral part of the world that we live in: from the air that we breathe, to the waters around us, to the rocks beneath our feet. Each of these topics is primarily a branch of inorganic chemistry with its own name: atmospheric chemistry, aquatic chemistry, and geochemistry. The living organisms on this planet depend upon many chemical elements for their functioning and this subject, too, has its own identity, that of bioinorganic chemistry.

Nature is not the only context in which inorganic chemistry is applied. Our modern civilization depends upon the synthesis of inorganic compounds, from the enormous quantities of such chemicals as ammonia and sulfuric acid to the much smaller quantities of cadmium sulfide, used as a paint pigment. Thus industrial inorganic chemistry is one of the cornerstones of our modern economy.

But more than this, inorganic chemistry is part of our future, a part of materials science, the synthesis of new and exotic materials for the 21st century will enable us to live better, more comfortable, environmentally-friendly lives.

In the following features, we have tried to select a few examples of the incredible range of applications of inorganic chemistry. We will see that inorganic chemistry is in space, beneath the seas, in the earth, in medical facilities, and in the materials that surround us.

Memory Metal: the Shape of Things to Come

Though we depict science as progressing through well-thought advances, it is amazing how many of our discoveries take place by accident. One of the most interesting examples of chance is provided by the discovery of memory metal. The story begins with attempts to develop a fatigue-resistant alloy for Navy missile nose cones. The metallurgist, William J. Buehler, discovered that a equimole alloy of titanium and nickel had exactly the desired properties. He named the alloy Nitinol (Nickel Titanium Naval Ordnance Laboratory). As demonstrations, he took long straight bands of Nitinol and folded them into an accordion shape. He would show how the metal could be stretched repeatedly without breaking. This flexibility, in itself, was a very useful property. At one such demonstration, one of the attendees produced a lighter and idly heated the metal. Much to everyone's amazement, the strip straightened out! — The metal had "remembered" its original shape.

Chemosynthesis: Redox Chemistry on the Sea Floor

On the surface of the Earth, life relies on photosynthesis to drive the redox cycles that make our life possible. What, then, drives the biological cycles in pitch-black cold environments? Life is not distributed evenly about the ocean floor but it is concentrated about vents, openings in the sea floor from which issue highly toxic plumes of boiling hot water saturated with toxic hydrogen sulfide and equally toxic heavy metal sulfides.[1] On the edge of this unlikely environment, a tremendous range of organisms survive and flourish. The most interesting are the mouthless, gutless tubeworms. These enormous creatures rely on bacteria living inside them to obtain energy by the oxidation of the hydrogen sulfide ion to sulfate ion, the process of chemosynthesis:

$$HS^-(aq)+4H_2O(l) \rightleftharpoons SO_4^{2-}(aq)+9H^+(aq)+8e^-$$

This energy is then used by the worms for the conversion of seawater-dissolved carbon dioxide to the complex carbon-based molecules in their structures. For every mole of hydrogen sulfide ion consumed, nine moles of hydrogen ion are produced. Hence the worms have to possess an efficient biochemical mechanisms to "pump out" the excess acid otherwise they would die from the low pH. The worms survive in the poisonous hydrogen sulfide environment by selectively absorbing the hydrogen sulfide ion rather than hydrogen sulfide itself. The HS^- ion is present at much lower concentrations than the hydrogen sulfide molecule as a result of the acid-base equilibrium below:

$$H_2S(aq)+H_2O(l) \rightleftharpoons H_3O^+(aq)+HS^-(aq)$$
$$K_{a1}=9.5 \times 10^{-8}$$

Concrete: an Old Material with a New Future

Though chemists are devising new and novel materials, there are some timeless materials that will always be the backbone of civilization and concrete is one of these. Most of our larger buildings are of concrete construction such as highways, bridges, dams, tunnels, and so on. In fact, of all the building materials, we probably depend upon concrete the most. In fact, about one tonne is used per person on Earth per year.

The crucial component of concrete is cement. To make cement, limestone (calcium carbonate) is mixed with clay or shale (a mixture of aluminosilicates) and heated to about 2000℃. This process produces lumps of material called "clinker," a mixture of about 50% tricalcium silicate, Ca_3SiO_5, 30% dicalcium silicate, Ca_2SiO_4, with the remainder being calcium aluminate, $Ca_3Al_2O_6$, and calcium ferroaluminate, $Ca_4Al_2Fe_2O_{10}$. The clinker is ground with gypsum (calcium sulfate dihydrate) to give cement powder. Cement reacts with water to form an inorganic "glue" holding together a matrix of sand and aggregate (small rocks).[2] A typical hydration reaction is:

$$2Ca_2SiO_4(s)+4H_2O(l) \rightleftharpoons Ca_3Si_2O_7 \cdot 3H_2O(s)+Ca(OH)_2(s)$$

The silicate product, known as tobermorite, forms strong crystals that adhere by means of strong silicon-oxygen bonds to the sand and aggregate.

However, even such a traditional substance as concrete has been reborn as one of our new materials. Autoclaved aerated concrete (AAC) promises to be a major building material of the 21st century. AAC is synthesized by mixing cement with lime (calcium hydroxide), silicate sand (silicon dioxide), water and aluminum powder.[3] In addition to the reaction above, the aluminum metal reacts with the hydroxide ion from the added calcium hydroxide to produce hydrogen gas.

$$2Al(s)+2OH^-(aq)+6H_2O(l) \rightleftharpoons 2[Al(OH)_4]^-(aq)+3H_2(g)$$

The millions of tiny gas bubbles cause the mixture to swell to five times its original volume. When the concrete has set, it is cut into blocks or slabs of required size then steam-cured in an oven (autoclave). The hydrogen gas diffuses out of the structure, being replaced by air. This low density building material has high thermal insulation properties and it can be made using fly ash, an unwanted product of coal-fired power plants, instead of silica sand. At the end of a building's life, the panels can be disassembled and reused or crushed and remade into new building materials, hence it is probably the most environmentally-friendly construction material.

New Minerals: Going beyond the Limitations of Geochemistry

Many minerals are formed in the Earth under conditions of high temperature and pressure and often over hundreds of thousands or millions of years. Now chemists have the ability to synthesize minerals using innovative reaction methods. One particular synthesis is that of the precious stone, lapis lazuli, also called ultramarine. Finely powdered ultramarine is important as an intensely-blue paint and plastics pigment (and eyeshadow) that is non-toxic and stable to light, unlike organic dyes which soon fade in light.[4] This compound has the formula $(Na, Ca)_8[SiAlO_4]_6(S, SO_4)$ where the ratios of sodium to calcium and sulfide to sulfate are variable. Its structure consists of AlO_4 and SiO_4 tetrahedra with the other ions filling holes in the framework. Natural ultramarine suffers from several disadvantages, one of the most important being that it often contains impurities, such as calcium carbonate and iron disulfide. Another problem is its rarity and hence, expense. Two chemists, Sandra Dann and Mark Weller, have produced a synthetic ultramarine that is free of impurities and has a consistent bright blue color. The compound has an exact chemical formula—$Na_8[SiAlO_4]_6(S_2, S_3)$. An advantage of mineral synthesis is that components can be altered to generate minerals that do not exist naturally, a field known as geomimetics. For example, the color of ultramarine is due to the anionic sulfur species. Replacement by chromate gives an equally stable and non-toxic yellow pigment.[5]

The minerals produced on Earth largely reflect the abundances of the constituent elements in the Earth's crust. Thus one avenue of research is to synthesize minerals that match the formula of known minerals but with one or two elements substituted by rare elements of the same group in the periodic table.[6] A good example is provided by sodalite $Na_8[SiAlO_4]Cl_2$. Dann and Weller have synthesized the analog $Na_8[GeGaO_4]Br_2$ in which silicon, aluminum, and chlorine are replaced by the element below them in the periodic table. Such a mineral would never be found in nature as the abundances of the replacement elements are of the order of 108 less than those in sodalite itself. Such novel compounds have potential as pigments, fluorescers, ferroelectrics, ion exchange materials, catalysts, and magnetic storage devices.

Glass: Ancient Bottles and Modern Lenses

Glass is an unusual substance in that it is not crystalline but an amorphous (shapeless) solid. The oldest glass objects, glass beads found in the near East, date back to about 3000 B. C. . But the first glass industry was founded about 1500 B. C. in ancient Egypt. The glass workers quickly developed sophistication to make useful and beautiful glass objects. From Egypt, the skills passed to the Roman Empire and then it was the Islamic world that kept the craft alive during the western dark ages (the 8th to 14th centuries). During the Renaissance, glass composition and working techniques became so important to the economy of the city state of Venice that glass workers were forbidden by law to leave Venice or divulge the secrets that they knew. Even today, Venetian glass is prized for its outstanding beauty and its complexity of decoration.

Glass science and technology is always at the "cutting-edge," providing us with new and novel transparent materials. The best example is that of photogrey glasses, glasses that darken on exposure to high light levels. This glass contains crystals of colorless silver chloride trapped between the silicon dioxide tetrahedrons. In the presence of ultraviolet light, a charge transfer reaction occurs:

$$AgCl + h\nu \rightleftharpoons Ag^0 + Cl^0$$

The reaction would immediately reverse except for the presence of copper(I) chloride as a deliberate impurity within the silver chloride crystal. The copper(I) reduces the chlorine atom back to chloride ion:

$$Cu^+ + Cl^0 \rightleftharpoons Cu^{2+} + Cl^-$$

The silver atoms migrate to the surface of the silver chloride crystal and aggregate into small, colloidal particles of silver metal. These particles absorb and reflect the ultraviolet and visible light, lowering the glass transmittance from about 85% to 22%. When the user returns indoors, the copper(II) ions slowly migrate to the crystal surface where they reoxidize the silver metal to silver ions:

$$Cu^{2+} + Ag^0 \rightleftharpoons Cu^+ + Ag^+$$

The silver ions, in turn, migrate back into the structure of the silver chloride crystal. And so the cycle is ready to begin again.

New Words and Expressions

wondrous ['wʌndrəs] adj. 奇妙的，惊奇的
geochemistry [,dʒi(:)əu'kemistri] n. 地球化学
pigment ['pigmənt] n. 色素，颜料
exotic [ig'zɔtik] adj. 外来的，奇异的
depict [di'pikt] vt. 描述，描写
cone [kəun] n. 锥形物，圆锥体；vt. 使成锥形
metallurgist [me'tælədʒist] n. 冶金家
stretch [stretʃ] v. 伸展，拉紧
attendee [ə,ten'di:] n. 出席者
flexibility [,fleksə'biliti] n. 弹性，适应性，机动性，挠性
pitch-black 漆黑的，墨黑的
plume [plu:m] n. 羽毛，飘升之物，烟羽，羽流，羽状物
vent [vent] n. 通风孔，出烟孔，出口
saturate ['sætʃəreit] v. 使饱和，浸透，充满
hydrogen sulfide ['haidrədʒən 'sʌl,faid] n. 硫化氢
flourish ['flə:riʃ] vi. 繁荣，茂盛；n. 挥舞，挥动
gutless ['gʌtlis] adj. 无肠道的，无消化道的
tubeworm n. 多毛虫
bacteria [bæk'tiəriə] n. 细菌
oxidation [,ɔksi'deiʃ(ə)n] n. 氧化

chemosynthesis [,keməu'sinθəsis] n. 化学合成
cement [sə'ment] n. 水泥，接合剂
limestone ['laimstəun] n. 石灰石
clinker ['kliŋkə] n. 熟料，水泥熟料，灰渣
grind [graind] v. 磨(碎)，碾(碎)，折磨
gypsum ['dʒipsəm] n. 石膏，石膏肥料
aggregate ['ægrigeit] n. 集料，骨料，粒料；vt. 聚集
tobermorite [təubə'mɔ:rait] n. 雪硅钙石，水化硅酸钙
lapis lazuli [leipis 'læzjulai] n. 天青石，青金石，天青石色
mimetism ['mimitizəm] n. 模仿性
sodalite ['səudəlait] n. 方钠石
amorphous [ə'mɔ:fəs] adj. 无定形的，无组织的
sophistication [sə,fisti'keiʃən] n. 复杂的，精致的工艺或产品
islamic [iz'læmik] adj. 伊斯兰的，伊斯兰教的
craft [krɑ:ft] n. 工艺，手艺
renaissance [ri'neisəns] n. 文艺复兴时期
divulge [dai'vʌldʒ] vt. 泄露，暴露
transparent [træns'peərənt] adj. 透明的，显然的，明晰的

Phrases

autoclaved aerated concrete　自动高压加气混凝土
by accident　偶然
rely on (upon)　依靠，信任，信赖
in that　由于，因为，既然
date back　回溯至
as a result of …　作为……结果

Affixes

geo-［'dʒiːəu］　表示"地球，土地"；如 geology 地质学，geochemistry 地球化学，geobiology 地球生物学

tetra- 或 tetr- 表示"四"；如 tetraacetate 四乙酸盐，tetraborate 四硼酸盐，tetrabasic 四碱价的。从"一到十"分别表示为：mono-、di-、tri-、tetra-、penta、hexa-、hepta-、octa-、nona-、deca-

Notes

1. Life is not distributed evenly about the ocean floor but it is concentrated about vents, openings in the sea floor from which issue highly toxic plumes of boiling hot water saturated with toxic hydrogen sulfide and equally toxic heavy metal sulfides. 参考译文：在海底，生命并不是均匀分布的，而是集中在出口，即海底的开口附近，在那里冒出含有饱和有毒硫化氢和同样有毒的重金属硫化物的沸腾热水的羽状物。

2. The clinker is ground with gypsum (calcium sulfate dihydrate) to give cement powder. Cement reacts with water to form an inorganic "glue" holding together a matrix of sand and aggregate (small rocks). 参考译文：水泥熟料与石膏（二水合硫酸钙）一起研磨得到水泥粉。水泥粉与水反应生成一种无机"胶水"，它可以将沙子与其他粒料（如小石子）粘在一起。

3. Autoclaved aerated concrete (AAC) promises to be a major building material of the 21st century. AAC is synthesized by mixing cement with lime (calcium hydroxide), silica sand (silicon dioxide), water and aluminum powder. 参考译文：蒸气加压混凝土有望成为 21 世纪的一种主要建筑材料，它是通过将水泥、石灰（氢氧化钙）、硅砂（二氧化硅）、水、铝粉混合而制成的。

4. Finely powdered ultramarine is important as an intensely-blue paint and plastics pigment (and eyeshadow) that is non-toxic and stable to light, unlike organic dyes, which soon fade in light. 参考译文：天青石细粉非常重要，可以用作一种深蓝色油漆和塑料颜料（还可作为眼影），它无毒、对光稳定，不像有机颜料那样容易见光褪色。

5. An advantage of mineral synthesis is that components can be altered to generate minerals that do not exist naturally, a field known as geomimetics. For example, the color of ultramarine is due to the anionic sulfur species. Replacement by chromate gives an equally stable and non-toxic yellow pigment. 参考译文：矿物合成的优点之一在于可以改变矿物组成来得到自然界中本不存在的矿石，这被称为地质拟态学。例如，天青石的颜色来自含硫的阴离子，用铬来代替可以得到同样稳定且无毒的黄色颜料。

6. Thus one avenue of research is to synthesize minerals that match the formula of known minerals but with one or two elements substituted by rare elements of the same group in the periodic table. 参考译文：因此，研究的途径之一就是合成与已知矿物质分子式相匹配的矿物质，但是其中一种或两种元素被元素周期表中同族的稀土元素取代。

4. The Map of Organic Chemistry

The term organic literally means "derived from living organisms". Originally, the science of organic chemistry was the study of compounds such as sugar, urea, starch, waxes, and plant oils, which were considered "organic", and people accepted vitalism: the belief that natural products need a "vital force" to create them. Organic chemistry, then, was the study of compounds having the vital force. Inorganic chemistry was the study of gases, rocks, minerals and the compounds that could be made from them.

In the nineteenth, experiments showed that organic compounds could be synthesized from inorganic compounds. In 1828, the German chemist Friedrich Wöhler converted ammoniums cyanate made from ammonia and cyanic acid, to urea simply by heating it in the absence of oxygen.

Urea had always come from living organisms and was presumed to contain the vital force, yet ammonium cyanate is inorganic and thus lacks the vital force. [1] Some chemists claimed that a trace of vital force from Wöhler's hand must have contaminated the reaction, but most recognized the possibility of synthesizing organic compounds from inorganic. Many other syntheses were carried out, and the vital force theory was eventually discarded.

Since Vitalism was disproved in the early nineteenth century, you'd think it would be extinct by now. And, you'd be wrong! Vitalism lives on today in the minds of those who believe that "natural" (plant-derived) vitamins, flavor compounds, etc. are somehow different and more healthful than the identical "artificial" (synthesized) compounds. [2]

As chemists, we know that plant-derived compounds and the synthesized compounds are identical. Assuming they are pure, the only way to tell them apart is through ^{14}C dating. [3] Compounds synthesized from petrochemicals have a lower content of radioactive ^{14}C and appear old because their ^{14}C has decayed over time. Plant-derived compounds are recently synthesized from CO_2 in the air. They have a high content of radioactive ^{14}C. Some large chemical suppliers provide isotope ratio analyses to show that "natural" have high ^{14}C contents and are plant-derived. Such a sophisticated analysis lends a high-tech flavor to this twenty-first-century form of Vitalism.

Even though, organic compounds do not need a vital force, they are still distinguished from inorganic compounds. The distinctive feature of organic compounds is that they all contain one or more carbon atoms. Still, not all carbon compounds are organic substances. Diamond, graphite, carbon dioxide, ammonium cyanate, and sodium carbonate are derived from minerals and have typical inorganic properties, while most of the millions of carbon compounds are classified as organic, however. [4]

The modern definition of Organic Chemistry is the chemistry of carbon compounds. What is so special about carbon that a whole branch of chemistry is devoted to its compounds? Unlike most other elements, carbon forms strong bonds to the other carbon atoms and to a wide variety of other elements. Chains and rings of carbon atoms can build up to form an endless variety of molecules. It is this diversity of carbon compounds that provide basis for life on Earth. Living creatures are composed largely of complex organic compounds that serve structure, chemical, or genetic functions.

Life is based on carbon's ability to bond with other carbon atoms to form diverse structures. Reflecting this fact, the branch of chemistry that is the study of carbon-containing compounds has come to be known as organic chemistry. Today, more than 13 million organic compounds are known, and about 100000 new ones are added to the list each year. This includes those discovered in nature and those synthesized in the laboratory. By contrast, there are only 200000 to 300000 known inorganic compounds, those based on elements other than carbon.

Although carbon is not among the ten most abundant elements in Earth's crust, surface water, and atmosphere, carbon is the third most abundant element in the human body in terms of number of atoms and the second most common in terms of mass. We ourselves are composed largely of organic molecules, and we are nourished by the organic compounds in our food. The proteins in our skin, the lipids in our cell membranes, the glycogen in our livers, and the DNA in the nuclei of our cells are all organic compounds. Our bodies are also regulated and defended by complex organic compounds. Water makes up 60%～90% of all living matter. However, of the remaining 10%～40% of living matter, less than 4% is inorganic, the remainder is organic.

Chemists have learned to synthesize or simulate many of these complex molecules. The synthetic products serve as drugs, medicines, plastics, pesticides, paints, and fibers. Many of the most important advances in medicine are actually advances in organic chemistry. New synthetic drugs are developed to combat disease, and new polymers are molded to replace failing organs. Organic chemistry has gone full circle. It began as the study of compounds derived from "organs", and now it gives us the drugs and materials we need to save or replace those organs.

Organic molecules are classified according to the functional groups they contains, where a functional groups is defined as a combination of atoms that behave as a unit. [5] Most functional groups are distinguished by the heteroatoms they contain. Carbon atoms are bond to one another and to hydrogen atoms in many ways, which results in an incredibly large number of hydrocarbons. But carbon atoms can bond to atoms of other elements as well, further increasing the number of possible organic molecules. In organic chemistry, any atom other than carbon and hydrogen in an organic molecule is called a heteroatom, where hetero- means "different from either C or H." The role heteroatoms play in determining the properties of each class is the underlying theme. As you study this material, focus on understanding the chemical and physical properties of the various classes of compounds, for doing so will give you greater appreciation of the remarkable diversity of organic molecules and their many applications. [6]

A hydrocarbon structure can serve as a frame work to which various heteroatoms can be attached. [7] This is analogous to a Christmas tree serving as the scaffolding on which ornaments are hung. Just as the ornaments give character to the tree, so do heteroatmos give character to an organic molecule. [8] In other words, heteroatoms can have profound effects on the properties of an organic molecule.

Consider ethane, C_2H_6, and ethanol, C_2H_6O, which differ from each other by only a single oxygen atom. Ethane has a b. p. $-88°C$, making it a gas at room temperature, and it does not dissolve in water very well. Ethanol, by contrast, has a b. p. of $+78°C$, making it a liquid at room temperature. It is infinitely soluble in water and is the active ingredient of alcoholic beverages. Consider further ethylamine, C_2H_7N, which has a nitrogen atom is a corrosive, pungent, highly toxic gas, most unlike ethane or ethanol.

Organic chemistry can be divided into three interrelated areas: determination of structure, reactions and synthesis, and the mechanisms by which reactions take place. Organic chemistry is too large a field to be summarized in some words.

New Words and Expressions

urea ['juəriə] n. 尿素
starch [stɑːtʃ] n. 淀粉
wax [wæks] n. 蜡, 蜡状物; vt. 上蜡于
ethylamine [eθiːˈlæmiːn] n. 乙胺
vitalism [ˈvaitəlizəm] n. 生机论, 生机说
ammonium [əˈməunjəm] n. 铵
cyanate [ˈsaiəneit] n. 氰酸盐
cyanic acid [saiˈænikˈæsid] n. 氰酸
contaminate [kənˈtæmineit] v. 污染, 弄脏
discard [diˈskɑːd] v. 丢弃, 抛弃
flavor [ˈfleivər] n. 味 (道), 特色; v. 给……调味, 加味于
decay [diˈkei] v. &n. 腐烂, 腐朽
membrane [ˈmembrein] n. 膜, 隔膜
nourish [ˈnəːriʃ] vt. 滋养, 施肥于, 抚养
lipid [ˈlipid] n. 脂质
glycogen [ˈglaikəudʒen] n. 肝糖, 糖原质
nuclei [ˈnjuːkliai] n. 核, 核心, 原子核
remainder [riˈmeindər] n. 剩余物, 其他人员
hydrocarbon [ˌhaidrəˈkɑːrbən] n. 碳氢化合物
heteroatom [ˈhetərəuˌætəm] n. 杂原子, 杂环原子
diversity [daiˈvəːsiti] n. 差异, 多样性
interrelated [intəriˈleitid] adj. 相关的
mechanism [ˈmekənizəm] n. 机理, 机制
scaffolding [ˈskæfəuldiŋ] n. 搭脚手架的材料
ornament [ˈɔːnəmənt] n. 装饰物, 教堂用品; vt. 装饰, 修饰
corrosive [kəˈrəusiv] adj. 腐蚀性的
pungent [ˈpʌndʒənt] adj. 刺激性的, 辛辣的

Phrases

such as...   例如
in the absence of...   在缺少……时
be known as...   被认为是
functional group   官能团

Affixes

in- [in] 表示 "否定, 与……相反"; 如 inorganic 无机的, inaccurate 不准确的, inartistic 非艺术的

pre- [pri] 表示 "……之前, 预先"; 如 presumed 假定的, preexist 先于……存在, preact 预作用

re- [re] 表示 "又, 再"; 如: recognized 经过验证的, reable 使 (病人) 复原, react 起反应

dis- [dis] 表示 "分开, 分离, 否定, 不"; 如 disprove 反驳, disability 无能, disagree 不同意

iso- [ˈaisəu] 表示 "相等的, 相同的", (元音前作 is-); 如 isotope 同位素, isoalkyl 异烷基, isoallyl (＝propenyl) 丙烯基

-ate [eit] 表示 "酸盐"; 如 carbonate 碳酸盐, sulfate 硫酸盐, phosphate 磷酸盐

hetero- [ˈhetərəu] 表示 "其他的, 不同的, 异"(元音之前作 heter-); 如 heteroatom 杂原子, 杂环原子, heterocyclic 杂环的, heterochromatic 异色的

hydro- [ˈhaidrəu] 表示 "水, 液, 流体; 氢的, 含氢的"; 如 hydrocarbon 碳氢化合物, hydrochloride 氯化氢, hydroelectric 水电的

inter- [ˈintə(r)] 表示 "之间的"; 如 interrelated 相关的, international 国际的

Notes

1. Urea had always come from living organisms and was presumed to contain the vital

force, yet ammonium cyanate is inorganic and thus lacks the vital force. 参考译文：尿素过去一直来自有机体，所以人们推测其含有生命力，而氰酸铵是无机的，因而没有生命力。

2. Vitalism lives on today in the minds of those who believe that "natural" (plant-derived) vitamins, flavor compounds, etc. are somehow different and more healthful than the identical "artificial" (synthesized) compounds. 复合句，"who"引导的定语从句修饰"those"。参考译文：直到今天，生命论仍然存在于一些人的思想中，他们认为自然的（源于植物的）维生素、香料等和完全相同的人工（合成的）化合物有点不同，更健康。

3. Assuming they are pure, the only way to tell them apart is through ^{14}C dating. 参考译文：假定它们都是纯品，区别它们的唯一办法是通过^{14}C测定年代。

4. Diamond, graphite, carbon dioxide, ammonium cyanate, and sodium carbonate are derived from minerals and have typical inorganic properties, while most of the millions of carbon compounds are classified as organic, however. 参考译文：金刚石、石墨、二氧化碳、氰酸铵还有碳酸钠都来源于矿物质，具有典型的无机性质，然而数百万种含碳化合物被归为有机化合物。

5. Organic molecules are classified according to the functional groups they contains, where a functional groups is defined as a combination of atoms that behave as a unit. 参考译文：有机分子是根据它们所包含的官能团来分类的，官能团被定义为作为一个整体起作用的原子组合。

6. As you study this material, focus on understanding the chemical and physical properties of the various classes of compounds, for doing so will give you greater appreciation of the remarkable diversity of organic molecules and their many applications. 该句是主从复合句，"As..."为时间状语从句，主句省略主语"you"，"for doing so…"作原因状语修饰主句。参考译文：研究这些物质时，要注意各类化合物的化学和物理性质，这样能让人更好地理解有机分子显著的多样性及其应用。

7. A hydrocarbon structure can serve as a frame work to which various heteroatoms can be attached. 参考译文：碳氢化合物结构可以作为一个框架，不同的杂原子可以和它相连。

8. Just as the ornaments give character to the tree, so do heteroatoms give character to an organic molecule. 该并列句为"as…as (so)…"结构，"tree"指前文所讲圣诞树。参考译文：就像装饰物让圣诞树有了特色一样，杂原子赋予一个有机分子不同的特征。

5. Introduction to Analytical Chemistry

Is there any iron in moon dust? How much aspirin is there in a headache tablet? What trace metals are there in a tin of tuna fish? What is the purity and chemical structure of a newly prepared compound? These and a host of other questions concerning the composition and structure of matter fall within the realms of analytical chemistry. The answers may be given by simple chemical tests or by the use of costly and complex instrumentations. The techniques and methods employed and the problems encountered are so varied as to cut right across the traditional divisions of inorganic, organic and physical chemistry as well as embracing aspects of such areas as bio-chemistry, physics, engineering and economics. Analytical chemistry is therefore a subject which is broad in its scope whilst requiring a specialist and disciplined approach. An enquiring and critical mind, a keen sense of observation and the ability to pay scrupulous attention to detail are desirable characteristics in anyone seeking to become proficient in the subject.[1] However, it is becoming increasingly recognized that the role of the analytical chemist is not to be tied to a bench using a burette and balance, but to become involved in the broader aspects of the analytical problems which are encountered. Thus, discussions with scientific and commercial colleagues, customers and other interested parties, together with on-site visits can greatly assist in the choice of method and the interpretation of analytical data thereby minimizing the expenditure of time, effort and money.

The Scope of Analytical Chemistry

Analytical chemistry has bounds which are amongst the widest of any technological discipline. An analyst must be able to design, carry out, and interpret measurements with the context of the fundamental technological problem with which he or she is presented. The selection and utilization of suitable chemical procedures requires a wide knowledge of chemistry, whilst familiarity with and the ability to operate a varied range of instruments is essential. Finally, analysts must have a sound knowledge of the statistical treatment of experimental data to enable them to gauge the meaning and reliability of the results that they obtain.[2]

When an examination is restricted to the identification of one or more constituents of a sample, it is known as qualitative analysis, while an examination to determine how much of a particular species is present constitutes a quantitative analysis. Sometimes information concerning the spatial arrangement of atoms in a molecule or crystalline compound is required or confirmation of the presence or position of certain organic functional groups is sought. Such examinations are described as structural analysis and they may be considered as more detailed forms of analysis. Any species that are the subjects of either qualitative or quantitative analysis are known as analytes.

There is much in common between the techniques and methods used in qualitative and quantitative analysis. In both cases, a sample is prepared for analysis by physical and chemical "conditioning", and then a measurement of some property related to the analyte is made. It is in the degree of control over the relation between a measurement and the amount of analyte present that the major difference lies. For a qualitative analysis it is sufficient to be able to apply a test which has a known sensitivity limit so that negative and positive results may be seen in the right perspective. Where a quantitative analysis is made, however, the relation between measurement and analyte must obey a strict and measurable proportionality; only then can the amount of analyte in the sample be derived from the measurement. To maintain this proportionality it is generally essential that all reactions used in the preparation of a sample for measurement are controlled and reproducible and that the conditions of measurement remain constant for all similar measurements. A premium is also placed upon careful calibration of the methods used in a quantitative analysis. These aspects of chemical analysis are a major pre-occupation of the analyst.

The Function of Analytical Chemistry

Chemical analysis is an indispensable servant of modern technology whilst it partly depends on that modern technology for its operation. The two have in fact developed hand in hand. From the earliest days of quantitative chemistry in the latter part of the eighteenth century, chemical analysis has provided an important basis for chemical development. For example, the combustion studies and the atomic theory proposed by Dalton had their bases in quantitative analytical evidence.

The transistor provides a more recent example of an invention which would have been almost impossible to develop without sensitive and accurate chemical analysis.[3] This example is particularly interesting as it illustrates the synergic development that is so frequently observed in differing fields. Having underpinned the development of the transistor, analytical instrumentation now makes extremely wide use of it. In modern technology, it is impossible to over-estimate the importance of analysis. Some of the major areas of application are listed below.

(1) Fundamental Research

The first steps in unraveling the details of an unknown system frequently involve the identification of its constituents by qualitative chemical analysis. Follow-up investigations usually require structural information and quantitative measurements. This pattern appears in such diverse areas as the formulation of new drugs, the examination of meteorites, and studies on the results of heavy ion bombardment by nuclear physicists.

(2) Product Development

The design and development of a new product will often depend upon establishing a link between its chemical composition and its physical properties or performance. Typical examples are the development of alloys and of polymer composites.

(3) Product Quality Control

Most manufacturing industries require a uniform product quality. To ensure that this requirement is met, both raw materials and finished products are subjected to extensive chemical analysis. On the one hand, the necessary constituents must be kept at the optimum levels, while on the other impurities such as poisons in foodstuffs must be kept below the maximum allowed by law.

(4) Monitoring and Control of Pollutants

Residual heavy metals and organo-chlorine pesticides represent two well-known pollution problems. Sensitive and accurate analysis is required to enable the distribution and level of a pollutant in the environment to be assessed and routine chemical analysis is important in the control of industrial effluents.[4]

(5) Assay

In commercial dealings with raw materials such as ores, the value of the ore is set by its metal content. Large amounts of material are often involved, so that taken overall small differences in concentration can be of considerable commercial significance. Accurate and reliable chemical analysis is thus essential.

(6) Medical and Clinical Studies

The levels of various elements and compounds in body fluids are important indicators of physiological disorders. A high sugar content in urine indicating a diabetic condition and lead in blood are probably the most well-known examples.

Analytical Problems and Their Solutions

The solutions of all analytical problems, both qualitative and quantitative, follow the same basic pattern. This may be described under seven general headings.

(1) Choice of Method

The selection of the method of analysis is a vital step in the solution of an analytical problem. A choice cannot be made until the overall problem is defined, and where possible a decision should be taken by the client and the analyst in consultation.[5] Inevitably, in the method selected, a compromise has to be reached between the sensitivity, precision and accuracy desired of the results and the costs involved.

(2) Sampling

Correct sampling is the cornerstone of reliable analysis. The analyst must decide in conjunction with technological colleagues how, where, and when a sample should be taken so as to be truly representative of the parameter that is to be measured.

(3) Preliminary Sample Treatment

For quantitative analysis, the amount of sample taken is usually measured by mass or volume. Where a homogeneous sample already exists, it may be subdivided without further treatment. With many solids such as ores, however, crushing and mixing are prior requirement. The sample often needs additional preparation for analysis, such as drying, ignition and dissolution.

(4) Separations

A large proportion of analytical measurements is subject to interference from other constituents of the sample. Newer methods increasingly employ instrumental techniques to distinguish between analyte and interference signals. However, such distinction is not always possible and sometimes a selective chemical reaction can be used to mask the interference. If this approach fails, the separation of the analyte from the interfering component will become necessary. Where quantitative measurements are to be made, separations must also be quantitative or give a known recovery of the analyte.[6]

(5) Final Measurement

This step is often the quickest and easiest of the seven but can only be as reliable as the preceding stages. The fundamental necessity is a known proportionality between the magnitude of the measurement and the amount of analyte present.

(6) Method Validation

It is pointless carrying out the analysis unless the results obtained are known to be meaningful. This can only be ensured by proper validation of the method before use and subsequent monitoring of its performance. The analysis of validated standards is the most satisfactory approach. Validated standards have been extensively analysed by a variety of methods, and an accepted value for the appropriate analyte obtained. A standard should be selected with a matrix similar to that of the sample. In order to ensure continued accurate analysis, standards must be re-analysed at regular intervals.

(7) The Assessment of Results

Results obtained from an analysis must be assessed by the appropriate statistical methods and their meaning considered in the light of the original problem.

It is common to find analytical methods classified as classical or instrumental, the former comprising "wet chemical" methods such as gravimetry and titrimetry. Such a classification is historically derived and largely artificial as there is no fundamental difference between the methods in the two groups. All involve the correlation of a physical measurement with the analyte concentration. Indeed, very few analytical methods are entirely instrumental, and most involve chemical manipulations prior to the instrumental measurement.

Trends in Analytical Methods and Procedures

There is constant development and change in the techniques and methods of analytical chemistry. Better instrument design and a fuller understanding of the mechanics of analytical processes enable steady improvements to be made in sensitivity, precision, and accuracy.[7] These same changes contribute to more economic analysis as they frequently lead to the elimination of time-consuming separation steps. The ultimate development in this direction is a non-destructive method, which not only saves time but also leaves the sample unchanged for further examination or processing.

The automation of analysis, sometimes with the aid of laboratory robots, has become increasingly important. For example, it enables a series of bench analyses to be carried out more rapidly and efficiently, and with better precision, whilst in other cases continuous monitoring of an analyte in a production process is possible. Two of the most important developments in recent years have been the incorporation of microprocessor control into analytical instruments and their interfacing with micro- and minicomputers. The microprocessor has brought improved instrument control, performance and, through the ability to monitor the condition of component parts, easier routine maintenance. Operation by relatively inexperienced personnel can be facilitated by simple interactive keypad dialogues including the storage and re-call of standard methods, report generation and diagnostic testing of the system. Micro-computers with sophisticated data handling and graphics software packages have likewise made a considerable impact on the collection, storage, processing, enhancement and interpretation of analytical data. Laboratory Information and Management Systems (LIMS), for the automatic logging of large numbers of samples, Chemometrics, which involve computerized and often sophisticated statistical analysis of data, and Expert Systems, which provide interactive computerized guidance and assessments in the solving of analytical problems, have all become important in optimizing chemical analysis and maximizing the information it provides.

Analytical problems continue to arise in new forms. Demands for analysis at 'long range' by instrument packages steadily increase. Space probes, 'borehole logging' and deep sea studies exemplify these requirements. In other fields, such as environmental and clinical studies, there is increasing recognition of the importance of the exact chemical form of an element in a sample rather than the mere level of its presence.[8] Two well-known examples are the much greater toxicity of organo-lead and organo-mercury compounds compared with their inorganic counterparts. An identification and determination of the element in a specific chemical form presents the analyst with some of the more difficult problems.

New Words and Expressions

aspirin [ˈæspərin] n. 阿司匹林，乙酰水杨酸
tablet [ˈtæblət] n. 药片，丸，匾，便笺本
tuna fish 金枪鱼
scrupulous [ˈskruːpjuləs] adj. 小心谨慎的，细心的
disciplined [ˈdisəplind] adj. 受过训练的，遵守纪律的
bench [bentʃ] n. 实验台，工作台，长凳
burette [bjuəˈret] n. 滴管，量管
constitute [ˈkɔnstiˌtjuːt] v. 组成，构成
arrangement [əˈreindʒmənt] n. 排列，安排，筹划，布置
crystalline [ˈkristəlain] adj. 水晶的，结晶质的，清澈的
confirmation [ˌkɔnfə(r)ˈmeiʃ(ə)n] n. 证实，确认书
conditioning [kənˈdiʃəniŋ] n. （老化）处理，条件作用，训练
proportionality [prəˌpɔːʃəˈnæləti] n. 比例，均衡(性)
premium [ˈpriːmjəm] n. 高度重视，重要价值，额外费用，奖金
indispensable [ˌindiˈspensəbl] adj. 不可缺少的，绝对必要的
composite [ˈkɔmpəzit] adj. 混合成的，复合的，拼成的；n. 合成物，复合材料
combustion [kəmˈbʌstʃən] n. 燃烧
transistor [trænˈzistə] n. 晶体管
synergic [siˈnəːdʒik] adj. 协作的，合作的
underpin [ˌʌndəˈpin] v. 巩固，支撑
unravel [ʌnˈrævəl] v. 拆开，解开
alloy [ˈæloi] n. 合金；vt. 使成合金
monitoring [ˈmɔnitəriŋ] n. 监测，监视
chlorine [ˈklɔːriːn] n. 氯

effluent [ˈefluənt] n. 污水，排水道；adj. 发出的，流出的
ore [ɔː(r)] n. 矿石
fluorescence [fluːəˈresəns] n. 荧光，荧光性
cornerstone [ˈkɔːnəstəun] n. 基础，里程碑
homogeneous [ˌhəuməˈdʒiːniəs] adj. 同性质的，同类的
subdivide [ˌsʌbdiˈvaid, ˈsʌbdiˌvaid] vt. 再分，细分；vi. 细分，再分
ignition [igˈniʃən] n. 燃烧，着火，点火
dissolution [ˌdisəˈluːʃən] n. 溶解，融化
mask [mæsk] n. 面具，口罩，面膜；v. 掩饰，遮住
validate [ˈvælideit] vt. 使合法化，使生效，批准，确认，证实
matrix [ˈmeitriks] n. 基质，矩阵，模型
gravimetric [ˌgræviˈmetrik] adj. （测定）重量的，重量分析的
titrimetry [taiˈtrimitri] n. 滴定测量
mercury [ˈməːkjuri] n. 水银，汞
maintenance [ˈmeintənəns] n. 维持，保养，维护
facilitate [fəˈsiliteit] v. 促进，使便利
logging [ˈlɔgiŋ] n. 记录，存入，航行日志
chemometrics [ˈkeməuˈmetriks] n. 化学计量学，化学统计学
lead [liːd, led] n. 铅，榜样，主角，狗绳
borehole [ˈbɔːhəul] n. 地上凿洞
exemplify [igˈzemplifai] v. 例证，是……的典范
toxicity [tɔkˈsisiti] n. 毒性
counterpart [ˈkauntəpɑːrt] n. 职能（或地位）相当的人，对应的事物

Phrases

be able to... 能够
carry out... 贯彻，执行
in common 共同
depend on... 依靠
hand in hand 联合，携手
a variety of... 许多

Affixes

micro- [ˈmaikrəu] 表示"微小的"；如 microprocessor 微处理器，microcircuit 微型电路，microwave 微波

un- [ʌn] 表示"不，否定"；如 unravel 拆开，unusual 不经常的，unwise 不明智的

Notes

1. An enquiring and critical mind, a keen sense of observation and the ability to pay scrupulous attention to detail are desirable characteristics in anyone seeking to become proficient in the subject. 句中"An enquiring and critical mind""a keen sense of observation""the ability to pay scrupulous attention to detail"三个并列短语共同作主语。"seeking to become proficient in the subject"作后置定语修饰"anyone"；"the subject"指上文提到的分析化学。参考译文：任何人想在分析化学领域拥有一席之地，需要具有善于探索和批判性的头脑、敏捷的观察和关注细节的能力。

2. Finally, analysts must have a sound knowledge of the statistical treatment of experimental data to enable them to gauge the meaning and reliability of the results that they obtain. 参考译文：最后，分析人员必须具备良好的实验数据统计分析知识，使他们能判断所得结果的意义和可靠性。

3. The transistor provides a more recent example of an invention which would have been almost impossible to develop without sensitive and accurate chemical analysis. 参考译文：晶体管是一个最近的发明例子，若没有灵敏精确的化学分析，该发明几乎是不可能的。

4. Sensitive and accurate analysis is required to enable the distribution and level of a pollutant in the environment to be assessed and routine chemical analysis is important in the control of industrial effluents. 是并列句。"Sensitive and accurate analysis"为前一句话的主语，"routine chemical analysis"为后一句话的主语，"to be assessed"修饰"the environment"。参考译文：环境中污染物的分布和含量评估需要灵敏和准确的分析，化学常规分析对工业废水的控制很重要。

5. A choice cannot be made until the overall problem is defined, and where possible a decision should be taken by the client and the analyst in consultation. 参考译文：只有当所有的问题都确定之后才能做出选择，很可能会在客户和分析人员商讨后做出决定。

6. Where quantitative measurements are to be made, separations must also be quantitative or give a known recovery of the analyte. 参考译文：在做定量测定时，分离也必须量化或者给出被分析物的确定回收率。

7. Better instrument design and a fuller understanding of the mechanics of analytical processes enable steady improvements to be made in sensitivity, precision, and accuracy. 参考译文：更好的仪器设计以及更全面了解分析过程的机制，能逐步提高灵敏度、精密度和准确度。

8. In other fields, such as environmental and clinical studies, there is increasing recognition of the importance of the exact chemical form of an element in a sample rather than the mere level of its presence. 参考译文：在其他领域，比如环境和临床研究，人们越来越认识到在样品中元素化学形态的重要性，而不是它的含量。

6. What is Physical Chemistry?

Physical chemistry is an empirical science. A science is a set of constructs, called theories, that link fragments of experience into a consistent description of natural phenomena. The adjective "empirical" refers to the common experiences from which the theories grow, that is, to experiments. Simple working hypotheses are guessed by imaginative insight or intuition or luck, usually from a study of experiments. This repetitive interplay in time leads to the formulation of theories that correlate the accumulated experimental information and that can predict new phenomena with accuracy. [1]

Traditionally, there are three principal areas of physical chemistry: thermodynamics (which concerns the energetics of chemical reactions), quantum chemistry (which concerns the structures of molecules), and chemical kinetics (which concerns the rates of chemical reactions).

Physical chemistry is the branch of chemistry that establishes and develops the principles of the subject. Its concepts are used to explain and interpret observations on the physical and chemical properties of matter. Physical chemistry is also essential for developing and interpreting the modern techniques used to determine the structure and properties of matter, such as new synthetic materials and biological membranes. [2]

Physical chemistry is the study of the physical basis of phenomena related to the chemical composition and structure of substances. It has been pursued from two levels, the macroscopic and the molecular. Knowledge in physical chemistry available today provides a rich, comprehensive view of the world of atoms and molecules that connects their nature with macroscopic properties and phenomena of materials and substances. A starting point for an introduction to physical chemistry is the concept of energy levels in atoms and molecules, distributions among these energy levels, and something familiar, temperature.

Physical chemistry is the study of the underlying physical principles that govern the properties and behavior of chemical systems. [3]

Physical chemistry, like a table with four legs, is built upon four major theoretical areas: thermodynamics, kinetics (or, more generally, transport processes), quantum mechanics, and statistical mechanics. This is not all of physical chemistry, no more than a table is only legs. Physical chemistry is a widely diverse subject that cannot be summarized adequately in any brief definition, and there are important parts of physical chemistry that do not fit neatly into this quadrivium. [4]

Physical Chemistry is a fascinating field of study. It can reasonably be claimed that many parts of physics and all parts of chemistry are included within physical chemistry and its applications. Furthermore, it is the course in which most chemistry students first have the opportunity to synthesize what they have learned in mathematics, physics, and chemistry courses into a coherent pattern of knowledge.

We see it as the quantitative interpretation of the macroscopic world in terms of the atomic-molecular world. To achieve this interpretation, we must organize our observations of macroscopic phenomena, as we do in thermodynamics and in parts of kinetics. We must advance our studies of atoms and molecules, as we do, for example, in quantum mechanics and spectroscopy. Then we must bring these studies together. This coming together is woven into much of the fabric of a modern physical chemistry course.

Physical chemistry is the application of the methods of physics to chemical problems. It includes the qualitative and quantitative study, both experimental and theoretical, of the general principles determining the behavior of matter, particularly the transformation of one substance into another. Although the physical chemist uses many of the methods of the physicist, he applies them to chemical structures and chemical processes. Physical chemistry is not so much concerned with the description of chemical substances and their reactions—this is the concern of organic and inorganic chemistry—as with theoretical principles and with quantitative problems.

It is said that there are more than four million chemical compounds. If you add composite materials like alloys and minerals and intermediate species like the free radicals to this list, it becomes truly staggering. The list of properties that interest scientists, even though modest compared to the above list, is also vast. The fascinating aspect of science is that only a few principles are needed to understand the behavior of the huge number of substances and their properties.[5] Physical chemistry is the study of these principles.

Two approaches are possible in a physicochemical study. In what might be called a systemic approach, the investigation begins with the very basic constituents of matter—the fundamental particles—and proceeds conceptually to construct larger systems from them.[6] The adjective microscopic is used to refer to these tiny constituents. In this way, increasingly complex phenomena can be interpreted on the basis of the elementary particles and their interactions.

In the second approach, the study starts with investigations of macroscopic material, such as a sample of liquid or solid that is easily observable with the eye. Measurements are made of macroscopic properties such as pressure, temperature, and volume. In the phenomenological approach, more detailed studies of microscopic behavior are made only insofar as they are needed to understand the macroscopic behavior in terms of the microscopic.

The topics of the traditional physical chemistry course can be grouped into several areas: (1) the study of the macroscopic properties of systems of many atoms or molecules; (2) the study of the processes which systems of many atoms or molecules can undergo; (3) the study of the properties of individual atoms and molecules; and (4) the study of the relationship between molecular and macroscopic properties.

Physical chemistry provides the theoretical basis for all of chemistry and many subjects related to it. Hence I feel, along with many instructors, that the first course in physical chemistry should lead to a critical understanding of primary theoretical concepts and their use in explaining crucial experiments.

Universal lessons of physical chemistry are quantitative reasoning, problem solving, rigorous and exact thinking. Many students may never directly use the factual knowledge gained in a course of physical chemistry, but all can benefit from the skills and habits learned. In the opinion of some, this emphasis leads to excessive detail in certain places. But attention to detail is the essence of good science and, in any case, it is easier to ignore unnecessary details than to add vital ones that are missing.[7]

Your education in chemistry has trained you to think in terms of molecules and their interactions, and we believe that a course in physical chemistry should reflect this viewpoint. The focus of modern physical chemistry is on the molecule. Current experimental research in physical chemistry uses equipment such as molecular beam machines to study the molecular details of gas-phase chemical reactions, high vacuum machines to study the structure and reactivity of molecules on solid interfaces, lasers to determine the structures of individual molecules and the dynamics of chemical reactions, and nuclear magnetic resonance spectrometers to learn about the structure and dynamics of molecules. Modern theoretical research in physical chemistry uses the tools of classical mechanics, quantum mechanics, and statistical mechanics along with computers to develop a detailed understanding of chemical phenomena in terms of the structure and dynamics of the molecules involved. For example, computer calculations of the electronic structure of molecules are providing fundamental insights into chemical bonding, and computer simulations of the dynamical interaction between molecules and proteins are being used to understand how proteins function.

Chemistry works with an enormous number of substances; it is an extensive science. Physics on the other hand works with rather few substances; it is an intensive science. Physical chemistry is the child of these two sciences; it has inherited the extensive character from chemistry. Upon this depends its all-embracing feature, which has attracted so great admiration. Physical chemistry may be regarded as an excellent school of exact reasoning for all students of natural sciences.

New Words and Expressions

empirical [im'pirikl] adj. 经验(主义)的
intuition [,intju(:)'iʃən] n. 直觉，直觉的知识
interplay ['intə(r),plei] v. & n. 相互影响
formulation [fɔ:(r)mju'leiʃ(ə)n] n. 公式化，配方
quantum ['kwɑntəm] n. 量子，定量，总量
macroscopic [,mækrəu'skɔpik] adj. 肉眼可见的，宏观的
fabric ['fæbrik] n. 织物，结构
energy level 能级
distribution [,distri'bju:ʃn] n. 分布，分配
quadrivium [kwɔ'driviəm] n. 四门学科（指算术、几何、天文、音乐）
coherent [kəu'hiərənt] adj. 黏着的，连贯的，一致的
woven ['wəuvən] weave 的过去分词；n. 机织织物
staggering ['stægəriŋ] adj. 难以置信的，惊愕的
approximate [ə'prɔksimeit] adj. 近似的，大约的；v. 近似，约计
statistical thermodynamics 统计热力学
physicochemical [,fizikəu'kemikəl] adj. 物理化学的，理化的
phenomenological [finɔminə'lɔdʒikl] adj. 现象学的，现象的
insofar [,insəu'fɑ:] adv. 在……的范围
instructor [in'strʌktə] n. 指导者，教师
ignore [ig'nɔ:] vt. 不理睬，忽视
vital ['vaitl] adj. 生死攸关的，重大的，至关重要的，所必需的
interface ['intə(:),feis] n. 界面
vacuum ['vækju:m] n. 真空，空虚，清洁；v. 用真空吸尘器清扫
laser ['leizər] n. 激光，激光器，镭射器
nuclear magnetic resonance 核磁共振
spectrometer [spek'trɔmitə(r)] n. 分光仪
inherit [in'herit] vt. & vi. 继承
simulation [,simju'leiʃən] n. 模仿，模拟
inordinately [in'ɔ:dinətli] adv. 无度地，非常地

Phrases

along with 连同……一起，随同……一起
in terms of 根据，在……方面
be concerned with… 与……有关，参与，干预

Affixes

therm- [θə:m-] 表示"热,热电";如 thermodynamics 热力学,thermochemistry 热化学

macro- ['mækrəu] 表示"巨大的";如 macroeconomics 宏观经济学

Notes

1. This repetitive interplay in time leads to the formulation of theories that correlate the accumulated experimental information and that can predict new phenomena with accuracy. 两个"that"引导的从句都用来修饰"formulation of theories"。参考译文:经过一段时间的这种反复相互作用得到了理论公式,该公式能把累积的实验信息关联起来并能准确预测新现象。

2. Physical chemistry is also essential for developing and interpreting the modern techniques used to determine the structure and properties of matter, such as new synthetic materials and biological membranes. 参考译文:物理化学对于开发和解释用于确定物质结构和性质的现代技术也很重要,比如新型合成材料和生物膜。

3. Physical chemistry is the study of the underlying physical principles that govern the properties and behavior of chemical systems. 参考译文:物理化学是对支配化学体系性质和行为的基本物理原理的研究。

4. Physical chemistry is a widely diverse subject that cannot be summarized adequately in any brief definition, and there are important parts of physical chemistry that do not fit neatly into this quadrivium. 参考译文:物理化学是一门内容广泛的学科,不能用任何简单的定义来恰当地概括,物理化学还有许多重要内容不能归入以上四个部分。

5. The fascinating aspect of science is that only a few principles are needed to understand the behavior of the huge number of substances and their properties. 科学吸引人的地方在于你只需要一些原理就能了解很多物质的行为和特征。

6. In what might be called a systemic approach, the investigation begins with the very basic constituents of matter— the fundamental particles— and proceeds conceptually to construct larger systems from them. 参考译文:在所谓的系统方法中,研究从物质最基本的组成——基本粒子——着手,进而研究由其构成的更大体系。

7. But attention to detail is the essence of good science and, in any case, it is easier to ignore unnecessary details than to add vital ones that are missing. 参考译文:但是专注细节是科学的精髓,无论如何,忽略不必要的细节比缺乏重要细节要容易得多。

7. Working in the Lab

Safety in the Lab

Chemical experimentation, like driving a car or operating a household, creates hazards. The primary safety rule is to familiarize yourself with the hazards and then to do nothing that you (or your instructor or supervisor) consider to be dangerous. If you believe that an operation is hazardous, discuss it first and do not proceed until sensible precautions are in place.

Preservation of a habitable planet demands that we minimize waste production and responsibly dispose of waste that is generated.[1] Recycling of chemicals is practiced in industry for economic as well as ethical reasons; it should be an important component of pollution control in your lab.[2]

Before working, familiarize yourself with safety features of your laboratory. You should wear goggles or safety glasses with side shields at all times in the lab to protect your eyes from liquids and glass, which fly around when least expected.[3] Contact lenses are not recommended in the lab because vapors can be trapped between the lens and your eye. You can protect your skin from spills and flames by wearing a flame-resistant lab coat. Use rubber gloves when pouring concentrated acids. Never eat food in the lab.

Organic solvents, concentrated acids, and concentrated ammonia should be handled in a fume hood. Air flowing into the hood keeps fumes out of the lab. The hood also dilutes fumes with air before expelling them from the roof. Never generate large quantities of toxic fumes that are allowed to escape through the hood. Wear a respirator when handling fine powders, which could produce a cloud of dust that might be inhaled.

Clean up spills immediately to prevent accidental contact by the next person who comes along. Treat spills on your skin first by flooding with water. In anticipation of splashes on your body or in your eyes, know where to find and how to operate the emergency shower and eyewash. If the sink is closer than an eye wash, use the sink first for splashes in your eyes. Know how to operate the fire extinguisher and how to use an emergency blanket to extinguish burning clothing. A first aid kit should be available, and you should know how and where to seek emergency medical assistance.

Label all vessels to indicate what they contain. An unlabeled bottle left and forgotten in a refrigerator or cabinet presents an expensive disposal problem, because the contents must be analyzed before it can be legally discarded. National Fire Protection Association labels identify hazards associated with chemical reagents. A Material Safety Data Sheet provided with each chemical sold in the United States lists hazards and safety precautions for that chemical. It gives first aid procedures and instructions for handling spills.

Disposal of Chemical Waste

If carelessly discarded, many chemicals that we use are harmful to plants, animals, and people. For each experiment, your instructor should establish procedures for waste disposal. Options include (1) pouring solutions down the drain and diluting with tap water, (2) saving the waste for disposal in an approved landfill, (3) treating waste to decrease the hazard and then pouring it down the drain or saving it for a landfill, and (4) recycling. Chemically incompatible wastes should never be mixed with each other, and each waste container must be labeled to indicate the quantity and identity of its contents.[4] Waste containers must indicate whether the contents are flammable, toxic, corrosive, or reactive, or have other dangerous properties.

A few examples illustrate different approaches to managing lab waste. Dichromate ($Cr_2O_7^{2-}$) is reduced to Cr^{3+} with sodium hydrogen sulfite ($NaHSO_3$), treated with hydroxide to make insoluble $Cr(OH)_3$, and evaporated to dryness for disposal in a landfill. Waste acid is mixed with waste base until nearly neutral (as determined with pH paper) and then poured down the drain. Waste iodate (IO_3^-) is reduced to I^- with $NaHSO_3$, neutralized with base, and poured down the drain. Waste Pb^{2+} solution is treated with sodium metasilicate (Na_2SiO_3) solution to precipitate insoluble $PbSiO_3$ that can be packaged for a landfill. Waste silver or gold is treated to recover the metals. Toxic gases used in a fume hood are bubbled through a chemical trap or burned to prevent escape from the hood.

The Lab Notebook

The critical functions of your lab notebook are to state what you did and what you observed, and it should be understandable by a stranger. The greatest error, made even by experienced scientists, is writing incomplete or unintelligible notebooks.[5] Using complete sentences is an excellent way to prevent incomplete descriptions.

Beginning students often find it useful to write a complete description of an experiment, with sections dealing with purpose, methods, results, and conclusions. Arranging a notebook to accept numerical data prior to coming to the lab is an excellent way to prepare for an experiment. It is good practice to write a balanced chemical equation for every reaction you use. This practice helps you understand what you are doing and may point out what you do not understand about what you are doing.[6]

The measure of scientific "truth" is the ability of different people to reproduce an experiment. A good lab notebook will state everything that was done and what you observed and will allow you or anyone else to repeat the experiment.[7]

Record in your notebook the names of computer files where programs and data are stored. Paste hard copies of important data into your notebook. The lifetime of a printed page is an order of magnitude (or more) greater than the lifetime of a computer disk.[8]

New Words and Expressions

experimentation [iks‚perimen'teiʃən] n. 实验，试验，实验法
household ['haus‚həuld] n. 家庭，一家人; adj. 家庭的，家常的
hazard ['hæzəd] n. 危险
preservation [‚prezər'veiʃn] n. 保存，保护
habitable ['hæbitəbl] adj. 可居住的
ethical ['eθikəl] adj. 合乎道德的
goggle ['gɔgl] n. 护目镜，（复数）风镜
contact lens 隐形镜
trap [træp] v. 收集，吸收，卡住，夹住
flame-resistant [fleim riz'istənt] adj. 耐火的
spill [spil] n. 溢出，溅出
respirator ['respəreitə] n. 呼吸器
inhale [in'heil] vt. 吸入; vi. 吸气
anticipation [‚æntisi'peiʃən] n. 预期，预料
splash ['splæʃ] n. 溅上的液体，溅洒后留下的污渍; v. 溅，泼，溅湿
sink [siŋk] n. 水槽，水池
extinguisher [ik'stiŋgwiʃə(r)] n. 灭火器
first aid kit 急救箱
label ['leibl] v. 贴标签于，用标签表明
eyewash ['aiwɔʃ] n. 洗眼器

emergency [i'mə:dʒənsi] n. 紧急情况，突然事件
assistance [ə'sistəns] n. 协助，援助
precaution [pri'kɔ:ʃən] n. 预防，警惕，防范
refrigerator [ri'fridʒəreitə] n. 电冰箱，冷藏库
disposal [dis'pəuzəl] n. 处理，安排
drain [drein] n. 排水管，下水道
dilute [dai'lu:t] v. 冲淡，稀释
landfill ['lændfil] n. 垃圾填埋地（或场）
incompatible [,inkəm'pætəbl] adj. 不相容的，不兼容的，矛盾的
illustrate ['iləstreit] vt. 举例说明，图解，阐明；vi. 举例
dichromate [dai'krəumeit] n. 重铬酸盐

insoluble [in'sɔljubl] adj. 不能溶解的
iodate ['aiədeit] vt. 以碘处理；n. 碘酸盐
metasilicate [,metə'silikit] n. 硅酸盐
neutralize ['nu:trəlaiz] vt. 中和，使中立化
precipitate [pri'sipiteit] vt. 使沉淀；n. 沉淀物，产物
sulfite ['sʌlfait] n. 亚硫酸盐
evaporated [i'væpəreitid] adj. 浓缩的，脱水的，蒸发干燥的
critical ['kritikəl] adj. 临界的，关键的
description [dis'kripʃən] n. 描写，记述，说明书，描述
unintelligible [ʌnin'telidʒəb(ə)l] adj. 难解的，无法了解的，莫名其妙的
magnitude ['mægnitju:d] n. 大小，量级

Phrases

flow into 流入
keep….out of 关在门外，不准入内
in anticipation (of) 预先，预料，期待
dilute with 用……稀释

Affixes

pre- [pri] 表示"……前的，预先"；如 preheat 预热，precoat 预涂，precursor 前辈、前驱
osmo- ['ɔzməu] 表示"渗透，嗅觉"；如 osmometry 渗透压力测定法，osmose 渗透，osmoceptor 渗透压感受器、嗅觉感受器
dif- [dif-] 表示"不，否定，分开"；如 differ 不同，diffraction 衍射，differential 差别，diffuse 散开

Notes

1. Preservation of a habitable planet demands that we minimize waste production and responsibly dispose of waste that is generated. 参考译文：保护宜居星球要求我们制造最少的废物，并能够负责任地处理产生的废物。

2. Recycling of chemicals is practiced in industry for economic as well as ethical reasons; it should be an important component of pollution control in your lab. 这是并列句，前一分句中"as well as"意思是"也"。参考译文：工业中要对化学药品回收利用，这不仅有经济原因，也有伦理方面的因素；这是实验室中污染控制的一个重要部分。

3. You should wear goggles or safety glasses with side shields at all times in the lab to protect your eyes from liquids and glass, which fly around when least expected. 参考译文：在实验室，你应该一直戴着护目镜或者有侧护板的防护眼镜，以保护你的眼睛免遭意外溅出的液体和玻璃的危害。

4. Chemically incompatible wastes should never be mixed with each other, and each waste container must be labeled to indicate the quantity and identity of its contents. 参考译

文：化学上不相容的废弃物绝对不能相互混合，并且每个废弃物容器必须贴上标签说明其中物品的数量和特性。

5. The greatest error, made even by experienced scientists, is writing incomplete or unintelligible notebooks. 参考译文：甚至是经验丰富的科学家，犯的最大错误是写了不完整的或莫名其妙的实验记录本。

6. This practice helps you understand what you are doing and may point out what you do not understand about what you are doing. 参考译文：这种做法帮助你理解你正在做的事情，也许还能指明其中你不理解的东西。

7. A good lab notebook will state everything that was done and what you observed and will allow you or anyone else to repeat the experiment. 参考译文：一个好的实验记录本，应该记录所做的和观察到的，可以让你或他人能够重复实验。

8. The lifetime of a printed page is an order of magnitude (or more) greater than the lifetime of a computer disk. 参考译文：印刷制品的寿命比电脑磁盘的寿命要大一个数量级，甚至更多。

8. Basic Laboratory Apparatus and Manipulation

Analytical Balance

An electronic balance uses an electromagnet to balance the load on the pan. A typical analytical balance with a capacity of 100~200g and a sensitivity of 0.01~0.1mg. The sensitivity is the smallest increment of mass that can be measured. The microbalance weighs milligram quantities with a sensitivity of 0.1μg.

To weigh a chemical, first place a clean receiving vessel on the balance pan. The mass of the empty vessel is called the tare. On most balances, you can press a button to reset the tare to 0. Add the chemical to the vessel and read its new mass. If there is no automatic tare operation, subtract the tare mass from that of the filled vessel. Chemicals should never be placed directly on the weighing pan. This precaution protects the balance from corrosion and allows you to recover all the chemical being weighed.

An alternate procedure, called "weighing by difference", is used routinely by many people and is necessary for hygroscopic reagents, which rapidly absorb moisture from the air.[1] First weigh a capped bottle containing dry reagent. Then quickly pour some reagent from that weighing bottle into a receiver. Cap the weighing bottle and weigh it again. The difference is the mass of reagent delivered from the weighing bottle.

The object on a balance pushes the pan down with a force equal to mg, where m is the mass of the object and g is the acceleration of gravity. The electronic balance uses electromagnetic force to return the pan to its original position. The electric current required to generate the force is proportional to the mass, which is displayed on a digital readout.

When a mass is placed on the pan, the null detector senses a displacement and sends an error signal to the circuit that generates a correction current. This current flows through the coil beneath the balance pan, thereby creating a magnetic field that is repelled by a permanent magnet under the pan. As the deflection decreases, the output of the null detector decreases. The correction current required to restore the pan to its initial position is proportional to the mass on the pan.[2]

A mechanical balance should be in its arrested position when you load or unload the pan and in the half-arrested position when you are dialing weights. This practice prevents abrupt forces that wear down the knife edges and decrease the sensitivity of the balance.

Burets

The buret is a precisely manufactured glass tube with graduations enabling you to measure the volume of liquid delivered through the stopcock (the valve) at the bottom.[3] The 0mL mark is near the top. If the initial liquid level is 0.83mL and the final level is 27.16mL, then you have delivered 27.16−0.83=26.33mL. Class A burets (the most accurate grade) are certified to meet the tolerances. If the reading of a 50mL buret is 27.16mL, the true volume can be anywhere in the range 27.21 to 27.11mL and still be within the tolerance of ±0.05mL.

When reading the liquid level in a buret, your eye should be at the same height as the top of the liquid. If your eye is too high, the liquid seems to be higher than it really is. If your eye is too low, the liquid appears too low. The error that occurs when your eye is not at the same height as the liquid is called parallax.

For precise location of the end of a titration, we deliver less than one drop at a time from the buret near the end point (a drop from a 50mL buret is about 0.05 mL). To deliver a fraction of a drop, carefully open the stopcock until part of a drop is hanging from the buret tip. (Some people prefer to rotate the stopcock rapidly through the open position to expel part of a drop.) Then touch the inside glass wall of the receiving flask to the buret tip to transfer the droplet to the wall of the flask. Carefully tip the flask so that the main body of liquid washes over the newly added droplet. Swirl the flask to mix the contents. Near the end of a titration, tip and rotate the flask often to ensure that droplets on the wall containing unreacted analyte contact the bulk solution.

Liquid should drain evenly down the wall of a buret. The tendency of liquid to stick to glass is reduced by draining the buret slowly ($<$20mL/min). If many droplets stick to the wall, then clean the buret with detergent and a buret brush. If this cleaning is insufficient, soak the buret in peroxydisulfate-sulfuric acid cleaning solution, which eats clothing and people, as well as grease in the buret. Never soak volumetric glassware in alkaline solutions, which attack glass.

When you fill a buret with fresh solution, it is a wonderful idea to rinse the buret several times with small portions of the new solution, discarding each wash. It is not necessary to fill the buret with wash solution. Simply tilt the buret to allow all surfaces to contact the wash liquid. This same technique should be used with any vessel (such as a spectrophotometer cuvet or a pipet) that is reused without drying.

The digital titrator is convenient for use in the field where samples are collected. The counter tells how much reagent has been dispensed. The precision of 1‰ is 10 times poorer than that of a glass buret, but many measurements do not require higher precision. The battery-operated electronic buret fits on a reagent bottle and delivers up to 99.99mL in 0.01mL increments. For titrations requiring the very highest precision measure, the mass of reagent, instead of the volume, is delivered from a buret or syringe. Mass can be measured more precisely than volume.

Volumetric Flasks

A volumetric flask is calibrated to contain a particular volume of solution at 20℃ when the bottom of the meniscus is adjusted to the center of the mark on the neck of the flask.[4] Most flasks bear the label "TC 20℃", which means to contain at 20℃. The temperature of the container is relevant because both liquid and glass expand when heated.

To use a volumetric flask, dissolve the desired mass of reagent in the flask by swirling with less than the final volume of liquid. Then add more liquid and swirl the solution again. Adjust the final volume with as much well-mixed liquid in the flask as possible. For good control, add the final drops of liquid with a pipet, not a squirt bottle. Finally, hold the cap firmly in place and invert the flask 20 times to mix well.

Transfer Pipets

Using a rubber bulb or other pipet suction device, not your mouth, suck liquid up past the calibration mark. Discard one or two pipet volumes of liquid to rinse traces of previous reagents from the pipet. After taking up a third volume past the calibration mark, quickly replace the bulb with your index finger at the end of the pipet. Gently pressing the pipet against the bottom of the vessel while removing the rubber bulb helps prevent liquid from draining below the mark while you put your finger in place. Wipe the excess liquid off the outside of the pipet with a clean tissue. Touch the tip of the pipet to the side of a beaker and drain the liquid until the bottom of the meniscus just reaches the center of the mark. Touching the beaker draws liquid from the pipet without leaving part of a drop hanging when the liquid reaches the calibration mark.

Transfer the pipet to a receiving vessel and drain it by gravity while holding the tip against the wall of the vessel. After the liquid stops, hold the pipet to the wall for a few more seconds to complete draining. The pipet should be nearly vertical at the end of delivery. When you finish with a pipet, you should rinse it with distilled water or soak it until you are ready to clean it. Solutions should never be allowed to dry inside a pipet because removing internal deposits is very difficult.

Micropipets

Micropipets deliver volumes of 1 to $1000 \mu L$ ($1 \mu L = 10^{-6} L$). Liquid is contained in the disposable polypropylene tip, which is stable to most aqueous solutions and many organic solvents except chloroform ($CHCl_3$). The tip is not resistant to concentrated nitric or sulfuric acids.

To use a micropipette, place a fresh tip tightly on the barrel. Keep tips in their package or dispenser so that you do not contaminate the tips with your fingers. Set the desired volume with the knob at the top of the pipet. Depress the plunger to the first stop, which corresponds to the selected volume. Hold the pipet vertically, dip it 3～5mm into the reagent solution, and slowly release the plunger to suck up liquid. Withdraw the tip from the liquid by sliding it along the wall of the vessel to remove liquid from the outside of the tip. To dispense liquid, touch the micropipet tip to the wall of the receiver and gently depress the plunger to the first stop. Wait a few seconds to allow liquid to drain down the wall of the pipet tip, then depress the plunger further to squirt out the last liquid. It is a good idea to clean and wet a fresh tip by taking up and discarding two or three squirts of reagent. The tip can be discarded or rinsed well with a squirt bottle and reused.

The volume of liquid taken into the tip depends on the angle at which the pipet is held and how far beneath the liquid surface the tip is held during uptake. Each person attains slightly different precision and accuracy with a micropipette.

Filtration

In gravimetric analysis, the mass of product from a reaction is measured to determine how much unknown was present. Precipitates from gravimetric analyses are collected by filtration, washed, and then dried. Most precipitates are collected in a fritted-glass funnel (also called a Gooch filter crucible) with suction applied to speed filtration. The porous glass plate in the funnel allows liquid to pass but retains solid. The empty funnel is first dried at 110℃ and weighed. After collecting solid and drying again, the funnel and its contents are weighed a second time to determine the mass of collected solid. Liquid from which a substance precipitates or crystallizes is called the mother liquor. Liquid that passes through the filter is called filtrate.

In some gravimetric procedures, ignition (heating at high temperature over a burner or in a furnace) is used to convert a precipitate to a known, constant composition. For example, Fe^{3+} precipitates as hydrous ferric oxide, $FeOOH \cdot xH_2O$, with variable composition. Ignition converts it to pure Fe_2O_3 prior to weighing. When a precipitate is to be ignited, it is collected in ashless filter paper, which leaves little residue when burned.

To use filter paper with a conical glass funnel, fold the paper into quarters, tear of one corner (to allow a firm fit into the funnel), and place the paper in the funnel. The filter paper should fit snugly and be seated with some distilled water. When liquid is poured in an unbroken stream of liquid should fill the stem of the funnel. The weight of liquid in the stem helps speed filtration.

For filtration, pour the slurry of precipitate down a glass rod to prevent splattering. (A slurry is a suspension of solid in liquid.) Particles adhering to the beaker or rod can be dislodged with a rubber policeman, which is a flattened piece of rubber at the end of a glass rod.[5] Use a jet of appropriate wash liquid from a squirt bottle to transfer particles from the rubber and glassware to the filter. If the precipitate is going to be ignited, particles remaining in the beaker should be wiped onto a small piece of moist filter paper. Add that paper to the filter to be ignited.

Drying

Reagents, precipitates, and glassware are conveniently dried in an oven at 110℃. (Some chemicals require other temperatures.) Anything that you put in the oven should be labeled. Use a beaker and watch glass to minimize contamination by dust during drying. It is good practice to cover all vessels on the benchtop to prevent dust contamination.

The mass of a gravimetric precipitate is measured by weighing a dry, empty filter crucible before the procedure and reweighing the same crucible filled with dry product after the procedure.[6] To weigh the empty crucible, first bring it to "constant mass" by drying it in the oven for 1h or longer and then cooling it for 30min in a desiccator. Weigh the crucible and then heat it again for about 30min. Cool it and reweigh it. When successive weighings agree to ± 0.3mg. The filter has reached "constant mass". You can use a microwave oven instead of an electric oven for drying reagents and crucibles. Try an initial heating time of 4min, with subsequent 2min heatings. Take 15min to cool down before weighing.

A desiccator is a closed chamber containing drying agent called a desiccant. The lid is greased to make an airtight seal and desiccant is placed in the bottom beneath the perforated disk. Another useful desiccant is 98% sulfuric acid. After placing a hot object in the desiccator, leave the lid cracked open for a minute until the object has cooled slightly. This practice prevents the lid from popping open when the air inside warms up. To open a desiccator, slide the lid sideways rather than trying to pull it straight up.

New Words and Expressions

electromagnet [iˌlektrəuˈmægnit] n. 电磁铁
increment [ˈinkrimənt] n. 增加,增量
microbalance [ˌmaikrəuˈbæləns] n. 微量天平
vessel [ˈvesl] n. 容器,船
tare [teə(r)] n. 量皮重,去皮
automatic [ˌɔːtəˈmætik] n. 自动机械; adj. 自动的,机械的
corrosion [kəˈrəuʒən] n. 侵蚀,腐蚀

hygroscopic [ˌhaigrəˈskɔpik] adj. 吸湿的
moisture [ˈmɔistʃə] n. 潮湿,湿气
acceleration [ækˌseləˈreiʃən] n. 加速度
readout [riːdaut] n. 读出器,读出
null [nʌl] adj. 零值的,等于零的
arrest [əˈrest] v. 阻止,逮捕
graduation [ˌgrædʒuˈeiʃn] n. 刻度,毕业(典礼)
stopcock [ˈstɔpkɔk] n. 活塞,旋塞阀

tolerance ['tɔlərəns] n. 公差，限度，宽容
swirl [swərl] vi. 旋转；vt. 使成漩涡，打转
detergent [di'tə:rdʒənt] n. 洗涤剂，去垢剂
soak [səuk] vt. 浸泡，浸透
peroxydisulfate 过二硫酸盐
grease [gri:s] n. 动物油脂，润滑油；vt. 涂油脂于
dislodge [dis'lɔdʒ] vt. 把……移动，驱逐；vi. 移走，离开原位
parallax ['pærəlæks] n. 视差
meniscus [mə'niskəs] n. 弯月面，弯液面
tilt [tilt] vt. 使倾斜
titrator ['taitreitə] n. 滴定仪
counter ['kauntər] n. 计数器，柜台，对立面，反驳；v. 抵制；adv. 逆向地
dispense [di'spens] v. 分配，实施
volumetric [vɔlju'metrik] adj. 测定体积的
bear [beər] v. 显示，带有，忍受
squirt bottle 喷瓶，洗瓶
invert [in'və:rt] vt. 使……前后倒置，使反转
suction [sʌkʃn] n. 吸，抽吸，吸出
suck [sʌk] v. 吮吸，吸引；n. 吸入物
rinse [rins] vt. 漂洗，冲洗；n. 冲洗
distilled [di'stild] adj. 由蒸馏得来的
deposit [di'pɔzit] n. 沉淀物，押金，存款；v. 使沉淀，存放，存入银行账户

disposable [di'spəuzəbl] adj. 一次性的
polypropylene [pɔli'prəupəli:n] n. 聚丙烯
chloroform ['klɔrəfɔrm] n. 氯仿，三氯甲烷
package ['pækidʒ] n. 包装盒，包裹
knob [nɔb] n. 旋钮，球形把手
depress [di'pres] v. 按下，使抑郁，使萧条
plunger ['plʌndʒər] n. 活塞，柱塞，撞针杆
uptake [ʌpteik] n. 吸入，举起，摄入
fritted ['fritid] adj. 烧结的，熔块的
funnel ['fʌnl] n. 漏斗，烟囱，通风井
crystallize ['kristə,laiz] v. （使）结晶，（使）成形
filtrate ['filtreit] n. 滤出液
flatten ['flætn] v. 变平，停止增长
glassware [glɑ:sweə(r)] n. 玻璃器具类
filter ['filtər] n. 过滤器；v. 过滤，渗透
benchtop ['bentʃtɔp] 台式
crucible ['kru:səb(ə)l] n. 坩埚，熔炉
desiccator ['desi,keitə] n. 干燥器
chamber ['tʃeimbər] n. 室，腔，房间，议会
desiccant ['desəkənt] n. 干燥剂
airtight ['eə(r)tait] adj. 不透气的，密封的
seal [si:l] n. 密封处/物/垫，印章；v. 密封
perforate ['pərfəreit] v. 穿孔于，在……上打眼
crack [kræk] v. （使）破裂，裂开；n. 缝隙
slide [slaid] v. 滑动；n. 滑行，降低

Phrases

subtract…from… 从……中减去……
be proportional to 与……成正比
enable to 使能够
squirt out 喷出来

at the bottom of 在……底部
be convenient for 方便，便利
gravimetric analysis 重量分析（法）
ashless filter paper 无灰滤纸

Affixes

electro- [i'lektrəu] 表示"电的"；如 electrobath 电镀浴，electrode 电极，electrochemistry 电化学
poly- ['pɔli] 表示"多的，多个的"；如 polyacid 多酸的，polyamide 聚酰胺，polyatomic 多原子的

Notes

1. An alternate procedure, called "weighing by difference", is used routinely by many

people and is necessary for hygroscopic reagents, which rapidly absorb moisture from the air. 参考译文：通常许多人使用另一种方法，被称为"差减称量法"，对于快速吸收空气中水分的吸湿性试剂需要使用该方法。

2. The correction current required to restore the pan to its initial position is proportional to the mass on the pan. 参考译文：恢复托盘到初始位置所需要的校正电流与托盘上的质量成正比。

3. The buret is a precisely manufactured glass tube with graduations enabling you to measure the volume of liquid delivered through the stopcock (the valve) at the bottom. 参考译文：滴定管是一种带有刻度的精密加工的玻璃管，能够测量通过底部活塞（阀）放出的液体体积。

4. A volumetric flask is calibrated to contain a particular volume of solution at 20℃ when the bottom of the meniscus is adjusted to the center of the mark on the neck of the flask. 参考译文：当调节（溶液）弯月面底部到容量瓶瓶颈上刻度线中心的时候，容量瓶就被校准为 20℃时具有一特定的容积。

5. Particles adhering to the beaker or rod can be dislodged with a rubber policeman, which is a flattened piece of rubber at the end of a glass rod. 参考译文：沾附在烧杯或搅拌棒上的微粒，可以用橡胶刮勺来除去，橡胶刮勺是玻璃棒末端的一块扁平橡胶。

6. The mass of a gravimetric precipitate is measured by weighing a dry, empty filter crucible before the procedure and reweighing the same crucible filled with dry product after the procedure. 参考译文：重量法测量沉淀物的质量是先称量实验开始前干燥的空过滤坩埚的质量，然后再称量实验后装有干燥产物的相同坩埚的质量。

Part B

Basic Knowledge of Chemical Engineering

1. Chemical Engineering

Chemical engineering creatively combines the three basic physical sciences—chemistry, physics, and biology—along with mathematics to address the world's needs by creating new technology and solving problems in existing technology. The use of all three basic sciences and mathematics makes chemical engineering extremely versatile, since nearly all physical phenomena can be described by the combination of these four sciences.

Those working in the field of chemical engineering are involved in a variety of areas. Chemical engineering is found in research and development, in process design, plant design and construction, sales, management.

Chemical engineering deals mainly with industrial or commercial processing to produce value-added products from raw materials. Chemical engineering has ranged from petroleum and petrochemical products to products coming from natural minerals and deposits. Chemical engineering has produced gasoline, packaging film and is working on developing fuel cells for the future electric car.

address [ə'dres] v. 演说，处理，演讲，对付
versatile ['və:(r)sətail] adj. 多用途的，通用的，多方面的
involve [in'vɔlv] vt. 包括，包含
plant [plɑ:nt] n. 工厂，车间

deposit [di'pɔzit] n. 矿藏，矿床
fuel cell 燃料电池

2. The Difference Between Engineering and Science

The major difference between engineering and science is methodology. The differences between engineers and scientists fall into the following categories:

a. Purpose. The scientist wants to understand the way the universe (or some particular part of it) works; the engineer wants to design some mechanism or system to work according to known laws

methodology [ˌmeθə'dɔlədʒi] n. 方法，方法论，方法学

and applies to specific needs.

b. Routine. The scientist will develop a theory and test it — when the field allows. In some fields the scientist will collect and analyze data and "then" develop a theory to describe the results. (This theory may lead to an equation or some other tools used by the engineer.) The engineer will instead collect information, draw up a plan, build and test a prototype, iterate and iron out the kinks, and go to production and marketing.

3. Pipe Lines

The movement of liquids and gases through pipelines is highly specialized and extremely important. Without the gas pipelines, the movement of large volumes of gases over great distances would be an economic impossibility. The liquid pipelines, used mostly for either crude or refined petroleum, and for water, are an important part of the general transportation system. Pipe-line transportation has the following general characteristics: (a) one-material service or service to a class of material, (b) fixed loading point and terminus, (c) high initial investment, and (d) the lowest ton-mile cost for overland transportation.

It is estimated that more than 50 percent is liquid line in the petroleum and gas pipeline system, the remainder is gasline.

Pipeline size is governed by the amount of material to be transported through the line. Lines may vary anywhere from a diameter of 3 or 4 inches for the liquid collection lines to 48 inches for the gas trunk lines. The oil lines tend toward the smaller sizes, the gas toward the larger.

The pipe line, once installed, offers the cheapest method of transporting petroleum and natural gas, and certain other liquids and gases such as water, chlorine, hydrogen, and steam, and solids such as powdered fuel between points separated by land only. The cost of the operation of a line is low.

4. Valve

Often the peculiarities of the material being handled or the service required limit the material the valve can be made of and these, in turn, dictate valve design. Many materials which are adequately resistant to corrosion are difficult to machine, and can be successfully worked only by casting and grinding. Threads and

routine [ruˈtin] n. 程序，常规
prototype [ˈprəutəˌtaip] n. 原型，模型
iron out 烫平，消除，解决
kink [kiŋk] n. 扭结，绞缠，缺陷

specialized [ˈspeʃəlaizd] adj. 专业的，特殊的
refine [riˈfain] vt. 精炼，精制
transportation [ˌtrænspɔː(r)ˈteiʃ(ə)n] n. 运输，运送
terminus [ˈtəː(r)minəs] n. 终点站，末端
remainder [riˈmeində] n. 残余，剩余物

trunk [trʌŋk] n. 干线，主干

chlorine [ˈklɔrin] n. 氯
powdered fuel 粉状燃料，褐煤粉及石煤粉

peculiarity [piˌkjuːliˈærəti] n. 特点；特性
casting 铸造
grinding 磨削
thread [θred] n. 螺纹

screws must be avoided if possible. Such valves are expensive, and must be made simple in design to keep their cost within reasonable limits. Since much of the cost of the valve is in the machining rather than in the material, valves tend, in general, to be made of somewhat more expensive material than those used in pipes.

The various valves have a number of features in common. Each valve has a handle or hand-wheel for its operation; a stem to transmit the motion of the hand-wheel to the closure; a closure, which may be a gate, plug or disk; and the seat in or on which this device rests. The valve is encased in a body shaped to fit the valve closure.

There is a trend to make valves, even those remotely controlled, responsive to automatic control by instruments. These instruments may measure any one of any number of elements and convert the results into automatic control of hydraulic or electrical circuits, which in turn operate the valves. Such controls are often expensive, but so effective and so free from the erratic control of manual operation that they are attracting much attention. Many production processes today are becoming "push button" in character.

5. Centrifugal Pump

Fluids are often forced to move through pipes by pumps. The chief use of pump is to add energy to the fluid. Energy is considered to be the capacity to do work. The energy to be added will serve to raise the pressure, elevation, and velocity.

The terms "air pumps" and "vacuum pumps" are used to name the machines to compress a gas, but commonly pumps are regarded as devices with which to handle liquids.

It is impossible for a pump to work by itself. Therefore a motor or a steam engine is employed to make the pump run.

Pumps are said to be of great importance in industry. We consider it is important to build more pump plants so as to meet the growing needs of our socialist construction. Now great progress has been made in this respect. Various kinds of pumping equipments are widely used here. Although a wide range of pumps are available for numerous applications, most fit into one of two main groups. These are: rotodynamic pumps and positive displacement pumps.

There are many different types of positive displacement pumps, including reciprocating pumps, controlled volume pumps, air operated double diaphragm pumps, and rotary pumps.

There are many different types of rotodynamic pumps suited to varying applications, including centrifugal pumps, peripheral pumps and other types of rotodynamic pumps. Centrifugal pumps are classified into three general categories depending on the type of impeller used: radial flow, mixed flow, and axial flow pumps.

screw [skru:] n. 螺丝钉，螺旋，螺杆，螺孔

feature ['fi:tʃə(r)] n. 特征，容貌
plug 堵头
encase [in'keis] vt. 装入，包住，围
instrument ['instrəmənt] n. 仪器，工具
hydraulic [hai'drɔ:lik] adj. 水力的，水压的，油压的

centrifugal [ˌsentri'fju:gl] adj. 离心的

compress [kəm'pres] vt. 压缩

rotodynamic pump 转子动力泵
positive displacement pump 容积泵
reciprocate [ri'siprəˌkeit] v. 往复，互换
controlled volume pump 计量泵
air operated double diaphragm pump 气动双隔膜泵
peripheral [pə'rifərəl] adj. 外周的
peripheral pumps 涡流泵
radial ['reidiəl] adj. 放射状的，径向的

Centrifugal pump is one of the simplest pieces of equipment. Its purpose is to convert energy of an electric motor or engine into velocity or kinetic energy and then into pressure of a fluid that is being pumped. The energy changes occur into two main parts of the pump, the impeller and the volute. The impeller is the rotating part that converts driver energy into the kinetic energy. The volute is the stationary part that converts the kinetic energy into pressure.

Liquid enters the pump suction and then the eye of the impeller. When the impeller rotates, it spins the liquid sitting in the cavities between the vanesoutward and imparts centrifugal acceleration. As the liquid leaves the eye of the impeller a low-pressure area is created at the eye allowing more liquid to enter the pump inlet.

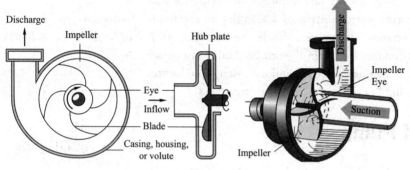

6. Cyclone Separator

Cyclone separators are very useful piece of equipments for the removal from air streams of particles above 10 micrometers in diameter.

In the conventional cyclone, the gas enters a cylinder tangentially, where it spins in a vortex as it proceeds down the cylinder. A cone section causes the vortex diameter to decrease until the gas reverses on it and spins up the center to the outlet pipe or vortex finder. A cone causes flow reversal to occur sooner and makes the cyclone more compact. Dust particles are centrifuged toward the wall and collected by inertial impingement. The collected dust flows down in the gas boundary layer to the cone apex where it is discharged through an air lock or into a dust hopper serving one or more parallel cyclones. Although conventional cyclones can be built to larger diameter, they are commonly 600 to 915 millimeters in diameter.

Cyclone separators can be classified according to either their geometrical configuration (tangential inlet axial discharge, tangential inlet peripheral discharge, axial inlet and discharge, and axial inlet peripheral discharge) or their efficiency in high efficient (98%～99%), moderate efficient (70%～80%), and low efficient (50%).

Cyclones can be used for separating particles from liquids as well as from gases and they can also be used for separating liquid droplets from gases. In industries such as food and chemical industries, cyclones are used for removing the dry product from the air. In synthetic detergent production, fast reactor cyclones are used in separating a cracking catalyst from vaporized reaction products.

detergent [di'tə:dʒənt] n. 清洁剂，去垢剂

7. Cooling Tower

Cooling towers are a very important part of many chemical plants. They represent a relatively inexpensive and dependable means of removing low-grade heat from cooling water.

The make-up water source is used to replenish water lost to evaporation. Hot water from heat exchangers is sent to the cooling tower. The water exits the cooling tower is sent back to the exchangers or to other units for further cooling.

Cooling towers fall into two main subdivisions: natural draft and mechanical draft. Natural draft designs use very large concrete chimneys to introduce air through the media. Due to the tremendous size of these towers (500 ft high and 400 ft in diameter at the base) they are generally used for water flow rates above 200 000 gal/min. Usually these types of towers are only used by utility power stations in the United States. Mechanical draft cooling towers are much more widely used. These towers utilize large fans to force air through circulated water. The water falls downward over fill surfaces that help increase the contact time between the water and the air. This helps maximize heat transfer between the two phases.

make-up water
补充水
replenish [ri'pleniʃ] v. 补充，重新装满
exchanger [iks'tʃendʒər] n. 换热器，交换器
natural draft
自然通风

utility power stations
电站

circulate ['sə:kjuleit] v. (使)流通,(使)循环

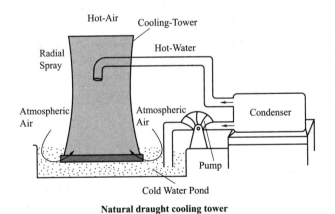

Natural draught cooling tower

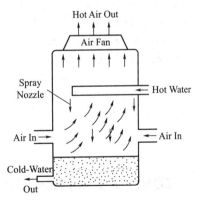

Mechanical draft cooling tower

8. Membrane

Membranes can be defined essentially as a barrier, which separates two phases and restricts transport of various chemicals in a selective manner. A membrane can be homogenous or heterogeneous, symmetric or asymmetric in structure, solid or liquid, can carry a

homogenous [hə'mɔdʒənəs] adj. 同质的，均相的
heterogeneous [,hetərə'dʒi:niəs] adj. 不同种类的，异类的

positive or negative charge or be neutral or bipolar. Transport through a membrane can be effected by convection or by diffusion of individual molecules, induced by an electric field or concentration, pressure or temperature gradient. The membrane thickness may vary from as small as 100 micros to several millimeters.

A membrane separation system separates an influent stream into two effluent streams known as the permeate and the concentrate. The permeate is the portion of the fluid that has passed through the semi-permeable membrane. Whereas the concentrate stream contains the constituents that have been rejected by the membrane.

The ongoing evolution of membrane technology allows greater flexibility in designing systems that function under a variety of operating conditions. The development of new membranes continues to expand both the range of chemical compatibilities and physical operating conditions (including pressure, temperature, and pH) of membrane systems.

9. Diffusion Process

In its simplest form, diffusion is the transport of a material or chemical by molecular motion. If molecules of a chemical are present in an apparently motionless fluid, they will exhibit microscopic erratic motions due to being randomly struck by other molecules in the fluid. Individual particles or molecules will follow paths sometimes known as "random walks".

In such processes, a chemical initially concentrated in one area will disperse. That is, there will be a net transport of that chemical from regions of high concentration to regions of low concentration.

An analogous form of diffusion is called conduction. In this case, heat is the "chemical" that is transported by molecular motion. As in chemical diffusion, heat migrates from regions of high temperature to regions of low temperature. The mathematics describing both conduction and diffusion are the same.

10. Reverse Osmosis

Diffusion is the movement of molecules from a region of higher concentration to a region of lower concentration. Osmosis is a special case of diffusion in which the molecules are water molecules and the concentration gradient occurs across a semi-permeable membrane. The semi-permeable membrane allows the passage of water molecules, but not ions (e.g., Na^+, Ca^{2+}, Cl^-) or larger molecules (e.g., glucose, urea, bacteria). Diffusion and osmosis are thermodynamically favorable and will continue until equilibrium is reached. Osmosis can be slowed, stopped, or even reversed if sufficient pressure is applied to the membrane from the "concentrated" side of the membrane.

Reverse osmosis occurs when the water is moved across the membrane against the concentration gradient, from lower concentration to higher concentration. To illustrate, imagine a semi-permeable membrane with fresh water on one side and a concentrated aqueous solution on the other side. If normal osmosis takes place, the fresh water will cross the membrane to dilute the concentrated solution. In reverse osmosis, pressure is exerted on the side with the concentrated solution to force the water molecules across the membrane to the fresh water side.

Reverse osmosis is often used in commercial and residential water filtration. It is also one of the methods used to desalinate seawater. Sometimes reverse osmosis is used to purify liquids in which water is an undesirable impurity (e.g., ethanol).

11. Filtration

Filtration is one of the most common applications of the flow of fluids through packed beds. As carried out industrially, it is exactly analogous to the filtration carried out in a chemical laboratory using a filter paper in a funnel. The object is still the separation of a solid from the fluid in which it is carried. In every case, the separation is accomplished by forcing the fluid through a porous membrane. The solid particles are trapped within the pores of the membrane and build up a layer on the surface of this membrane. The fluid, which may be either gas or liquid, passes through the bed of solids and through the retaining membrane.

Industrial filtration differs from laboratory filtration only in the bulk of material handled and in the necessity that it be handled at low cost. Thus, to attain a reasonable throughput with a moderate-sized filter, the pressure drop for flow may be increased, or the resistance to flow may be decreased. Most industrial equipments decrease the flow resistance by making the filtering area as large as possible without increasing the over-all size of the filter apparatus. The choice of filter equipment depends largely on economics, but the economic advantages will vary depending on the following factors: fluid viscosity, density, and chemical reactivity, solid particle size, size distribution, shape, flocculation tendencies, and deformability, feed slurry concentration, amount of material to be handled, absolute and relative values of liquid and solid products, completeness of separation required, relative costs of labor, capital, and power consumption etc.

12. Evaporation

The objective of evaporation is to concentrate a solution consisting of a nonvolatile solute and a volatile solvent. In the great majority of evaporations the solvent is water. Evaporation is conducted by vaporizing a portion of the solvent to produce a concentrated solution or thick liquor. Evaporation differs from drying in that the residue is a liquid (sometimes a highly viscous one) rather than a solid; it differs from distillation in that the vapor is a single component, and even when the vapor is a mixture, no attempt is made in the evaporation step to separate the vapor into fractions; it differs from crystallization in that emphasis is placed on concentrating a solution rather than forming and building crystals. In certain situations, e.g., in the evaporation of brine to produce common salt, the line between evaporation and crystallization is far from sharp. Evaporation sometimes produces slurry of crystals in saturated mother liquor.

Normally, in evaporation the thick liquor is the valuable product and the vapor is condensed and discarded. In one specific situation, however, the reverse is true. Mineral-bearing water is often evaporated to give a solid-free product for boiler feed, for special process requirements, or for human consumption. This technique is often called water distillation, but technically it is evaporation. Large-scale evaporation process is being developed and used for recovering potable water from seawater. Here the condensed water is the desired product. Only a fraction of the total water in the feed is recovered, and the remainder is discarded.

volatile ['vɔlətail] adj. 挥发性的
thick liquor 稠液，浓酒
viscous ['viskəs] adj. 黏性的，黏滞的，胶黏的
fraction ['frækʃən] n. 分馏，馏分

brine [brain] n. 盐水
saturated ['sætʃəreitid] adj. 饱和的

condense [kən'dens] v. 冷凝，凝结

water distillation 水蒸馏（法）

potable ['pəutəbl] adj. 适于饮用的

13. Crystallization

Crystallization from liquid solution is important industrially because of the variety of materials are marketed in the crystalline forms. Its wide use is based on the fact that a crystal formed from an impure solution is itself pure (unless mixed crystals occur) and that crystallization affords a practical method of obtaining pure chemical substances in a satisfactory condition for package and storing.

It is clear that good yield and high purity are important objectives in operating a crystallization process, but these two factors are not the only ones to be considered. The appearance and size range of a crystalline product are also significant. It is especially necessary that the crystals should be of reasonable and uniform size. If they are to

crystalline ['kristəlain] adj. 结晶的，晶状的，晶体的

be further processed, reasonable size and uniformity are desirable for washing, filtering, reacting with other chemicals, transporting, and storing the crystals. If the crystals are to be marketed as a final product, customers require individual crystals to be strong, nonaggregated, uniform in size, and noncaking in the package. For these reasons, crystal size distribution (CSD) must be under control; it is a prime objective in the design and operation of crystallizers.

In general, crystallization may be analyzed from the standpoint of purity, yield, energy requirements, rates of formation, and growth of crystals.

14. Drying

In general, drying a solid means the removal of relatively small amounts of water or other liquid from the solid material to reduce the content of residual liquid to an acceptably low value. Drying is usually the final step in a series of operations, and the product from a dryer is often ready for final packing.

Water or other liquids may be removed from solids mechanically by filtration or centrifugation or thermally by vaporization. It is generally cheaper to remove water mechanically than thermally. The utmost use should be made of these mechanical processes. In a simple instance a centrifugal will remove 2 tons of water from a ton of granular solid with a power cost of about 10 KWh; the steam equivalent of this will be at most 300 lb. If the water is evaporated in a steam heated dryer, the steam consumption must be at least 4 480 lb. Thus it is advisable to reduce the moisture content as much as possible before feeding the material to a heated dryer.

The moisture content of a dried substance varies from product to product. Occasionally the product contains no water. More commonly, the product does contain some water. Dried table salt, for example, contains about 0.5 percent water, dried coal about 4 percent, and dried casein about 8 percent. Drying is a relative term and means only that there is a reduction in moisture content from an initial value to a final one.

15. Mixing

Many processing operations depend for their success on the effective mixing of materials. The practical aims of mixing are four:

a. To produce simple physical mixtures, such as that of two or more miscible fluids, two or more uniformly divided solids, or a mixture of phases where no reaction or changes of particle size take place.

---

uniformity [ˌjuːniˈfɔːməti] n. 均匀性(度)，一致
noncaking adj. 不黏结的，无黏性的
distribution [ˌdistriˈbjuːʃ(ə)n] n. 分配，分布状态
standpoint [ˈstændpɔint] n. 立场，观点

mechanically [miˈkænikəli] adv. 机械地
centrifugation [senˌtrifjuˈgeiʃən] n. 离心法，离心过滤
granular [ˈgrænjulə(r)] adj. 颗粒的，粒状的
moisture [ˈmɔistʃər] n. 水分，湿气，潮湿

casein [ˈkeisiːn] n. 酪蛋白

miscible [ˈmisəbl] adj. 可混合的，互溶的，可混溶的

b. To accomplish physical change, such as the solution of one component in another, the formation of crystals from a supersaturated solution, the selective adsorption of minor constituents by adsorbents such as fullers earth, and so on.

c. To accomplish dispersion, wherein a quasi-homogeneous product is produced from two or more immiscible fluids, or more fluids with finely divided solids.

d. To promote a reaction. This latter is perhaps the most important use of mixing in the chemical industry since intimacy of contact between reacting phases is a necessary condition of proper reaction.

The requirements of a satisfactory mixer, in general, are (1) that it yield a desired degree of mixing at the point of most intense agitation, (2) that a satisfactory rate and direction of motion of the entire body of material must be established and maintained, and (3) that it require the minimum expenditure of power and the shortest, most economical period of time. Whether a particular type of mixer will meet these requirements in a given problem can often be determined only by experiment.

16. Distillation

Distillation is a common chemistry process used to separate materials by changing their states of matter. Distillation is widely used for separating mixtures based on differences in the conditions required to change the state of components of the mixture. To separate a mixture of liquids, the liquid can be heated to force components, which have different boiling points, into the gas phase. The gas is then condensed back into liquid form and collected. Repeating the process on the collected liquid to improve the purity of the product is called double distillation. Although the term is most commonly applied to liquids, the reverse process can be used to separate gases by liquefying components using changes in temperature and/or pressure.

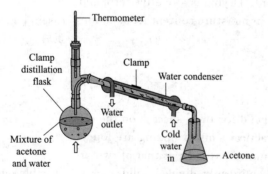

Distillation is used for many commercial processes, such as production of gasoline, distilled water, xylene, alcohol, paraffin, kerosene, and many other liquids.

Types of distillation include simple distillation (described here), fractional distillation (different volatile "fractions" are collected as they are produced), and destructive distillation (usually, a material is heated so that it decomposes into compounds for collection).

17. Adsorption

Adsorption is the binding of molecules or particles to a solid surface, which must be distinguished from absorption. The binding to the surface is usually weak and reversible. But compounds with color and those that have taste or odor tend to bind strongly. Compounds that contain chromogenic groups (atomic arrangements that vibrate at frequencies in the visible spectrum) usually are strongly adsorbed on activated carbon. Decolorization can be wonderfully efficient by adsorption and with negligible loss of other materials.

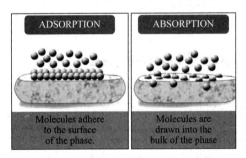

The most common industrial adsorbents are activated carbon, silica gel, and alumina, because they present enormous surface areas per unit weight.

A surface already heavily contaminated by adsorbates is not likely to have much capacity for additional binding, but further heating will drive off these compounds to produce a surface with high adsorptive capacity.

Temperature effects on adsorption are profound, and measurements are usually at a constant temperature. Graphs of the data are called isotherms.

18. Reciprocating Compressor

The reciprocating compressor can furnish gas at pressures of a few pounds or at extremely high pressures, such as 35 000 psi. The characteristic features of reciprocating compressors are the same as those of reciprocating pumps — a piston, a cylinder with suitable intake and exhaust valves, and a crankshaft with drive. Single-stage or multistage operation is common, with double-acting cylinder usage being general.

Gas being compressed enters and leaves the cylinder through valves, which are set to be actuated when the pressure difference between cylinder contents and outside conditions is desired. If multistage compression is used, it is general practice to cool the gas between stages.

Discharge characteristics of reciprocating compressors are similar to those of reciprocating pumps. Compressor operation is fundamentally thought of as being isentropic, and efficiencies are reported relative to this isentropic basis. Thermodynamic losses and fluid friction are grouped together as compression inefficiency. Mechanical friction losses are termed mechanical inefficiency. The over-all compressor efficiency will be the product of the compression and mechanical efficiency. The over-all efficiency of most reciprocating compressors is 65 to 80 percent.

19. Batch and Continuous Processes

Many industrial operations can be carried out in either of two ways, which may be called batch and continuous operations. This is the simple case of heating a solution with steam. In the batch process the solution, at its original temperature, is pumped into a tank, and then heated as a batch by admission of steam to a surrounding jacket or to internal coils. When the solution in the tank has reached the desired temperature, it is discharged, a new batch of cool solution is added, and the process repeated. In the continuous process the solution can be passed slowly but continuously through a pipe coil which is heated by steam, the rate of flow being adjusted so that the solution leaves the outlet end of the coil at the desired temperature.

The continuous process, although requiring more carefully designed equipment than the batch process, can ordinarily be handled in less space, fits in with other continuous steps more smoothly, and can be conducted at any prevailing pressure without release to atmospheric pressure. The temperature of each part of the equipment remains substantially constant during operation, thus avoiding the fluctuating, which is unavoidable with the batch procedure.

Continuous operation of processes has many advantages and is ordinarily a goal in engineering design. Batch operations are frequently found in lab and pilot-plant.

20. Removal of Dust from Gases

In general, gas must be cleaned from dust for one or more of the following three purposes:

a. the dust contained in the gas may be valuable and separated from it as another product from the process;

b. the gas itself may be required for use in a further process;

c. it may be an effluent gas which must be cleaned before discharge into atmosphere to avoid nuisance or damage to amenities.

Gas cleaning can be a very expensive process, particularly if almost complete removal of all of the dust is required and great care must be given to the selection of the most economic equipment for a particular purpose, bearing in mind capital charges and running costs, and the value of the collected particles. It is necessary, therefore, to have an adequate knowledge of the principal features and fields of application of the various types of gas cleaning equipments available.

The simplest method of removing particles from a moving gas stream is to allow them to settle out under the force of gravity. Large particles will often do so in a simple settling chamber. It is considered as an efficient collector of coarse particles.

Cyclones are another type of dust removal systems, where particles are removed from spinning gases by centrifugal forces. They are simple to construct and have no moving parts.

The centrifugal force on particles in a spinning gas stream is much greater than gravity, therefore cyclones are more effective in the removal of much smaller particles than gravitational settling chambers, and require much less space to handle the same gas volumes. On the other hand, the pressure drop in a cyclone is greater, and power consumption is much higher.

There are still other types of gas cleaning equipments. They will not be discussed here.

effluent gas 废气，烟道气

nuisance ['nju:səns] n. 讨厌的人或东西，麻烦事，损害

amenity [ə'mi:nəti] n. 舒适，宜人

gravity ['græviti] n. 重力

settling chamber 降尘室

coarse [kɔ:s] adj. 粗粒的，粗糙的

spin [spin] v. 旋转

power consumption 能耗

21. Centrifugal Settling Processes

A given particle in a given fluid settles under gravitational force at a fixed maximum rate. To increase the settling rate the force of gravity acting on the particle may be replaced by a much stronger centrifugal force. Centrifugal separators have to a considerable extent replaced gravity separators in production operation because of their greater effectiveness with fine drops and particles and their much smaller size for a given capacity.

Most centrifugal separators for removing particles from gas streams contain no moving parts. The typical example is a cyclone.

centrifugal [,sentri'fju:gl,] adj. 离心的

separator ['sepə,reitə] n. 分离器，分离者

capacity [kə'pæsəti] n. 生产能力，容积，产量

It consists of a vertical cylinder with a conical bottom, a tangential inlet near the top, and an outlet for dust at the bottom of the cone. The inlet is usually rectangular. The outlet pipe is extended into the cylinder to prevent short-circuiting of gas from inlet to outlet.

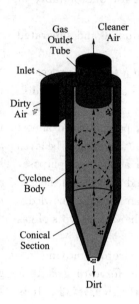

The incoming dust-laden gas receives a rotating motion on entrance to the cylinder. The vortex so formed develops centrifugal force, which acts to throw the particles radially toward the wall. Basically, a cyclone is a settling device in which strong centrifugal force acting radially is used in place of relatively weak gravitational force acting vertically. The centrifugal force in a cyclone is from 5 times gravity in large, low-velocity units to 2500 times gravity in small, high-pressure units.

The path of the gas in the cyclone follows downward vortex, or spiral, adjacent to the wall and reaching to the bottom of the cone. The gas stream then moves upward in a tighter spiral, concentric with the first, and leaves through the outlet pipe, still whirling. Both spirals rotate in the same direction.

In the cyclone, dust particles are precipitated against the wall, along which they slide down toward the cone bottom.

Muticyclone is an assembly of small tube-type cyclones. It is often used to handle a large quantity of gas with small particles.

22. Heat Transfer

Heat is always being transferred in one way or another, wherever there is any difference in temperature. Just as water will run downward, always flowing to the lowest possible level, so heat is transferred from the hot to the cold objects. The rate at which heat flows depends on the amount of temperature difference as well as on the properties of the material through which it has to flow.

There are three ways in which heat is transferred-conduction, convection, and radiation. Since heat itself is the energy of molecular activity, the simplest mode of transfer of heat, called conduction is the direct communication of molecular disturbance through a substance by means of the collisions of neighboring molecules. Metals contain so-called "free" electrons, which make them good conductors of electricity; these electrons also contribute to the conduction of heat, so metals have high thermal conductivities.

conduction [kən'dʌkʃən] n. 传导
convection [kən'vekʃən] n. 对流，传送
radiation [ˌreidi'eiʃən] n. 辐射
disturbance [dis'təːbəns] n. 湍动，扰动
contribute to 归因于

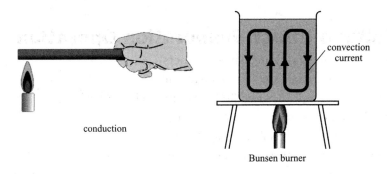

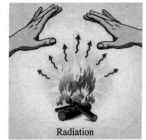

Bunsen burner

Radiation

Convection is the transfer of heat from one place to another by actual motion of the hot material. Heat transfer is accomplished also by a combination of radiation and absorption. Radiation is the only mode of heat transfer which does not require a material medium. Thermal energy is transformed into radiant energy, similar in nature to light. While in the form of radiation, the energy may travel a tremendous distance before being absorbed or changed back into heat. For example, energy radiated from the surface of the sun is converted into heat at the surface of the earth only eight minutes later.

23. Heat Exchanger

Very commonly in a chemical process, the temperature of a stream of fluid must be altered. This can be done by passing the fluid through a heat exchanger in which it is in thermal contact (but usually not in direct physical contact) with some other fluid at a different temperature. The most common arrangement by which this is achieved is to pass one of the fluids through a metal tube immersed in the other fluid. The fluid to be heated passes through the inner tube and the hot fluid that provides the heat passes through a coaxial outer tube.

Because of the mechanical difficulties encountered in supporting one

heat exchanger 换热器

immerse [i'məːs] vt. 沉浸，使陷入
coaxial [kəu'æksiəl] adj. 同轴的，共轴的

tube concentrically in another, a more common physical arrangement is known as the shell and tube heat exchanger, where one fluid passes through a large number of tubes (often up to 100) in parallel supported on a large cylindrical container. The other fluid passes through the cylinder, the so-called shell side, and is constrained to flow in a zigzag manner backwards and forwards across the tubes. This result in a great deal of turbulence that increases the rate of heat transfers and also ensures good mixing. The temperature of the fluid on the shell side is, therefore, nearly constant at any section so that the only variation is in an axial direction.

Most heat exchangers are liquid-liquid, but gases and noncondensing vapors can also be treated in them.

24. Single and Multiple-Effect Evaporation Operation

Most evaporators are heated by steam condensing on metal tubes. Nearly always the material to be evaporated flows inside the tubes. Usually the steam is at a low pressure, below 3 atm (abs), and the boiling temperature of the liquid is under a moderate vacuum, up to about 0.05 atm (abs). Reducing the boiling temperature of the liquid increases the temperature difference between the steam and the boiling liquid and thereby increases the heat-transfer rate in the evaporator.

When a single evaporator is used, the vapor from the boiling liquid is condensed and discarded. This method is called single-effect evaporation, and although it is simple, it utilizes steam ineffectively. To evaporate 1 lb of water from a solution, from 1 000 to 1 200 Btu needed, and this calls for from 1 to 1.3 lb of steam. If the vapor generated in the first evaporator is used as the heating fluid for a second evaporator and the vapor from the second is then sent to a condenser, the operation becomes double-effect. The heat in the original steam is reused in the second effect, and the evaporation achieved by a unit mass of steam fed to the first effect is approximately doubled. The method is feasible if the second evaporator is operated at a lower pressure than the first. It is clear that several evaporators can be connected in series in this way. Thus, additional effects can be added in the same manner. This method of evaporator operation in series is called multiple-effect evaporation.

25. Extraction

Solvent extraction is the transfer of a solute species from its initial location to a solvent known as the extracting solvent. When the solute is in solution the extraction process is called liquid-liquid extraction, and the extracting solvent must be substantially immiscible with the original solvent. If, on the other hand, the solute forms part of a solid, the process is termed solid-liquid extraction and will be discussed later on.

In liquid-liquid extraction, the extracting solvent must have a suitably selective affinity for the appropriate solute, which sometimes occurs in company with materials other than the original solvent. This selectivity is very important because the essence of liquid-liquid extraction is the separation of a particular solute from other materials by means of selective transfer to the extracting solvent. It must be remembered that the solute extracted is not always the most valuable product of the separation process; the aim might be to purify the original solvent by removal of an unwanted solute, or perhaps to remove one of two solutes from the original solution.

The technique of separation by solvent extraction is often attractive in circumstances where distillation is unsuitable. If, for example, the solute is heat sensitive, or present in very low concentration, then liquid-liquid extraction may be appropriate.

In solid-liquid extraction, one constitution of a solid is transferred into an extracting solvent and thereby separated from the rest of the solid. The extracted material is not necessarily a solid but may be present in the bulk solid in a liquid form. Some solids even have an intrinsic solvent content, which becomes evident during the subdivision process.

Since solid does not flow, the equipment for solid-liquid extraction is different from that for liquid-liquid extraction.

26. The Phenomenon of Fluidization

If a fluid is passed upward through a bed of fine particles at a low flow rate, the fluid merely percolates through the void spaces between stationary particles. This is called a fixed bed.

With an increase in flow rate, the particles move apart and a few of them vibrate and move about in restricted regions. This is called an expanded bed.

At a even higher velocity, a point is reached where all the particles are just suspended by the upward flowing gas or liquid. At this point the fractional force between particles and fluid counterbalances the weight of the particles, the vertical component of the compressive force between adjacent particles disappears, and the pressure drop through any section of the bed nearly equals the weight of fluid and particles in that section. The bed is considered to be just fluidized and is referred to as an incipiently fluidized bed or a bed at minimum fluidization.

In liquid-solid systems an increase in flow rate above minimum fluidization usually results in a smooth, progressive expansion of the bed. Gross flow instabilities are damped and remain small, and large-scale bubbling or heterogeneity is not observed under normal conditions. A bed such as this is called a homogeneously fluidized bed, a smoothly fluidized bed, or simply a liquid fluidized bed.

Gas-solid systems generally behave in quite a different manner. With an increase in flow rate beyond minimum fluidization, large instabilities with bubbling and channeling of gas are observed. At higher flow rates agitation becomes more violent and the movement of solids becomes more vigorous. In addition, the bed does not expand much beyond its volume at minimum fluidization. Such a bed is called an aggregative fluidized bed, a heterogeneously fluidized bed, a bubbling fluidized bed, or simply a gas fluidized bed.

In a few rare cases liquid-solid systems will not fluidized smoothly and gas-solid systems will not bubble. At present such beds are only laboratory curiosities of theoretical interest.

Both gas and liquid fluidized beds are considered to be dense-phase fluidized beds as long as there is a fairly clearly defined upper limit or surface to the bed. However, at a sufficiently high fluid flow rate the terminal velocity of the solids is exceeded, the upper surface of the bed disappears, entrainment becomes appreciable, and solids are carried out of the bed with the fluid stream. In this state we have a disperse-, dilute- or lean-phase fluidized bed with pneumatic transport of solids.

Compared with other methods of gas-solid contacting, gas fluidized beds have some rather unusual and useful properties. This is not shared to the same extent with liquid-solid systems. Thus practically all the important industrial applications of fluidization are gas-fluidized systems.

27. Applications of Size Reduction

In the chemical industry, size reduction is usually carried out in order to increase the surface. Because in most reactions involving solid particles, the rate is directly proportional to the area of contact with a second phase. Thus the rate of combustion of solid particles is proportional to the area presented to the gas, though a number of secondary factors may also be involved, for instance, the free flow of gas may be impeded because of the higher resistance to flow of a bed of small particles. Again in leaching, not only is the rate of extraction increased by virtue of the increased area of contact between the solvent and the solid, but the distance the solvent has to penetrate into the particles in order to gain access to the more remote pockets of solute is also reduced. This factor is also important

heterogeneity [ˌhetərədʒəˈniːəti] n. 异质性，不均匀性

aggregative fluidized bed 聚式流化床

entrainment [inˈtreinmənt] n. 带走，夹带
disperse [disˈpəːs] v. （使）分散，（使）散开
lean-phase 疏相，稀相

size reduction 粉碎，磨碎，粒度细化
combustion [kəmˈbʌstʃən] n. 燃烧

leach [liːtʃ] vt. 过滤，萃取

gain access to 可以使用，可以理解

in the drying of porous solids, where reduction in size causes both an increase in area and a reduction in the distance the moisture must travel within the particles in order to reach the surface; in this case the capillary forces acting on the moisture are also affected.

There are a number of other reasons for effecting size reduction. For example, it may be necessary to break a material into very small particles in order to separate two constituents, especially where one is dispersed in small isolated pockets. Further, the properties of a material may be considerably influenced by the particle size, for example, the chemical reactivity of fine particles is greater than that of coarse particles, and the color and covering power of a pigment is considerably affected by the size of the particles. Again, far more intimate mixing of solids can be achieved if the particle is small.

28. Screening

Screening is a method of separating particles according to size alone. In industrial screening the solids are dropped on, or thrown against, a screening surface. The undersize, or fines, pass through the screen openings; oversize, or tails, do not. A single screen can make a single separation into two fractions. These are called unsized fractions, because although either the upper or lower limit of the particle sizes they contain is known, the other limit is unknown. Material passed through a series of screens of different sizes is separated into sized fractions, i.e., fractions in which both the maximum and minimum particles sizes are known. Screening is occasionally done wet but much more commonly dry. The discussion in this section is limited to the screening of dry particulate solids.

Industrial screens are made of metal bars, perforated or slotted metal plates, woven wire cloth, or fabric, such as silk bolting cloth. Metals used include steel, stainless steel, bronze, copper, and nickel. The mesh size of woven screens ranges from 4 into 400 mesh, but screens finer than 100 or 150 mesh are rarely used. With very fine particles other methods of separation are usually more economical. Many varieties and types of screens are available for different purposes.

In most screens the particles drop through the screen opening by gravity. In a few designs, they are pushed through by a brush or by centrifugal force. Coarse particles drop quickly and easily through large openings in a stationary surface; with finer particles the screening surface must be agitated in some way. Common ways are revolving a cylindrical screen by a horizontal axis; or shaking, gyrating, vibrating a flat screen by machine or electricity.

29. Instrumentation and Control

In all chemical processes it is necessary to know such process data as flow rates, compositions, pressures, and temperatures, so that the operator and engineer can tell whether the process is functioning properly. In the typical chemical process many instruments are used to measure, indicate, and record the necessary process data.

It is often desirable to use an automatic control because not only does the instrument measure and record a variable, but it also maintains the variable at a predetermined value. If the variable begins to change from the proper value, the automatic control initiates corrective action to return the variable to its proper value. For example, the temperature in a chemical reactor must often be controlled to give the desired yield of products. If the reaction is endothermic, the reactor might have a steam jacket to supply heat. A temperature-sensing instrument, such as a thermocouple, measures the temperature of the materials in the reactor. The signal is transmitted to a paper-chart recorder to give the operator a record of the temperature variations with time. The temperature signal is also sent to the controller, which has been set by the operator to maintain the desired temperature. If the temperature of the reactor begins to fall below the desired value, the controller opens the steam valve to supply more heat to the heating jacket on the reactor. Conversely, if the reactor temperature is too high, the controller closes the steam valve. The steam valve may be in any position between fully open and fully closed.

Automatic control may be applied to almost any process variable that can be measured. Control of a variable is often maintained by the measurement of another more easily measured variable. Automatic control reduces the number of human operators. It can give faster and more accurate control than a human operator.

The coupling of automatic controllers to electronic computers makes it possible to run a process with no human control. Such plants are now in operation. The engineer determines the best operating conditions, designs the process, and controls computer to give the optimum results. In operation, the instruments transmit process information to the computer; the computer uses the information to determine whether the process is operating at the best conditions. If it is not, the computer initiates corrective action through the control system.

Although automatic process control has eliminated many low-skill human operators, it is still necessary to have one or more highly skilled operators to observe that the plant is functioning properly. It is also necessary to have a large highly trained mainte-

predetermined value
预定值
endothermic
[ˌendəu'θə:mik] adj.
吸热(性)的
steam jacket 蒸汽套
thermocouple
['θə:məuˌkʌpl] n. 热电偶

conversely ['kɔnvə:sli]
adv. 反之

process variable 工艺变量，工艺参数

coupling ['kʌpliŋ] n.
联结，接合

optimum ['ɔptiməm]
adj. 最适宜的; n. 最适宜

corrective [kə'rektiv]
adj. 纠正的，矫正的;
n. 矫正物，中和物

nance staff to repair the process and control system when it breaks down. The more complex the control system is, the greater the chance for breakdown. Of course, automated chemical plants are more expensive to build and require engineers with wide knowledge of designing and operating.

Although the principles of chemical reactions, unit operations, instrumentation, and control can be studied separately, in the design of a chemical process all these areas are closely interrelated. It is therefore necessary to consider the interaction of the components of a process to determine the over-all behavior of the process; this is often an extremely difficult and complex job. A consideration of process dynamics must be included in any complete process design.

instrumentation [ˌinstrumenˈteɪʃ(ə)n] n. 仪器

process design 工艺流程设计, 工艺过程设计

30. The Material Balance

If matter may be neither created nor destroyed, the total mass of all materials entering an operation equals the total mass of all materials leaving that operation, except for any material that may be retained or accumulated in the operation. By the application of this principle, the yields of a chemical reaction or engineering operation are computed.

In continuous operations, material is usually not accumulated in the operation, and a material balance consists simply in charging (or debiting) the operation with all material entering and crediting the operation with all material leaving, in the same manner as used by any accountant. The result must be a balance.

As long as the reaction is chemical and does not destroy or create atoms, it is proper and frequently very convenient to employ atoms as the basis for the material balance. The material balance may be made for the entire plant or for any part of it as a unit, depending upon the problem at hand.

debit [ˈdebit] n. 借方, 借记; vt. 记入借方
credit [ˈkredit] n. 信用, 信贷; v. 存钱, 把……归于

at hand 在手边, 在附近, 即将到来

31. The Energy Balance

Similarly, an energy balance may be made around any plant or unit operation to determine the energy required to carry on the operation or to maintain the desired operating conditions. The principle is just as important as that of the material balance, and it is used in the same way. The important point to keep in mind is that all energy of all kinds must be included, although it may be converted to a single equivalent.

unit operation 单元操作

equivalent [iˈkwivələnt] n. 等价物, 相等物

32. The Ideal Contact (the equilibrium stage model)

Whenever the materials being processed are in contact for any length of time under specified conditions, such as temperature, pressure, chemical composition, or electrical potential, they tend to approach a definite condition of equilibrium which is determined by the specified conditions. In many cases the rate of approach to these equilibrium conditions is so rapid or the length of time is sufficient that conditions are practically attained at each contact. Such a contact is known as an equilibrium or ideal contact. The calculation of the number of ideal contacts is an important step required in understanding those unit operations involving transfer of material from one phase to another, such as leaching, extraction, absorption, and dissolution.

equilibrium [,i:kwi'libriəm] n. 平衡，均衡
specify ['spesifai] vt. 指定，详细说明，列入清单
dissolution [,disə'lu:ʃ(ə)n] n. 溶化，溶解

33. Rates of an Operation (the rate of transfer model)

In most operations equilibrium is not attained either because of insufficient time or because it is not desired. As soon as equilibrium is attained no further change can take place and the process stops, but the engineer must keep the process going. For this reason, rate operations, such as rate of energy transfer, rate of mass transfer, and rate of chemical reaction, are of the greatest importance and interest. In all such cases the rate and direction depend upon a difference in potential or driving force. The rate usually may be expressed as proportional to a potential drop divided by a resistance. An application of this principle to electrical energy is similar to Ohm's law for steady or direct current.

resistance [ri'zistəns] n. 阻力，电阻，阻抗
Ohm's law 欧姆定律

In solving rate problems as in heat transfer or mass transfer with this simple concept, the major difficulty is the evaluation of the resistance terms that are generally computed from an empirical correlation of many determinations of transfer rates under different conditions.

The basic concept that rate depends directly upon a potential drop and inversely upon a resistance may be applied to any rate operation, although the rate may be expressed in different ways, particular coefficients for particular cases.

coefficient [kəui'fiʃənt] n. 系数

34. Application of Computers in Chemical Engineering

Computers are revolutionizing chemical engineering. Long tedious calculations are greatly speeded up, thereby releasing engineers for other more creative work. It is now possible to take into account more variables and to arrive at a more rigorous solution of

rigorous ['rigərəs] adj. 严格的，严厉的，严酷的，严峻的

complex problems. Computers permit more adequate analysis and correlation of experimental data. Designs of chemical processes may be optimized, i.e., computers perform the complex calculations which is necessary to find the best possible combination of dozens of design variables. Computers are used to run actual experiments. For example, a chemical process or a whole chemical plant may be simulated in a computer, and the effect of changing process variables may be studied without ever building the plant. Computers may be used to control chemical processes, assuring greater reliability of operation. One of the largest uses of computers is in the business aspects of industry, such as payroll, inventory and sales records, materials and process scheduling, and market research.

Computers may be used wherever a basic calculation must be carried out many times with various combinations of variables. It is seldom practical to use a computer for a single solution of a problem, because of the substantial time needed to set up the problem for machine calculation. Computers have been called mechanical brains. One of their advantage is speed. Great ingenuity is required of the engineer who must set up a problem for machine computation. He must thoroughly understand the physical situation so that he can describe it accurately to the computer. Accurate description in the simple terms a computer understands requires complex applied mathematics such as numerical methods. Thus, computers have released the engineer from the drudgery of tedious calculations and have, at the same time, challenged his ingenuity in developing methods of calculation on the computer. To meet this challenge, the modern chemical engineer needs a higher level of understanding of mathematics and of the fundamental physical mechanisms of chemical processes.

From this short description it is apparent that, although computers may be considered as "super slide rules", they are really much more versatile than this. Their ability to explore a much wider range of possible approaches to a problem and to simulate a system are more important and of wider usefulness than their ability to perform more rapidly the same computations now being done by hand.

35. Chemical Manufacturing Process

The basic components of a typical chemical process are shown in Fig. 1, in which each block represents a stage in the overall process for producing a product from the raw materials. Fig. 1 represents a generalized process; not all the stages will be needed for any particular process, and the complexity of each stage will depend on the nature of the process. Chemical engineering design is con-

optimize ['ɔptimaiz] vt. 使最优化
variable ['vɛəriəb(ə)l] n. 变量，可变因素
reliability [ri‚laiə'biliti] n. 可靠性
payroll ['pei‚rəul] n. 工资单，工资表
inventory ['invəntəri] n. 库存，存货清单
scheduling ['ʃedjuːliŋ] n. 行程安排，时序安排

ingenuity [‚indʒi'njuːiti] n. 独创性，灵活性

applied mathematics 应用数学
drudgery ['drʌdʒəri] n. 单调乏味的工作，单调沉闷的工作

slide rule 计算尺
versatile ['vəːsətail] adj. 通用的，万能的，多面手的

manufacture [‚mænju'fæktʃə] vt. 制造，加工
block [blɔk] n. 模块

arrangement [ə'reindʒmənt] n. 排列，安排

cerned with the selection and arrangement of the stages, and the selection, specification and design of the equipment required to perform the stage functions.

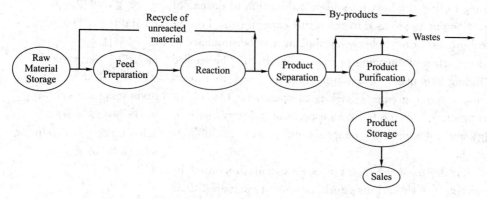

Fig. 1　The typical chemical process

(a) Raw material storage

Unless the raw materials (also called essential materials, or feed stocks) are supplied as intermediate products (intermediates) from a neighboring plant, some provision will have to be made to hold several days, or weeks storage to smooth out fluctuations and interruptions in supply. Even when the materials come from an adjacent plant some provision is usually made to hold a few hours, or even days, supply to decouple the processes. The storage required will depend on the nature of the raw materials, the method of delivery, and what assurance can be placed on the continuity of supply. If materials are delivered by ship (tanker or bulk carrier) several weeks stocks may be necessary; whereas if they are received by road or rail, in smaller lots, less storage will be needed.

(b) Feed preparation

Some purification, and preparation, of the raw materials will usually be necessary before they are fed to the reaction stage. For example, acetylene generated by the carbide process contains arsenical and sulphur compounds, and other impurities, which must be removed by scrubbing with concentrated sulphuric acid (or other processes) to make it sufficiently pure for reaction with hydrochloric acid to produce dichloroethane. Liquid feeds will need to be vaporized before being fed to gas-phase reactors, and solids may need crushing, grinding, and screening.

(c) Reactor

The reaction stage is the heart of a chemical manufacturing process. In the reactor the raw materials are brought together under conditions that promote the production of the desired product; invariably, by-products and unwanted compounds (impurities) will also formed.

(d) Product separation

In this first stage after the reactor, the products and by-products are separated from any unreacted material. If in sufficient quantity, the unreacted material will be recycled to the reactor. They may be returned directly to the reactor or to the feed purification and preparation stage. The by-products may also be separated from the products at this stage.

(e) Purification

Before sale, the main product will usually need purification to meet the product specification. If produced in economic quantities, the by-products may also be purified for sale.

(f) Product storage

Some inventory of finished product must be held to match production with sales. Provision for product packaging and transport will also be needed, depending on the nature of the product. Liquids will normally be dispatched in drums and in bulk tankers (road, rail, and sea), solids in sacks, cartons or bales. The stock held will depend on the nature of the product and the market.

product specification 产品技术规格
inventory ['inv(ə)nt(ə)ri] n. 库存,清单
packaging ['pækidʒiŋ] n. 包装
dispatch [dis'pætʃ] vt. 派出,发出
sack [sæk] n. 大袋,麻布袋
carton ['kɑːt(ə)n] n. 硬纸盒,纸板箱
bale [beil] n. 大包
biotechonology n. 生物技术

36. Biotechnology

Scientists have turned to nature for help in destroying toxic substances. Some microorganisms in soil, water, and sediments can adapt their diets to a wide variety of organic chemicals; they have been used for decades in conventional waste treatment systems. Researchers are now attempting to coax even higher levels of performance from these gifted microbes by carefully determining the optimal physical, chemical, and nutritional conditions for their existence. Their efforts may lead to the design and operation of a new generation of biological waste treatment facilities. A major advance in recent years is the immobilization of such microorganisms in bioreactors, anchoring them in a reactor while they degrade waste materials. Immobilization permits high flow rates that would flush out conventional reactors, and the use of new, highly porous support materials allows a significant increase in the number of microorganisms for each reactor.

microbe ['maikrəub] n. 微生物,细菌
immobilization [i,məubəlai'zeiʃ(ə)n] n. 固定
anchor ['æŋkə] v. 紧固,锚定
flush out (彻底)冲洗

37. Genetic Engineering

Genetic engineering is essentially the art and science of "cutting and stitching" deoxyribonucleic acid (DNA) into what is known as recombinant DNA or rDNA, carrying the desired genetic information. It is one of the most promising divisions of bioengineering as it offers a means of introducing into a bacterial host cell

genetic engineering 基因工程
recombinant [ri'kɔmbinənt] n. 重组

the genetic code, or genes, from practically any organism, including the human being, thus converting it into a highly efficient protein factory for medicine, agriculture, and industry. When suitable foreign genes are "stitched" into the cells of bacteria, these cells will then manufacture human protein, such as interferon, insulin, growth hormones, and other valuable drugs and diagnostic reagents. It also offers a means for the improvement and/or development of highly efficient bacterial strains for the manufacture of antibiotics, amino acids, vitamins, and new microbial cultures that can in turn be utilized in the chemical process and food industries and as energy sources.

Genetic engineering has proved a success in plant breeding. By introducing new genes into plant cells, it is possible to endow plants with qualities that will enhance their resistance to environmental factors and step up photosynthesis rate, and with the ability to fix molecular nitrogen from the air into usable forms by themselves or to establish symbiotic relating high-rate photosynthesis and nitrogen-fixing abilities, wheat, rice, and other cereal crops can be converted into varieties of an extremely high protein content without having to put in more fertilizers. As a corollary, this will also save energy, notably gas and petroleum which are used as feed stocks in the manufacture of nitrogen fertilizers.

38. Tissue Culture

It comprises isolating and growing isolated cells. These cells could be from plants, animals including human beings. The isolated cells are put in a media which could nourish them, where they multiply. Techniques have also been developed to allow them to grow rapidly. Plant cells grow relatively more easily, while human tissue is most difficult to grow.

39. Cloning

When a single cell or tissue is placed in a medium and where they multiply, they reproduce identical cells, i. e., cells possessing similar characteristics. These are clones. This method is useful for replicating some characteristics in a large number of cells. The technique is useful for reproducing a large number of cells to meet a specific purpose, as for example in the production of a particular substance, a chemical, through cell metabolism. It is also useful in producing a plant which is resistant to a particular disease.

40. Fermentation Technology

Fermentation technology, or the use of enzymes as biocatalysts in the industrial production of a wide gamut of substances, is a highly promising division of bioengineering. Enzymes increase the rate of reaction millions of times. As they do so, they also allow a substantial reduction in the temperature and pressure used in chemical processes, thus making them less energy-intensive and independent of expensive inorganic catalysts. Importantly, fermentation synthesis of polymers does not pollute the atmosphere in which respect it compares favorably with the chemical synthesis of these materials.

In some cases, enzymes are immobilized, or trapped, in a suitable substrate—this makes them more convenient to handle and to be used repeatedly.

Among other things, fermentation technology is to be used for the preparation of prostaglandins, biologically active substances of high value to medicine, livestock breeding, and veterinary science. Work is under way on fermentation process for the production of glucose from the cellulose of cotton lint. When commercialized, the process will help to expand the production of this valuable product many times and to obtain better economic benefit.

fermentation 发酵
enzyme ['enzaim] n. 酶
gamut ['gæmət] n. 整个范围, 全部

trap [træp] vt. 捕获
substrate ['sʌbstreit] n. 培养基
prostaglandin [ˌprɔstə'glændin] n. 前列腺素
livestock ['laivstɔk] n. 家畜, 牲畜
veterinary ['vetrənəri] adj. 兽医的

Part C

General Chemistry

1. Introduction of General Chemistry

Chemistry deals with the composition, structure, and properties of matter and the changes that matter undergoes. Matter is anything that occupies space; all matter is made of chemicals. A substance is a distinct kind of matter. All samples of a substance from anywhere in the universe have the same properties; a substance has the same properties throughout the whole sample. Properties that do not involve substances changing into other substances are called physical properties. Properties that involve substances changing into other substances are called chemical properties. The changes are called chemical changes or chemical reactions. Substances that react rapidly with many other substances are said to be reactive. Reactions in which substances combine to form more complex substances are called combination reactions and reactions in which substances break down (decompose) into simpler substances are called decomposition reactions.[1]

There are two kinds of substances, elements and compounds. Elements cannot be broken down into simpler substances by chemical reaction. Compounds are substances composed of two or more of the 118 known elements. Compounds can be broken down into simpler substances by decomposition reactions. About eleven million compounds are known.

Although compounds can be decomposed into simpler substances by chemical reactions, they cannot be separated into simpler substances by physical changes. Mixtures have varying compositions and can be separated by physical changes. Substances making up mixtures are called components. Homogeneous mixtures have only one phase and are called solutions. A phase is a sample of matter that is uniform in composition and physical state and is separated from other phases by definite boundaries. The term aqueous refers to a water solution. Mixtures that do not have the same properties throughout are called heterogeneous mixtures.

Chemistry, like all sciences, is based on observations. In science, a law is a summary of many observations and a theory is an explanation of a law. As soon as a new theory has been proposed, scientists start thinking of experiments to test it. Science progresses by cycles of proposed theories and tests by experiment. A theory can be proved wrong but it can never be proved right beyond any shadow of a doubt. The overturning of an important theory opens new frontiers in science. Scientists must be careful not to jump to conclusions based on too few or wrong observations; they must be alert to observations that do not fit their theories.

The law of constant composition states that the percent by weight of each element in a compound is always the same. This law is explained by the atomic theory. According to Dalton's atomic theory everything is made of small particles called atoms. All atoms of an element are alike and atoms of different elements are different. Atoms of one element cannot be changed into atoms of another element by chemical reactions. In chemical reactions, atoms are combined in new ways; the relative number of each kind of atom in a compound is always the same.

According to modern atomic theory, atoms are pictured as being made up of a small, dense, positively charged nucleus that contains protons. Protons are small particles with a unit positive charge. The number of protons in the nucleus determines the atomic number of the element. All atoms of an element have the same atomic number. The nucleus is surrounded by rapidly moving electrons, which are very small particles with a unit negative charge. Atoms are electrically neutral, that is, they have no net charge; therefore, the number of electrons outside the nucleus must be equal to the number of protons in the nucleus (and to the atomic number).

The periodic table is one of the most useful organizers of chemical information. It can be used to predict many chemical and physical properties from a few observations. In the modern periodic table, the elements are arranged in rows in order of increasing atomic number. The table is constructed so that elements in a vertical column have similar properties; the vertical columns are called groups or families. The groups are numbered. Some of the groups also have names: Group IA, alkali metals; Group IIA, alkaline earth metals; Group VIIA, halogens; Group 0, noble gases. The properties of the elements in a group usually change gradually going from top to bottom of the group. In Groups IVA through VI A, properties change from nonmetallic to metallic. Horizontal rows in the periodic table are called periods; properties change from metallic to nonmetallic across periods. The elements in Groups IIIB through IIB and those in the lanthanide and actinide series are called transition elements. All the other elements are called main group elements.

When atoms combine to form compounds, some of their electrons arrange around the nuclei in a way different from the arrangement in the atoms. When atoms of nonmetals combine to form compounds, molecules result. A molecule is the smallest particle of an element or compound that has the chemical properties of the element or compound; a molecule does not have a net electric charge. [2] Molecules made up of two atoms are called diatomic molecules. Compounds that have molecules as units are referred to as molecular compounds.

Ions are charged particles formed by transfer of electrons. When atoms of the metals of Groups IA and the reactive metals toward the bottom of Group IIA combine with atoms of nonmetals to form compounds, enough electrons are transferred to give each atom the same number of electrons as the noble gas with the closest atomic number. [3] Positively charged ions are called cations and negatively charged ions are called anions. Monatomic ions are formed from a single atom; polyatomic ions are formed from more than one atom. Ions combine to form compounds so that charges cancel and the compounds are electrically neutral. [4] Compounds composed of ions are called ionic compounds. In crystals of ionic compounds, oppositely charged ions are held together by electrostatic force, the attraction between opposite charges.

Inorganic compounds are compounds of all elements except carbon. Some simple carbon compounds are also usually classified as inorganic. All organic compounds contain carbon; most also contain hydrogen. Most compounds are named according to the IUPAC system. In naming inorganic compounds according to the IUPAC system, Roman numerals are used to distinguish between different compounds of a metal with the same anion. Prefixes are used to distinguish between different compounds of the same nonmetals.

Chemical equations summarize information about chemical reactions. In equations, compounds and molecules of elements are represented by formulas, and atoms of elements are represented by symbols.[5] Reactants, substances present before reaction, are written on the left. Products, substances formed in a reaction, are written on the right. Equations must be balanced (made to show the same number of atoms of each kind on both sides) by using the smallest possible whole numbers for coefficients. Equations may show the states of the reactants and products and the conditions necessary for reaction.

New Words and Expressions

composition [ˌkɑːmpəˈziʃn] n. 成分，构成，组成
matter [ˈmætə] n. 物质，实质
substance [ˈsʌbstəns] n. 物质，实质，主旨
reactive [ri(ː)ˈæktiv] adj. 反应的，活性的
decompose [ˌdiːkəmˈpəuz] v. 分解
decomposition [ˌdiːkɔmpəˈziʃən] n. 分解
compound [ˈkɔmpaund] n. 化合物
component [kəmˈpəunənt] n. 成分，组分
aqueous [ˈeikwiəs] adj. 水的
overturn [ˌəuvə(r)ˈtəː(r)n] v. 推翻，颠覆
nucleus [ˈnjuːkliəs] n. 原子核
proton [ˈprəutən] n. 质子

family [ˈfæmili] n. 周期表中的族
halogen [ˈhælədʒən] n. 卤素
period [ˈpiəriəd] n. 周期
metalloid [ˈmetəlɔid] n. 准金属，类金属
nonmetal [ˌnɔnˈmetl] n. 非金属(元素)
cation [ˈkætaiən] n. 阳离子
anion [ˈænaiən] n. 阴离子
numeral [ˈnjuːmərəl] n. 数字，数码
formula [ˈfɔːmjulə] n. 公式，分子式，化学式
symbol [ˈsimbəl] n. 符号，记号，象征
balance [ˈbæləns] v. 保持平衡

Phrases

combination reaction   化合反应
decomposition reaction   分解反应
law of constant composition   定组成定律
Dalton's atomic theory   道尔顿原子理论
atomic number   原子序数
periodic table   (元素)周期表
alkali metals   碱金属
alkaline earth metals   碱土金属
noble gases   惰性气体

transition elements   过渡元素
main group elements   主族元素
diatomic molecules   双原子分子
molecular compounds   分子化合物
monatomic ions   单原子离子
polyatomic ions   多原子离子
electrostatic force   电子引力
chemical equations   化学方程式

Affixes

non- [nɔn-] 表示"非,不,无",如 nonmetal 非金属, nonelectrolyte 非电解质, noninflammable 不可燃的

di- [dai-] 表示"二,双,联,重,偶",如 dibenzoyl 联苯甲酰, dichromate 重铬酸盐, dipole 偶极

-on [-ɔn, ən] 名词词尾;1. 组成原子的微粒,如 proton 原子, neutron 中子, ion 离子, electron 电子;2. 非金属元素词尾,如 argon 氩, boron 硼, carbon 碳, silicon 硅

-ic [-ik] 形容词词尾,如 ionic 离子的, periodic 周期的, atomic 原子的, catalytic 催化的

-ide [-aid] 表示"……化物(名词词尾)",如 oxide 氧化物, chloride 氯化物, hydride 氢化物, halide 卤化物, nitride 硝化物

Notes

1. Reactions in which substances combine to form more complex substances are called combination reactions and reactions in which substances break down (decompose) into simpler substances are called decomposition reactions. 这是一个并列句,每个分句中还有一个 which 引导的定语从句。参考译文:物质结合形成复杂物质的反应称为化合反应,物质分解为简单物质的反应称为分解反应。

2. A molecule is the smallest particle of an element or compound that has the chemical properties of the element or compound; a molecule does not have a net electric charge. 这是一个并列句,分号前面为一个含有"that"引导的定语从句的复合句,分号后为一个简单句。句中"net"意思是"净",即正负抵消之后所剩的电荷。参考译文:分子是具有元素或化合物化学性质的元素或化合物,分子不带净电荷(即为电中性)。

3. When atoms of the metals of Groups ⅠA and the reactive metals toward the bottom of Group ⅡA combine with atoms of nonmetals to form compounds, enough electrons are transferred to give each atom the same number of electrons as the noble gas with the closest atomic number. 这是复合句,其中"when"引导的句子为时间状语从句,主句中的"the same... as..."表示"……与……相同"。参考译文:当第一主族金属原子和第二主族底部活性金属原子与非金属原子形成化合物时,足够多的电子被转移,使每个原子都具有与其原子数最接近的惰性元素气体相同的电子数。

4. Ions combine to form compounds so that charges cancel and the compounds are electrically neutral. 参考译文:离子结合成化合物所以电荷相互抵消,化合物变成电中性。

5. In equations, compounds and molecules of elements are represented by formulas, and atoms of elements are represented by symbols. 参考译文:在方程式中,元素的化合物和分子用分子式表示,元素的原子用原子符号表示。

2. Chemical Bond and Bonding Theory

Chemical Bonds

The forces that hold atoms together in compounds are called chemical bonds. Two kinds of bonds connect atoms in compounds: ionic bonds and covalent bonds. Formation of both ionic and covalent bonds is exothermic and leads to a state of lower energy and greater stability.

Ionic bonds are the attraction between positively and negatively charged ions. Most of the energy released by the formation of ionic bonds is lattice energy. Lattice energy is the energy required to separate the ions of an ionic solid to an infinite distance.

Covalent bonds consist of pairs of electrons shared between two atoms. One, two, or three pairs of electrons can be shared between two atoms leading to single, double, and triple bonds. The average energy needed to break a given type of bond is called the bond energy of that type of bond. If bonds between the same two atoms are compared, triple bonds are shorter and stronger than double bonds, which are shorter and stronger than single bonds. The number of bonds between two atoms in a molecule or ion is called bond order. A pair of electrons that is shared between two atoms is called a bonding pair. Only the outer electrons are involved in bond formation; the outer electrons used in bond formation are called valence electrons and the outer shell is called the valence shell. Valence electrons that are not shared are referred to as unshared pairs, lone pairs, or nonbonding electrons.

Lewis (electron-dot) formulas are used to represent molecules and polyatomic ions composed of main-group elements. Many compounds follow the octet rule that there should be eight electrons around each atom except hydrogen. However, although the octet is a very stable grouping of electrons, not all atoms have octets in compounds.[1] Three types of species involving main-group elements are exceptions to the octet rule: (1) species with more than eight electrons around the central atom, (2) species with fewer than eight electrons around the central atom, and (3) species with an odd total number of electrons. Species that have one or more unpaired electrons are called free radicals.

The shapes of molecules and ions that have main-group elements as central atoms can be predicted from their Lewis structures by means of valence shell electron pair repulsion (VSEPR). According to the VSEPR model, electron pairs around a central atom tend to be located as far apart from each other in space as possible. The total coordination number of an atom is the total number of atoms and unshared electron pairs around a central atom. The shapes of molecules depend on the positions occupied by the atoms attached to the central atom. Stereochemical formulas must be used to show the shapes of three-dimensional species.

Bonds in which electron pairs are shared equally are called nonpolar bonds. Bonds in which electron pairs are not shared equally are called polar bonds. A pair of equal and opposite charges separated by a distance is called a dipole. Dipole moment, μ, is a quantitative measure of the polarity of a molecule. Dipole moments are vectors, that is they have both magnitude and direction. All molecules that have one polar covalent bond are polar. Whether or not molecules with more than one polar bond are polar depends on their shape.

Electronegativity is the ability of an atom to attract to itself an electron pair that is shared with another atom. Electronegativity is a periodic property. It usually increases from left to right across rows of the periodic table and from bottom to top of groups. Differences in electronegativity are useful in predicting the direction of polarization of covalent bonds and whether bonds are slightly polar, very polar, or ionic. The greater the difference in electronegativity between bonded atoms, the more polar the bond. Bonds vary from nonpolar to slightly polar to very polar to mainly ionic, depending on the difference in electronegativity between the bonded atoms.

Sometimes more than one Lewis formula must be written to describe a molecule or polyatomic ion. The different Lewis formulas are called resonance structures. The real structure of the molecule or ion is a hybrid of the resonance structures.

Theory of Bonding

Approximations must be used to solve the Schrödinger equation for the wave functions of electrons in all molecules. The valence bond method is one method of approximating and the molecular orbital method is another.

In the valence bond method, formation of bonds is pictured as resulting from overlap of atomic orbitals so that electrons move in the region of space between two nuclei. The valence bond method uses Lewis formulas including resonance structures to describe molecules and polyatomic ions. Hybrid orbitals, orbitals formed by combination of atomic orbitals on the same atom, are needed to explain the number of bonds that some atoms form and the directions in space of the bonds. The number of hybrid orbitals formed must be the same as the number of atomic orbitals combined.

Sigma(σ) bonds are pictured as formed by endwise (head-on) overlap of atomic orbitals on different atoms. All single bonds are sigma bonds. Rotation about single bonds is free; the different arrangements of parts of a molecule in space that result from rotation about sigma bonds are called conformations. Pi(π) bonds are pictured as formed by sidewise overlap of atomic orbitals on different atoms. Multiple bonds consist of one sigma bond and one or more pi bonds. Rotation about pi bonds is not possible unless the pi bond is broken. Pi bonding is very important in the chemistry of the elements in the second period of the periodic table.

Binding energy curves show how the energy of the system changes as atoms move toward each other. For a stable bond to form, there must be a minimum in the binding energy curve; the distance between the atoms at the minimum is the bond length. The difference between the energy at the minimum and the energy of the two separate atoms is the bond dissociation energy, the energy that is required to break a specific bond in a certain molecule. [2]

The molecular orbital method supposes that electrons in molecules occupy molecular orbitals that may extend over the whole molecule. The energies of the molecular orbitals are calculated using the Schrödinger equation. Electrons are then assigned to the molecular orbitals using the aufbau approach and following the same rules (Hund's rule and the Pauli exclusion principle) followed in placing electrons in atomic orbitals. The molecular orbital method successfully explains the paramagnetism of the oxygen molecule and molecular spectra and avoids the need for resonance structures. [3]

The atomic orbitals that are combined to form a molecular orbital come from different atoms. The atomic orbitals that are combined to form a molecular orbital must occupy the same region in space and have similar energies; the number of molecular orbitals formed must be equal to the number of atomic orbitals combined. [4] A bonding molecular orbital is lower in energy than the atomic orbitals from which it is formed. Electron density is concentrated between the bonded atoms. An antibonding molecular orbital weakens the chemical bond between two atoms and help to raise the energy of the molecule relative to separate atoms. Such an orbital has one or more nodes in the bonding region between the nuclei. The density of the electrons in the orbital is concentrated outside the bonding region and acts to pull one nucleus away from the other and tends to cause mutual repulsion between the two atoms.

If three or more p orbitals are perpendicular to adjacent atoms that lie in the same plane, the electrons of the pi bonds formed by sidewise overlap are delocalized and move over three or more atoms. Structures with delocalized electrons always have lower energy (greater stability) than similar structures without delocalized electrons.

New Words and Expressions

exothermic [,eksəu'θə:mik] adj. 发热的，放热的
octet [ɔk'tet] n. 八位组，八位字节，八重
coordination [kəu,ɔ:di'neiʃn] n. 协调，配合，配位
stereochemical [steri:əu'kemikl] adj. 立体化学的
dipole ['daipəul] n. 双极子，偶极
polarity [pə'lærəti] n. 极性
vector ['vektər] n. 向量，矢量
magnitude ['mægnitju:d] n. 大小，数量
electronegativity [elektrəunigə'tiviti] n. 电负性
resonance ['rezənəns] n. 共振，谐振，共鸣
hybrid ['haibrid] n. 杂化，杂交，混合物; adj. 杂化的，杂交的，混合的

approximation [ə,prɔksi'meiʃən] n. 接近，近似法
polyatomic [,pɔliə'tɔmik] adj. 多原子的
combination [,kɔmbi'neiʃən] n. 结合，组合
endwise ['endwaiz] adj. 末端朝前或向上的
conformation [,kɔnfɔ:'meiʃən] n. 构象
sidewise ['said,waiz] adj. 侧向的，横向的
multiple ['mʌltipl] adj. 多样的，多重的
paramagnetism [,pærə'mægnitizəm] n. 顺磁性
spectra ['spektrə] n. 光谱（spectrum 的名词复数）
antibonding ['æntibɔndiŋ] n. 反键
delocalize [di:'ləukəlaiz] vt. 离域，使离开原位

Phrases

lattice energy　晶格能，点阵能
covalent bond　共价键
bond order　键级
bonding pair　成键电子对
valence electron　价电子
valence shell　价电子层，价层
unshared pair　非共用电子对
lone pair　孤对电子
nonbonding electron　非键合电子
Lewis formulas　路易斯（电子结构）式
octet rule　八隅律，八隅体规则
electron pair repulsion　电子对互斥
total coordination number　总配位数
stereochemical formulas　立体化学式

nonpolar bond　非极性键
dipole moment　偶极矩
resonance structure　共振结构
Schrödinger equation　薛定谔方程
wave function　波函数
valence bond method　价键法
molecular orbital method　分子轨道法
hybrid orbital　杂化轨道
binding energy curve　结合能曲线
bond dissociation energy　键解离能
Aufbau principle　构造原理，电子充填原理
Hund's rule　洪特规则
Pauli exclusion principle　泡利不相容原理
bonding molecular orbital　成键分子轨道

Affixes

exo- [eksəu-] 表示"外"；如 exoatmosphere 外大气层，exotic 外来的，异国的

Notes

1. Many compounds follow the octet rule that there should be eight electrons around each atom except hydrogen. However, although the octet is a very stable grouping of electrons, not all atoms have octets in compounds. 参考译文：很多化合物都符合八隅规则，即除氢以外，每个原子周围都应有八个电子。然而，尽管八个是很稳定的电子组合，但并不是化合物中所有原子都有八个电子。

2. The difference between the energy at the minimum and the energy of the two separate atoms is the bond dissociation energy, the energy that is required to break a specific bond in a certain molecule. 参考译文：（结合能曲线上的）最低能量与两个独立原子的能量之差，就是键解离能，即用于断裂分子中某个特定键所需的能量。

3. The molecular orbital method successfully explains the paramagnetism of the oxygen molecule and molecular spectra and avoids the need for resonance structures. 参考译文：分子轨道理论成功地解释了氧分子的顺磁性及其分子光谱，并且不必使用共振结构。

4. The atomic orbitals that are combined to form a molecular orbital must occupy the same region in space and have similar energies; the number of molecular orbitals formed must be equal to the number of atomic orbitals combined. 参考译文：那些能组合形成分子轨道的原子轨道，必须在空间上占据相同的区域并具有相似的能量；形成的分子轨道数一定等于用于组合的原子轨道数。

3. Brønsted Acids and Bases

Johannes Brønsted in Demark and Thomas Lowry in England proposed (in 1932) that the essential feature of an acid-base reaction is the transfer of a proton from one species to another. In the context of the Brønsted-Lowry definitions, a proton is a hydrogen ion, H^+. They suggested that any substance that acts as a proton donor should be classified as an acid, and any substance that acts as a proton acceptor should be classified as a base.[1] Substances that act in this way are now called Brønsted acids and Brønsted bases, respectively. The definitions make no reference to the environment in which proton transfer occurs, so they apply to proton transfer behavior in any solvent and even in no solvent at all.

An example of a Brønsted acid is hydrogen fluoride, HF, which can donate a proton to anther molecule, such as H_2O, when it dissolves in water. An example of a Brønsted base is ammonia, NH_3, which can accept a proton from a proton donor.

As these two examples show, water is an example of an amphiprotic substance, a substance that can act as both a Brønsted acid and a Brønsted base.

When an acid donates a proton to a water molecule, the latter is converted into a hydronium ion, H_3O^+. The dimensions of the hydronium ion are taken from the crystal structure of $H_3O^+ClO_4^-$. However, the structure H_3O^+ is the almost certainly an oversimplified description of the ion in water, for it participates in extensive hydrogen bonding. If a simple formula is required, the hydronium ion in water is probably best represented as $H_9O_4^+$. Gasphase studies of water clusters using mass spectrometry suggest that a cage of 20 H_2O molecules can condense around one H_3O^+ ion in a regular pentagonal dodecahedral arrangement, resulting in the formation of the species $H^+(H_2O)_{21}$.[2] As these structures indicate, the most appropriate description of a proton in water varies according to the environment and the experiment under consideration.

Proton transfer equilibria in water

Proton transfer between acids and bases is fast in both directions, so the dynamic equilibria:

$$HF(aq) + H_2O(l) \rightleftharpoons H_3O^+(aq) + F^-(aq)$$
$$H_2O(l) + NH_3(aq) \rightleftharpoons NH_4^+(aq) + OH^-(aq) \quad (1)$$

give a more complete description of the behavior of the acid HF and the base NH_3 in water than the forward reaction alone. The central feature of Brønsted acid-base chemistry in aqueous solution is that of rapidly attained proton transfer equilibrium, and we concentrate on this aspect.

Conjugate acids and bases

The symmetry of each of the two forward and reverse reactions in eqn (1), both of which depend on the transfers of a proton from an acid to a base, is expressed by writing the general Brønsted equilibrium as:

$$Acid_1 + Base_2 \rightleftharpoons Acid_2 + Base_1 \quad (2)$$

The species $Base_1$ is called the conjugate base of $Acid_1$, and $Acid_2$ is the conjugate acid of $Base_2$. The conjugate base of an acid is the species that is left after a proton is lost. The conjugate acid of a base is the species formed when a proton is gained. Thus, F^- is the conjugate base of HF and H_3O^+ is the conjugate acid of H_2O. There is no fundamental distinction between an acid and a conjugate acid or a base and a conjugate base: a conjugate acid is just another acid and a conjugate base is just another base.

Dissociation equilibrium constant of Brønsted acids and bases

The relative strengths of Brønsted acids is often described in terms of an acid-dissociation equilibrium constant (or "acid ionization constant", "acidity constant"), K_a. The value of K_a for acid, such as HF, in aqueous solution is calculated from the following equation:

$$HF(aq) + H_2O(l) \rightleftharpoons H_3O^+(aq) + F^-(aq)$$

$$K_a = \frac{[H_3O^+][F^-]}{[HF]} \tag{3}$$

In this definition, $[X]$ denotes the numerical value of the molar concentration of the species X (so, if the molar concentration of HF molecules is $0.001 mol \cdot L^{-1}$, then $[HF] = 0.001$). A value $K_a \ll 1$ implies that proton retention by the acid favored. The experimental value of K_a for hydrogen fluoride in water is 3.5×10^{-4}, indicating that under normal conditions, only a very small fraction of HF molecules are deprotonated in water. The actual fraction deprotonated can be calculated as a function of acid concentration from the numerical value of K_a as described in any introductory chemistry text.

The proton transfer equilibrium characteristic of a base, such as NH_3 in water can also be expressed in terms of an equilibrium constant, the basicity constant, K_b:

$$NH_3(aq) + H_2O(l) \rightleftharpoons NH_4^+(aq) + OH^-(aq)$$

$$K_b = \frac{[NH_4^+][OH^-]}{[NH_3]} \tag{4}$$

If $K_b \ll 1$, the base is a weak proton acceptor and its conjugate acid is present in low abundance in solution. The experimental value of K_b for ammonia in water is 1.8×10^{-5}, indicating that under normal conditions, only a very small fraction of NH_3 molecules are protonated in water. As for the acid calculation, the actual fraction of base protonted can be calculated from the numerical value of K_b.

Because water is amphiprotic, a proton transfer equilibrium exists even in the absence of added acids or bases. The proton transfer from one water molecule to another is called autoprotolysis (or autoionization). The extent of autoprotolysis and the composition of the solution at equilibrium is described by the water autoprotolysis constant, K_w:

$$2H_2O(l) \rightleftharpoons H_3O^+(aq) + OH^-(aq)$$

$$K_w = [H_3O^+][OH^-] \tag{5}$$

The experimental value of K_w is 1.00×10^{-14} at 25℃, indicating that only a very tiny fraction of water molecules is present as ions in pure water.

An important role for the autoprotolysis constant of a solvent is that it enables us to express the strength of a base in terms of the strength of its conjugates acid. Thus, the value of K_b for the equilibrium in Eq. (4) is related to the value K_a for the equilibrium:

$$NH_4^+ + H_2O \rightleftharpoons H_3O^+(aq) + NH_3(aq)$$

By

$$K_a K_b = K_w \tag{6}$$

This relation may be verified by multiplying together the expression for the acidity constant of NH_4^+ and the basicity constant of NH_3.[3] The implication of Eq. (6) is that the larger the value of K_b, the smaller the value of K_a. That is, the stronger the base, the weaker its conjugate acid. A further implication of Eq. (6) is that the strengths of bases may be reported in terms of the acidity constants of their conjugate acids.

Because molar concentrations and acidity constants span many orders of magnitude, it proves convenient to report them as their common logarithms (logarithms to the base 10) by using:
$$pH = -\lg[H_3O^+]; \quad pK = -\log K$$
where K may be any of the constants we have introduced. At 25℃, for instance, $pK_w = 14.00$. It follows from this definition and the relation in Eq. (6) that:
$$pK_a + pK_b = pK_w$$
A similar expression applies to the strengths of conjugate acids and bases in any solvent, with pK_w replace by the appropriate autoprotolysis constant of the solvent, pK_{sol}.

The strength of acids and bases

A substance is classified as a strong acid if the proton transfer equilibrium lies strongly in favor of donation to water. Thus, a substance with $pK_a < 0$ (corresponding to $K_a > 1$ and usually to $K_a \gg 1$) is a strong acid. Such acids are commonly regarded as being fully deprotonated in solution (but it must never be forgotten that that is only an approximation). For example, hydrochloric acid is regarded as a solution of hydronium ions and chloride ions, and a negligible concentration of HCl molecules. A substance with $pK_a > 0$ (corresponding to $K_a < 1$) is classified as a weak acid; for such species, the proton transfer equilibrium lies in favor of nonionized acid. Hydrogen fluoride is a weak acid in water, and hydrofluoric acid consists of hydronium ions, fluoride ions, and a high proportion of HF molecules.

A strong base is a species that is virtually fully protonated in water. An example is the oxide ion, O^{2-}, which is immediately converted into OH^- ions in water. A weak base is only partially protonated in water. An example is NH_3, which is present almost entirely as NH_3 molecules in water, with a small proportion of NH_4^+ ions. The conjugate base of any strong acid is a weak base, because it is thermodynamically unfavorable for such a base to accept a proton.

Polyprotic acids

A polyprotic acid is a substance that can donate more than one proton. An example is hydrogen sulfide, H_2S, a diprotic acid. For a diprotic acid, there are two successive proton donations and two acidity constants:

$$H_2S(aq) + H_2O(l) \rightleftharpoons HS^-(aq) + H_3O^+(aq) \quad K_{a1} = \frac{[H_3O^+][HS^-]}{[H_2S]}$$

$$HS^-(aq) + H_2O(l) \rightleftharpoons S^{2-}(aq) + H_3O^+(aq) \quad K_{a2} = \frac{[H_3O^+][S^{2-}]}{[HS^-]}$$

In which, $K_{a1} = 9.1 \times 10^{-8}$ ($pK_{a1} = 7.04$) and $K_{a2} \approx 10^{-19}$ ($pK_{a2} = 19$). The second acidity constant, K_{a2} is almost always smaller than K_{a1} (and hence pK_{a2} is generally larger than pK_{a1}). The decrease in K_a is consistent with an electrostatic model of the acid in which, in the second deprotonation, a proton must separate from a center with one more negative charge than in the first deprotonation. Because additional electric work must be done to remove the positively charged proton, the deprotonation is less favorable.[4]

The clearest representation of the concentrations of the species that are formed in the successive proton transfer equilibria of polyprotic acids is a distribution diagram. In such a diagram, the fraction, $\alpha(X)$, of a specified species X is plotted against the pH. Consider, for instance, the triprotic acid H_3PO_4, which releases three protons in succession to give $H_2PO_4^-$, HPO_4^{2-}, and PO_4^{3-}. The distribution diagram shows the fraction of each of these species as a function of pH; for the fraction of H_3PO_4 molecules, for instance:

$$\alpha(H_3PO_4) = \frac{[H_3PO_4]}{[H_3PO_4]+[H_2PO_4^-]+[HPO_4^{2-}]+[PO_4^{3-}]}$$

the variation of α with pH reveals the relative importance of each acid and its conjugate base at each pH. Conversely, the diagram indicates the pH of the solution that contains a particular fraction of the species.[5] We see, for instance, that if $pH < pK_{a1}$, corresponding to high hydronium ion concentrations, the dominant species is the fully protonated H_3PO_4 molecule. However, if $pH > pK_{a3}$, corresponding to low hydronium ion concentrations, the dominant species is the fully deprotonated PO_4^{3-} ion. The intermediate species are dominant at pH values that lie between the relevant pK_{as}.

New Words and Expressions

amphiprotic [æmfip'rɔtik] adj. 两性的
hydronium [hai'drəuniəm] n. 水合氢离子
condense [kən'dens] v. (使)浓缩，凝结
pentagonal [pen'tægənl] adj. 五角的，五边形的
dodecahedral [,dəudekə'hi:drəl] adj. 十二面体的
retention [ri'tenʃn] n. 保留，滞留，扣留
protonate ['prəutə,neit] vt. 使质子化
autoprotolysis [,ɔ:təprəu'tɔlisis] n. 质子自递作用
multiply ['mʌltiplai] v. 乘，增加
span [spæn] v. 横跨，包括，涵盖
magnitude ['mægnitju:d] n. 数量，量级
logarithm ['lɔgəriðəm] n. 对数
virtually ['və:rtʃuəli] adv. 实际上，几乎
protic ['prəutik] adj. 质子的

Phrases

be classified as　分类为，定义为
in terms of　根据，按照
dissociation equilibrium constant　解离平衡常数
in the absence of　缺乏……时，当……不在时
in favor of　赞同，有利于
polyprotic acid　多元酸
diprotic acid　二元酸
electric work　电功
distribution diagram　分布曲线图
triprotic acid　三元酸

Affixes

de- 表示"向下，剥夺，分离"；如 deprotonate 去质子化，decolor 脱色，漂白，defrost 除霜，dehydrogenation 脱氢，dehydrate 脱水
amphi- ['æmfi] 表示"两，两者"；如 amphiprotic（酸碱）两性的，amphibious 两栖的，amphipathic 同时具有亲水和厌水部分的，两性分子的

Notes

1. They suggested that any substance that acts as a proton donor should be classified as an acid, and any substance that acts as a proton acceptor should be classified as a base. 参考译文：他们认为任何能提供质子的物质应归为酸，任何能接收质子的物质应归为碱。

2. However, the structure H_3O^+ is the almost certainly an oversimplified description of the ion in water, for it participates in extensive hydrogen bonding. If a simple formula is re-

quired, the hydronium ion in water is probably best represented as $H_9O_4^+$. Gasphase studies of water clusters using mass spectrometry suggest that a cage of 20 H_2O molecules can condense around one H_3O^+ ion in a regular pentagonal dodecahedral arrangement, resulting in the formation of the species $H^+(H_2O)_{21}$. 参考译文：然而，对水中离子用 H_3O^+ 描述肯定是过于简化了，因为它还参与了大量的氢键。如果需要一个简单的分子式的话，水合氢离子最好表示为 $H_9O_4^+$。水分子团簇的气相质谱研究表明，20 个水分子以规则的五边形十二面体构型聚集在一个 H_3O^+ 周围，形成 $H^+(H_2O)_{21}$。

3. This relation may be verified by multiplying together the expression for the acidity constant of NH_4^+ and the basicity constant of NH_3. 参考译文：这种关系（$K_a K_b = K_w$）可以通过将 NH_4^+ 的酸常数和 NH_3 的碱常数的表达式相乘来验证。

4. The decrease in K_a is consistent with an electrostatic model of the acid in which, in the second deprotonation, a proton must separate from a center with one more negative charge than in the first deprotonation. Because additional electric work must be done to remove the positively charged proton, the deprotonation is less favorable. 参考译文：（多元酸）K_a 的减小与其静电模型是一致的，其中，在二级解离中，质子必须从比第一级解离时多一个负电荷的中心脱离出来。由于需要额外的电功来去掉这个带正电荷的质子，因此第二级解离更困难。

5. The distribution diagram shows the fraction of each of these species as a function of pH; for the fraction of H_3PO_4 molecules, for instance, the variation of α with pH reveals the relative importance of each acid and its conjugate base at each pH. Conversely, the diagram indicates the pH of the solution that contains a particular fraction of the species. 参考译文：分布曲线图表明这些物质的分配系数均是 pH 的函数；如对 H_3PO_4 的分配系数来说，α 随 pH 值的变化显示了在各 pH 值时每种酸及其共轭碱的相对多少。反过来，该图也表明了含有一定组成的溶液所对应的 pH 值。

4. Chemical Reaction and Equilibrium

Reactions in Solution

Solutions are homogeneous mixtures. If a solution is in the same state as one of the materials that make up the mixture, that material is usually called the solvent. If all the substances in a solution are in the same state when pure, the substance present in greatest amount in the solution is called the solvent. The other substances are called solutes. Chemists use solutions to carry out reactions because they are easy to handle and the solute particles can move around and hit each other so that reaction can take place at a practical rate.

A saturated solution contains as much solute as it can dissolve in the presence of undissolved solute at a given temperature; the quantity of solute that will dissolve is called solubility of the solute.[1] Unsaturated solutions contain less dissolved solute than a saturated solution. Supersaturated solutions contain more solute than a saturated solution and are unstable. Solid that separates from a solution is called precipitate.

Electrolytes are compounds that conduct an electric current when dissolved or melted. The ability to conduct electricity is called conductivity. In a solution of an electrolyte or in a molten electrolyte, the current consists of moving ions. In solutions of strong electrolytes most of the solute is in the form of ions; there are few molecules of solute. In solutions of weak electrolytes most of the solute is in the form of molecules; only a little is in the form of ions. Solutions of nonelectrolytes do not contain any ions; all of the solute is in the form of molecules. Acids, bases, and salts are electrolytes. Acids increase the concentration of hydrogen ions when dissolved in water. Bases increase the concentration of hydroxide ions when dissolved in water. Acids and bases neutralize each other and form water and salts, which are compounds composed of metals (or polyatomic cations such as the ammonium ion, NH_4^+) and nonmetals (including polyatomic anions such as the nitrate ion, NO_3^-). Metal hydroxides and oxides are classified as bases, not salts.

Reactions take place between ions in solution whenever at least one of the possible products is either insoluble or nonelectrolyte. Reactions in solution can be represented by molecular, complete ionic, and net ionic equations. Molecular equations show all substances as if they exist in solution as molecules. Ionic equations show compounds that exist as ions in solution. Molecular formulas are used for weak electrolytes and insoluble compounds. Net ionic equations show only the species that take part in the reaction. Ions that are present but do not take part in the reaction are called spectator ions. Ionic equations must show the same number of atoms of each kind and the same charge on both sides.

In a single replacement reaction, one element takes the place of another element in a compound. There is a change in properties from metallic to nonmetallic across rows in the periodic table. The reactivity of metals in Groups IA and IIA (and aluminum) decreases across a row and increases going down a group. The reactivity of transition metals and nonmetals decreases down a group.

Reactions in solution can be used for dissolving insoluble compounds, for making compounds (synthesis), and for qualitative and quantitative analysis. Titration is a method of determining the amount of substance present in a solution by adding a solution of known concentration, called a standard solution, from a buret until the endpoint is reached. Indicators are used to signal endpoints.

Concentration of a solution is the amount of solute dissolved in a given quantity of solvent or solution. Dilute solutions have relatively low concentrations of solute; concentrated solutions have relatively high concentrations of solute. In everyday life, concentration is often expressed as mass percent or volume percent. Molarity is the unit most used in laboratory work because it provides a conversion factor between volume of solution and moles of solute. Molarity, M, is the number of moles of solute per liter of solution:

$$\text{molarity}, M = \frac{\text{number of moles of solute}}{\text{volume of solution in liters}}$$

Solutions of known molarity can be prepared either from pure solute or by diluting a concentrated solution of known molarity. Once a solution of known molarity is available, it can be used to measure amounts of solute simply by measuring volume. When pure solvents and concentrated solutions are mixed, the total volume is not necessarily equal to the sum of the individual volumes. However, the total volume of mixtures of dilute solutions is equal to the sum of the volumes mixed. Using molarity as a unit of concentration simplifies solving stoichiometry problems involving solutions.

Equilibrium

Whether the equilibrium in any acid-base reaction lies to the right or to the left can be predicted from the positions of the acid and base in a table of K_a values.[2] In general, all acid-base reactions favor the direction where a stronger acid and base react to form a weaker acid and base. The value of the equilibrium constant can be calculated from the values of the equilibrium constants for the acid and base by making use of the fact that the equilibrium constant for a reaction that is the sum of two or more reactions is equal to the product of the equilibrium constants for the individual reactions.[3]

The strengths of acids and bases in aqueous solutions are a result of a combination of factors of which bond polarity, bond strength, and solvation are the most important. Fortunately, a few empirical rules that relate acidity to structure happen to work reasonably well at room temperature. The acidity of the binary compounds (compounds consisting of two elements) of hydrogen increases from left to right across rows and from top to bottom down groups in the periodic table. The hydrides of the reactive metals of Groups I A and II A are strong bases; the hydrides of many nonmetals are acids.

The hydroxides of the reactive metals are also strong bases. The hydroxides of nonmetals are acidic and the hydroxides of elements near the metal-nonmetal borderline are amphoteric. The acidity of oxo acids is related to the electronegativity of the central atom and to the number of extra oxygens attached to the central atom. The acidity of organic acids is increased by substitution of more electronegative atoms for hydrogens close to the —COOH group.

Hydrated cations also act as Brønsted-Lowry acids. If charge and electronegativity are similar, the smaller the radius of the ion, the more acidic the hydrated cation is. The acidity of hydrated cations decreases down groups of the periodic table. If radii and electronegativities are similar, the higher the charge, the more acidic the hydrated cation. If charge and radius are similar, the greater the electronegativity of the metal, the more acidic the hydrated cation.

The basicity of anionic and cationic weak bases can be deduced from the acidity of their conjugate acids. Anions that contain one or more ionizable hydrogens, such as HCO_3^-, are amphoteric.

Most metal oxides are basic. Oxides of some metals near the metal-nonmetal borderline are amphoteric. Most nonmetal oxides are acidic and many nonmetal oxides react with water to form oxo acids. When an element forms more than one kind of oxides, the oxide with the higher proportion of oxygen reacts with water to form a stronger acid. A few nonmetal oxides are neither acidic nor basic. Acidic and basic oxides often react directly to form salts.

Lewis acids are not limited to compounds that contain hydrogen. A Lewis acid is a species that can accept an electron pair to form a covalent bond. A Lewis acid must have an empty valence orbital for the electron pair to go into. Species with incomplete octets, small cations with high charges, and species with multiple bonds are Lewis acids. A Lewis base is a species that has an unshared electron pair that can form a covalent bond. Lewis acid-base reactions can be regarded as substitution reactions in which one Lewis base takes the place of another Lewis base.

Complexes are species in which a central atom is surrounded by Lewis bases that are covalently bonded to the central atom. The Lewis bases are usually referred to as ligands. Complexes can be either ions or molecules. Formation of complexes other than aqua complexes in water solution involves substitution of other ligands for water; substitution of other ligands for water takes place in steps and is reversible.[4] The values of the equilibrium constants for successive steps decrease although differences between equilibrium constants are small and solutions usually contain mixtures of complexes. Complex ion equilibria are too complicated to deal with quantitatively in general chemistry unless an excess of the ligand is present so that a single species is predominant.

The solubility product constant or solubility product, K_{sp}, is equal to the product of the molar concentrations of the ions in a saturated solution of a slightly soluble salt, each raised to the power of its coefficient in the balanced equation.[5] For a few slightly soluble salts and hydroxides, solubility is quantitatively related to the value of the equilibrium constant. For most, actual solubilities are higher than solubilities calculated from K_{sp}. For some, the observed solubility is many powers of ten greater than the calculated solubility. The common ion effect, the salt effect, side reactions such as hydrolysis and complex ion formation, and incomplete dissociation and ion pair formation are important in solubility equilibria. A salt effect is an increase in solubility caused by the presence in the solution of ions that are not common ions.

Some slightly soluble salts and metal hydroxides can be dissolved by complex ion formation. Others can be dissolved by Bronsted-Lowry acid-base reactions.

New Words and Expressions

solvent ['sɔlvənt] n. 溶剂
solute ['sɔljuːt] n. 溶解物，溶质
dissolve [di'zɔlv] v. （使）溶解，解散，解除
solubility [,sɔlju'biliti] n. 溶解度，溶解性
precipitate [pri'sipiteit] n. 沉淀物
electrolyte [i'lektrəulait] n. 电解，电解质
conductivity [,kɔndʌk'tiviti] n. 传导性，传导率
base [beis] n. 碱
synthesis ['sinθəsis] n. 合成
titration [tai'treiʃən] n. 滴定
buret [bjuə'ret] n. 滴定管，移液管
endpoint ['endpɔint] n. 端点，终点

indicator ['indikeitə] n. 指示剂
molarity [mɔu'læriti] n. 物质的量浓度
stoichiometry [,stɔiki'ɔmitri] n. 化学计量学，化学计量法，计量化学
equilibrium [,iːkwi'libriəm] n. 平衡，均衡（复数形式为 equilibria）
polarity [pɔu'læriti] n. 极性
solvation [sɔl'veiʃən] n. 溶剂化
empirical [im'pirikl] adj. 经验主义的，以经验（或实验）为依据的
binary ['bainəri] adj. 由两个东西组成的，二态的，二元的，二进制的
hydride ['haidraid] n. 氢化物

hydroxide [hai'drɔksaid, -sid] n. 氢氧化物
borderline ['bɔːdəlain] n. 边界线
amphoteric [ˌæmfə'terik] adj. 两性的
oxo ['ɔksəu] adj. 含氧的
basicity [bə'sisiti] n. 碱度，碱性
conjugate ['kɔndʒugeit] adj. 成对的，结合的，共轭的；n. 结合物

complex [kəm'pleks] n. 复数，复合物
ligand ['ligənd] n. 配合基，配体
aqua ['ækwə] adj. 含水的，水合的
successive [sək'sesiv] adj. 连续的，相继的，继承的
predominant [pri'dɔminənt] adj. 主要的，占主导地位的，占优势的

Phrases

saturated solution　饱和溶液
unsaturated solution　不饱和溶液
supersaturated solution　过饱和溶液
molecular equation　分子方程式
ionic equation　离子方程式
net ionic equation　净离子方程式
spectator ion　旁观离子
replacement reaction　置换反应
standard solution　标准溶液
dilute solution　稀溶液
concentrated solution　浓溶液

empirical rule　经验法则
binary compound　二元化合物
Brønsted-Lowry acid-base theory　布朗斯特-劳里酸碱理论，即酸碱质子理论
hydrated cation　水合阳离子
conjugate acid　共轭酸
Lewis acid　路易斯酸
aqua complex　水合物，水络合物
successive steps　逐步，逐级
common ion effect　同离子效应
solubility product constant　溶度积常数

Affixes

extra- [ekstrə] 表示"在外，外面，离开"；如 extractive 萃取的, extrapolate 推断
en- [in-, en-] 表示"置于……之中；使处于……状态；使成为"；如 enable, enlarge, encase, endanger, enrich, encapsulate
-phile [-fail] （名词后缀）表示"亲，爱好，嗜"；如 nucleophile 亲核试剂, electrophilic 亲电的, hydrophile 亲水（性）
co- [kəu-] 表示"联合，伴同"；如 coabsorption 共吸收, coactivate 共活化剂, coprecipitation 共沉淀
hydro- [hai'drəu] 表示"水，液，流体"，"氢的，含氢的"；如 hydrophobic 疏水的, hydroalkylation 加氢烷基化, hydrogel 水凝胶, hydrolysis 水解, hydroxcopicity 吸湿性

Notes

1. A saturated solution contains as much solute as it can dissolve in the presence of undissolved solute at a given temperature; the quantity of solute that will dissolve is called solubility of the solute. 这是一个并列句，"as much as"是"和……一样多"的意思，后一分句为含有"that"引导的定语从句的复合句。参考译文：一定温度下，饱和溶液含有溶质的量等于仍有未被溶解溶质时所溶解溶质的量，所溶解的溶质的量称为该溶质的溶解度。

2. Whether the equilibrium in any acid-base reaction lies to the right or to the left can be predicted from the positions of the acid and base in a table of K_a values. 参考译文：酸碱平衡落在左边还是右边可以通过酸碱在 K_a 值表中的位置来推断。

3. The value of the equilibrium constant can be calculated from the values of the equilibrium constants for the acid and base by making use of the fact that the equilibrium constant

for a reaction that is the sum of two or more reactions is equal to the product of the equilibrium constants for the individual reactions. 参考译文：利用两个或多个反应加和得到的一个反应的平衡常数等于每个反应平衡常数的乘积这一事实，可以利用酸和碱的平衡常数值来计算反应的平衡常数。

4. Formation of complexes other than aqua complexes in water solution involves substitution of other ligands for water; substitution of other ligands for water takes place in steps and is reversible. 参考译文：水溶液中除了水合物，复合物的形成都涉及其他配体对水的取代；其他配体取代水是逐步进行的，并且可逆。

5. The solubility product constant or solubility product, K_{sp}, is equal to the product of the molar concentration of the constituent ions in a saturated solution of a slightly soluble salt, each raised to the power of its coefficient in the balanced equation. 句中，"each"作为代词，代替前面的"the molar concentration"；"its"指代前面的"the constituent ions"。参考译文：溶度积常数或溶度积，K_{sp}，等于微溶盐饱和溶液中组成离子物质的量浓度的乘积，每个浓度都以平衡方程式中该离子的系数做幂指数。

5. Structure and Nomenclature of Hydrocarbons

The Saturated Hydrocarbons, or Alkanes

Compounds that contain only carbon and hydrogen are known as **hydrocarbons**. Those that contain as many hydrogen atoms as possible are said to be saturated. The saturated hydrocarbons are also known as alkanes. A common "ane" suffix identifies these compounds as alkanes.

The simplest alkane is methane: CH_4. The Lewis structure of methane can be generated by combining the four electrons in the valence shell of a neutral carbon atom with four hydrogen atoms to form a compound in which the carbon atom shares a total of eight valence electrons with the four hydrogen atoms.

Methane is an example of a general rule that carbon is **tetravalent**; it forms a total of four bonds in almost all of its compounds. To minimize the repulsion between pairs of electrons in the four C—H bonds, the geometry around the carbon atom is tetrahedral, as shown in the figure below.

The names, formulas, and physical properties for a variety of alkanes with the generic formula $C_n H_{2n+2}$ are given in the table below. The boiling points of the alkanes gradually increase with the molecular weight of these compounds. At room temperature, the lighter alkanes are gases; the midweight alkanes are liquids; and the heavier alkanes are solids, or tars.

The alkanes in the table below are all straight-chain hydrocarbons, in which the carbon atoms form a chain that runs from one end of the molecule to the other. The generic formula for these compounds can be understood by assuming that they contain chains of CH_2 groups with an additional hydrogen atom capping either end of the chain.[1] Thus, for every n carbon atoms there must be $2n+2$ hydrogen atoms: $C_n H_{2n+2}$.

The Saturated Hydrocarbons, or Alkanes

Name	Molecular Formula	Melting Point/℃	Boiling Point/℃	State at 25℃
methane	CH_4	−182.5	−164	gas
ethane	$C_2 H_6$	−183.3	−88.6	gas
propane	$C_3 H_8$	−189.7	−42.1	gas

continued

Name	Molecular Formula	Melting Point/°C	Boiling Point/°C	State at 25°C
butane	C_4H_{10}	−138.4	−0.5	gas
pentane	C_5H_{12}	−129.7	36.1	liquid
hexane	C_6H_{14}	−95	68.9	liquid
heptane	C_7H_{16}	−90.6	98.4	liquid
octane	C_8H_{18}	−56.8	124.7	liquid
nonane	C_9H_{20}	−51	150.8	liquid
decane	$C_{10}H_{22}$	−29.7	174.1	liquid
undecane	$C_{11}H_{24}$	−24.6	195.9	liquid
dodecane	$C_{12}H_{26}$	−9.6	216.3	liquid
icosane	$C_{20}H_{42}$	36.8	343	solid
triacontane	$C_{30}H_{62}$	65.8	449.7	solid

Because two points define a line, the carbon skeleton of the ethane molecule is linear, as shown in the figure below.

Because the bond angle in a tetrahedron is 109.5°, alkanes molecules that contain three or four carbon atoms can no longer be thought of as "linear", as shown in the figure below.

Propane   Butane

In addition to the straight-chain examples considered so far, alkanes also form branched structures. The smallest hydrocarbon in which a branch can occur has four carbon atoms. This compound has the same formula as butane (C_4H_{10}), but a different structure. Compounds with the same formula and different structures are known as isomers. When it was first discovered, the branched isomer with the formula C_4H_{10} was therefore given the name isobutane.

$$\text{CH}_3-\underset{\underset{\text{CH}_3}{|}}{\text{CH}}-\text{CH}_3 \quad \text{Isobutane}$$

The best way to understand the difference between the structures of butane and isobutane is to compare the ball-and-stick models of these compounds shown in the figure below.[2]

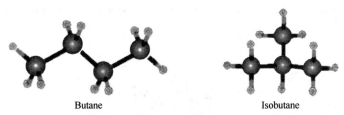

Butane   Isobutane

Butane and isobutane are called constitutional isomers because they literally differ in their constitution. One contains two CH_3 groups and two CH_2 groups; the other contains three CH_3 groups and one CH group.

There are three constitutional isomers of pentane, C_5H_{12}. The first is "normal" pentane, or n-pentane.

$$CH_3-CH_2-CH_2-CH_2-CH_3 \quad n\text{-Pentane}$$

A branched isomer is also possible, which was originally named isopentane. When a more highly branched isomer was discovered, it was named neopentane (the new isomer of pentane).

$$\begin{array}{cc} \text{CH}_3 & \text{CH}_3 \\ | & | \\ \text{CH}_3-\text{CH}-\text{CH}_2-\text{CH}_3 & \text{CH}_3-\text{C}-\text{CH}_3 \\ & | \\ & \text{CH}_3 \end{array}$$

Isopentane   Neopentane

Ball-and-stick models of the three isomers of pentane are shown in the figure below.

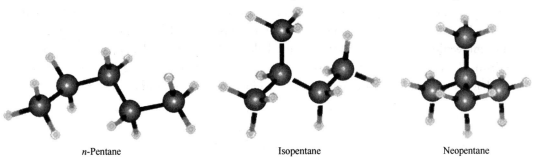

n-Pentane   Isopentane   Neopentane

There are two constitutional isomers with the formula C_4H_{10}, three isomers of C_5H_{12}, and five isomers of C_6H_{14}. The number of isomers of a compound increases rapidly with additional carbon atoms. There are over 4 billion isomers for $C_{30}H_{62}$, for example.

The Cycloalkanes

If the carbon chain that forms the backbone of a straight-chain hydrocarbon is long enough, we can envision the two ends coming together to form a cycloalkane. One hydrogen atom has to be removed from each end of the hydrocarbon chain to form the C—C bond that closes the ring. Cycloalkanes therefore have two less hydrogen atoms than the parent alkane and a generic formula of C_nH_{2n}. Hydrocarbons having more than one ring are common, and are referred to as bicyclic (two rings), tricyclic (three rings) and in general, polycyclic compounds.

The smallest alkane that can form a ring is cyclopropane, C_3H_6, in which the three carbon atoms lie in the same plane. The angle between adjacent C—C bonds is only 60°, which is very much smaller than the 109.5° angle in a tetrahedron, as shown in the figure below. Cyclopropane is therefore susceptible to chemical reactions that can open up the three-membered ring.

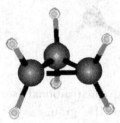

Any attempt to force the four carbons that form a cyclobutane ring into a plane of atoms would produce the structure shown in the figure below, in which the angle between adjacent C—C bonds would be 90°.

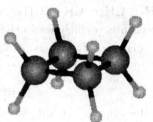

One of the four carbon atoms in the cyclobutane ring is therefore displaced from the plane of the other three to form a "puckered" structure that is vaguely reminiscent of the wings of a butterfly.[3]

The angle between adjacent C—C bonds in a planar cyclopentane molecule would be 108°, which is close to the ideal angle around a tetrahedral carbon atom. Cyclopentane is not a planar molecule, as shown in the figure below, because displacing two of the carbon atoms from the plane of the other three produces a puckered structure that relieves some of the repulsion between the hydrogen atoms on adjacent carbon atoms in the ring.[4]

By the time we get to the six-membered ring in cyclohexane, a puckered structure can be formed by displacing a pair of carbon atoms at either end of the ring from the plane of the other four members of the ring. One of these carbon atoms is tilted up, out of the ring, whereas the other is tilted down to form the "chair" structure shown in the figure below.[5]

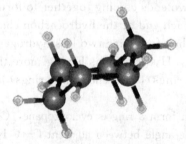

The Nomenclature of Alkanes

Common names such as pentane, isopentane, and neopentane are sufficient to differentiate between the three isomers with the formula C_5H_{12}. They become less useful, however, as the size of the hydrocarbon chain increases.

The International Union of Pure and Applied Chemistry (IUPAC) has developed a systematic approach for naming alkanes and cycloalkanes based on the following steps.

• Find the longest continuous chain of carbon atoms in the skeleton structure. Name the compound as a derivative of the alkane with this number of carbon atoms. The following compound, for example, is a derivative of pentane because the longest chain contains five carbon atoms.

• Name the substituents on the chain. Substituents derived from alkanes are named by replacing the -ane ending with -yl. This compound contains a methyl (CH_3—) substituent.

• Number the chain starting at the end nearest the first substituent and specify the carbon atoms on which the substituents are located. Use the lowest possible numbers. This compound, for example, is 2-methylpentane, not 4-methylpentane.

• Use the prefixes di-, tri-, and tetra- to describe substituents that are found two, three, or four times on the same chain of carbon atoms.

• Arrange the names of the substituents in alphabetical order.

The Unsaturated Hydrocarbons: Alkenes and Alkynes

Carbon not only forms the strong C—C single bonds found in alkanes, but also forms strong C=C double bonds. These compounds are called alkenes. The simplest alkene has the formula C_2H_4 and the following Lewis structure.

The relationship between alkanes and alkenes can be understood by thinking about the following hypothetical reaction. We start by breaking the bond in an H₂ molecule so that one of the electrons ends up on each of hydrogen atoms. We do the same thing to one of the bonds between the carbon atoms in an alkene. We then allow the unpaired electron on each hydrogen atom to interact with the unpaired electron on the carbon atom to form a new C—H bond.

$$\underset{\underset{H}{\overset{H}{\diagdown}}C=C\underset{H}{\overset{H}{\diagup}}}{H-H} \longrightarrow \underset{H\ H}{H-\overset{H\cdot}{\underset{|}{C}}-\overset{H\cdot}{\underset{|}{C}}-H} \longrightarrow \underset{H\ H}{H-\overset{H\ H}{\underset{|}{C}}-\overset{}{\underset{|}{C}}-H}$$

Thus, in theory, we can transform an alkene into the parent alkane by adding an H₂ molecule across a C=C double bond. In practice, this reaction only occurs at high pressures in the presence of a suitable catalyst, such as piece of nickel metal.

$$\underset{H\quad H}{\overset{H\quad H}{\diagdown\diagup}}C=C\quad + \quad H_2 \quad \xrightarrow{Ni} \quad \underset{H\ H}{H-\overset{H\ H}{\underset{|}{C}}-\overset{}{\underset{|}{C}}-H}$$

Because an alkene can be thought of as a derivative of an alkane from which an H₂ molecule has been removed, the generic formula for an alkene with one C=C double bond is C_nH_{2n}.

Alkenes are examples of unsaturated hydrocarbons because they have fewer hydrogen atoms than the corresponding alkanes. They were once named by adding the suffix -ene to the name of the substituent that carried the same number of carbon atoms.

$$CH_2=CH_2 \qquad CH_2=CH-CH_3$$
$$\text{Ethylene} \qquad\qquad \text{Propylene}$$

The IUPAC nomenclature for alkenes names these compounds as derivatives of the parent alkanes. The presence of the C=C double bond is indicated by changing the -ane ending on the name of the parent alkane to -ene.

$$CH_3-CH_3 \qquad CH_2=CH_2$$
$$\text{Ethane} \qquad\qquad \text{Ethene}$$

$$CH_3-CH_2-CH_3 \qquad CH_3-CH=CH_2$$
$$\text{Propane} \qquad\qquad \text{Propene}$$

The location of the C=C double bond in the skeleton structure of the compound is indicated by specifying the number of the carbon atom at which the C=C bond starts.

$$CH_2=CH-CH_2-CH_3 \qquad CH_3-CH=CH-CH_3$$
$$\text{1-Butene} \qquad\qquad \text{2-Butene}$$

The names of substituents are then added as prefixes to the name of the alkene.

Compounds that contain C≡C triple bonds are called **alkynes.** These compounds have four less hydrogen atoms than the parent alkanes, so the generic formula for an alkyne with a single C≡C triple bond is C_nH_{2n-2}. The simplest alkyne has the formula C_2H_2 and is known by the common name *acetylene*.

$$H-C\equiv C-H \qquad \text{Acetylene}$$

The IUPAC nomenclature for alkynes names these compounds as derivatives of the parent alkane, with the ending -yne replacing -ane.

$$CH_3C\equiv CCH_2CH_3 \qquad \text{2-Pentyne}$$

$$HC\equiv CCH_2CH_3 \qquad \text{1-Butyne}$$

$$CH_3C\equiv CCH_2\overset{\underset{\displaystyle CH_3}{|}}{C}HCH_2CH_3 \qquad \text{5-Methyl-2-heptyne}$$

In addition to compounds that contain one double bond (*alkenes*) or one triple bond (*alkynes*), we can also envision compounds with two double bonds (*dienes*), three double bonds (*trienes*), or a combination of double and triple bonds.

$$CH_3CH=CHCH_2C\equiv CH \qquad \text{4-Hexen-1-yne}$$

$$CH_2=CHCH=CH_2 \qquad \text{1,3-Butadiene}$$

New Words and Expressions

nomenclature [nəuˈmenkleitʃə] *n.* 命名法
saturated [ˈsætʃəreitid] *adj.* 饱和的
alkane [ˈælkein] *n.* 烷烃
valence [ˈveiləns] *n.* （化合）价，原子价
tetravalent [ˌtetrəˈveilənt] *adj.* 四价的
methane [ˈmeθein] *n.* 甲烷，沼气
tetrahedral [ˌtetrəˈhedrəl] *adj.* 四面体的
generic [dʒiˈnerik] *adj.* 一般的，普通的
tar [tɑː] *n.* 焦油，柏油
skeleton [ˈskelitən] *n.* 骨架，骨骼，基干
ethane [ˈeθein] *n.* 乙烷
propane [ˈprəupein] *n.* 丙烷
butane [ˈbjuːtein] *n.* 丁烷
branched [brɑːntʃid] *adj.* 有枝的，支链的
isomer [ˈaisəmə(r)] *n.* 异构体
constitutional [ˌkɔnstiˈtjuːʃənəl] *adj.* 构成的
pentane [ˈpentein] *n.* 戊烷
neopentane [ˌniːəuˈpentein] *n.* 新戊烷，季戊烷
backbone [ˈbækbəun] *n.* 骨干，支柱，脊柱
envision [inˈviʒən] *vt.* 想象，预想
adjacent [əˈdʒeisnt] *adj.* 邻近的，毗邻的
tetrahedron [ˌtetrəˈhiːdrən] *n.* 四面体

susceptible [səˈseptəbl] *adj.* 易受影响的
displace [disˈpleis] *v.* 替换，取代，转移
pucker [ˈpʌkə] *v.* 折叠，皱起，使起褶子
vaguely [ˈveigli] *adv.* 模糊地，依稀地
reminiscent [remiˈnis(ə)nt] *adj.* 提醒的，使人想起……的
planar [ˈpleinə] *adj.* 平面的，平坦的
tilt [tilt] *vt.* 使倾斜
differentiate [ˌdifəˈrenʃieit] *v.* 区分，辨别
derivative [diˈrivətiv] *n.* 衍生物
substituent [sʌbˈstitʃuənt] *n.* 取代；*adj.* 取代的
prefix [ˈpriːfiks] *n.* 前缀
alphabetical [ˌælfəˈbetikəl] *adj.* 按字母（表）顺序的，字母的
alkene [ˈælkiːn] *n.* 烯烃，链烯
alkyne [ˈælkain] *n.* 炔
hypothetical [ˌhaipəuˈθetikəl] *adj.* 假设的，假定的
unpaired [ʌnˈpeəd] *adj.* 不成双的
acetylene [əˈsetiliːn] *n.* 乙炔，电石气
diene [ˈdaiiːn] *n.* 二烯（烃）
triene [ˈtraiiːn] *n.* 三烯

Phrases

boiling point 沸点
molecular weight 分子量
straight-chain 直链
branched structure 支链结构

ball-and-stick model 球棍模型
constitutional isomer 构型异构体
by the time… 当……时
tilt up 翘起

"chair" structure 椅式结构   be thought of… 被认为……

Affixes

-ane [ein] 表示"……烷";如 propane 丙烷, methane 甲烷, ethane 乙烷
tetra- [tetrə] 表示"四";如 tetrahedral 四面体, tetrachloride 四氯化物, tetravalent 四价的
iso- ['aisəu] 表示"相等、相同";如 isobutane 异丁烷, isomer 异构体, isopentane 异戊烷
n- 表示"正",如:*n*-pentane 正戊烷
neo- [ni:əu] 表示"新的,新式的";如 neopentane 新戊烷, neophyte 初学者,新手
cyclo- ['saikləu] 表示"圆,圆周";cycloalkane 环烷烃, cyclopropane 环丙烷
-ene [i:n] 表示"……烯";如 ethene 乙烯, propylene 丙烯, butylene 丁烯
-yne [ain] 表示"……炔";如 ethyne 乙炔, alkyne 炔烃
-yl [il, ail] 表示"……基";如 methyl 甲基, ethyl 乙基
tri- [trai] 表示"三";如 triene 三烯, triacetamide 三乙酰胺

Notes

1. The generic formula for these compounds can be understood by assuming that they contain chains of CH$_2$ groups with an additional hydrogen atom capping either end of the chain. 是含有介词宾语从句（by assuming that...）的复合句,主句为被动语态。参考译文:这些化合物的分子通式可以这样理解,即它们包含由 CH$_2$ 基团组成的链,链的两端各加了一个氢原子。

2. The best way to understand the difference between the structures of butane and isobutane is to compare the ball-and-stick models of these compounds shown in the figure below. 参考译文:了解丁烷和异丁烷结构之间差异的最好方法是比较它们如下图所示的球棍模型。

3. One of the four carbon atoms in the cyclobutane ring is therefore displaced from the plane of the other three to form a "puckered" structure that is vaguely reminiscent of the wings of a butterfly. 文中主句为被动语态,"that"引导定语从句修饰不定式宾语"structure"。参考译文:因此,在环丁烷环中,四个碳原子中的其中一个不在另外三个碳原子所处的平面上,形成了一种"折起的"结构,这似乎让我们想起了蝴蝶的翅膀。

4. The angle between adjacent C—C bonds in a planar cyclopentane molecule would be 108°, which is close to the ideal angle around a tetrahedral carbon atom. Cyclopentane is not a planar molecule, as shown in the figure below, because displacing two of the carbon atoms from the plane of the other three produces a puckered structure that relieves some of the repulsion between the hydrogen atoms on adjacent carbon atoms in the ring. 文中"would be"表示虚拟语气,"because"引导原因状语从句,"produces"为该从句的谓语,"that"引导定语从句。参考译文:在平面环戊烷分子中,相邻 C—C 键的键角应该为 108°,这接近于一个正四面体碳原子的理想角度。如下图所示,实际上环戊烷不是一个平面分子,这是因为两个碳原子偏离另外三个碳原子组成的平面,形成了一个折叠结构,缓解了环中相邻碳原子上氢原子之间的部分斥力。

5. One of these carbon atoms is tilted up, out of the ring, whereas the other is tilted down to form the "chair" structure shown in the figure below. 文中"ring"指由其他四个碳原子所组成的圆环,"one"和"the other"是指六元环中两端的两个碳原子。参考译文:（六元环中两端两个碳原子中的）一个向上翘起,偏离（由其他四个碳原子所组成的）环平面,而另一端的一个碳原子向下翘,形成了下图所示的"椅式"结构。

6. Type of Organic Chemical Reactions

The process in which substance are converted to their constituent atoms is called "cracking" and is common to all compounds, organic or inorganic. Also common to all organic compounds is the reaction with oxygen that yields the oxides of the constituent atoms in a process known as combustion.

The importance of combustion reaction cannot be minimized; most of the heat and power (except that generated by falling water, wind, sun, compressed steam and within the earth, or nuclear sources) comes from the burning with very complicated oxidative processes in which compounds of carbon are ultimately converted to carbon dioxide and water. The combustion reactions are usually not very interesting. Seldom to be captured by reactions in which only a few bonds in the molecule are changed at a time.

Selective reactions are such reactions in which relatively small changes occur in the transformation of reactants to products. Hundreds of such reactions are now known to the organic chemists, and many of these will be presented in the fields of organic syntheses. To introduce this large and important segment of organic chemistry, let us first focus our attention on some of the reactions that are characteristic of the various types of carbon frameworks that we have discussed previously. To do this, we shall organize the discussion on the basis of four major types of reactions: viz., addition reactions, substitution reactions, elimination reactions, and oxidation reactions.

Addition reactions of alkenes. The most generally useful reaction of alkenes involves the addition of various reagents to the double bond, converting the double bond to a single bond in processes that we can represent as Fig. 1.

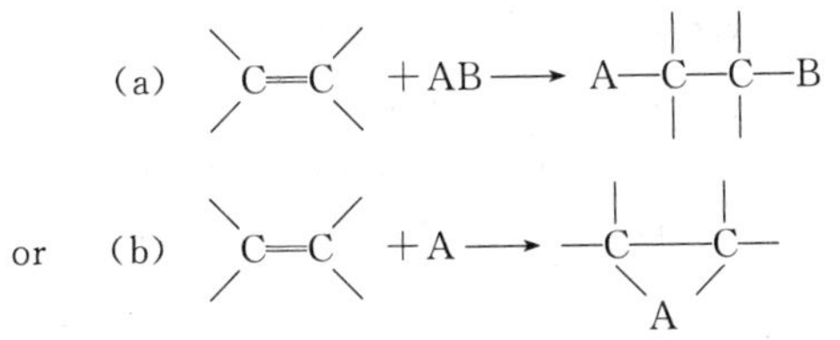

$$(a) \quad \diagup_{\diagdown}C=C\diagup^{\diagdown} + AB \longrightarrow A-\overset{|}{\underset{|}{C}}-\overset{|}{\underset{|}{C}}-B$$

$$or \quad (b) \quad \diagup_{\diagdown}C=C\diagup^{\diagdown} + A \cdot \longrightarrow -\overset{|}{\underset{\diagdown}{C}}-\overset{\diagup}{\underset{A}{C}}-$$

Fig. 1 Reaction of alkenes involving the addition of various reagents

Although the majority of addition processes involving alkenes occur via carbonium ion intermediates, a few follow a different pathway and involve radical intermediates. One of the most interesting of these is the addition of hydrogen bromide in the presence of peroxide reagents. In the absence of peroxide, hydrogen bromide adds to propene via the Markovnikov pathway to yield isopropyl bromide.[1] In the presence of peroxides, however, the order of addition is reversed, and the product is n-propyl bromide; the addition in this case is said to be anti-Markovnikov. This is interpreted in terms of initiation of the addition reaction by bromine atom, Br·, rather than by a proton, as is the case for electrophilic addition. The bromine atom, formed by the action of a free radical on hydrogen bromide (e.g., RO· + HBr ⟶ ROH + Br·), adds to the double bond of propene at either C-1 to form a secondary radical or C-2 to form a primary radical.[2] Since the stabilities of radicals follow the same order as that of carbonium ions, the reaction occurs preferentially via the secondary radical, which subsequently collides with a molecule of hydrogen bromide to form n-propyl bromide and a bromine atom. Once this stage of the reaction sequence is reached, the process becomes self-propagating; every time a carbon radical abstracts a hydrogen from hydrogen bromide another bromine atom is formed, which adds to propene to form another carbon radical.

Substitution reactions of alkanes. The most characteristic reaction of alkanes, which are much less reactive compounds than alkenes, alkynes, or arenes is a substitution process in which a hydrogen is replaced by some other atom or group, $R-H + Y \cdot \longrightarrow R-Y + H \cdot$. Among the several examples of this type of reactions, the generally most useful ones involve chlorine or bromine. For example, when a mixture of n-butane and chlorine is heated or irradiated, a reaction takes place to produce a mixture of 1-chlorobutane and 2-chlorobutane (Fig. 2).

$$CH_3CH_2CH_2CH_3 + X_2 \longrightarrow CH_3CH_2CH_2CH_2X + \begin{array}{c} CH_3CH_2 \\ \diagdown \\ H_3C \diagup \end{array} CHX$$

n-Butane
28%(X=Cl) 72%(X=Cl)
2%(X=Br)   98%(X=Br)

Fig. 2 Reaction between n-butane and chlorine or bromine molecules

A variety of pieces of evidence indicate that this reaction commences with the dissociation of molecular chlorine to chlorine atoms ($Cl_2 =\!\!=\!\!= Cl \cdot + Cl \cdot$), and that a chlorine atom then collides with a molecule of n-butane to abstract a hydrogen atom to form hydrogen chloride and a butyl radical. If the collision occurs at the C—H bond of the methyl group, a primary radical is produced ($CH_3CH_2CH_2\dot{C}H_2$); if it occurs at the C—H bond of the methylene carbon, a secondary radical is produced ($CH_3CH_2\dot{C}HCH_3$). Subsequent collisions of these radicals with molecular chlorine then yield 1-chlorobutane and 2-chlorobutane, respectively, along with chlorine atoms. At this stage of the reaction sequence, we have the same situation that we encountered in the peroxide-induced addition of hydrogen bromide to alkenes, viz., a self-propagating of chain reaction.[3] As in that case, here also the chain does not continue indefinitely, for various chain-terminating reactions occur, requiring new chlorine atoms to be constantly supplied to keep the reaction going. However, as many as 10^4 cycles of the self-propagating steps may take place before the chain is broken.

Elimination Reactions. Addition reactions, as we have seen, proceed from a less saturated reactant to a more saturated product. Elimination reactions represent the reciprocal case and proceed from a more saturated reactant to a less saturated product. We have already alluded to one type of elimination reaction at the beginning where we discussed the cracking reaction, in which carbon-hydrogen and carbon-carbon bonds are broken to yield, ultimately, atomic carbon and hydrogen. A comparable reaction more generally useful for laboratory synthesis involves the partial removal of hydrogen from six-membered alicyclic compounds to yield aromatic compounds. For example, when cyclohexane is treated at an elevated temperature with platinum, palladium, sulfur, or selenium, hydrogen is removed and benzene is formed (Fig. 3). In similar fashion, tetralin and decalin can be converted to naphthalene:

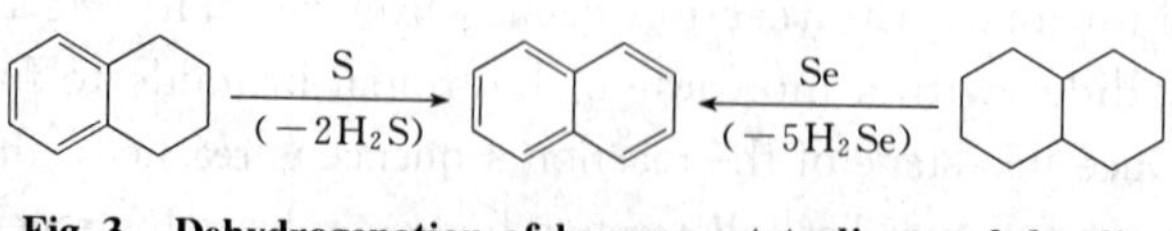

Fig. 3 Dehydrogenation of benzene, tetralin, and decalin

The process of removing hydrogen from six-membered alicyclic compounds is called dehydrogenation and finds useful application in the determination of the structure of alicyclic compounds. Aromatic compounds are generally crystallizable and less stereochemically complicated than their alicyclic precursors; also, they are more likely to be known compounds or, if unknown, to be accessible by easy synthesis. From the structure of the dehydrogenated product, then, the structural details of the alicyclic compound can be inferred. Caution must be exercised in using such information, however, because rearrangements and loss of functional groups sometimes occur during dehydrogenation.

Oxidation reactions of alkenes and alkynes. For the present discussion, we shall define oxidation reactions as processes in which C—H or C—C bonds are converted to C—O bonds or in which carbon-carbon multiple bonds are converted to C=O bonds.

Alkenes and alkynes are far less resistant to oxidation than alkanes and undergo cleavage of the C=C, or C≡C bond in the presence of a variety of oxidizing agents. A particularly useful oxidizing agent is ozone, which converts alkenes of structure $RCH=CH_2$ or $RCH=CHR'$ to aldehydes, alkenes of structure $R_2C=CR_2'$ to ketones, and alkenes of structure $R_2C=CHR'$ to mixtures of an aldehyde and ketone. Alkynes also react with ozone, yielding carboxylic acids, but the reaction is slower than alkenes, and may yield mixtures containing other compounds in addition to or instead of carboxylic acid. Ozonolysis provides a most useful way for locating the position of a C=C bond in a compound. For example, suppose that we have a sample of a material that we know to be either compound (a) or compound (b) in Fig. 4. If it is compound (a), both products of ozonolysis are ketones; if it is compound (b), one of the product of ozonolysis is a ketone and the other is an aldehyde.

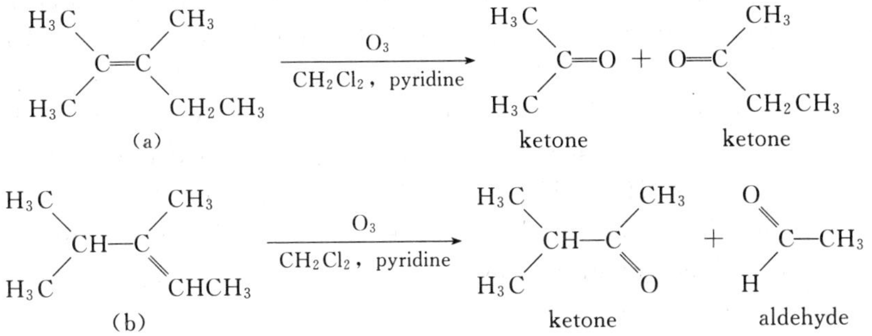

Fig. 4 Ozonolysis of isomeric dimethylpentenes

To be able to use reactions such as those shown above in the design of organic syntheses, we must, of course, remember what kinds of reactants give what kinds of product. For example, we must remember that when bromine reacts with propene the product is 1,2-dibromopropane. Rather than learn each reaction as an isolated fact, however, it is essential that we discern general patterns by means of which we can predict with some certainty how a particular set of compounds will react even though we may not have encountered the specific compounds previously.[4] For example, knowing how propene and bromine react, we can predict, correctly, that cyclohexene will react with chlorine to form 1,2-dichlorocyclohexane. In fact, we can rely on this kind of reaction as a general diagnostic test for the presence of a carbon-carbon multiple bond in a molecule. Thus if treatment of an unknown compound with a dilute solution of bromine in carbon tetrachloride (pale brown-red color) causes the solution to turn colorless, it is a reasonable inference that the compound contains a carbon-carbon multiple bond to which the bromine in the solution has added. To furnish substance to predictions and extrapolations of this sort, however, it is useful that we have some knowledge of how the reactions take place—i. e., by what faith mechanisms they occur. Although it is dangerous to place unquestioning faith in many of the generalizations of organic chemistry, certain ones, nevertheless, are useful to the person who is encountering this material for the first time.[5] Despite the exceptions, generalizations provide very useful focal points around which to organize one's thoughts. Recognizing the potential pitfalls, we suggest the following:

① The characteristic reaction of the saturated alkanes is free radical substitution; that of the alkenes and alkynes is addition (both ionic and free radical); and that of aromatic compounds is electrophilic substitution.

② The relative reactivity of C—H bonds with respect to hydrogen atom abstraction decreases in the following order:

$$C=C-\overset{|}{\underset{|}{C}}-H \approx Ar-\overset{|}{\underset{|}{C}}-H > R_3CH > R_2CH_2 > RCH_3 > CH_4$$

③ The resistance of various carbon frameworks to oxidation decreases in the following order: arene>alkane>alkyne>alkene. This must be accepted with reservation, however, for the reaction conditions and the arene is oxidized by potassium permanganate at the methyl group rather than at the benzene ring, but ozone attacks the benzene ring preferentially.

The compounds whose reactions are discussed above are those composed solely of carbon and hydrogen. We have already seen, however, that hetero atoms and groups can be attached to carbon frameworks, and it is not surprising to find that the chemistry of the original carbon framework may be changed as a result. For example, chloroform ($CHCl_3$) has a hydrogen that is sufficiently acidic to be removed by strong bases; tetrafluoroethylene ($CF_2=CF_2$) is inert to electrophilic addition and, instead, reacts readily with nucleophiles; benzoic acid (C_6H_5COOH) is much less susceptible to electrophilic substitution than benzene; and p-hydroxytoluene ($HO-C_6H_4-CH_3$) undergoes oxidation in the aromatic ring rather than the methyl group. Thus the attached groups (i. e., the functional groups) may alter the properties of the carbon frameworks even to the point of reversing the chemical behavior that is observed in the parent systems.

New Words and Expressions

cracking [ˈkrækiŋ] n. 破裂，裂化
viz. [viz] 即，就是
carbonium [kɑːˈbəuniəm] n. 碳正离子
intermediate [ˌintə(r)ˈmiːdiət] n. 中间体
peroxide [pəˈrɔksaid] n. 过氧化物，过氧化氢，双氧水
bromide [ˈbrəumaid] n. 溴化物
electrophilic [ilektrəuˈfilik] adj. 亲电子的
propene [ˈprəupiːn] n. 丙烯

preferentially [ˌprefəˈrenʃəli] adv. 优先地
propyl [ˈprəupəl] n. 丙烷基，丙基
propagate [ˈprɔpəgeit] vt. 传递
commence [kəˈmens] v. 开始
butyl [ˈbjuːtil] n. 丁基
methylene [ˈmeθiliːn] n. 亚甲基
allude [əˈluːd] v. 暗指，影射，间接提到
alicyclic [ˌæliˈsaiklik] adj. 脂环的，脂环族的

aromatic [ˌærəuˈmætik] adj. 芳香的，芳香族的；n. 芳香物质，芳香族化合物
platinum [ˈplætinəm] n. 铂，白金
palladium [pəˈleidiəm] n. 钯
selenium [siˈli:niəm, -njəm] n. 硒
tetralin [ˈtetrəlin] n. 萘满，1,2,3,4-四氢化萘
decalin [ˈdekəlin] n. 十氢化萘，萘烷
naphthalene [ˈnæfθəli:n] n. 萘（球），卫生球
cleavage [ˈkli:vidʒ] n. 分裂，劈开
ozone [ˈəuzəun, əuˈz-] n. 臭氧
ketone [ˈki:təun] n. 酮类

carboxylic [ˌkɑbɔkˈsilik] adj. 羧基的
ozonolysis [əuzəuˈnɔlisis] n. 臭氧分解
pale [peil] adj. 浅色的，苍白的，暗淡的
furnish [ˈfə:rniʃ] vt. 陈设，提供，供应
extrapolation [ikˌstræpəˈleiʃ(ə)n] n. 推断，外推
generalization [ˌdʒen(ə)rəlaiˈzeiʃ(ə)n] n. 一般化，普通化，归纳，概括
pitfall [ˈpitˌfɔ:l] n. 隐患，危险，陷阱，缺陷
arene [əˈri:n] n. 芳烃，芳香烃
nucleophilic [nju:kliəuˈfilik] adj. 亲核的
benzoic [benˈzəuik] adj. 安息香的

Phrases

addition reaction 加成反应
substitution reaction 取代反应
elimination reaction 消除反应
electrophilic addition 亲电加成

chain-terminating reaction 链终止反应
potassium permanganate 高锰酸钾
carbon framework 碳骨架，碳架

Affixes

per- [pə:] 表示"过，高"；如 peroxide 过氧化物，perchloric acid 高氯酸，permanganate 高锰酸盐

-philic [filik] 表示"喜……的，嗜……的，亲……的"；如 electrophilic 亲电的，nucleophilic 亲核的

cyclo- [saikləu] 表示"圆，环"；如 cyclohexane 环己烷，cyclodextrin 环糊精

stereo- [ˈsteriəu] 表示"立体的"；如 stereochemical 立体化学的

chloro- [ˈklɔ:rəu] 表示"氯，氯代"；如 chloroform 氯仿，chloride 氯化物，perchloric acid 高氯酸

-one [əun] 表示"酮"；如 ketone 酮类，acetone 丙酮

hydroxy- [haiˈdrɔksi] 表示"氢氧根的，羟基的"；如 hydroxytoluene 羟基甲苯

Notes

1. In the absence of peroxide, hydrogen bromide adds to propene via the Markovnikov pathway to yield isopropyl bromide. 参考译文：当不存在过氧化物时，溴化氢和丙烯的加成通过马氏路径生成 2-溴丙烷。

2. The bromine atom, formed by the action of a free radical on hydrogen bromide (e.g., RO· + HBr ⟶ ROH+Br·), adds to the double bond of propene at either C-1 to form a secondary radical or C-2 to form a primary radical. 参考译文：自由基和 HBr 作用（例如，RO· + HBr ⟶ ROH+Br·）生成的溴原子加成到丙烯双键的 C-1 位生成仲自由基，或加成到 C-2 位生成伯自由基。

3. At this stage of the reaction sequence, we have the same situation that we encoun-

tered in the peroxide-induced addition of hydrogen bromide to alkenes, viz. a self-propagating of chain reaction. "that"引导的定语从句修饰宾语"situation"。参考译文：在反应的这个阶段，情况与过氧化物诱导的溴化氢与烯烃加成反应相同，即链反应的自传递。

4. Rather than learn each reaction as an isolated fact, however, it is essential that we discern general patterns by means of which we can predict with some certainty how a particular set of compounds will react even though we may not have encountered the specific compounds previously. 句中，"it"是代词，指代"that"引导的从句，"which"引导定语从句修饰"general patterns"，"even though"引导让步状语从句。参考译文：然而，不能把每一个反应当成孤立的来看，重要的是能够察觉出一般规律，利用该规律能够基本预测某一类化合物会如何反应，即使我们之前可能没有遇到过这类化合物。

5. Although it is dangerous to place unquestioning faith in many of the generalizations of organic chemistry, certain ones, nevertheless, are useful to the person who is encountering this material for the first time. 该句包含"Although"引导的状语从句，"who"引导的定语从句修饰"the person"。参考译文：尽管完全相信有机化学中的许多规律是危险的，然而当我们初次接触这类物质时，某些规律还是有用的。

7. Briefing on Chemical Thermodynamics and Chemical Kinetics

Chemical Thermodynamics

The law of conservation of energy is the first law of thermodynamics. According to the first law, energy cannot be created or destroyed. The second law makes possible prediction of the direction of change. According to the second law, although the entropy of a system may decrease, the entropy of the universe is increasing. The third law says that the entropy of perfect crystalline substances is zero at temperature of absolute zero Kelvin; however, it is impossible to reach absolute zero Kelvin.

The average amount of energy needed to break a covalent bond in a polyatomic molecule is called bond energy. Bond energies can be used to estimate standard enthalpies of reactions ($\Delta H_{rxn}^{\ominus}$) for reactions involving species so reactive that they cannot be isolated or standard enthalpies of formation for compounds that have not yet been prepared. [1]

Entropy is a measure of the disorder of a system and of the probability that a system will be in a given state. The more arrangements that are possible for the molecules of a sample or the more energy levels that can be occupied, the greater the entropy. [2] Entropy increases with increasing temperature. Although all spontaneous changes increase the entropy of the universe, the entropy of a system can either increase or decrease in a spontaneous change. If the entropy of the system decreases, the entropy of the surroundings must increase more. Standard entropy, $S^{\ominus}$, is the entropy of a substance in a standard state. Entropy is a state function; calculation of standard entropy changes from standard entropies is similar to calculations of standard enthalpy changes from standard enthalpies of formation.

Gibbs free energy, G, combines enthalpy and entropy in a single state function. The equation relating standard Gibbs free energy change to changes in standard enthalpy and standard entropy is:

$$\Delta G^{\ominus} = \Delta H^{\ominus} - T \Delta S^{\ominus}$$

Standard Gibbs free energy changes can be calculated from the definition of standard free energy changes or from standard free energy changes of formation. For spontaneous changes, ΔG is negative. If ΔH and ΔS both have the same sign, temperature determines the direction of spontaneous change. If ΔH and ΔS are assumed not to change with temperature, the definition of free energy change can be used to estimate free energy changes at different temperatures.

The free energy change of the reaction in any state, ΔG, is related to the standard free energy change of the reaction, $\Delta G^{\ominus}$, according to the equation:

$$\Delta G = \Delta G^{\ominus} + RT \ln Q$$

where Q is the reaction quotient. At equilibrium, $\Delta G = 0$ and Q become equal to the equilibrium constant, K. Hence the equation becomes:

$$\Delta G^{\ominus} = -RT \ln K$$

This relationship can be used to calculate the value of K from known $\Delta G^{\ominus}$, or, if K is known, to calculate $\Delta G^{\ominus}$. The free energy lost by the system during a spontaneous change at constant temperature and pressure is the maximum amount of energy that is free to do useful work. The free energy gained by the system during a nonspontaneous change at constant temperature is the minimum amount of work needed to bring about that change. [3]

Thermodynamics tells whether a change can take place spontaneously and how far a change goes before reaching equilibrium. It does not provide any information about how fast a change will take place or about how changes take place.

Chemical Kinetics

Chemical kinetics deals with the rates of chemical reactions. Studies of reaction rates are an important source of information about reaction mechanisms, detailed pictures of how a reaction takes place. Mechanisms are theories and can never be proved to be correct although they can be shown to be wrong.[4] They are useful in organizing information about chemical reactions.

Because the rates of formation of products and disappearance of reactants are related by the equation for the reaction, the rate of a reaction can be followed by measuring the amount or concentration of any reactant or product at intervals. The rate of a chemical reaction depends on the identity of the reactants and their concentrations, temperature, presence of catalysts, the solvent, and, for heterogeneous reactions, particle size and mixing.

The dependence of reaction rate on concentration of reactants is described by the rate law for a reaction. Rate laws must be determined by experiment. Many rate laws have the form rate $=k[A]^x[B]^y \cdots$, where k is a constant called the rate constant. The value of the rate constant depends on all the factors that affect the rate of a reaction except concentration of reactants. If the exponent of the concentration of a reactant in the rate law is zero, the reaction is zero order with respect to that substance, and the rate of the reaction is independent of the concentration of that substance. If the exponent is one, the reaction is first order with respect to that substance, and the rate doubles when the concentration of that reactant is doubled. If the exponent is two, the reaction is second order with respect to that substance and the rate increases fourfold when the concentration of that substance is doubled. The overall order of the reaction is obtained by adding the orders with respect to each reactant.

The rate law can be found by observing initial rates or by graphing. The half-life of a reaction, $t_{1/2}$, is the time required for one-half of the quantity of reactant originally present to react.

The rates of almost all reactions increase as the temperature is raised; quantitatively, the relationship is given by the Arrhenius equation, $k = A e^{-E_a/RT}$. The dependence of reaction rates on concentration and temperature is explained by the collision and activated complex (transition state) theories.

The collision theory explains chemical reactions as involving collisions between molecules or ions. According to the collision theory, particles must collide with a minimum amount of energy, called the activation energy, and with the correct orientation in order for a reaction to take place.[5] According to the activated complex theory, reactants follow the reaction coordinate, that is, the lowest energy path available, from reactants to activated complex to products. The activated complex is the highest energy arrangement of atoms along the reaction coordinate. Reaction profiles are graphs showing how potential energy changes as the reactants proceed along the reaction coordinate from reactants to activated complex to products.

Most reaction mechanisms consist of a series of simple steps called elementary processes. Molecularity of an elementary process is the number of particles that must collide to form the activated complex for the elementary process. For elementary processes, the exponents in the rate law are the same as the coefficients in the equation. If the exponents in the rate law for an overall reaction are different from the coefficients in the equation for the reaction, the mechanism must consist of more than one step. If the exponents in the rate law for the overall reaction are the same as the coefficients in the chemical equation, the reaction may take place in a single step, but it does not necessarily do so. The elementary steps in a mechanism must add to give the net chemical equation for the overall reaction, the mechanism must lead to the experimentally observed rate law, and the mechanism must account for any other observations that have been made of the reaction. [6]

Intermediates are species that are formed in one step and used up in another step. In a steady state, the concentration of an intermediate is constant because the intermediate is being formed in one step and used up in a later step. Rate-determining step is the slowest step in a sequence of elementary processes making up a reaction mechanism that determines the rate of the overall reaction.

Catalysts provide another mechanism with lower activation energy and/or increase the frequency of collisions with the right orientation. Catalysts may be homogeneous or heterogeneous.[5] Catalysts are present both at the beginning and at the end of a reaction; they are used up in one step and formed again in another. According to the principle of microscopic reversibility, the reverse reaction takes place by the same path as the forward reaction but in the opposite direction.

Enzymes are complex substances produced in living cells that catalyze biological reactions. The reactant in an enzyme-catalyzed reaction is known as the substrate. The substrate fits in the active site of the enzyme.

New Words and Expressions

thermodynamics [θə:məudai'næmiks] n. 热力学
entropy ['entrəpi] n. 熵
crystalline ['kristəlain] adj. 结晶的，晶状的
enthalpy [en'θælpi] n. 焓
disorder [dis'ɔ:də] n. 杂乱，混乱，无序状态
spontaneous [spɔn'teinjəs] adj. 自发的
interval ['intəvəl] n. 间隔，距离，幕间休息
quotient ['kwəuʃ(ə)nt] n. 商，商数
identity [ai'dentiti] n. 身份，同一性，特征
exponent [iks'pəunənt] n. 指数，幂

half-life 半衰期
orientation [,ɔ:riən'teiʃ(ə)n] n. 方向，方位，取向
molecularity [məlekju'læriti] n. 分子状态，反应分子数
stoichiometric [stɔiki'ɔmitrik] adj. 化学计量的
intermediate [,intə'mi:diət] n. 中间体
homogeneous [,həuməu'dʒi:niəs] adj. 由同类事物（或人）组成的，均匀的
heterogeneous [,hetərəu'dʒi:niəs] adj. 由很多种类组成的，各种各样的，异类的
substrate ['sʌbstreit] n. 底物，基质

Phrases

law of conservation of energy 能量守恒定律
bond energy 键能

standard entropy 标准熵
state function 状态函数
Gibbs free energy 吉布斯自由能

chemical kinetics　化学动力学
reaction mechanism　反应机理（历程，机制）
rate law　速率定律，速率法则
rate constant　速率常数
zero order　零级
overall order　总级数
collision theory　碰撞理论
activation energy　活化能
activated complex theory　活化复合物理论
reaction coordinate　反应坐标
reaction profile　反应（势能）剖面图
elementary process　基元反应
account for　由于，解释，说明……的原因
use up　用完，耗尽
steady state　稳态，定态
rate-determining step　速率控制步骤
principle of microscopic reversibility　微观可逆性原则
active site　活性位

Affixes

thermo- [θəːməu-] 表示"热，热电"；如 thermometer 温度计，thermocouple 热电偶，thermochemistry 热化学

inter- [inˈtə(r)] 表示"在一起，交互"；如 intermolecular 分子间的，interrelate 相互关联，interchangeable 可互换的

homo- [ˈhəuməu] 表示"同类的"；如 homocentric 同中心的，homothermic 同温的，homopolar 同极的，单极的

hetero- [ˈhetərəu] 表示"异类，异种"；如 heteroatom 杂原子，heterocycle 杂环，heterosexual 异性的

Notes

1. Bond energies can be used to estimate standard enthalpies of reactions ($\Delta H_{rxn}^{\ominus}$) for reactions involving species so reactive that they cannot be isolated or standard enthalpies of formation for compounds that have not yet been prepared. 句中"or"连接两个并列成分"standard enthalpies of reactions"和"standard enthalpies of formation"，第一个"that"引导定语从句修饰"species"，第二个"that"引导定语从句修饰"compounds"。参考译文：键能可以用来估算难以分离的活性组分参与反应的标准反应焓变，或还未被制备出来的化合物的生成焓。

2. The more arrangements that are possible for the molecules of a sample or the more energy levels that can be occupied, the greater the entropy. 此句是"the more…the more…"句型。参考译文：样品分子的可能排列越多，或可被占据的能级越多，那么其熵就越大。

3. The free energy gained by the system during a nonspontaneous change at constant temperature is the minimum amount of work needed to bring about that change. 参考译文：恒温下，一个非自发变化中体系增加的自由能，等于使该变化发生所需的最小功。

4. Studies of reaction rates are an important source of information about reaction mechanisms, detailed pictures of how a reaction takes place. Mechanisms are theories and can never be proved to be correct although they can be shown to be wrong. 参考译文：对反应速率的研究是关于反应机理的一个重要信息来源，反应机理详细描述了一个反应是怎样发生的。机理是理论，从来不能被证明是正确的，尽管可以证明机理是错误的。

5. According to the collision theory, particles must collide with a minimum amount of energy, called the activation energy, and with the correct orientation in order for a reaction to take place. "according to the collision theory"是现在分词短语，作为状语。参考译文：依

据碰撞理论，粒子必须具有被称为活化能的最小能量，并且以适当的方向碰撞，才能使一个反应发生。

6. If the exponents in the rate law for the overall reaction are the same as the coefficients in the chemical equation, the reaction may take place in a single step, but it does not necessarily do so. The elementary steps in a mechanism must add to give the net chemical equation for the overall reaction, the mechanism must lead to the experimentally observed rate law, and the mechanism must account for any other observations that have been made of the reaction. 参考译文：如果总反应速率方程中的指数和化学方程式里的系数一样，该反应可能是一步发生的，但也不一定。机理中的基元反应步骤必须加起来才能给出总反应的净化学方程式，机理必须能导出实验观测的速率方程，并且能解释反应产生的任何其他现象。

8. Applied Chemistry

Engineering students often ask "Why is another chemistry course required for non-chemical engineers?" There are many answers to this question but foremost is that the professional engineer must know when to consult a chemist and be able to communicate with him. When this is not done, the consequences can be disastrous due to faulty design, poor choice of materials, or inadequate safety factors. Examples of blunders abound and only a few will be described in an attempt to convince the student to take the subject matter seriously.

The Challenger space shuttle disaster which occurred in January 1986 was attributed to the cold overnight weather which had hardened the O-rings on the booster rockets while the space craft sat on the launchpad. During flight, the O-ring seals failed, causing fuel to leak out and ignite. The use of a material with a lower glass transition temperature (T_g) could have prevented the disaster. A similar problem may exist in automatic transmissions used in vehicles. The use of silicone rubber O-rings instead of neoprene may add to the cost of the transmission but this would be more than compensated for by an improved and more reliable performance at $-40°C$ where neoprene begins to harden; whereas the silicone rubber is still flexible.[1]

A new asphalt product from Europe incorporates the slow release of calcium chloride ($CaCl_2$) to prevent icing on roads and bridges. Predictably, this would have little use in Winnipeg, Canada, where $-40°C$ is not uncommon in winter.

The heavy water plant at Glace Bay, Nova Scotia, was designed to extract D_2O from sea water. The corrosion of the plant eventually delayed production and the redesign and use of more appropriate materials added millions to the cost of the plant.

A chemistry colleague examined his refrigerator which failed after less than 10 years of use. He noted that a compressor coil made of copper was soldered to an expansion tube made of iron. Condensing water had corroded the—guess what? —iron tube. Was this an example of designed obsolescence or sheer stupidity. One wonders, since the savings by using iron instead of copper is a few cents and the company is a well-known prominent world manufacturer of electrical appliances and equipment.

With the energy problems now facing our industry and the resulting economic problems, the engineer will be required to make judgments which can alter the cost-benefit ratio for his employer. One must realize that perpetual motion is impossible even though the US Supreme Court has ruled that a patent should be granted for a device which the Patent Office considers to be a Perpetual Motion Machine. An example of this type of proposal appeared in a local newspaper which described an invention for a car which ran on water. This is accomplished by a battery which is initially used to electrolyze water to produce H_2 and O_2 that is then fed into a fuel cell which drives an electrical motor that propels the car. While the car is moving, an alternator driven by the automobile's motion charges the battery.[2] Thus, the only consumable item is water. This is an excellent example of perpetual motion.

A similar invention of an automobile powered by an air engine has been described. A compressed air cylinder powers an engine which drives the automobile. A compressor which is run by the moving car recompresses the gas into a second cylinder which is used when the first cylinder is empty. Such perpetual motion systems will abound and the public must be made aware of the pitfalls.

An engineer responsible for the application of a thin film of a liquid adhesive to a plastic was experiencing problems. Bubbles were being formed which disrupted the even smooth adhesive coat. The answer was found in the dissolved gases since air at high pressure was used to force the adhesive out of the spreading nozzle. The engineer did not believe that the air was actually soluble in the hexane used to dissolve the glue. When helium was used instead of air, no bubbles formed because of the lower solubility of He compared to O_2 and N_2 in the solvent. Everything is soluble in all solvents, only the extent of solution varies from nondetectable (by present methods of measurement) to completely soluble. The same principle applies to the permeability of one substance through another.

An aluminum tank car exploded when the broken dome's door hinge was being welded. The tank car, which had been used to carry fertilizer (aqueous ammonium nitrate and urea), was washed and cleaned with water—so why had it exploded? Dilute ammonium hydroxide is more corrosive to aluminum than the concentrated solution. Hence, the reaction

$$3NH_4OH + Al \longrightarrow Al(OH)_3 + 3NH_3 + 1.5H_2$$

produced hydrogen which exploded when the welding arc ignited the H_2/O_2 mixture. The broad explosive range of hydrogen in air makes it a dangerous gas when confined.

Batteries are often used as a back-up power source for relays and, hence, stand idle for long periods. To keep them ready for use they are continuously charged. However, they are known to explode occasionally when they are switched into service because of the excess hydrogen produced due to overcharging. This can be avoided by either catalyzing the recombination of the H_2 and O_2 to form water

$$2H_2 + O_2 \longrightarrow 2H_2O$$

by a nickel, platinum, or palladium catalyst in the battery caps, or by keeping the charging current equal to the inherent discharge rate which is about 1% per month for the lead-acid battery.

It has recently been shown that the flaming disaster of the Hindenburg Zeppelin in 1937, in which 36 lives were lost, may have been caused by static electricity igniting the outer fabric. This was shown to contain an iron oxide pigment and reflecting powdered aluminum. Such a combination, known as a thermite mixture, results in the highly exothermic Gouldshmidt reaction (first reported in 1898):

$$Fe_2O + 2Al \longrightarrow Al_2O + 2Fe$$

In the early days of the railway, rails were welded with the molten iron formed in this reaction. The combination of powdered aluminum and a metal oxide has been used as a rocket fuel and evidence has been obtained to indicate that after the disaster the Germans replaced the aluminum by bronze which does not react with metal oxides. Thus, the bad reputation hydrogen has had as a result of the accident is undeserved and the resulting limiting use of the airship was due to faulty chemistry and could have been avoided.

The original design and structure of the Statue of Liberty, built about 100 years ago, took into account the need to avoid using different metals in direct contact with each other. However, the salt sea spray penetrated the structure and corroded the iron frame which supported the outer copper shell. Chloride ions catalyzed the corrosion of iron. The use of brass in a steam line valve resulted in corrosion and the formation of a green solid product. The architect was apparently unaware of the standard practice to use amines such as morpholine as a corrosion inhibitor for steam lines. Amines react with copper in the brass at high temperatures in the presence of oxygen to form copper-amine complexes similar to the dark blue copper ammonium complex, $Cu(NH_3)J^+$.

Numbers are a fundamental component of measurements and of the physical properties of materials. However, numbers without units are meaningless. Few quantities do not have units, e. g. , specific gravity of a substance is the ratio of the mass of a substance to the mass of an equal volume of water at 4℃. To ignore units is to invite disaster. Two examples will illustrate the hazards of the careless or nonuse of units. During the transition from Imperial to SI (metric) units in Canada, an Air Canada commercial jet (Boeing 767) on a trans Canada flight (No 143) from Montreal to Edmonton on July 23, 1983, ran out of fuel over Winnipeg.[3] Fortunately the pilot was able to glide the airplane to an abandoned airfield used for training pilots during World War II. The cause of the near disaster was a mix-up in the two types of units involved for loading the fuel and the use of a unitless conversion factor.

The second example of an error in units cost the USA (NASA) $94,000,000. A Mars climate probe missed its target orbit of 150 km from the Mars' surface and approached to within 60 km and burned up. The error was due to the different units used by two contractors which were not interconverted by the NASA systems engineering staff.

The above examples show how what may be a simple design or system can fail due to insufficient knowledge of chemistry. Applied chemistry will give you the vocabulary and basis on which you can build your expertise in engineering.

New Words and Expressions

blunder [ˈblʌndə(r)] n. 愚蠢（或粗心）的错误
abound [əˈbaund] v. 大量存在，有许多
booster [ˈbuːstə(r)] n. 助推器，引爆剂
neoprene [ˈniːəpriːn] n. 氯丁橡胶
asphalt [ˈæsfælt] n. 沥青，柏油
Winnipeg [ˈwinipeg] 温尼伯（加拿大城市）
Glace Bay, Nova Scotia 新斯科舍省格莱斯湾（加拿大）
obsolescence [ˌɔbsəˈles(ə)ns] n. 淘汰，陈旧
perpetual [pə(r)ˈpetʃuəl] adj. 不间断的，持续的，长久的，一再反复的
rule [ruːl] v. 统治，控制，支配，裁定
dome [dəum] n. 穹顶，圆顶状物
hinge [hindʒ] n. 铰链，合页
ignite [igˈnait] v. 点燃，（使）燃烧
relay [riːˈlei] n. 接力赛，接班人，继电器
thermite [ˈθəːmit] n. 铝粉焊接剂，铝热剂，铝热反应

undeserved [ˌʌndiˈzəː(r)vd] adj. 不应得的，冤枉的，不公正的，受之有愧的
faulty [ˈfɔːlti] adj. 不完美的，有错误的，有缺陷的
amine [əˈmiːn] n. 胺
morpholine [ˈmɔːfəliːn] n. 吗啉（一种吸湿性液体，用作溶剂和乳化剂等）
trans n. 反，反式，横过，贯通，横跨
Montreal [ˌmɔntriˈɔːl] 蒙特利尔（加拿大城市）
Edmonton [ˈedməntən] 埃德蒙顿（加拿大城市）
NASA National Aeronautics and Space Administration 美国太空总署，美国宇航局，美国国家航空航天局
contractor [kənˈtræktə(r)] n. 承包商，承包人
interconvert [intəkənˈvəːt] v. 互相转换，相互转化

Phrases

take… seriously 重视，认真对待，高度重视

Challenger space shuttle 挑战者号航天飞机
be attributed to 被认为是……所为，归因于
booster rocket 火箭助推器
launchpad （火箭等的）发射台
glass transition temperature 玻璃转变温度
automatic transmission 自动变速器
compensate for 补偿，抵偿
US Supreme Court 美国高等法院
Patent Office 专利局
Perpetual Motion Machine 永动机
welding arc 焊弧，焊接电弧
stand idle 闲置，袖手旁观，停产

Hindenburg Disaster 兴登堡号空难，1937年5月6日，兴登堡号飞艇（airship）在一场灾难性事故中被大火焚毁。当时，这艘大飞艇正在新泽西州莱克赫斯特海军航空总站上空准备着陆，仅32秒的时间就被烧毁，起火原因目前尚不清楚，不过人们认为是由于发动机放出的静电或火花点燃了降落时放掉的氢气所致
Zeppelin 齐柏林公司
Statue of Liberty （美国纽约港的）自由女神像
corrosion inhibitor 防腐剂

Affixes

-en 表示"做，使成为……，使变成……"；如 harden 使变硬, flatten 使变平, strengthen 加强, moisten 弄湿, deepen 加深

hex-, hexa- 表示"六"；如 hexane 己烷, hexachromic 六色的, hexagon 六边形, hexadiine 己二炔

therm(o)- 表示"热/热的"；如 thermometer 温度计, thermos 热水瓶, isotherm 等温线, thermal 热的

Notes

1. The use of silicone rubber O-rings instead of neoprene may add to the cost of the transmission but this would be more than compensated for by an improved and more reliable performance at -40℃ where neoprene begins to harden; whereas the silicone rubber is still flexible. 参考译文：尽管使用硅橡胶O圈代替氯丁橡胶可能会增加变速器的成本，但在零下40摄氏度提升的和更可靠的操作性能能弥补了这一缺点。在零下40摄氏度氯丁橡胶开始硬化，而硅橡胶仍然有弹性。

2. This is accomplished by a battery which is initially used to electrolyze water to produce H_2 and O_2 that is then fed into a fuel cell which drives an electrical motor that propels the car. While the car is moving, an alternator driven by the automobile's motion charges the battery. 第一句里共有三个定语从句，第一个"which"引导定语从句修饰"battery"，"that"引导另一个定语从句来修饰"H_2 and O_2"，最后面的"which"又作为定语从句来修饰"a fuel cell"。参考译文：这是通过一个电池实现的，首先使用这个电池来制氢气和氧气，然后输入到一个燃料电池，该燃料电池驱动一个电动马达来驱使汽车。当汽车运动的时候，汽车的运动驱使一个交流发电机来给电池充电。

3. During the transition from Imperial to SI (metric) units in Canada, an Air Canada commercial jet (Boeing 767) on a trans Canada flight (No 143) from Montreal to Edmonton on July 23, 1983, ran out of fuel over Winnipeg. 参考译文：在加拿大，从英制到国际单位转换中，（因转换错误）1983年7月23日，一架加拿大航空商业飞机（波音767）在一次从蒙特利尔到埃德蒙顿横跨加拿大的飞行中（No 143），在温尼伯上空耗尽了燃料。

9. High Performance Liquid Chromatography and Capillary Electrophoresis

High Performance Liquid Chromatography

Liquid chromatography was first discovered in 1903 by M. S. Tswett, who used a chalk column to separate the pigments of green leaves.[1] Only in 1960's the more and more emphasis was placed on the development of liquid chromatography. High Performance Liquid Chromatography (HPLC) is one mode of chromatography, the most widely used analytical technique. Chromatographic processes can be defined as separation techniques involving mass-transfer between stationary and mobile phases. HPLC utilizes a liquid mobile phase to separate the components of a mixture. These components (or analytes) are first dissolved in a solvent, and then forced to flow through a chromatographic column under a high pressure. In the column, the mixture is resolved into its components. The amount of resolution is important, and is dependent upon the extent of interaction between the solute components and the stationary phase. The stationary phase is defined as the immobile packing material in the column. The interaction of the solute with mobile and stationary phases can be manipulated through different choices of both solvents and stationary phases. As a result, HPLC acquires a high degree of versatility not found in other chromatographic systems and it has the ability to easily separate a wide variety of chemical mixtures.

The basic components of an HPLC system include a solvent reservoir, pump, injector, analytical column, detector, recorder and waste reservoir (Fig. 1). Other important elements are an inlet solvent filter, post-pump inline filter, sample filter, precolumn filter, guard column, back-pressure regulator and/or solvent sparging system. The function of each of these components is briefly described below.

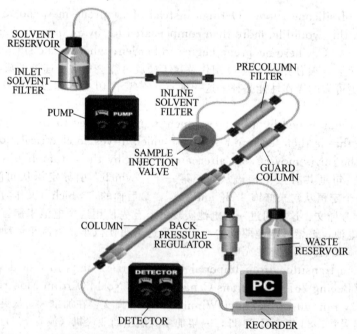

Fig. 1　The basic components of an HPLC system

An HPLC system begins with the solvent reservoir, which contains the solvent used to carry the sample through the system. The solvent should be filtered with an inlet solvent filter to remove any particles that could potentially damage the system's sensitive components. Solvent is propelled through the system by the pump. This often includes internal pump seals, which slowly break down over time. As these seals break down and release particles into the flow path, an inline solvent filter prevents any post-pump component damage. The next component in the system is the sample injector, also known as the injection valve. This valve, equipped with a sample loop of the appropriate size for the analysis being performed, allows for the reproducible introduction of sample into the flow path. Because the sample often contains particulate matter, it is important to utilize either a sample filter or a precolumn filter to prevent valve and column damage. Following the injector, an analytical column allows the primary sample separation to occur. This is based on the differential attraction of the sample components for the solvent and the packing material within the column. However, a sacrificial guard column is often included just prior to the analytical column to chemically remove components of the sample that would otherwise foul the main column. [2]Following the analytical column, the separated components pass through a detector flow cell before they pass into the waste reservoir. The sample components' presence in the flow cell prompts an electrical response from the detector, which is digitized and sent to a recorder. The recorder helps analyze and interpret the data. As a final system enhancement, a back pressure regulator is often installed immediately after the detector. This device prevents solvent bubble formation until the solvent is completely through the detector. This is important because bubbles in a flow cell can interfere with the detection of sample components. Alternatively, an inert gas sparging system may be installed to force dissolved gasses out of the solvent being stored in the solvent reservoir.

Let us consider a separation of a two component mixture dissolved in the eluent. Assume that component A has the same interaction with the adsorbent surface as an eluent, and component B has strong excessive interaction. [3]Being injected into the column, these components will be forced through by eluent flow. Molecules of the component A will interact with the adsorbent surface and retard on it by the same way as an eluent molecules. Thus, as an average result, component A will move through the column with the same speed as an eluent. Molecules of the component B being adsorbed on the surface (due to their strong excessive interactions) will sit on it much longer. Thus, it will move through the column slower than the eluent flow. Figure below represents the general shape of the chromatogram for this mixture (Fig. 2).

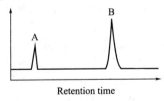

Fig. 2 The general shape of two component mixture

Usually a relatively narrow band is injected (5~20μL injection volume). During the run, the original chromatographic band will be spread due to the nonevenly flows around and inside the porous particles, slow adsorption kinetics, longitudinal diffusion, and other factors. These processes together produce so called band broadening of the chromatographic zone. In general, the longer the component retained on the column, the broader its zone (peak on the chromatogram). Separation performance depends on both component retention and band broadening. Band broadening is, in general, a kinetic parameter, dependent on the adsorbent particle size, porosity, pore size, column size, shape, and packing performance. On the other hand, retention does not depend on the above mentioned parameters, but it reflects molecular surface interactions and depends on the total adsorbent surface.

Today, HPLC is the most widely used analytical separation method. The method is popular because it is non-destructive and may be applied to thermally labile compounds (unlike GC); it is also a very sensitive technique since it incorporates a wide choice of detection methods.[4] With the use of post-column derivatization methods to improve selectivity and detection limits, HPLC can easily be extended to trace determination of compounds that do not usually provide adequate detector response.[5] The wide applicability of HPLC as a separation method makes it a valuable separation tool in many scientific fields.

Liquid chromatography is useful for a multitude of applications in industry and academia. Its use can be broken down into two classifications, analytical LC and preparative LC. In analytical LC the goal is identification and quantification of given components within a sample, usually in the picogram to milligram range. In preparative LC, the objective is to isolate or collect the separated components of the sample in the mg to kg range.

High Performance Capillary Electrophoresis

Electrophoresis refers to the migration of charged electrical species when dissolved, or suspended, in an electrolyte through which an electric current is passed. Cations migrate toward the negatively charged electrode (cathode) and anions are attracted toward the positively charged electrode (anode). Neutral solutes are not attracted to either electrode. Conventionally electrophoresis has been performed on layers of gel or paper. The traditional electrophoresis equipment offered a low level of automation and long analysis times. Detection of the separated bands was performed by post-separation visualization. The analysis times were long as only relatively low voltages could be applied before excessive heat formation caused loss of separation.

The advantages of conducting electrophoresis in capillaries were highlighted in the early 1980's by the work of Jorgenson and Lukacs who popularized the use of CE. Performing electrophoretic separations in capillaries was shown to offer the possibility of automated analytical equipment, fast analysis times and on-line detection of the separated peaks. Heat generated inside the capillary was effectively dissipated through the walls of the capillary which allowed high voltages to be used to achieve rapid separations. The capillary was inserted through the optical centre of a detector which allowed on-capillary detection.

Capillary electrophoresis (CE) has grown to become a collection of a range of separation techniques which involve the application of high voltages across buffer filled capillaries to achieve separations. Many of the CE separation techniques rely on the presence of an electrically induced flow of solution (electroosmotic flow, EOF) within the capillary to pump solutes towards the detector. Generally, CE is performed using aqueous based electrolytes, however there is a growing use of non-aqueous solvents in CE.

Operation of a CE system involves application of a high voltage (typically $10 \sim 30 kV$) across a narrow bore ($25 \sim 100 \mu m$) capillary. The capillary is filled with electrolyte solution which conducts current through the inside of the capillary. The ends of the capillary are dipped into reservoirs filled with the electrolyte. Electrodes made of an inert material such as platinum are also inserted into the electrolyte reservoirs to complete the electrical circuit. A small volume of sample is injected into one end of the capillary. The capillary passes through a detector, usually a UV absorbance detector, at the opposite end of the capillary. Application of a voltage causes movement of sample ions towards their appropriate electrode usually passing through the detector. The plot of detector response with time is generated which is termed an electropherogram. A flow of electrolyte, known as electroosmotic flow, EOF, results in a flow of the solution along the capillary usually towards the detector. This flow can significantly reduce analysis times or force an ion to overcome its migration tendency towards the electrode it is being attracted to by the sign of its charge.

Commercially available CE instruments (Fig. 3) are PC controlled and consist of a buffer filled capillary passing through the optical centre of a detector, a means of introducing the sample into the capillary, a high voltage power supply and an autosampler.

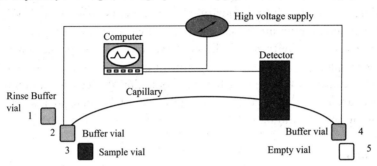

Fig. 3 Typical CE separation system

The typical voltages used are in the range of 5~30kV which results in currents in the range of 10~100μA. Higher currents than this can cause problems of heating inside the capillary which can broaden peaks resulting in loss of resolution.

- **Capillaries**

The capillaries used are normally fused silica capillaries covered with an external polyimide protective coating to give them increased mechanical strength as bare fused silica is extremely fragile. A small portion of this coating is removed to form a window for detection purposes. The window is aligned in the optical centre of the detector. Capillaries are typically 25~100cm long with 50 and 75 micron being the most commonly employed inner diameters. Capillary volumes are in the order of a few 1μL, for example, the approximate volume of a 50μm wide 50 cm long capillary is 1μL.

On standard commercial CE instruments the capillary is often held in a housing device such as a cartridge to facilitate ease of capillary insertion into the instrument and to protect the delicate detection window area. The inner surface of the capillary can be chemically modified by covalently binding (coating) different substances onto the capillary wall. These coatings are used for a variety of purposes such as to reduce sample adsorption or to change the ionic charge on the capillary wall.

- **Temperature control**

It is important to regulate the temperature of the environment around the capillary to ensure consistent separations. To achieve this capillaries are often inserted into cartridges which are placed in the CE instrument. Temperature controlled air or liquid coolant is then forced through the cartridge to regulate the temperature.

- **Sample introduction**

Sample solution is forced into the end of the capillary furthest from the detector.

Typical injection volumes are 10~100nL. The most frequently used injection mode is to dip the capillary into the sample solution vial. The vial is then pressurized causing a volume of solution to be forced into the capillary. An alternative, a less popular sample injection procedure is to dip the capillary and electrode into the sample solution vial and to apply a voltage. If the sample is ionized and the appropriate voltage polarity is used, sample ions will migrate into the capillary. This type of injection is known as electrokinetic sampling.

- **Detectors**

The most frequently used detector is a UV absorbance detector which is standard on commercial CE instruments. The majority of instruments also have UV diode detectors available. Alternative detector modes commercially available include fluorescence, laser induced fluorescence, conductivity and indirect detection. The hyphenation of CE and mass spectrometers is frequently used to give structural information on the resolved peaks.

The detectors can be interfaced with data acquisition devices to calculate results. Integrated peak areas are routinely used for quantitation as these give increased dynamic ranges compared to use of peak heights.

- **Power supply**

Separations are normally performed employing voltages in the region of 5~30kV. Electrolyte ionic strengths are generally selected during method development such that application of these voltages generates currents of 10~100μA. Operations with currents above this level may lead to unstable, irreproducible operating conditions. On many instruments it is possible to operate by applying constant voltage (most common), constant current or constant power across the capillary. However, constant voltage is the most commonly employed operational mode.

New Words and Expressions

chromatography [ˌkrəuməˈtɔgrəfi] n. 色谱法，层析法，色层分析法
capillary [kəˈpiləri] n. 毛细血管，毛细管
electrophoresis [iˌlektrəufəˈriːsis] n. 电泳（法），电泳技术
chalk [tʃɔːk] n. 白垩，粉笔，石灰石
column [ˈkɔləm] n. 柱，支柱，圆柱
pigment [ˈpigmənt] n. 色素，颜料
stationary [ˈsteiʃ(ə)nəri] adj. 固定的
analyte [ˈænəlait] n. （被）分析物
immobile [iˈməubail] adj. 固定的，静止的
pack [pæk] v. 填充，包装，压紧
manipulate [məˈnipjuleit] vt. 操纵，使用
versatility [ˌvəːsəˈtiləti] n. 多功能性，多面性，多样性，通用性
injector [inˈdʒektə] n. 注射器，针管
filter [ˈfiltə] n. 过滤器，筛选；v. 过滤
regulator [ˈregjuleitə] n. 调节器，稳定器

sparge [ˈspɑːdʒ] v. 喷射，喷洒，喷雾于
propel [prəˈpel] v. 推进，推动，驱动，驱使
seal [siːl] n. 封条，图章，密封；v. 封闭
loop [luːp] n. 环，回路，循环；v. 使成环
reproducible [ˌriːprəˈdjuːsəbl] adj. 能复制的，能繁殖的，可再生的，可重现的
particulate [pɑːrˈtikjələt] adj. 微粒的，粒子的；n. 微粒，粒子
sacrificial [ˌsækriˈfiʃəl] adj. 牺牲的
foul [faul] vt. 弄脏，对（对手）犯规
digitize [ˈdidʒitaiz] vt. （使数据）数字化
eluent [ˈeljuːənt] n. 洗脱液，淋洗液
retard [riˈtɑːd] vt. 减慢，减缓，延迟
retention [riˈtenʃən] n. 保留，保持
longitudinal [ˌlɔŋgiˈtjuːdin(ə)l] adj. 纵的，纵向的，纵观的
porosity [pɔːˈrɔsiti] n. 多孔性，孔隙率
non-destructive adj. 无破坏性的，无害的

labile ['leibail] adj. 易变化的，易分解的，不稳定的
derivatization [dəˌrivəˌtizeiʃən] n. 衍生作用，衍生化，衍生反应
pictogram ['pikəgræm] n. 皮克（10^{-12}克）
visualization [ˌviʒuəlaiˈzeiʃn] n. 形象化，显现，可视化，视觉化
dissipated ['disipeitid] adj. 浪费的，分散的
buffer ['bʌfə] n. 缓冲液，缓冲剂，缓冲器
electroosmotic [iˌlektrəuɔzˈməutik] adj. 电渗的

electropherogram [elektrəfərəgˈræm] n. 电泳图谱
autosampler [ˌɔːtəˈsæmplə] n. 自动进样器
polyimide [pɔliˈimaid] n. 聚亚胺，聚酰亚胺
fragile ['frædʒail] adj. 易碎的，脆的
cartridge ['kɑːtridʒ] n. 盒，筒，芯，囊，管
coolant ['kuːlənt] n. 冷冻剂，冷却液
vial ['vaiəl] n. 小瓶，小玻璃瓶，药水瓶
hyphenation [ˌhaifəˈneiʃ(ə)n] n. 用连字号的连接，连字符，连字符连接

Phrases

high Performance Liquid Chromatography 高效液相色谱法
high Performance Capillary Electrophoresis 高效毛细管电泳法

break down 毁掉，倒塌，垮掉，分解
interfere…with 干涉，干扰，妨碍
be interfaced with 与……连接

Affixes

re- 表示"又，再"；如 reproducible 可重现的，rebuild 重建，refresh 刷新
pre- 表示"之前"；如 preposition 介词，precolumn 柱前，prefix 前缀，predict 预言

Notes

1. Liquid Chromatography was first discovered in 1903 by M. S. Tswett, who used a chalk column to separate the pigments of green leaves. "who"引导的非限制性定语从句修饰"Tswett"。参考译文：液相色谱最早是由 M. S. Tswett 发现的，他使用石灰柱分离了绿叶中的色素。

2. However, a sacrificial guard column is often included just prior to the analytical column to chemically remove components of the sample that would otherwise foul the main column. "that"引导的定语从句修饰"components"。"prior to"的意思是"在前，居先"。参考译文：通常紧靠分析柱前还会有一个牺牲保护柱，其功能是用化学方法除去样品中可能污染主分析柱的组分。

3. Assume that component A has the same interaction with the adsorbent surface as an eluent, and component B has strong excessive interaction. "the same…as"的意思是"与……一样"。参考译文：假定 A 组分和洗脱液对吸附剂表面有相同的作用，而 B 组分对吸附剂表面的作用大得多。

4. The method is popular because it is non-destructive and may be applied to thermally labile compounds (unlike GC); it is also a very sensitive technique since it incorporates a wide choice of detection methods. 句中"the method"和三个"it"都是指 HPLC。参考译文：高效液相色谱因其非破坏性以及可用于检测热不稳定成分（与气相色谱不同）而被广泛使用；高效液相色谱也是非常灵敏的技术，因为它可以使用多种检测方法。

5. With the use of post-column derivatization methods to improve selectivity and detection limits, HPLC can easily be extended to trace determination of compounds that do not usually provide adequate detector response. "that"引导的定语从句用来修饰"compounds"。参考译文：采用柱后衍生法提高选择性和检测限，高效液相色谱可扩展到痕量组分检测，这些痕量组分通常情况下不能产生足够的检测响应。

10. Structure Determination

Every time a reaction is run, the product must be identified. Determining the structure of an organic molecule was a difficult and time-consuming process in the nineteenth and early twentieth centuries, but extraordinary advances have been made in the past few decades. Powerful techniques and specialized instruments that greatly simplify structure determination are now available. We'll look four most useful such techniques—infrared (IR) spectroscopy, ultraviolet (UV) spectroscopy, and nuclear magnetic resonance (NMR) spectroscopy, mass spectrometry (MS)—each of which yields a different kind of structural information.

Electromagnetic spectrum

Infrared spectroscopy is a method of structure determination that depends on the interaction of molecules with IR radiant energy. Before beginning a study of IR spectroscopy, however, we need to look into the nature of radiant energy and the electromagnetic spectrum.

Visible light, X-rays, microwaves, radiowaves, and so forth, are all different kinds of electromagnetic radiation. Collectively, they make up the electromagnetic spectrum (Fig. 1). The electromagnetic spectrum is loosely divided into regions, with the familiar visible region accounting for only a small portion of the overall spectrum, from 3.8×10^{-7} to 7.8×10^{-7} m in wavelength.[1] The visible region is flanked by the IR and UV regions.

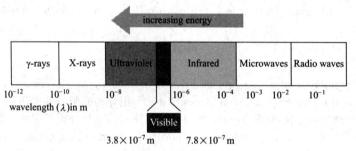

Fig. 1　The electromagnetic spectrum

Electromagnetic radiation has dual behavior. In some respects it has the properties of a particle (called a photon), yet in other respects it behaves as an energy wave traveling at the speed of light. Like all waves, electromagnetic radiation is characterized by frequency or wavelength, and amplitude. The frequency, ν (Greek nu), is the number of wave peaks that pass a fixed point per unit time, usually given in reciprocal second (s^{-1}), or hertz, Hz ($1 Hz = 1 s^{-1}$). The wavelength, λ (Greek lambda), is the distance from one wave maximum to the next. The amplitude is the height of the wave, measured from the midpoint between peak and trough to the maximum. The intensity of radiant energy, whether a feeble beam or a blinding glare, is proportional to the square of the wave's amplitude.

Multiplying the length of a wave in meters (m) by its frequency in reciprocal second (s^{-1}) gives the speed of the wave in meters per second (m/s). The rate of travel of all electromagnetic radiation in a vacuum is a constant value, commonly called the "speed of light" and abbreviated c. It's numerical value is defined as exactly 2.99792458×10^8 m/s, usually rounded off to 3.00×10^8 m/s.

$$\lambda(m) \times \nu(s^{-1}) = c(m/s)$$

which can be rewritten as:
$$\lambda = c/\nu \quad \text{or} \quad \nu = c/\lambda$$

Electromagnetic energy is transmitted only in discrete amounts, called quanta. The amount of energy E corresponding to 1 quantum of energy (or 1 photon) with a given frequency ν is expressed by the equation:
$$E = h\nu = hc/\lambda$$

E = Energy of 1 photon (1 quantum)
h = Planck's constant (6.62×10^{-34} J·s = 1.58×10^{-34} cal·s)
ν = Frequency (s^{-1})
λ = Wavelength (m)
c = Speed of light (3.00×10^8 m/s)

This equation says that the energy of a given photon varies directly with its frequency ν but inversely with its wavelength λ. High frequencies and short wavelengths correspond to high-energy radiation such as gamma rays; low frequencies and long wavelengths correspond to low-energy radiation such as radio waves.

When molecules absorb energy from electromagnetic radiation, they undergo changes. The changes depend on the amount of energy absorbed. When a molecule absorbs visible radiation, the energy causes an electron in the molecule to move from a lower-energy orbital to a higher-energy orbital. When infrared radiation is absorbed by a molecule, a bond or group of bonds in the molecule begins to vibrate more vigorously. The energy in microwave radiation can cause small molecules to rotate faster, which is what it does to water molecules in a microwave oven. All of these changes give information about how electrons and atoms are arranged in molecules, and together can be used to determine the structure of molecules. If we irradiate an organic compound with energy of many wavelengths and determine which are absorbed and which are transmitted, we can determine the absorption spectrum of the compound. The results are displayed on a plot of wave number or wavelength versus the amount of radiation transmitted.

Infrared spectroscopy

The infrared region of the electromagnetic spectrum covers the range from just above the visible (7.8×10^{-7} m) to approximately 10^{-4} m, but only the middle of the region is used by organic chemists. This mid-portion extends from 2.5×10^{-5} to 2.5×10^{-6} m, and wavelengths are usually given in micrometers (μm; $1\mu m = 10^{-6}$ m). Frequencies are usually given in wavenumbers (σ), rather than in hertz. The wavenumber is equal to the reciprocal of the wavelength in centimeters and is thus expressed in units of reciprocal centimeters (cm^{-1}):
$$\text{Wavenumber}: \sigma(cm^{-1}) = 1/\lambda(cm)$$

Photon energies associated with this part of the infrared (from 1 to 15kcal/mol) are not large enough to excite electrons, but may induce vibrational excitation of covalently bonded atoms and groups. All molecules have a certain amount of energy, which causes bonds to stretch and contract, atoms to wag back and forth, and other molecular motions to occur.[2] Although we usually speak of bond lengths as if they were fixed, the numbers given are really average because bonds are constantly stretching and bending, lengthening and contracting. Thus, a typical C—H bond length of 110pm is actually vibrating at a specific frequency, alternately stretching and compressing as if there were a spring connecting the two atoms.

Why does a molecule absorb some wavelengths of infrared energy but not others? The amount of energy a molecule contains is not continuously variable but is quantized. That is, a molecule can vibrate only at specific frequencies corresponding to specific energy levels. Take bond stretching as an example. When the molecule is irradiated with electromagnetic radiation, energy is absorbed if the frequency of the radiation matches the frequency of the vibration. The result of energy absorption is an increased amplitude for the vibration; in other words, the "spring" connecting the two atoms stretches and compressed a bit further. Since each frequency absorbed by a molecule corresponds to a specific molecular motion, we can find what kind of motions a molecule has by measuring its IR spectrum. By then interpreting those motions, we can find out what kinds of bonds (function groups) are present in the molecule.

IR spectrum → What molecular motions? → What functional groups?

The full interpretation of an IR spectrum is difficult because most organic molecules are so large that they have dozens of different bond stretching and bending motions. Thus, an IR spectrum usually contains dozens of absorptions. Fortunately, we don't need interpret an IR spectrum fully to get useful information because functional groups have characteristic IR absorption that don't change from one compound to another.[3] The $C=O$ absorption of ketone almost always in the range 1680 to 1750cm^{-1}, the O—H absorption of a alcohol is almost is always in the range 3400 to 3650cm^{-1}, the $C=C$ absorption of an alkene is almost in the range 1640 to 1680cm^{-1}, and so forth. By learning to recognize where characteristic functional-group absorptions occur, it's possible to get structural information from IR spectra.

Look at the IR spectra of cyclohexanol and cyclohexanone in Fig. 2 to see how they can be used. Although both spectra contain many peaks, the characteristic absorptions of the different functional groups allow the compounds to be distinguished. Cyclohexanol shows a characteristic alcohol O—H adsorption at 3300cm^{-1} and a C—O adsorption at 1060cm^{-1}; cyclohexanone show a characteristic ketone $C=O$ peak at 1715cm^{-1}.

One further point about infrared spectroscopy: It's also possible to obtain structural information from an IR spectrum by noticing which absorptions are *not* present. If the spectrum of an unknown does *not* have absorption near 3400cm^{-1}, the unknown is not an alcohol; if the spectrum does not have an absorption near 1715cm^{-1}, the unknown is not a ketone; and so on.

It helps in remembering the position of various IR absorption to divide the infrared range from 4000cm^{-1} to 200cm^{-1} into four parts, as shown in Fig. 3.

• The region from 4000 to 2500cm^{-1} corresponds to N—H, C—H, and O—H single-bond stretching motions. Both N—H and O—H bonds absorb in the 3300 to 3600cm^{-1} range, whereas C—H bond stretching occurs near 3000cm^{-1}. Since almost all organic compounds have C—H bonds, almost all IR spectra have an intense absorption in this region.

• The region from 2500 to 2000cm^{-1} is where triple-bond stretching occur. Both nitriles (RC≡N) and alkynes (RC≡CR[1]) absorb here.

• The region from 2000 to 1200cm^{-1} is where $C=O$, $C=N$, and $C=C$ double-bond absorb. Carbonyl groups generally absorb from 1670 to 1780cm^{-1}, and alkene stretching normally occurs in the narrow ranged from 1640 to 1680cm^{-1}. The exact position of a $C=O$ absorption is often diagnostic of the exact kind of carbonyl group in the molecule. Esters usually absorb at 1735cm^{-1}, aldehydes at 1725cm^{-1}, and open-chain ketones at 1715cm^{-1}.

• The region below 1500cm^{-1} is the so-called fingerprint region. A large number of

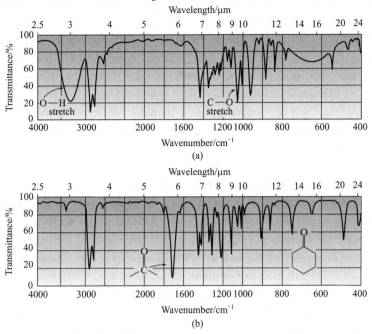

Fig. 2 IR spectra of cyclohexanol (a) and cyclohexanone (b)

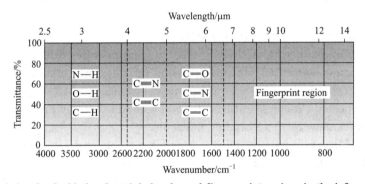

Fig. 3 Single-bond, double-bond, triple-bond, and finger-print regions in the infrared spectrum

absorptions due to various C—O, C—C, and C—N single-bond vibrations occur here, forming a unique pattern that acts as an identifying "fingerprint" of each molecule.

Ultraviolet Spectroscopy

The ultraviolet (UV) region of the electromagnetic spectrum extends from the low-wavelength end of the visible region (4×10^{-7} m) to 10^{-8} m. The portion of greatest interest to organic chemists, though, is the narrow range from 2×10^{-7} m to 4×10^{-7} m. Absorptions in this region are measured in nanometers (nm), where $1 \text{nm} = 10^{-9}$ m $= 10^{-7}$ cm. Thus, the ultraviolet range of interest is from 200 to 400nm.

We have known that an organic molecule either absorbs or transmits electromagnetic energy when irradiated, depending on the radiation's energy. With IR radiation, the energy absorbed corresponds to the amount necessary to raise the amplitude of molecular bending or stretching vibrations. Instead of causing molecular vibrations, UV light can excite electrons in one orbital into an orbital of higher energy. The electrons that are most easily promoted are those in conjugated π-bonds. With UV radiation, the energy absorbed corresponds to the amount necessary to raise the energy level of a π electron in an unsaturated molecule.

Ultraviolet spectra are recorded by irradiating a sample with UV light of continuously changing wavelength. When the wavelength of light corresponds to the amount of energy required to promote a π electron in an unsaturated molecule to a higher level, energy is absorbed. The absorption is detected and displayed on a chart that plots wavelength versus percent radiation absorbed.

Unlike IR spectra, which generally have many peaks, UV spectra are usually quite simple. Often, there is only a single broad peak, which is identified by noting the wavelength at the very top (λ_{max}).

Interpreting Ultraviolet Spectra: The Effect of Conjugation

The wavelength of radiation necessary to raise the energy of a π electron in an unsaturated molecule depends on the nature of the π electron system in the molecule. One of the most important factors is the extent of conjugation. It turns out that the energy required for an electronic transition decreases as the extent of conjugation increases. Thus, 1,3-butadiene shows an absorption at $\lambda_{max}=217$nm, 1,3,5-hexatriene absorbs at $\lambda_{max}=258$nm, and 1,3,5,7-octatetraene has $\lambda_{max}=290$nm. (Remember: Longer wavelength means lower energy.)

Other kinds of conjugated π electron systems besides dienes and polyenes also show ultraviolet absorptions. Conjugated enones, such as 3-buten-2-one, and aromatic molecules, such as benzene, also have characteristic UV absorptions that aid in structure determination.

Nuclear Magnetic Resonance Spectroscopy

We have seen up to this point that IR spectroscopy provides information about a molecule's functional groups and that UV spectroscopy provides information about a molecule's conjugated π electron system. Nuclear magnetic resonance (NMR) spectroscopy doesn't replace either of these techniques; rather, it complements them by providing a "map" of the carbon-hydrogen framework in an organic molecule.

How does NMR spectroscopy work? Many kinds of nuclei, including ^{1}H and ^{13}C, behave like a child's top spinning about an axis. Since they're positively charged, these spinning nuclei act like tiny magnets and interact with an external magnetic field (denoted B_0). In the absence of an external magnetic field, the nuclear spins of magnetic nuclei are oriented randomly. When a sample containing these nuclei is placed between the poles of a strong magnet, however, the nuclei adopt specific orientations, much as a compass needle orients itself in the earth's magnetic field.

A spinning ^{1}H or ^{13}C nucleus can orient so that its own tiny magnetic field is aligned either with (parallel to) or against (antiparallel to) the external field. The two orientations don't have the same energy and therefore aren't equally likely. The parallel orientation is slightly lower in energy, making this spin state slightly favored over the antiparallel orientation.

If the oriented nuclei are now irradiated with electromagnetic radiation of the right frequency, energy absorption occurs and the lower-energy state "spin-flips" to the higher-energy state. This amount of energy occurs in the microwave regin of the electromagnetic spectrum. When this spin-flip occurs, the nuclei are said to be in resonance with the applied radiation—hence the name nuclei magnetic resonance.

The exact frequency necessary for resonance depends both on the strength of the external magnetic field and on the identity of the nuclei.[6] If a very strong external field is applied, the energy difference between the two spin states is large, and higher-energy (higher-frequency) radiation is required. If a weaker magnetic field is applied, less energy is required to effect the transition between nuclear spin states.

The nature of NMR Absorptions

From the description thus far, you might expect all ^{1}H nuclei in a molecule to absorb energy at the same frequency and all ^{13}C nuclei to absorb at the same frequency. If this was true, we would observe only a single NMR absorption in the ^{1}H or ^{13}C spectrum of a molecule, a situation that would be of little use for structure determination. In fact, the absorption frequency is not the same for all ^{1}H or ^{13}C nuclei.

All nuclei are surrounded by circulating electrons. When an external magnetic field is applied to a molecule, the moving electrons around nuclei set up tiny local magnetic fields (B_{local}) of their own. These local in opposition to the applied field ($B_{applied}$) so that the effective field ($B_{effective}$) actually felt by the nucleus is bit weaker than the applied field:

$$B_{effective} = B_{applied} - B_{local}$$

In describing this effect of local fields, we say that the nuclei are shielded from the full effect of the applied field by their surrounding electrons. Since each specific ^{1}H or ^{13}C nucleus in a molecule is in a slightly different electronic environment, each specific nucleus is shielded to a slightly different extent and the effective magnetic field felt by each is not the same.[4] These slight differences can be detected, and we therefore see different NMR signals for each chemically distinct ^{1}H or ^{13}C nucleus.

Fig. 4 show both the ^{1}H and the ^{13}C NMR spectra of methyl acetate, $CH_3CO_2CH_3$. In both spectra, the horizontal axis tells the effective field strength felt by the nuclei, and the vertical axis indicates the intensity of absorption of rf energy. Each peak in the NMR spectrum corresponds to a chemically distinct hydrogen or carbon in the molecule. Note, though, that ^{1}H and ^{13}C spectra can't be observed at the same time on the same spectrometer because different amounts of energy are required to spin-flip the different kinds of nuclei. The two spectra must be recorded separately.

The ^{13}C spectrum of methyl acetate showed in Fig. 4(b) has three peaks, one for each of the three chemically distinct carbons in the molecule. The ^{1}H spectrum shows only *two* peaks (Fig. 4(a)), however, even though methyl acetate has *six* hydrogens. One peak is due to the $CH_3C=O$ hydrogens and the other to the $-OCH_3$ hydrogens. Because the three hydrogens in each methyl group have the same chemical (and magnetic) environment, they are shielded to the same extent and are said to be equivalent. Chemically equivalent nuclei show a single absorption. The two methyl groups themselves, however, are nonequivalent, so the two sets of hydrogens absorb at different positions.

Chemical Shifts

NMR spectra are displayed as a plot of the applied radio frequency increasing from left to right, vs. the absorption. Thus the left side of the plot is the low field or downfield side, and the right side is the high field or upfield side. Nuclei absorbing on the downfield side of the plot require a low field strength for resonance, implying they are relatively little shielded. Nuclei absorbing on the upfield side require a high field strength for resonance, implying strongly shielded.

The difference in resonance frequency between chemically different types of nucleus is called chemical shift. The radiofrequency energy required to bring a given nucleus into reso-

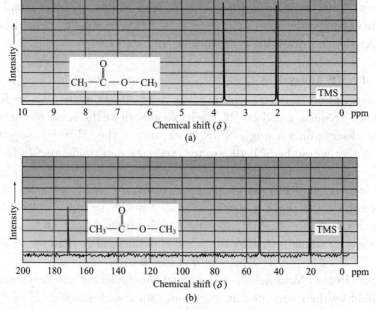

Fig. 4　The ^{1}H NMR spectrum (a) and the ^{13}C NMR spectrum (b) of methyl acetate

nance depends on the spectrometer's magnetic field strength. But because there are many different kinds of spectrometers with many different magnetic field strengths available, chemical shifts given in frequency units (Hz) vary from one instrument to another.[5] A resonance that occurs at 120 Hz downfield from TMS on one spectrometer might occur at 600 Hz downfield from TMS on another spectrometer with a more powerful magnet. This relationship could make it difficult to compare NMR spectra taken on spectrometers operating at different field strengths.

To avoid this problem, the NMR plot is calibrated and a reference point is used. In practice, a small amount of tetramethylsilane [TMS, $(CH_3)_4Si$] is added to the sample so that a reference absorption line is produced when the spectrum is run. TMS is used as a reference for both ^{1}H and ^{13}C spectra, because in both kinds of spectra it produces a single peak that occurs upfield (farther right on the chart) of other absorptions normally found in organic molecules. By convention, the chemical shift of TMS is set as the zero point, and other peaks normally occur downfield, to the left on the plot. The chemical shift of a nucleus, δ, is defined as:

$$\delta = \frac{\nu_{sample} - \nu_{TMS}}{\nu_{TMS}} \times 10^6$$

where ν_{sample} is the absolute resonance frequency of the sample and ν_{TMS} is the absolute resonance frequency of a standard reference compound, TMS, measured in the same applied magnetic field B_0.

Thus, an NMR signal observed at a frequency 300 Hz higher than the signal from TMS, where the TMS resonance frequency is 300 MHz, has a chemical shift with 1 ppm. Although the absolute resonance frequency depends on the applied magnetic field, the chemical shift is independent of external magnetic field strength. By using a system of measurement in which NMR absorptions are expressed in relative terms rather than in absolute terms (Hz), comparisons of spectra obtained on different instruments are possible. The chemical shift of an NMR absorption in δ units is constant, regardless of the operating frequency of the instrument. A ^{1}H nucleus that absorbs at 2.0ppm on a 100MHz instrument also absorbs at 2.0ppm on a 300MHz instrument. Almost all ^{1}H absorptions occur downfield within 10ppm of TMS. For ^{13}C NMR almost all absorptions occurs within 220ppm downfield of the C atom in TMS.

Mass Spectrometry

In contrast to other spectroscopic techniques, mass spectrometry (MS) does not involve the absorption of electromagnetic radiation, but operates on a completely different principle. MS is used for both qualitative and quantitative chemical analysis. It may be used to identify the elements and isotopes of a sample, to determine the masses of molecules, and as a tool to help identify chemical structures. The instrument used in MS is called mass spectrometer. Mass spectrum is obtained by injecting a very small amount of sample into a mass spectrometer, where it is subjected to bombardment by a high-energy electron beam. The first reaction that occurs in the mass spectrometer is the formation of molecular ions or parent ions by loss of an electron from the molecule, which then fragment into smaller ions. It produces a mass spectrum that plots the relative amount of each ion (called the relative abundance) as a function of the ionic mass (or m/z), such as that shown in Fig. 5. The masses of these ions may be used in making judgments about the structure of the compound that gives rise to them. The mass spectrum of a compound of any complexity is unique in the pattern of peaks and the relative intensities of those peaks. As such, it can serve as a fingerprint for the compound.

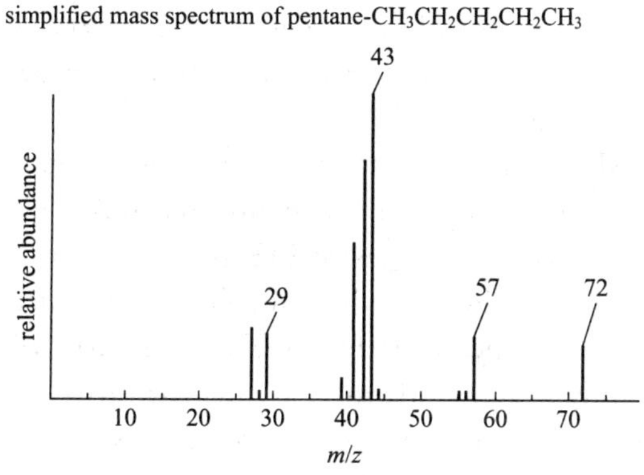

Fig. 5 Mass spectrum of pentane

Fragmentation of the molecular ion gives other radical-cations, carbocations, and neutral molecules. The positively charged species are separated according to their mass-to-charge ratios, m/z, by a variety of techniques. Most ions created in a mass spectrometer have a single positive charge; therefore, the separation is essentially done according to mass. Once the sample has been ionised, it is accelerated through an electric field before being passed through a magnetic field generated by an electromagnet, as shown in Fig. 6 The positively charged ions are deflected as they pass through this field, with the magnitude of the deflection dependent on the mass/charge ratio of the ion. Lighter ions are deflected more, whilst heavier ions are deflected less. Ions with a larger charge are also deflected more. Thus ions of different masses impinge separately on an electron multiplier (detector) and are recorded on a chart. The calibration of the instrument allows not only the masses of the ions to be recorded but the relative number of each kind.

The masses recorded by a mass spectrometer are exact masses; therefore, molecules of

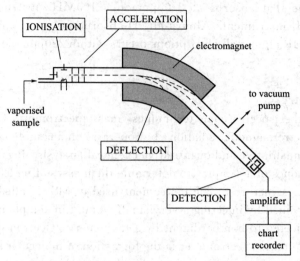

Fig. 6 Schematic diagram of a mass spectrometer

different isotopic composition give different molecular ions. For example, methyl bromide has two molecular ions of about equal abundance, one arising from $CH_3{}^{79}Br$ and the other from $CH_3{}^{81}Br$.

The fragmentation patterns seen for different types of compounds are typical of their structures. Fragmentations occur so as to produce stable cations or by the loss of stable neutral fragments. Rearrangements also occur, such as McLafferty rearrangement, in which a hydrogen atom from the γ-carbon atom is transferred to the oxygen atom in a radical-cation derived from a carbonyl compound.

A big advantage of MS over many other techniques is that it is incredibly sensitive (parts per million). It is an excellent tool for identifying unknown components in a sample or confirming their presence. Disadvantages of MS are that it isn't very good at identifying hydrocarbons that produce similar ions and it's unable to tell optical and geometrical isomers apart. The disadvantages are compensated for by combining MS with other techniques, such as gas-phase chromatography (GC), which separate mixtures efficiently, and computers, which automatically identify the components of mixtures by comparing mass spectral information with stored patterns for known compounds.[6]

Taken together, these four techniques often make it possible to find the structures of even very complex molecules.

IR spectroscopy	functional groups
UV spectroscopy	conjugated π-electron system
NMR spectroscopy	map of carbon-hydrogen framework
Mass spectrometry	mass, formula and isotope of a compound

New Words and Expressions

infrared [infrə'red] *adj.* 红外线的; *n.* 红外线

spectroscopy [spek'trɔskəpi] *n.* 光谱学, 波谱学

ultraviolet [ʌltrə'vaiəlet] *adj.* 紫外线的, 紫外的; *n.* 紫外线辐射

spectrometry [spek'trɔmitri] *n.* 光谱法, 光谱学

electromagnetic [ilektrəumæɡˈnetik] adj. 电磁的
microwave [ˈmaikrəweiv] n. 微波炉，微波
flank [flæŋk] v. 处于……之间，在……的侧面
amplitude [ˈæmplitjuːd] n. 振幅
reciprocal [riˈsiprəkəl] adj. 倒数的；n. 倒数
trough [trɔf] n. 波谷，谷底
transmit [trænzˈmit] v. 发射，传送，传播
discrete [diˈskriːt] adj. 不连续的，分立的
quanta [ˈkwɔntə] n. 量子（quantum 的复数）
vigorously [ˈvigərəsli] adv. 活泼地，有力地，猛力地
wag [wæɡ] v. 摆动，摇摆
quantize [ˈkwɔntaiz] v. 使量子化
irradiate [iˈreidieit] v. 照射
wavenumber [weiˈvinʌmbər] n. 波数
bend [bend] v. 弯曲，屈服
compound [ˈkɔmpaund] n. 混合物，化合物
cyclohexanol [saikləuˈheksənɔl] n. 环己醇
cyclohexanone [ˌsaikləuˈheksənəun] n. 环己酮
nitrile [ˈnaitril] n. 腈
carbonyl [ˈkɑːbənil] n. 羰基，碳酰
diagnostic [ˌdaiəɡˈnɔstik] n. 诊断

ester [ˈestə(r)] n. 酯，酯类，酯基
butadiene [ˌbjuːtəˈdaiiːn] n. 丁二烯
polyene [ˈpɔliiːn] n. 多烯（烃）
complement [ˈkɔmpləment] v. 补充，补足
nucleus [ˈnjuːkliəs] n. 核，原子核，（复数：nuclei）
framework [ˈfreimwəːk] n. 框架，结构
shield [ʃiːld] v. 给……加防护罩，屏蔽
acetate [ˈæsiteit] n. 醋酸盐，醋酸酯
equivalent [iˈkwivələnt] n. 等同物；adj. 等价的，同等的
radiofrequency [reidiəuˈfriːkwənsi] n. 射频
calibrate [ˈkælibreit] v. 校准
tetramethylsilane [tetrəˌmiθilˈsilein] n. 四甲基硅烷
isotope [ˈaisətəup] n. 同位素
bombardment [bɔmˈbɑːdmənt] n. 炮击，轰炸
fragmentation [ˌfræɡmenˈteiʃən] n. 分裂，破碎
carbocation [kɑːbəˈkeiʃən] n. 碳正离子，碳阳离子
deflect [diˈflekt] v. 使弯曲，偏转，偏离
impinge [imˈpindʒ] v. 冲击，撞击
rearrangement [ˌriːəˈreindʒmənt] n. 重排

Phrases

correspond to…　相应于……
be proportional to　与……成比例
multiply…by　乘以，乘上，使相乘
round off　四舍五入，舍入
range from…to…　范围从……到……
fingerprint region　指纹区
vary from…to…　从……到……都不同

spin-flip　自旋翻转
chemical shift　化学位移
by convention　按照惯例
be subjected to　遭受，服从，经受
McLafferty rearrangement　麦氏重排，麦克拉弗蒂重排反应
tell…apart　辨别，分别

Affixes

extra- [ˈekstrə] 表示"以外的，超过的"；如 extraordinary 非常的、特别的，extrapolate 推断，extracurriculum 课外的，extrasolar 太阳系以外的，extrovert 性格外向的
ultra- [ˈʌltrə] 表示"极端，过度"；如 ultraviolet 紫外线辐射，ultrasonic 超音速的，ultrapure 极纯的，ultrathin 极薄的
infra- [ˈinfrə] 表示"在下，下"；如 infrared 红外线，infrastructure 下部结构，infrasonic 低于声频的

nano- [ˈnænəu] 表示"纳，十亿分之一"；如 nanometer 纳米，nanoparticle 纳米颗粒，nanosecond 纳秒，nanotechnology 纳米技术

Notes

1. The electromagnetic spectrum is loosely divided into regions, with the familiar visible region accounting for only a small portion of the overall spectrum, from 3.8×10^{-7} to 7.8×10^{-7} m in wavelength. 现在分词独立结构"with the familiar visible region accounting for…"作非限制性定语修饰"regions"。参考译文：电磁波谱大致可以分为几个区域，我们熟悉的可见光区只占整个波谱区域的很小一部分，它的波长范围从 3.8×10^{-7} 米到 7.8×10^{-7} 米。

2. All molecules have a certain amount of energy, which causes bonds to stretch and contract, atoms to wag back and forth, and other molecular motions to occur. 主从复合句，包含"which…"引导的非限制性定语从句。参考译文：所有的分子都具有一定的能量，导致化学键的伸缩、原子的前后摇摆以及其他分子运动。

3. Fortunately, we don't need interpret an IR spectrum fully to get useful information because functional groups have characteristic IR absorption that don't change from one compound to another. 参考译文：幸运的是，我们不需要解析所有红外光谱峰来得到有用的信息，因为官能团有特征红外吸收，该吸收不会因化合物的不同而改变。

4. Since each specific ^{1}H or ^{13}C nucleus in a molecule is in a slightly different electronic environment, each specific nucleus is shielded to a slightly different extent and the effective magnetic field felt by each is not the same. 参考译文：由于一个分子中每一个特定的 ^{1}H 或 ^{13}C 核处于一个稍微不同的电子环境中，每一个特定的核被屏蔽的程度会略有不同，感应到的有效磁场也不同。

5. But because there are many different kinds of spectrometers with many different magnetic field strengths available, chemical shifts given in frequency units (Hz) vary from one instrument to another. 参考译文：但因为有很多不同种类的使用不同磁场强度的光谱仪，所以使用不同的仪器得到的用频率单位（赫兹）表示的化学位移就不相同。

6. The disadvantages are compensated for by combining MS with other techniques, such as gas-phase chromatography (GC), which separate mixtures efficiently, and computers, which automatically identify the components of mixtures by comparing mass spectral information with stored patterns for known compounds. 两个"which"分别引导两个非限制性定语从句来修饰"chromatography"和"computers"。参考译文：通过质谱和其他技术的结合，比如有效分离混合物的气相色谱和通过比较质谱信息与存储的已知化合物的谱图自动识别混合物组成的计算机，质谱的缺点可以得到弥补。

11. Electrochemistry

Electrochemistry deals with the use of spontaneous chemical reactions to supply electrical energy and the use of electrical energy to make nonspontaneous chemical reactions take place. In voltaic or galvanic cells, spontaneous chemical reactions are used to generate electricity. The oxidation and reduction reactions must be physically separated but connected by a wire and an electrolyte. An electric current is a flow of electric charge; charge is carried through an electrolyte by movement of ions and through a wire by movement of electrons. Reaction takes place at the surface of the electrodes, the conductors that carry charge into and out of an electrolyte. The electrode where oxidation takes place is named the anode and the electrode where reduction takes place is named the cathode. The reactions that take place at electrodes are called half-cell reactions or half reactions.

The electromotive force (emf), E, (or cell potential or cell voltage) of a cell is the difference in electric potential energy between the two half-cells that make up the cell. Potentials are measured in volts; $1V = 1J/C$. The standard cell potential, $E^\ominus$, is the cell potential when the cell is operating under standard conditions. By agreement among scientists, the voltage for the half-reaction:

$$2H^+ + 2e^- \longrightarrow H_2(g)$$

or its reverse under standard conditions is exactly zero. A half-cell that contains one molar hydrogen ion and hydrogen gas at a partial pressure of one atmosphere is called a standard hydrogen electrode, SHE. The potentials in tables of standard reduction potentials are measured with respect to the standard hydrogen electrode as the cathode.

A positive sign for the voltage of a half-reaction shows that the half-reaction has a greater tendency to take place than the reduction of hydrogen ion under standard conditions; a negative sign shows that a half-reaction has a lesser tendency to take place than the reduction of hydrogen ion.[1] Whether or not a given oxidation-reduction reaction will be spontaneous under standard conditions can be predicted on the basis of the diagonal relationship of the species to each other in the table of standard reduction potentials. When standard reduction potentials are listed in order of decreasing value, any species on the reactant side of a half-reaction equation will oxidize any species on the product side that is lower in the table.

Standard reduction potentials can be used to calculate standard cell potentials:

$$E^\ominus_{cell} = E^\ominus_{half\text{-}cell\ of\ reduction} - E^\ominus_{half\text{-}cell\ of\ oxidation}$$

Cell potentials under nonstandard conditions can be calculated from standard cell potentials by means of the Nernst equation:

$$E = E^\ominus - \frac{RT}{nF}\ln Q$$

where E is the cell potential under nonstandard conditions, $E^\ominus$ is the cell potential under standard conditions, R is the ideal gas constant, T is the temperature in kelvin, Q is the reaction quotient, n is the number of moles of electrons transferred, and F is the Faraday constant. The Faraday constant is the charge on 1mol of electrons, $9.65 \times 10^4 C$. Reactions that have positive potentials are spontaneous. A concentration cell produces an electric current as a result of a difference in concentration between solutions in the two half-cells.

Gibbs free energy is related to cell potential by the equation:

$$\Delta G = -nFE$$

which can be used to calculate $\Delta G^\ominus$ from experimental values for $E^\ominus$ and to calculate values for $E^\ominus$ that cannot be found experimentally from tabulated values of $\Delta G_f^\ominus$. By means of the relationship:

$$E^\ominus = \frac{RT}{nF}\ln K$$

equilibrium constants K for any oxidation-reduction reaction can be calculated from measurements of $E^\ominus$.

Batteries are compact, portable voltaic cells that contain all the reactants and store energy ready to be used whenever and wherever needed. Unlike a battery, fuel cells do not store chemical or electrical energy; fuel cells are voltaic cells that require a constant external supply of reactants to continuously convert chemical energy into electrical energy.[2] The spontaneous redox reactions that take place in batteries and fuel cells are very useful. On the other hand, the spontaneous redox reactions involved in corrosion, the deterioration of metals by chemical reactions, are extremely destructive. Metals can be protected against corrosion by painting, plating, equipping with sacrificial anodes, or alloying.

Oxidation-reduction reactions that are nonspontaneous can be made to take place by supplying electrical energy. An electrochemical cell in which a nonspontaneous reaction is made to take place is called an electrolytic cell. The process that takes place in an electrolytic cell is called electrolysis. As usual, the reaction that takes place depends on both thermodynamics and kinetics. The cell potential for a cell is the minimum voltage necessary to bring about electrolysis. Overpotential is additional voltage (beyond the thermodynamic requirement) needed to drive an electrochemical reaction at a practical rate.[3] Electrolytic cells are used to produce active metals, refine metals, for electroplating, and for synthesis of both inorganic and organic compounds.

The masses of products formed and reactants used up in electrochemical reactions are directly proportional to the quantity of electricity transferred at the electrodes and to the molar masses of the substances involved in the reaction.[4]

New Words and Expressions

electrochemistry [iˌlektrəuˈkemistri] n. 电化学
spontaneous [spɔnˈteiniəs] adj. 自发的，自然的
voltaic [vɔlˈteiik] adj. 电流的
galvanic [gælˈvænik] adj. 产生电流的
oxidation [ˌɔksiˈdeiʃən] n. 氧化
reduction [riˈdʌkʃən] n. 还原
electrode [iˈlektrəud] n. 电极
anode [ˈænəud] n. 阳极，正极
cathode [ˈkæθəud] n. 阴极
electromotive [iˌlektrəˈməutiv] adj. 电动的
tendency [ˈtendənsi] n. 趋向，倾向
diagonal [daiˈægən(ə)l] n. 对角线，斜线; adj. 斜线的，对角线的
quotient [ˈkwəuʃənt] n. 商
tabulate [ˈtæbjuleit] v. 列成表格，列表显示
redox [ˈredɔks] n. 氧化还原作用
deterioration [diˌtiəriəˈreiʃən] n. 变坏，退化，堕落
destructive [disˈtrʌktiv] adj. 破坏(性)的
electrolysis [iˌlekˈtrɔləsis] n. 电解
overpotential [ˈəuvəpəˈtenʃəl] n. 超电势，过电位
refine [riˈfain] v. 精炼，提纯，精制，提炼
electroplate [iˈlektrəˌpleit] v. 电镀; n. 电镀物品

Phrases

galvanic cell　原电池
electric current　电流
half-cell reaction　半电池反应
electromotive force　电动势
cell potential　电池电压
standard hydrogen electrode　标准氢电极

diagonal relationship　对角线关系
Nernst equation　能斯特方程
Faraday constant　法拉第常数
concentration cell　浓差电池
fuel cell　燃料电池
electrolytic cell　电解池

Notes

1. A positive sign for the voltage of a half-reaction shows that the half-reaction has a greater tendency to take place than the reduction of hydrogen ion under standard conditions; a negative sign shows that a half-reaction has a lesser tendency to take place than the reduction of hydrogen ion. 这是由两个分句组成的并列句。参考译文：半反应电势的正号表明在标准条件下该半反应有比氢离子还原更大的趋势；负号则表明该半反应有比氢离子还原更小的趋势。

2. Unlike a battery, fuel cells do not store chemical or electrical energy; fuel cells are voltaic cells that require a constant external supply of reactants to continuously convert chemical energy into electrical energy. 参考译文：不同于蓄电池，燃料电池不存储化学能或电能；燃料电池需要外部持续提供反应剂，把化学能持续转化为电能的电池。

3. The cell potential for a cell is the minimum voltage necessary to bring about electrolysis. Overpotential is additional voltage (beyond the thermodynamic requirement) needed to drive an electrochemical reaction at a practical rate. 参考译文：电池的电势差是发生电解所需要的最低电压。超电势是驱动一个电化学反应以切实可行的速率进行所需要的（超过热力学要求的）额外电压。

4. The masses of products formed and reactants used up in electrochemical reactions are directly proportional to the quantity of electricity transferred at the electrodes and to the molar masses of the substances involved in the reaction. 参考译文：电化学反应中产物生成和反应物消耗的质量与电极上转移的电量以及反应中物质的摩尔质量成正比。

12. How to Develop a New Pesticide

All pesticides have a number of characteristics in common, some of which are desirable and some undesirable. Ideally, they should be highly effective against pests without being injurious to beneficial or desired organisms. Unfortunately, most pesticides do not completely comply with this ideal. Many are broad-spectrum poisons and therefore injury beneficial species. Some are toxic to crop plants, kill beneficial insects and micro-organisms, taint the flavor of foods, or stain the desired product. As many of these undesirable features as possible are naturally avoided, and a high priority in agriculture is for chemicals with some degree of specificity. It has been difficult to obtain highly specific compounds. However, a growing interest in conserving beneficial species is increasing the demand for more specific chemical, and manufactures are finding it more profitable to produce them.

Chemical origins

Modern synthetic pesticides have, in general, arisen from the research programs in the laboratories of the large chemical industries. The discovery of radically new types of pesticide has not so far come about by logical processes of deduction from knowledge of biochemical or biophysical processes in pests and disease organisms but rather from novelty in chemical synthesis followed by biological screening tests to measure activity.[1] The synthetic chemists and biologists concerned with the discovery of new active structures may have ideas on molecular shapes and degrees of reactivity which suggest to them a likelihood of biological activity but the success of prediction in the field of radical new approach has been poor. Massive screening programs have, however, shown novel biological activity from time to time. Once it has been recognized, the exploration of related structures and the optimization of biological activity can proceed on an increasingly logical basis as knowledge is built up of the structure—activity relationship and of possible biochemical modes of action. Intellectually unsatisfactory though a screening procedure may be, it has produced and continues to produce results. Screening test for biological activity must cover a wide spectrum of types of activity against a range of organisms. A novel synthesis is likely to produce a small quantity of chemical, so that considerable ingenuity is required in the design of biological tests to use the minimum quantity of material and yet detect novel types of activity. Once activity of interest has been discovered, the demands of the testing procedure may become a little easier, in that large quantities of chemical are prepared and more timid criteria for activity can be set.

Biological Evaluation

The biological evaluation of a compound emerging from primary screening tests will normally proceed sequentially through laboratory and glasshouse tests to small plot trails in the field and ultimately to larger scale trails in a range of climatic and crop conditions in various parts of the world.[2] The progress of biological evaluation, however, becomes increasingly dependent upon progress in two other fields of investigation which proceed in parallel: the examination and costing of possible manufacturing processes and research upon toxicology and environmental impact. It is clear that an eventual pesticide must not only be effective in controlling the pest or disease in the field conditions in which it occurs but it must do it at a cost which is a little more than rapid in terms of increased crop yield or quality. It must also do it without imposing undue toxic risk to the farmer who uses it, to the consumer of the crop, or to the environment in general. In practice, since research in these various areas is concurrent, the criteria can only be met through a series of decision points as information becomes available. Such decision points would be built into the critical path analysis plan which is an essential part of the overall control of the program.

Toxicology and Environmental Impact

The wide range of species of animals and plants in the natural world have all undergone the process of organic evolution and are therefore, to some extent, related and have many biochemical patterns in common. The specificity of toxic substances is thus a relative matter and it is likely that an insecticide, for example will have some activity to forms of life other than insects. The trend of pesticide evolution over the past thirty years, however, has been toward increased specificity. It has moved away from general poisons, so that apples are no longer sprayed with lead arsenate, weeds sprayed with arsenic compounds or stores fumigated with hydrogen cyanide. The injury of a farm worker by chemical poisoning is today a rare event. The risk of injure is from using tractors or even falling off haystacks or imprudently taking liberties with bulls.

The toxicological evaluation of a new chemical starts with the measurement of the acute toxicity when administered by various routes to laboratory animals and is expressed as an LD_{50} value—the dose required to kill 50% of a batch of animals exposed. This is followed by the measurement of chronic toxicity, by the continued administration of small quantities by various routes, as in the food, by application to the skin, or by inhalation of contaminated air. This procedure will include the measurement of the expression of toxic effects in various ways, including carcinogenesis. Such toxicity measurement ultimately lead to the establishment of no-effect levels, defined as those levels which can be administered continuously without producing any measurable physiological response. The no-effect level is of use in setting safety margins in the allocation of permissible residue levels in foodstuffs and in the environment.

The marketing of pesticides throughout the world is controlled by official registration authorities and a condition of registration is the submission of satisfactory information not only upon toxicology but also upon environmental impact.[3] Under the later heading, information is required in two areas: the ultimate fate of the chemical in the environment and the effects of the use of the chemical upon the populations of living things which may be exposed to it.

Chemicals may be degraded by spontaneous decomposition, the action of light, or metabolic transformations by living organisms. The metabolic degradation of pesticides by microorganisms, is clearly a most important aspect of the fate of the pesticides in soil. Metabolic investigations today, depend heavily upon studies with radio-labelled materials and the full determination of the environmental fate of a chemical may well require the synthesis of a number of samples with the label, at known different locations in the molecule, so that the various fragments may be traced.

The investigation of the biological impact of residues of pesticides and of their major metabolites also progresses sequentially through the research. A primary requirement is early recognition of major problems of ecological damage, so that grossly unsuitable may be rejected before excessive expenditure upon them has taken place. Many long-term effects in the environment, such as those upon large predatory birds, or accumulation into fish, might not emerge in practical use until large areas of land had been treated for a number of years, so that there is a requirement for laboratory or small plot procedures which will detect such long-term possibilities at an early stage.

If early work in laboratory and small plot systems does not indicate unacceptable environmental impact, ecological investigations are extended to large areas to cover population studies on large forms of life. [4] Terrestrial invertebrates are studied, with particular attention to predatory and parasitic forms in crops and to honey bees. Aquatic work is done to investigate the fate of the chemical in water and to measure effects on aquatic invertebrates and fish; and large area trails are laid down to determine effects in the field on wild birds and mammals.

New Words and Expressions

injurious [in'dʒuəriəs] adj. 造成伤害的，有害的
beneficial [ˌbeni'fiʃ(ə)l] adj. 有利的，有用的，有益的
taint [teint] v. 污染，使腐坏，玷污
specificity [ˌspesi'fisəti] n. 特异性，专一性
radically ['rædikli] adv. 根本地，彻底地，激进地，完全地
ingenuity [ˌindʒə'njuːəti] n. 聪明才智，独创性
criteria [krai'tiəriən] n. 标准，准则，条件
sequentially [si'kwenʃəli] adv. 相继地，顺序地
trail [treil] n. 踪迹，痕迹；v. 跟踪，追踪
toxicology [ˌtɔksi'kɔlədʒi] n. 毒物学，毒理学
undue [ʌn'djuː] adj. 不适当的，过分的，过度的
concurrent [kən'kʌrənt] adj. 同时发生的，同时完成的，同时存在的
arsenate ['ɑːsəneit] n. 砷酸盐
arsenic ['ɑː(r)s(ə)nik] adj. 砷的
fumigate ['fjuːmigeit] v. 熏蒸，以烟熏消毒
cyanide ['saiənaid] n. 氰化物
haystack ['heistæk] n. 草垛，干草堆
imprudently [im'pruːdntli] adv. 鲁莽地，不小心地

administer [əd'ministə] v. 管理，给予，执行
chronic ['krɔnik] adj. 长期的，慢性的
inhalation [ˌinhə'leiʃ(ə)n] n. 吸入，吸入法
carcinogenesis [ˌkɑːsinəu'dʒenisis] n. 致癌作用；致癌性
establishment [i'stæbliʃmənt] n. 设立，制定
margin ['mɑːdʒin] n. 余地，边缘，极限
allocation [ˌælə'keiʃən] n. 分配，安置，分配额
submission [səb'miʃən] n. 提交，屈服，投降
metabolic [ˌmetə'bɔlik] adj. 新陈代谢的
microorganism [maikrəu'ɔːgəniz(ə)m] n. 微生物
expenditure [iks'penditʃə] n. 支出，花费
predatory ['predət(ə)ri] adj. 食肉的，掠夺性的
terrestrial [tə'restriəl] adj. 陆地的，陆栖的，陆生的，地球的
invertebrate [in'və:(r)tibrət] n. 无脊柱动物
parasitic [ˌpærə'sitik] adj. 寄生的，寄生虫的
aquatic [ə'kwætik] adj. 水的，水生的
mammal ['mæməl] n. 哺乳动物

Phrases

comply with   遵守，遵从，依从，服从
broad-spectrum   广谱的，效用广泛的

decision point 决策点
critical path analysis 关键路径分析
move away 离开，挪开
take liberties with 随意对待，对……采取随意自由的态度

no-effect level 无作用剂量
safety margin 安全系数
permissible residue level 最大容许残留量
metabolic transformation 代谢转化

Affixes

con- [ˈkən] 表示"共同，联合"；如 concentric 同中心的，contemporary 同时代的，comcourse 合流，汇合

carcino- [kɑːˈsiːnəu] 表示"癌"；如 carcinogen 致癌物，carcinogenic 致癌的，carcinogenesis 致癌作用

Notes

1. The discovery of radically new types of pesticide has not so far come about by logical processes of deduction from knowledge of biochemical or biophysical processes in pests and disease organisms but rather from novelty in chemical synthesis followed by biological screening tests to measure activity. 参考译文：迄今为止，全新农药的发现，不是来自害虫和病原生物中生化或生物物理过程知识的逻辑推理，而是来自以测定活性的生物筛选实验为指导的新型化学合成。

2. The biological evaluation of a compound emerging from primary screening tests will normally proceed sequentially through laboratory and glasshouse tests to small plot trials in the field and ultimately to large scale trials in a range of climatic and crop conditions in various parts of the world. 参考译文：从初步筛选实验得到的化合物的生物学评价，通常会依序进行实验室和温室实验、田间小范围跟踪，并最终在世界各地不同的气候和种植条件下大规模的跟踪。

3. The marketing of pesticides throughout the world is controlled by official registration authorities and a condition of registration is the submission of satisfactory information not only upon toxicology but also upon environmental impact. 参考译文：全世界的农药销售都受官方注册机关控制，注册的一个条件是不仅要提交有（该农药的）毒理学信息，还要提交它对环境影响方面的令人满意的信息。

4. If early work in laboratory and small plot systems does not indicate unacceptable environmental impact, ecological investigations are extended to large areas to cover population studies on large forms of life. 参考译文：如果前期实验室和小范围的实验没有显示出不可接受的环境影响，那么生态研究会拓展到大范围的实验，来覆盖大量物种的种群研究。

13. What is Materials Chemistry?

Life in the 21st century is ever-dependent on an unlimited variety of advanced materials. In our consumptive world, it is easy to take for granted the macro-, micro-, and nanoscale building blocks that comprise any item ever produced. We are spoiled by the technology that adds convenience to our lives, such as microwave ovens, laptop computers, cell phones and tablets, and improved modes of transportation. However, we rarely take time to think about and appreciate the materials that constitute these modern engineering feats.

The term material may be broadly defined as any solid-state substance or device that may be used to address a current or future societal need (Fig. 1). For instance, simple building materials such as glass, wood, aluminum, etc. address our need of shelter. Other more intangible materials such as nanoscale components are also considered as materials, even though they may not yet be widely proven for applications. However, liquid substances such as crude oil, or gaseous compounds such as propane, are more properly considered as precursors for materials.

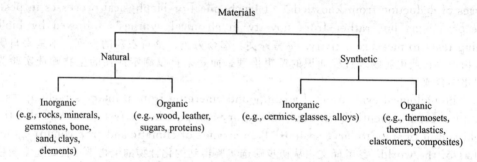

Fig. 1 Classification scheme for the various types of materials

The broadly defined discipline of materials chemistry is focused on understanding the relationships between the arrangement of atoms, ions, or molecules comprising a material, and its overall bulk structural and physical properties. By this designation, common disciplines such as polymer, solid-state, and surface chemistry would all be placed within the scope of materials chemistry. This broad field consists of studying the structures/properties of existing materials, synthesizing and characterizing new materials, and using advanced computational techniques to predict structures and properties of materials that have not yet been fabricated.

Historical Perspectives

By most accounts, Neolithic man (10000-300B. C.) was the first to realize that certain materials such as limestone, wood, shells, and clay were most easily shaped into materials used as utensils, tools, and weaponry. Applications for metallic materials date back to the Chalcolithic Age (4000-1500B. C.), where copper was used for a variety of ornamental, functional, and protective applications. This civilization was the first to realize fundamental properties of metals, such as malleability and thermal conductivity. More importantly, Chalcolithic man was the first to practice top-down materials synthesis, as they developed techniques to extract copper from oxide ores such as malachite, for subsequent use in various applications.

Fig. 2 presents the major developmental efforts related to materials science, showing the approximate year that each area was first investigated. Each of these areas is still of current interest, including the design of improved ceramics and metals, originally discovered by the earliest civilizations. Although building and structural materials such as ceramics, glasses, and asphalt have not dramatically changed since their invention, the world of electronics has undergone rapid changes. Many new architectures for advanced materials design are surely yet undiscovered, as scientists are now attempting to mimic the profound structural order existing in living creatures and plant life, which is evident as one delves into their microscopic and nanoscale regimes. [1]

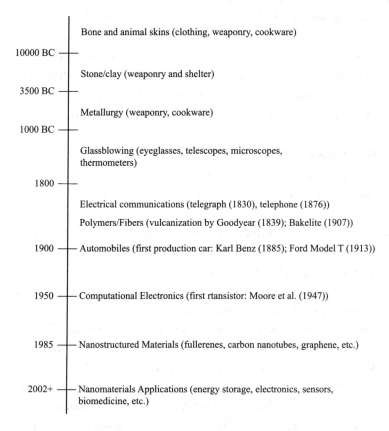

Fig. 2　Timeline of major developmental efforts related to materials science

"Bottom-up" Materials Synthesis

There are two rationales for the synthesis of materials, "top-down" and "bottom-up". Whereas the transformation of complex natural products into desirable materials occurs primarily via a top-down approach (e.g., gemstones from naturally occurring mineral deposits, etching features on silicon wafers for chip production), many important synthetic materials are produced using the bottom-up approach. This latter technique is the easiest to visualize, and is even practiced by children who assemble individual LEGO™ building blocks into more complex architectures. Indeed, the relatively new field of nanotechnology has drastically changed the conception of bottom-up processes, from the historical approach of combining/molding bulk precursor compounds, to the self-assembly of individual atoms and molecules. This capability of being able to manipulate the design of materials from the atomic level provides an unprecedented control over resultant properties. This will allow possibilities for an unlimited number of future applications, including faster electronic devices, efficient drug-delivery agents, and "green" energy alternatives such as hydrogen-based fuel cells and high-capacity batteries.

The recent discovery of self-repairing/autonomic healing materials is an example of the next generation of "smart materials", which offer bottom-up structural control of their properties. Analogous to the way our bodies are created to heal themselves, these materials are designed to undergo spontaneous physical change, with little or no human intervention. Imagine a world where cracks in buildings repair themselves, or automobile bodies transform to showroom condition shortly following an accident. Within the next few decades, these materials could be applied to eliminate defective parts on an assembly line, and could even find use in structures that are at present impractical or impossible to repair, such as integrated circuits or implanted medical devices.[2] An exciting world lies ahead of us; as we learn more about how to reproducibly design materials with specific properties from simple atomic/molecular subunits, the applications will only be limited by our imaginations!

Design of New Materials Through a "Critical Thinking" Approach

From the medical doctor that must properly diagnose an illness, to the lawyer that must properly follow logic to defend his/her client, critical thinking skills are a necessity for any career path. These skills are also very applicable for the design of new materials. Fig. 3 illustrates one example of a critical-thinking flowchart that could be applied to the design of a new material. Although there are many possibilities for such development, the following are essential components of any new development:

(i) Define the societal need and what type of material is being sought. That is, determine the desired properties of the new material.

(ii) Perform a comprehensive literature survey to determine what materials are currently being used. This must be done for the new product to successfully compete in the consumer/industrial market. It is essential to search both scientific and patent literature, so that extensive research efforts are not wasted by reinventing something that already exists.

(iii) It should be noted that any exercise in critical thinking will result in more questions than originally anticipated. This is illustrated in the flowchart above, where one will look for interesting products/reactions, and begin to think about the mechanism of the process. Such a "first-principle" understanding of the process is essential to increase yields of the material, and scale-up the technology for industrial applications.

(iv) After the new technology is protected by filing patents, publication in scientific literature is also important to foster continual investigations and new/improved materials. Top journals such as *Nature*, *Science*, *The Journal of the American Chemical Society*, *The Chemistry of Materials*, *Advanced Materials*, publish articles every week related to new developments in the most active areas of science. In recent years, the number of materials-related papers has increased exponentially. The continual compounding of knowledge fosters further development related to the synthesis, characterization, and modeling of materials. However, this may only take place as active researchers share their results with their worldwide colleagues.

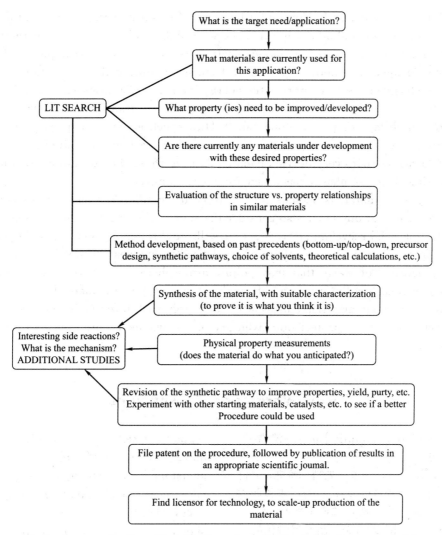

Fig. 3　An example of a critical thinking scheme for the design of a new material

Materials Sustainability

From the plastics that protect our electronic devices and encase our foods, to the metals that provide strength to buildings and various modes of transportation, we rely on the use of modern materials without giving much thought to their production. However, to ensure that our planet remains inhabitable for future generations, it is essential that we also understand the environmental impacts of materials production, use, and disposal. Such long-term planning is referred to as sustainable development, which entails balancing local and global efforts to meet the needs of the present without compromising the ability of future generations to meet their own needs. Accordingly, the selection of a material, processing technique, or end-use for a product should coincide with the three pillars of sustainability:
- Environmental—pollution prevention, natural resource use
- Social—better quality of life for all members of society
- Economic—fair distribution and efficient allocation of resources

Gauging the overall sustainability of a device or material is never an easy task, especially for the complex devices we encounter in today's society. For instance, consider the overall sustainability of a solar panel. You might be tempted to surmise that this would be consistent with the environmental pillar, but it's not as straightforward as you might think. Clearly, the replacement of fossil-fuel based electrical power stations with photovoltaic cells would result in lower greenhouse gas (GHG) emissions during their operation. However, how many GHGs were released during the energy-intensive processing steps required to convert sand to silicon? What about during the steps needed to transform the ultra-high purity silicon into a multilayered photovoltaic panel? How much energy is expended and environmental impacts generated by recycling solar panels after reaching their lifetime of use? It is important to realize that every device or material, even those that are more environmentally friendly during their use phase, has an environmental impact.

Not only must materials be chosen that are naturally abundant and easy to acquire, refine, and recycle, but one must also consider the source of electricity that is used during its use, production, and recycling efforts. As we will see throughout this book, the production of modern materials requires a plethora of specialized techniques, all involving inputs of energy and generation of waste that may pollute atmosphere, water, or land resources. To lower our global carbon footprint and offset the effects of global climate change, we need to incorporate sustainable materials, use sources of energy with fewer GHG emissions, and develop recycling efforts to protect our inventory of renewable resources and reduce environmental waste.[3]

New Words and Expressions

consumptive [kən'sʌmptiv] adj. 消费的，消耗性的
address [ə'dres] v. 演说，处理，演讲，对付
intangible [in'tændʒəb(ə)l] adj. 难以形容（或理解）的，无形的，触摸不到的
Neolithic [,ni:ə'liθik] adj. 新石器时代的
limestone ['laimstəun] n. 石灰岩，石灰石
utensil [ju:'tens(ə)l] n. 器皿，家什，器具
weaponry ['wepənri] n. 武器，兵器
Chalcolithic [,kælkə'liθik] 石器铜器并用时代，铜石并用时代
ornamental [,ɔ:(r)nə'ment(ə)l] adj. 装饰性的
malleability [,mæliə'biləti] n. （金属的）可锻性，柔顺性，可塑性，延展性
ore [ɔ:(r)] n. 矿，矿石，矿砂
malachite ['mæləkait] n. 孔雀石，碱式碳酸铜

asphalt ['æsfælt] n. 沥青，柏油
delve [delv] v. 钻研，掘
gemstone ['dʒem,stəun] n. 宝石
autonomic [,ɔ:tə'nɔmik] adj. 自治的，自主的，自发的
showroom ['ʃəuru:m] n. 商品陈列室，展厅
encase [in'keis] v. 把……装箱，包装
sustainability [sə,steinə'biləti] n. 可持续性
inhabitable [in'hæbitəb(ə)l] adj. 适于居住的
entail [in'teil] v. 需要，牵涉，使必要
coincide [,kəuin'said] v. 相符，同时发生
pillar ['pilə(r)] n. 支柱，柱子
gauge [geidʒ] n. 测量仪器；v. 估算，测量
surmise [sə'maiz] v. 猜测，估计，认为
photovoltaic [,fəutəuvɔl'teiik] adj. 光电（伏）的
plethora ['pleθərə] n. 过多，过量，过剩

Phrases

take for granted   认为……理所当然，视为当然

LEGO [ˈleɡəu] 乐高积木，乐高玩具
drug-delivery agent 药物缓释剂
integrated circuit 集成电路
implanted medical device 植入式医疗设备
Critical Thinking 批判性思维
flowchart 流程图；框图
first-principle 第一性原理，基本原理
coincide with 与……一致，与……相符，不谋而合，符合

Affixes

-ible，-able 表示"可……的，能……的"，或具有某种性质的；如 inflammable 易燃的，adaptable 可适应的，movable 可移动的，readable 可读的

auto- 表示"自己，自动"；如 autocriticsm 自我批评，autobiography 自传

photo- 表示"光"；如 photochemistry 光化学，photosynthesis 光合作用，photoelectric 光电的

multi- 表示"很多"；如 multilingual 多种语言的，multicultural 多种文化的，multimedia 多媒体的，multiple 多样的，多功能的，multiply 乘，繁殖

Notes

1. Many new architectures for advanced materials design are surely yet undiscovered, as scientists are now attempting to mimic the profound structural order existing in living creatures and plant life, which is evident as one delves into their microscopic and nanoscale regimes. 参考译文：当科学家们尝试模仿生物体内存在的重要结构次序时，很多先进材料设计的新构造方法还没被发现，随着人们的研究进入材料的微观和纳米领域，这是很显然的。

2. Within the next few decades, these materials could be applied to eliminate defective parts on an assembly line, and could even find use in structures that are at present impractical or impossible to repair, such as integrated circuits or implanted medical devices. 参考译文：在未来的几十年里，这些材料可以被用来消除一个装配线上的零件缺陷，甚至能用于目前不实际或不可修复的结构上，比如集成电路或植入式医疗设备。

3. To lower our global carbon footprint and offset the effects of global climate change, we need to incorporate sustainable materials, use sources of energy with fewer GHG emissions, and develop recycling efforts to protect our inventory of renewable resources and reduce environmental waste. 参考译文：为了降低全球的碳排放量和抵消全球气候变化的影响，我们需要实现可持续性材料、使用具有更少温室气体排放的能源、开发循环利用方法以保护我们的可再生资源和减少环境污染。

14. Materials Characterization

When a material is fabricated in the lab, how are we able to assess whether our method was successful? Depending on the nature of the material being investigated, a suite of techniques may be utilized to assess its structure and properties. Whereas some techniques are qualitative, such as providing an image of a surface, others yield quantitative information such as the relative concentrations of atoms that comprise the material. Recent technological advances have allowed materials scientists to accomplish something that was once thought to be impossible: to obtain actual two-dimensional/three-dimensional images of atomic positions in a solid, in real time. It should be noted that the sensitivity of quantitative techniques also continues to be improved, with techniques now being able to easily measure parts per trillion (ppt) concentrations of impurities in a bulk sample.

Here will focus on the most effective and widely used techniques available to characterize solid-state compounds. The primary objective is to provide a practical description of the methods used to characterize a broad range of materials. Rather than focusing on the theoretical aspects of each technique, which may be found in many other textbooks, our treatment will focus on method suitabilities and anticipated results.

Optical Microscopy

Of the many techniques available for the analysis of solid materials, perhaps the simplest is optical microscopy. Two modes of optical microscopy are typically employed, based on the measurement of transmitted or reflected light, from a transparent or opaque sample, respectively (Fig. 1). Often, a microscope is fitted with both modes, allowing one to analyze both types of samples. Most of the solid-state materials discussed thus far are nontransparent in their as-grown/as-deposited states. Further, it is usually difficult to prepare thin cross sections for transmission microscopy. Hence, materials scientists typically employ the reflection mode, also known as episcopic light differential interference contrast (DIC) microscopy. This technique is useful for imaging of a variety of reflective samples including minerals, metals, semiconductors, glasses, polymers, and composites. The semiconductor industry relies heavily on reflective DIC imaging for quality assessment of computer chip components.

Surface artifacts such as depressions and particulates create optical path differences in the reflected beam. Unlike the situation with transmitted light and semitransparent phase specimens, the image created in reflected light DIC can often be interpreted as a true three-dimensional representation of the surface geometry, provided a clear distinction can be realized between raised and lowered regions in the specimen.[1]

Electron Microscopy

Although optical microscopy may be extended into the nanoregime, other techniques must be used to clearly discern components below 100 nm. Indeed, the current "nanotechnology revolution" that we are experiencing would not have been possible if there were not suitable techniques in order to characterize nanomaterials.

There are two instruments that are used for electron imaging: transmission electron microscope (TEM) and scanning electron microscope (SEM). As the name implies, the transmission mode measures the intensity from an electron source after it has passed through a transparent sample (Fig. 2(a)). In contrast, SEM features the scanning of an electron beam over selected regions of an opaque sample (Fig. 2(b)).

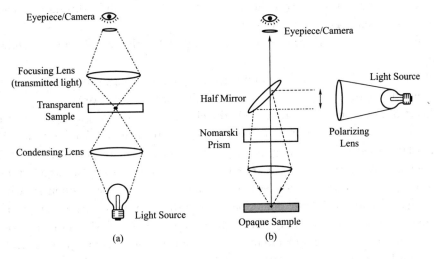

Fig. 1 Schematic of the components of (a) transmitted light optical microscope and (b) reflected light optical microscope

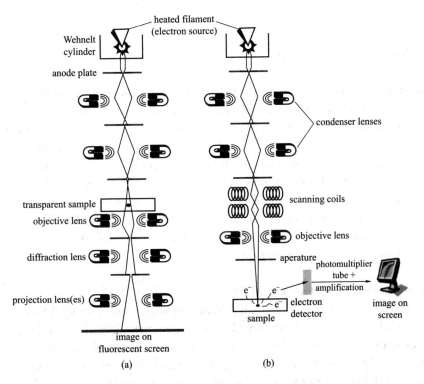

Fig. 2 Schematic of the major components of (a) transmission electron microscope (TEM) and (b) scanning electron microscope (SEM)

The basic principles that govern electron microscopy are analogous to optical microscopy. Whereas optical microscopes use light and optical lenses to illuminate and magnify the sample, electron microscopes utilize high-energy electrons and electromagnetic lenses. There are two types of lenses in electron microscopes (see below); TEM has an additional lens, the projector lens, which is used to project an amplified copy of the image onto a screen:

(ⅰ) Condenser-used to control the illumination of the sample through concentration of the electron beam generated from the source.

(ⅱ) Objective-used to magnify the sample (in TEM, the sample is inserted into the objective lens).

(ⅲ) Projector-used to project an amplified copy of the image onto a screen (photographic plate, computer screen, fluorescent screen, CCD camera/monitor).

The heart of any electron microscope is the electron source, or gun. In fact, the electron gun within microscopes is identical to that operating within modern televisions. Behind the TV monitor lays a cathode ray tube (CRT), containing a set of three tungsten filaments. The electrons generated from these filaments are accelerated toward an anode that is coated with phosphor particles, which emit either red, green, or blue light when struck with electrons. This light is focused onto individual pixels that comprise the monitor; if you look close at a television screen, you may notice the millions of tiny dots that comprise individual images. The picture we see on our monitors is a result of the electron guns being scanned sequentially from left to right in a fraction of a second, a process known as rastering. This is the exact mode that is operable in SEMs and scanning transmission electron microscopes (STEM), where the focused electron beam is allowed to scan across selected regions of a sample.

Transmission Electron Microscopy

A transmission electron microscope is analogous to a slide projector, with illumination from an electron beam rather than light. When an electron beam is impinged upon a sample, a black and white TEM image is formed from the passage of some electrons through the sample untouched, alongside the combination of interactions between other electrons and sample atoms (e.g., inelastic/elastic scattering, diffraction). If the undiffracted beam is selected to form the image, it is referred to as bright-field imaging; in contrast, selection of strongly diffracting regions of the sample, which would appear brighter than the transmitted beam, is known as dark-field imaging. It should be noted that electrons may also be absorbed by molecules containing large atoms, or by surface contamination (e.g., dust, grease). The absorption of a high density of electrons in a specific region will cause a buildup of heat, leading to sample destruction and poor image quality.

- **Nonimaging applications for TEM**

Due to the high spatial resolution and predictive scattering modes, TEMs are often employed to determine the three-dimensional crystal structure of solid-state materials. Thus, TEM may be considered as complementary to conventional crystallographic methods such as X-ray diffraction. When electrons (or X-rays) interact with a crystalline solid, comprising a regularly spaced three-dimensional array of atoms, the incoming beam is diffracted at specific angles, as predicted by the Bragg equation.

In addition to structural information from crystalline samples, quantitative analysis may also be carried out in tandem with TEM (and SEM) analyses. The interaction among high-energy electrons and sample atoms results in a variety of emissions (Fig. 3) that yield important information regarding the surface morphology and elemental composition of the sample.

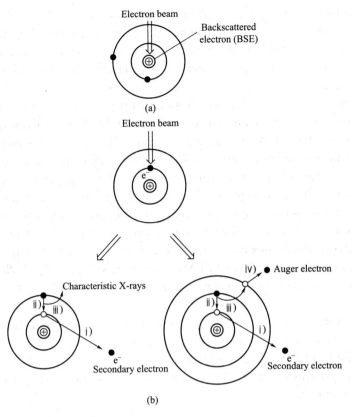

Fig. 3 Types of possible interactions between the primary electron beam and (a) the nucleus of surface atoms and (b) electrons of surface atoms comprising the sample. For simplicity, only K, L, and M shells (with no L and M subshells) are shown.

If the electron beam interacts with the nucleus of surface atoms, the electrons are elastically scattered. In this case, the trajectory of the electron changes with no change in the kinetic energy or velocity, a process known as backscattering. The number of backscattered electrons (BSE) that are produced from a given atom is proportional to the atomic number. That is, materials composed of heavy atoms will backscatter more electrons, resulting in brighter gray tones in the image relative to less dense materials. Hence, BSE produce an image that is related to material composition, providing both spatial and chemical information.

The primary electron beam may also be inelastically scattered through interaction with electrons from surface atoms. In this case, the collision displaces core electrons from filled shells (e.g., ns^2 (K) or np^6 (L)); the resulting atom is left as an energetic excited state, with a missing inner shell electron.[2] Since the energies of these secondary electrons are sufficiently low, they must be released from atoms near the surface in order to be detected. Electrons ejected from further within the sample are reabsorbed by the material before they reach the surface. As we will see in the next section (re SEM), as the intensity of the electron beam increases, or the density of the sample decreases, information from underlying portions of the sample may be obtained.

In order for the excited-state atom to return to its ground state (within a picosecond or so following secondary electron generation), the vacancy in the K shell is filled with an electron from shells farther from the nucleus (e.g., L shell). When such post-ionization atomic relaxation occurs, the excess energy may be released as either characteristic X-rays, or through nonradiative emission of an Auger electron (Fig. 3). Typically, a variety of X-rays are produced during atomic relaxation due to a cascading effect. By counting the number and energies of X-rays produced from electrons interacting the sample, it is possible to both qualitatively and quantitatively (using suitable standards) determine the chemical composition of the surface being analyzed.

There are two methods used to identify and quantify the X-ray emission: energy-dispersive X-ray spectroscopy (EDS), and wavelength-dispersive X-ray spectroscopy (WDS). In EDS, all of the characteristic X-ray energies reaching the detector are measured simultaneously. Hence, data acquisition is very rapid across the entire spectrum. By contrast, WDS measures a single wavelength at a time through use of a detecting crystal. As the characteristic X-rays are emitted from the sample, they are diffracted in a regular manner as discussed previously. Not only does this improve the resolution of WDS to an order of magnitude greater than EDS, but also improves the count rate and deconvolution of overlapping spectral peaks. Nevertheless, due to its simplicity and speed of analysis, EDS is the standard method for chemical analysis within TEM (and SEM) instruments. Typically, if WDS is desired, an instrument known as electron probe microanalyzer (EPMA) is utilized, often in tandem with SEM imaging.

In general, prerequisites for the best spatial resolution include a high-energy electron beam and extremely thin samples. Though the resolution limits of EDS/WDS will never match the imaging resolution, it is now possible to easily determine the elemental composition of individual nanoclusters in the 1-5nm size regime—as long as they are suitably dispersed with respect to one another.

- **Scanning transmission electron microscopy**

An imaging mode that merges both SEM and TEM is also possible on most modern TEM instruments. This method, referred to as scanning transmission electron microscopy (STEM), uses a LaB_6 source that produces a focused electron beam with a high current density and extremely small diameter. Instead of monitoring the transmitted electrons from a static beam as performed in standard TEM imaging, the beam within a STEM is scanned across the sample-analogous to SEM. Due to a higher beam intensity, thicker samples may be analyzed in a STEM; furthermore, staining is generally not necessary for low-Z elements due to a higher sensitivity to sample density/composition. In particular, it is possible to overlay the image with the EDS data-a technique known as elemental dot-mapping, widely used for SEM/EDS analysis.

A primary limitation of EDS and WDS is the inability to detect light (i. e., low-Z) elements. Since atomic energy levels are closely spaced for low-Z elements, the energies of the emitted X-rays will be relatively low. As a result, they are masked by the broad, continuous background spectrum (known as bremsstrahlung) that is most intense at energies below 1keV.

- **Electron energy-loss spectroscopy**

In order to increase the sensitivity toward the detection of light elements, a technique known as electron energy-loss spectroscopy (EELS) may be utilized. This method may be carried out within a (S) TEM, and consists of monitoring the loss in energy (due to inelastic scattering) of the beam electrons as they pass through the sample. Since it is more difficult to focus X-rays relative to electrons with appropriate lenses, the collection efficiency for EELS is *ca*. 80%—90%, relative to 5%—6% for EDS. This leads to a greater sensitivity and spatial resolution for EELS, with elemental mapping of *ca*. $\geqslant 2\text{Å}$. The intensity is greater than EDS for light elements since the signal generated by EELS represents the total sum of the number of X-ray photons and Auger electrons emitted from the sample. This technique is useful for elements with $Z > 1$, and like EDS, is amenable for elemental mapping of a sample surface.

In addition to detecting/quantifying particular elements in a sample, EELS also provides detailed elemental information such as the electronic structure, bonding, and nearest neighbor distribution of the atoms in the sample.

Scanning Electron Microscopy (SEM)

In contrast to TEM, with typical sample thicknesses in the range of 10nm—1μm, sample depths for SEM often extend into the 10—50mm range. As such, this technique is most often used to provide a topographic image of the sample surface. However, the electron beam is not confined to the top of the surface, but also interacts with lower depths of the sample. Consequently, SEM provides information regarding the species present at varying depths of the sample:

(ⅰ) Elastic scattering of electrons by atomic nuclei of the sample results in backscattered electrons (BSE)—useful for generating images based on Z-contrast.

(ⅱ) Inelastic scattering of electrons by sample atoms results in low-energy secondary electrons—useful for providing topographic information regarding the sample surface.

(ⅲ) Inelastic scattering of electrons by sample atoms results in X-ray generation (characteristic and Bremsstrahlung background X-rays) from lower sample depths—useful for chemical analysis of the bulk sample.

(ⅳ) Inelastic scattering results in Auger electrons emitted from sample atoms near the sample surface—useful for surface chemical analysis.

Photoelectron Spectroscopy

The photoelectric effect, first outlined by Einstein in the early 1900s, refers to the ejection of electrons from a surface due to photon impingement. However, it was not until the 1960s that this phenomenon was exploited for surface analysis-a technique referred to as X-ray photoelectron spectroscopy (XPS), or electron spectroscopy for chemical analysis (ESCA). This technique consists of the irradiation of a sample with monochromatic X-rays, which releases photoelectrons from the sample surface. Due to the short *mean free path* (MFP) of the photoelectrons in the solid, this technique provides compositional information from only the top 1—5nm of a sample.

Each atom in the sample has characteristic binding energies of their inner-shell electrons, referred to as absorption edges. In order to excite the electrons, the energy of the incident photons must be at least as large as the binding energy of the electrons. When this energy threshold is exceeded, a large absorption of energy takes place, followed by the release of photoelectrons with excess kinetic energy in order to relax the atom back to its stable ground state. Since the binding energy of an atom is altered by minute changes in its chemical environment (e.g., oxidation state, hybridization/geometry, *etc*.), XPS provides both elemental quantification and details regarding the chemical environment of the surface atoms.

In addition to using X-rays to irradiate a surface, ultraviolet light may be used as the source for photoelectron spectroscopy (PES). This technique, known as ultraviolet photoelectron spectroscopy (UPS), is usually carried out using two He lines (HeI at 21.2eV and HeII at 40.8eV), or a synchrotron source. This technique is often referred to as "soft PES," since the low photon energy is not sufficient to excite the inner-shell electrons, but rather results in photoelectron emission from valence band electrons—useful to characterize surface species based on their bonding motifs.[3] It should be noted that both UPS and XPS are often performed in tandem with an Ar^+ source, allowing for chemical analysis of the sample at depths of $\leq 1\mu m$ below the surface.

Scanning Probe Microscopy

The characterization techniques discussed thus far have involved the interaction of an incident beam of radiation (electrons, X-rays, ions, or light) with a sample. Subsequent scattering, transmission, and/or secondary emission is then used to provide an image of the sample, or delineate its chemical composition. This section will discuss a technique that does not involve irradiation, but rather features the scanning of a probe across a surface (hence, termed SPM). A tangible analogy of this technique is actually the precursor to modern CD players-the phonograph/record player. The heart of an antiquated phonograph is a cantilever-supported stylus that followed the grooves on the record. The mechanical movement of the stylus within the grooves resulted in an electrical response from a piezoelectric crystal, which was then converted into sound via the speaker system. Though this technology was abandoned for stereo applications in the 1980s, SPM represents a next-generation application for a stylus with a much sharper tip (radius of curvature of $<50nm$), to follow the surface topography of microscale and nanoscale materials. The resolution of SPM is among the best of all methods to date, with the possibility of atomic scale manipulation/imaging.

Analogous to record players, a SPM tip is supported by a flexible cantilever. During analysis, the tip is slowly rastered across the surface of a material—either a few Angstroms away from the surface (noncontact mode), or in contact with the sample (contact mode). There are two primary forms of SPM:

(i) Scanning tunneling microscopy (STM)—set the precedent for SPM in the early 1980s. The tip is held a few Angstroms from the sample surface during scans.

(ii) Atomic force microscopy (AFM)—the tip may interact with the sample surface through either contact or noncontact modes.

Both types of SPM are most often used to provide an image of the surface topography. Though both techniques are frequently carried out under ambient temperatures/pressures, or even in liquids, they may also be performed in an UHV chamber (*ca*. 10^{-11} Torr) in order to prevent sample contamination, prevent oxidation of the surface, or monitor the deposition of sputtered thin films in real time.[4] As a STM tip is scanned across the sample, a quantum mechanical tunneling current is established between the sample surface and a sharpened W or Pt/Ir tip (Fig. 4, top). The magnitude of the current is dependent on the distance between the tip and the surface, as well as the local density of states (DOS) of the surface. Accordingly, STM is typically performed on conductive and semiconductive surfaces. During topographic imaging, a feedback loop is established to maintain a constant current through varying the distance between the tip and surface ("constant current mode"). In this respect, STM is able to provide real-time, three-dimensional images of the surface with atomic resolution. The use of STM for nanofabrication also represents an important application that is

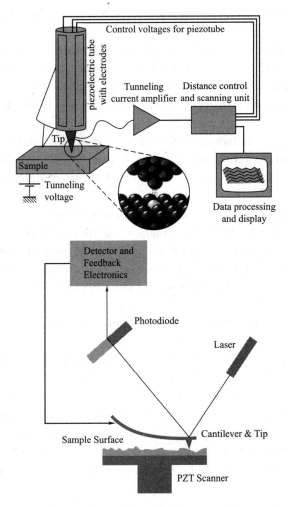

Fig. 4 Illustrations of STM (top) and AFM (bottom)

of increasing interest.

Rather than monitoring electronic tunneling phenomena, AFM measures the forces between the tip and surface, which depends on the nature of the sample, the probe tip, and the distance between them (Fig. 4, bottom). The deflection of the tip in response to surface-tip interfacial forces is recorded by using a laser focused on top of the Si or SiN cantilever, and reflected onto photodetectors. The signal emanating from the photodetector is used to generate a surface topographic map, or the direct measurement of surface intermolecular forces. As with STM, a feedback loop is present in the system, which controls the distance between the tip and sample *via* an electrical current sent to piezoelectric transducers. Such "constant force" scanning is used most frequently, since "constant-height" scanning could result in collisional damage between the tip and surface.

Bulk Characterization Techniques

The majority of characterization techniques discussed thus far have been surface-related, with some capable of analyzing sub-surface depths through *in situ* ion etching. This final section will focus briefly on a selection of common bulk techniques that may be used to characterize as-synthesized materials such as polymers, ceramics, etc. In particular, these additional resources, as well as countless others online, will highlight solid-state characterization techniques such as:

(ⅰ) Solid-state NMR—chemical environment of NMR-active nuclei; used to obtain physical, chemical, electronic, and structural information about constituent molecules.

(ⅱ) Raman spectroscopy—vibration, stretching, and bending of sample molecules (for the bulk sample, as well as adsorbed surface species); assessing defects in carbon nanotubes.

(ⅲ) IR spectroscopy (including surface-characterization modes such as attenuated total reflectance (ATR), diffuse reflectance infrared Fourier transform spectroscopy (DRIFT), and reflection absorption infrared spectroscopy (RAIRS))—complementary to Raman spectroscopy.

(ⅳ) UV-Vis spectroscopy—functional group information; sizes of nanoparticles.

(ⅴ) Mass spectrometry (MS)—information regarding isotopes, mass, and structure.

(ⅵ) BET surface area analysis—pore size and surface area of powders.

(ⅶ) Dynamic light scattering (DLS) and Coulter counting—particle size.

(ⅷ) Mössbauer spectroscopy—chemical environment of ^{57}Fe, ^{129}I, ^{119}Sn, or ^{121}Sb atoms in a sample.

(ⅸ) Single-crystal and powder X-ray diffraction—three-dimensional arrangement of atoms/ions/molecules.

A primary method that is used to characterize the thermal properties of a bulk material is thermogravimetric analysis (TGA). This method provides detailed information regarding the thermal stability and decomposition pathway of a material (e.g., stepwise loss of ligands for an organometallic compound), as well as structural information for complex composites. The operating principle of TGA is very simple—the solid is placed in a tiny microbalance pan and heated according to preset ramping conditions. The controlled thermolysis of the compound may be carried out in vacuo, or in the presence of a carrier gas such as O_2, N_2, or Ar.

New Words and Expressions

transparent [træns'pærənt] adj. 透明的，清澈的，易识破的
opaque [əu'peik] adj. 不透明的，不透光的
episcopic 反射的
artifact ['ɑː(r)tiˌfækt] n. 人工制品，人为现象
specimen ['spesəmin] n. 标本，样品，样本
discern [di'sə:(r)n] v. 识别，辨别，了解
projector [prə'dʒektə(r)] n. 投影仪，投影器
condenser [kən'densə(r)] n. 冷凝器，聚光镜
objective [əb'dʒektiv] n. 目标，目的，物镜
tungsten ['tʌŋstən] n. 钨，钨丝灯，钨灯
filament ['filəmənt] n. 细丝，灯丝

raster ['ræstə] n. 光栅，扫描 v. 扫描
rastering 光栅全方位模式，光栅扫描化
impinge [im'pindʒ] v. 侵犯，冲击，撞击
spatial ['speiʃ(ə)l] adj. 空间的
complementary [ˌkɔmpli'ment(ə)ri] adj. 互补的，补充的，相互补足的
crystallographic [ˌkristlə'ɡræfik] adj. 结晶的，结晶学的，晶体学的
tandem ['tændəm] n. 双人自行车，串联
morphology [mɔ:(r)'fɔlədʒi] n. 形态学，形态
backscattering 后向散射
displace [dis'pleis] v. 替换，迫使（某人）离开家园，移动
cascade [kæ'skeid] v. 串联，奔流

deconvolution [di:kɔnvəˈlu:ʃən] n. 去卷积
prerequisite [priːˈrekwəzit] n. 前提，必备条件；adj. 必须先具备的，先决条件的
stain [stein] v. 玷污，给……染色（或着色）
bremsstrahlung [ˈbremˌʃtrɑːlən] n. 韧致辐射
amenable [əˈmiːnəb(ə)l] adj. 适于的，顺从的，顺服的，经得起检验的
topographic [ˌtɔpəˈɡræfik] adj. 地形的
monochromatic [ˌmɔnəkrəˈmætik] adj. 单色光的
incident [ˈinsid(ə)nt] adj. 附带的，入射的
threshold [ˈθreʃˌhəuld] n. 阈值，临界值
hybridization [ˌhaibridaiˈzeiʃ(ə)n] n. 杂交，杂化，杂合反应
synchrotron [ˈsiŋkrəˌtrɔn] n. 同步辐射
motif [məuˈtiːf] n. 主题，要点，特色
delineate [diˈlinieit] v. 描述，描绘，叙述

phonograph [ˈfəunəɡræf] n. 留声机，唱机
cantilever [ˈkæntiˌliːvə(r)] n. 悬臂，悬臂梁
stylus [ˈstailəs] n. （唱机的）唱针，触针
groove [ɡruːv] n. 槽，沟，凹槽，沟槽
piezoelectric [paiˌizəuiˈlektrik] adj. 压电的
stereo [ˈsteriəu] adj. 立体（声）的
angstrom [ˈæŋstrəm] n. 埃（长度单位，等于 10^{-10} 米）
ambient [ˈæmbiənt] adj. 周围环境的，周围的
feedback [ˈfiːdbæk] n. 反馈，反馈意见
deflection [diˈflekʃ(ə)n] n. 偏斜，偏角，偏转
emanate [ˈeməneit] v. 产生，表现，发出
photodetector [fəutəudiˈtektə] n. 光电探测器，光检测器，光探测器
transducer [trænzˈdjuːsə(r)] n. 变换器，传感器，转换器

Phrases

optical microscopy　光学显微术，光学显微法
episcopic light differential interference contrast microscopy　反射光微分干涉差显微镜
transmission electron microscope (TEM)　透射电镜
scanning electron microscope (SEM)　扫描电镜
projector lens　投影透镜，投影镜
photographic plate　感光板，照相底片
scanning transmission electron microscope (STEM)　扫描透射电镜
in tandem with　同……合作，协同合作
secondary electron　二次电子
Auger electron　俄歇电子
cascading effect　层叠效应，级联效应
energy-dispersive X-ray spectroscopy　能量色散 X 射线谱
wavelength-dispersive X-ray spectroscopy　波长色散 X 射线谱
electron probe microanalyzer　电子探针显微分析仪
elemental dot-mapping　元素点映射

electron energy-loss spectroscopy (EELS)　电子能量损失谱
X-ray photoelectron spectroscopy (XPS)　X 射线光电子谱
electron spectroscopy for chemical analysis　化学分析电子光谱法
free mean path (FMP)　平均自由程
absorption edge　吸收限，吸收界限
photoelectron spectroscopy (PES)　光电子谱
ultraviolet photoelectron spectroscopy (UPS)　紫外光电子谱
scanning probe microscopy (SPM)　扫描探针显微镜，扫描探针显微术
radius of curvature　曲率半径
quantum mechanical tunneling　量子力学隧道效应
feedback loop　反馈回路，反馈电路
attenuated total reflectance　衰减全反射
diffuse reflectance　漫反射式
dynamic light scattering (DLS)　动态光散射
Coulter counting　库尔特计数法
Mössbauer spectroscopy　穆斯堡尔谱

thermogravimetric analysis (TGA) 热重分析

ramping condition 斜坡条件

in vacuo ['vækjuəu] 在真空中

Notes

1. Unlike the situation with transmitted light and semitransparent phase specimens, the image created in reflected light DIC can often be interpreted as a true three-dimensional representation of the surface geometry, provided a clear distinction can be realized between raised and lowered regions in the specimen. 参考译文：不同于透射光和半透明样品的情形，假如样品中的高区域和低区域之间能形成明显的差别，反射光微分干涉光差成像常常可反映出表面结构的真实三维形貌。

2. In this case, the collision displaces core electrons from filled shells (e.g., ns^2(K) or np^6(L)); the resulting atom is left as an energetic excited state, with a missing inner shell electron. 参考译文：这种情况下，碰撞使内层电子脱离满壳层（比如 K 壳层 ns^2 或 L 壳层 np^6），导致原子处于能量激发态并失去一个内层电子。

3. This technique is often referred to as "soft PES". since the low photon energy is not sufficient to excite the inner-shell electrons, but rather results in photoelectron emission from valence band electrons-useful to characterize surface species based on their bonding motifs. 参考译文：这种技术通常被称为"软光电子谱"，因为低光子能量不足以激发内壳层电子，而会导致价带电子的光电子发射，基于键合特点可对表面物种进行表征。

4. Though both techniques are frequently carried out under ambient temperatures/pressures, or even in liquids, they may also be performed in an UHV chamber ($ca.$ 10^{-11} Torr) in order to prevent sample contamination, prevent oxidation of the surface, or monitor the deposition of sputtered thin films in real time. 参考译文：尽管这两种技术经常是在环境温度或压力下，甚至在液体中使用，但也可以在高真空（UHV, ultra high vacuum）（约 10^{-11} 托，Torr：压强单位，1Torr 即 1mmHg）腔中进行，以防止样品污染和表面氧化，或实时监测溅射薄膜的沉积。

15. Nanotechnology

It has been said that a nanometer is "a magical point on the length scale, for this is the point where the smallest man-made devices meet the atoms and molecules of the natural world."[1]

Indeed, "nanotechnology mania" is sweeping through essentially all fields of science and engineering, and the public is becoming aware of the quote of the chemist and Nobel Laureate, Richard Smalley: "Just wait—the next century is going to be incredible. We are about to be able to build things that work on the smallest possible length scales, atom by atom. These little nanothings will revolutionize our industries and our lives."

In a recent report of the National Science Foundation to the President's Office of Science and Technology Policy it was stated that "Nanoscience and technology will change the nature of almost every human-made object in the next century."[2]

So what are these "nanothings" that are going to change our lives? Perhaps the best way to begin to convey the possibilities is to list topical areas that nanotechnology promises to affect.

Pharmacy

It may be possible to create biomolecules that carry out "pharmacy in a cell", that could release cancer-fighting nanoparticles or chemicals in response to a distress signal from an afflicted cell.[3]

Therapeutic Drugs

It is now possible to produce new solid state medicines by simply producing them in nanoparticle form. The high surface areas of these small particles allow them to be solubilized into the bloodstream where normal microparticles or larger particles cannot. Since over 50% of new drug formulations are never brought to market because of solubility problems, this simple transformation into a nano-form opens up broad new possibilities for drug synthesis and utilization.

Tagging of DNA and DNA Chips

Nanoparticle assay of DNA has been possible by coating gold nanoparticles with DNA strands. When these are exposed to complementary DNA, binding (hybridization) occurs, and this causes the colloidal gold particles to aggregate, and as a result a color change takes place.

Microarrays to detect and help identify DNA samples have been built by creating devices with up to 100000 different known DNA sequences. When the unknown target DNA sequences match with any of the DNA chip arrays, then binding (hybridization) occurs and the unknown sequence is identified by its position on the array.

Information Storage

Ultrafine dye particles often yield higher quality inks in terms of color, coverage, and colorfastness. Also, "nanopens" (atomic force microscope tips) can write letters with features as small as 5nm.

Actually, nanoparticles have already found their way into modern audio and videotapes and disks, which are dependent on magnetic and optical properties of fine particles. Further advances will be made with smaller and smaller sizes and with control of magnetic coercivity and optical absorption, so that much denser storage media should be possible.

Refrigeration

On a small scale it has been demonstrated that an entropic advantage can be gained in magnetic particle field reversal. Thus, upon application of a magnetic field, the entropy of a magnetic species changes, and if adiabatic conditions are maintained, the application of the field will result in a temperature change. This ΔT is the magnetocaloric effect, and the magnitude of this effect depends on the size of the magnetic moment, heat capacity, and temperature dependence of the magnetization. If nanoparticles with large magnetic moments and adequate coercivity can be obtained, the magnetocaloric effect may allow refrigeration on a practical scale. The promise of magnetic nanoparticle refrigerators, with no need for refrigeration fluids (Freons, HFC, etc.), has enticed many researchers, and success would mean tremendous benefits for society and the environment.

Chemical/Optical Computers

Organized two-dimensional or three-dimensional arrays of metal or semiconductor nanoparticles exhibit special optical and magnetic properties. These materials hold promise in numerous applications in the electronics industry, including optical computers.

Improved Ceramics and Insulators

The compression of nanoscale ceramic particles yields more flexible solid objects, apparently because of the multitude of grain boundaries that exist. After further development of compression techniques, so that highly densified nonporous materials can be prepared, these new materials may find uses as replacements for metals in many applications.

Harder Metals

Nanoparticulate metals when compressed into solid objects exhibit unusual surface hardness, sometimes as high as five times that of the normal microcrystalline metal.

Film Precursors

Similar to their use in inks, nonaqueous metallic colloidal solutions have proven useful as precursors for thin metallic film formation when used as spray paint. In particular, gold coating on silver artifacts has been accomplished with gold-acetone colloids.

Environmental/Green Chemistry

Solar Cells. Semiconductor nanoparticles, with size-tunable bandgaps, hold the potential for more efficient solar cells for both photovoltaics (electricity production) and water splitting (hydrogen production).

Remediation. Photoexcitation of fine particles of semiconductors leads to electron-hole pairs that are useful for both oxidation and reduction of pollutants, for use in decontaminating water.[4]

Water Purification. Reactive metal fine powders (Fe, Zn) show high reactivity toward chlorocarbons in an aqueous environment. These results have led to the successful implementation of porous metal powder-sand membranes for groundwater decontamination.

Destructive Adsorbents. Nanoparticulate metal oxides exhibit high intrinsic surface reactivities and high surface areas, and strongly chemisorb acidic gases and polar organics. Since dissociative chemisorption is usually observed, these new materials have been dubbed "destructive adsorbents", and are finding use in anti-chemical/biological warfare, in air purification, and as an alternative to incineration of toxic substances.[5]

Catalysts

Successful catalytic processes developed over the last six decades have led to a vital industry that contributes to the economy at least 20% of the GDP.

What is significant in the context of nanostructural materials in chemistry is that heterogeneous catalysis is dependent on nanoparticles of metals, and research on the effect of particle size (percent dispersion as a measure of the fraction of metal atoms on the surface and thus available to incoming reactants) and shape (crystal faces, edges, corners, defects that lead to enhanced surface reactivity) has been and continues to be a vigorous field.

Sensors

Porous aggregates of semiconductor nanoparticles can be prepared by low-load compression. These materials maintain their high surface areas, and when they undergo adsorption of various gases, their electrical conductivity changes. Since more of the gas to be detected (such as sulfur dioxide) is adsorbed per unit mass compared with normal compressed powders, the electrical changes are more pronounced. Thus, the use of nanoparticles yields a considerable advantage in sensor technology.

Nanostructured Electrodes

Nanoscale metal crystallites can be grown by rapid electrodeposition due to very high nucleation rates and thereby reduces crystallite (grain) growth.[6] Magnetic metals such as iron can then form dense magnetic solids with soft magnetic properties (low coercivity and high saturation magnetization). These materials are useful for transformers.

Improved Polymers

There are almost magical effects produced when nanopowders are add to polymer matrices. The nanopowders can be in the form of fine particles, needlelike structures, or platelets. There is a reinforcing effect such that strength of the composite is greatly increased.

The mechanism by which this reinforcement takes place is poorly understood at present. However, with further work and better understanding, the potential outcomes of improved polymers and plastics are easy to imagine. Stronger, lighter materials, wear-resistant tires, tougher coatings, replacements for body parts, flame-retardant plastics, replacements for metals, and more can be imagined.

Self-cleaning and Unusual Coloring in Paints

It has been demonstrated that when paints are doped with light-absorbing nanoparticles, such as TiO_2, the paints are self-cleaning.[7] The mechanism by which this happens is related to photooxidation of contaminants by TiO_2 in water discussed earlier. Organic greasy materials that adhere to paint can be oxidized by the electron-hole pair formed when TiO_2 nanoparticles absorb sunlight. Thus, the organic materials are cleaned off the paint film. It is perhaps surprising that the paint itself is not attacked by this powerful oxidation/reduction couple, and it may be found that such paints are not as long-lived as those that are not doped with TiO_2 nanoparticles.

Another interesting development is the use of gold nanoparticles to give paints a beautiful metallic reddish color, due to the special optical properties of such particles.

Better Batteries

Nanostructural materials in lithium ion batteries have proven to be very advantageous. For example, researchers at Fuji found that by placing nanocrystalline tin (7~10nm) within an amorphous glass-forming matrix yielded nanocrystalline islands of tin enclosed by an amorphous oxide network. Electrical conductivity can be maintained within such an electrode. The advantage of such a nanostructural material is that the rather open structure of the glass helps to accommodate strain associated with the volume expansion during insertion and removal of lithium from tin. Also, it is believed that the nanocrystalline nature of the tin prevents formation of bulk phases of Li-Sn alloys, which are harmful to the battery.

Other advantages have been gleaned from nanostructural materials, such as the rapid reaction of Li_2CO_3 and NiO to form a desired mixed oxide. Dragieva and coworkers have prepared a series of nickel-metal-hydride (Ni-M-H) batteries through the preparation of nickel nanoparticles by borohydride reduction in water.

In general, the ability to prepare metallic nanocrystals that can be consolidated into high-surface-area electrodes has certain inherent advantages, and further progress is sure to come.

Improved National Security

The use of high-surface-area reactive nanoparticles as destructive adsorbents for decontamination of chemical and biological warfare agents has proven quite effective.

Sensors for toxic airborne and waterborne materials are also possible through the unique adsorbent properties of consolidated nanocrystals. Indeed, there appear to be numerous areas where national security can be improved through advances in nanotechnology in electronics, optics, catalysts, and adsorbents.

Summary

It is quite apparent that there are innumerable potential benefits for society, the environment, and the world at large. Some of them have been briefly described, but the list is longer still.

New Words and Expressions

mania ['meinjə,-niə] n. 狂热，热衷
quote [kwəut] n. 引用语，名言
convey [kən'vei] v. 通知，表达，传达
pharmacy ['fɑːməsi] n. 药房，制药业
distress [di'stres] n. 痛苦，遇险，悲伤
afflict [ə'flikt] v. 使痛苦，折磨
therapeutic [ˌθerə'pjuːtik] adj. 治疗的，医疗的，治病的

strand [strænd] n. （绳子的）股，绞，海滨
complementary [ˌkɔmpliˈment(ə)ri] adj. 互补的；补充的
hybridization [ˌhaibridaiˈzeiʃən] n. 杂化（作用），杂交
colloidal [kəˈlɔidl] adj. 胶状的，胶体的
aggregate [ˈægrigeit] n. 合计，总计，集合体；v. 聚集，集合，合计
videotape [ˈvidiəuteip] n. 录像带
coercivity [kəuəːˈsiviti] n. 矫顽磁性，矫顽（磁）力
refrigeration [riˌfridʒəˈreiʃən] n. 冷藏，制冷，冷却
adiabatic [ˌædiəˈbætik] adj. 绝热的，不传热的
magnetocaloric [mægˈnitəukəˈlɔrik] adj. 磁（致）热的
Freon [ˈfriːɔn] n. 氟里昂
precursor [pri(ː)ˈkəːsə] n. 前驱物，前身，先驱
bandgap [ˈbændgæp] n. 能带隙
photovoltaics [ˌfəutə(u)vɔlˈteiiks] n. 光生伏打，太阳能光电板
remediation [riˌmiːdiˈeiʃən] n. 补救，纠正，修复
decontaminate [diːkənˈtæmineit] v. 净化，排除污染
chlorocarbon [ˌklɔːrəˈkɑːbən] n. 氯代烃，氯碳化合物
intrinsic [inˈtrinsik] adj. 固有的，本身的，内在的
chemisorb [ˈkemiˌsɔːb] v. 使用化学方法吸附，化学吸收
dissociative [diˈsəuʃiətiv] adj. 分离的，解离的
dub [dʌb] v. 把……戏称为，给……起绰号
incineration [inˌsinəˈreiʃ(ə)n] n. 焚毁，焚烧
nucleation [ˌnjuːkliˈeiʃən] n. 成核现象，晶核形成
platelet [ˈpleitlit] n. 小片，薄片
retardant [riˈtɑdənt] n. 延缓剂，阻止剂
contaminant [kənˈtæminənt] n. 致污物，污染物
lithium [ˈliθiəm] n. 锂（Li）
amorphous [əˈmɔː(r)fəs] adj. 无定形的，非晶质的
borohydride [ˌbɔːrəˈhaidraid] n. 硼氢化物
consolidate [kənˈsɔlideit] v. 合并，使巩固，强化
inherent [inˈhiərənt] adj. 固有的，内在的，与生俱来的

Phrases

flame-retardant 阻燃剂
sweep through… 席卷……
be dependent on… 依靠，依赖
it is believed that… 人们相信……

Affixes

bio- [ˈbaiəu] 表示"生命，生物"；如 biomolecule 生物分子，biology 生物学
de- 表示"去掉，相反"；如：decontaminate 净化，desalt 除去盐分，decompose 分解，decolour 使退色
-borne [bɔː(r)n] 表示"由……传播的"；如 airborne 空气传播的，waterborne 水传播的，水运的，mosquito-borne 蚊传播的

Notes

1. It has been said that a nanometer is "a magical point on the length scale, for this is the point where the smallest man-made devices meet the atoms and molecules of the natural world". 形式主语"it"代表的是"that"引导的从句。参考译文：一纳米被认为是"长度单位

上的一个神奇点,因为这是最小的人造设备能达到的自然界中原子和分子的尺度。"

2. In a recent report of the National Science Foundation to the President's Office of Science and Technology Policy it was stated that "Nanoscience and technology will change the nature of almost every human-made object in the next century." 参考译文:国家科学基金会在最近提交给总统科技政策办公室的一份报告中认为,"纳米科技将在未来一个世纪里改变几乎所有人造物体的性能。"

3. It may be possible to create biomolecules that carry out "pharmacy in a cell", that could release cancer-fighting nanoparticles or chemicals in response to a distress signal from an afflicted cell. 形式主语"it"指"create biomolecules","that carry..."和"that could..."两个并列从句用来修饰"biomolecules"。参考译文:制造实现"细胞中药店"的生物分子将成为可能,这些生物分子对来自受折磨细胞的病变信号做出响应,会释放出抗癌纳米颗粒或化学药品。

4. Photoexcitation of fine particles of semiconductors leads to electron-hole pairs that are useful for both oxidation and reduction of pollutants, for use in decontaminating water. "that"引导的从句修饰"electron-hole pairs"。参考译文:对半导体微粒进行光激发会形成电子空穴对,这些电子空穴可用于污染物的氧化还原反应以及用于净化水。

5. Since dissociative chemisorption is usually observed, these new materials have been dubbed "destructive adsorbents", and are finding use in anti-chemical/biological warfare, in air purification, and as an alternative to incineration of toxic substances. "these new materials"指的是上句中的"Nanoparticulate metal oxides"。参考译文:由于(金属氧化物纳米微粒的)解离化学吸附随处可见,这些新材料被称作"破坏性吸附剂",它们在反化学/生物战争、空气净化领域大有可为,也是一种替代有毒物质焚化处理的方法。

6. Nanoscale metal crystallites can be grown by rapid electrodeposition due to very high nucleation rates and thereby reduces crystallite (grain) growth. 参考译文:纳米级金属微晶可以用快速电沉积制得,因为该法的成核速度极快,从而减少了(大颗粒)微晶的生长。

7. It has been demonstrated that when paints are doped with light-absorbing nanoparticles, such as TiO_2, the paints are self-cleaning. 参考译文:已经证实,当在油漆中掺入能进行光吸收的纳米微粒,比如 TiO_2,该油漆就能自清洁。

16. Ceramic

The word ceramic, derives its name from the Greek *keramos*, meaning "pottery", which in turn is derived from an older Sanskrit root, meaning "to burn". Thus the word was used to refer to a product obtained through the action of fire upon earthy materials.

Ceramics make up one of three large classes of solid materials. The other material classes include metals and polymers. The combination of two or more of these materials together to produce a new material whose properties would not be attainable by conventional means is called a composite. [1]

Ceramics can be defined as inorganic, non-metallic materials that are typically produced using clays and other minerals from the earth or chemically processed powders. [2] Ceramics are typically crystalline in nature and are compounds formed between metallic and non-metallic elements such as aluminium and oxygen (Al_2O_3), silicon and nitrogen (Si_3N_4) and silicon and carbon (SiC). Glass is often considered a subset of ceramics. Glass is somewhat different from ceramics in that it is amorphous, or has no long range crystalline order.

Most people, when they hear the word ceramics, think of art, dinnerware, pottery, tiles, brick and toilets. The above mentioned products are commonly referred to as traditional or silicate-based ceramics. While these traditional products have been, and continue to be, important to society, a new class of ceramics has emerged that most people are unaware of. These advanced or technical ceramics are being used for applications such as space shuttle tile, engine components, artificial bones and teeth, computers and other electronic components, and cutting tools. [3]

History and Impact on Society

Archaeologists have uncovered human-made ceramics that date back to at least 24000 BC. These ceramics were made of animal fat and bone mixed with bone ash and a fine clay-like material. The first use of functional pottery vessels is thought to be in 9000 BC. These vessels were most likely used to hold and store grain and other foods. Ancient glass manufacture is thought to be closely related to pottery making, which flourished in Upper Egypt about 8000 BC. It is thought that it was not until 1500 BC that glass was produced independently of ceramics and fashioned into separate items.

Since these ancient times, the technology and applications of ceramics (including glass) has steadily increased. Lets us look at a few examples of the importance of ceramics in our lives.

Modern iron and steel and non-ferrous metal production would not be possible without the use of sophisticated refractory materials that are used to line high temperature furnaces and troughs. Refractory ceramics are enabling materials for other industries as well. The chemical, petroleum, energy conversion, glass and other ceramic industries all rely on refractory materials.

Much of the construction industry depends on the use of ceramic materials. This includes brick, cement, tile, and glass.

An important invention that changed the lives of millions of people was the incandescent light bulb. This important invention by Thomas Edison in 1879 would not be possible without the use of glass. Glass's properties of hardness, transparency, and its ability to withstand high temperatures and hold a vacuum at the same time made the light bulb a reality.

The electronic industry would not exist without ceramics. Ceramics can be excellent insulators, semiconductors, superconductors, and magnets. It's hard to imagine not having mobile phones, computers, television, and other consumer electronic products. Ceramic spark plugs, which are electrical insulators, have had a large impact on society. They were first invented in 1860 to ignite fuel for internal combustion engines and are still being used for this purpose today. Applications include automobiles, boat engines, and the like. High voltage insulators make it possible to safely carry electricity to houses and businesses.

Optic fibres have provided a technological breakthrough in the area of telecommunications. Information that was once carried electrically through hundreds of copper wires is now being carried through high-quality transparent silica (glass) fibres. Using this technology has increased the speed and volume of information that can be carried by orders of magnitude over that which is possible using copper cable. The reliability of the transmitted information is also greatly improved with optic fibres. In addition to these benefits, the negative effects of copper mining on the environment are reduced with the use of silica fibres.

Ceramics play an important role in addressing various environmental needs. Ceramics help decrease pollution, capture toxic materials and encapsulate nuclear waste. Today's catalytic converters in vehicles are made of cellular ceramics and help convert toxic hydrocarbons and carbon monoxide gases into non-toxic carbon dioxide and water. Advanced ceramic components are starting to be used in diesel and automotive engines. Ceramics' light weight and high-temperature and wear resistant properties results in more efficient combustion and significant fuel savings.

Reusable, lightweight ceramic tile make NASA's space shuttle program possible. These thermal barrier tile protect the astronauts and the shuttle's aluminium frame from the extreme temperatures (up to approximately 1600℃) encountered upon re-entry into the earth's atmosphere. While the list of examples could go on and on, I think you can get the picture of how important ceramics has been, and will continue to be to humankind.

Advanced Ceramics

Advanced ceramics, also known as engineering or technical ceramics, refer to materials which exhibit superior mechanical properties, corrosion/oxidation resistance, and thermal, electrical, optical or magnetic properties.[4]

Advanced ceramics are generally broken down into the following segments: structural ceramics, electrical and electronic ceramics, ceramics coatings, chemical processing and environmental ceramics.

Structural ceramics are useful in applications such as industrial wear parts, bioceramics, cutting tools, and engine components. The types of electronic ceramics, which have the largest share of the advanced ceramic market includes capacitors, insulators, substrates, integrated circuits packages, piezoelectrics, magnets and superconductors. Ceramic coatings find application in engine components, cutting tools, and industrial wear parts. The applications under chemical processing and environmental ceramics include filters, membranes, catalysts, and catalyst supports.

The beginning of the advanced ceramics era has been said to have started approximately 50 years ago with the expanding use of chemically prepared powders. Ceramic powders are a necessary ingredient for most advanced ceramics. These include oxides, nitrides, carbides, and borides.

Progress will continue in the area of ceramic matrix composites (CMCs). CMCs are attracting increasing attention due to the broader diversity of, and improvements in, the properties they can often provide. The major push for CMCs has been driven by the potential applications in heat engines. CMCs in this application would provide greater fuel efficiency and reduced exhaust emissions.

NASA Lewis Research Centre and the two leading aircraft engine manufacturers are developing the technology for an environmentally safe propulsion system for a High Speed Civil Transport. Because of this type of supersonic airliner's speed, a trip from Los Angeles to Tokyo, for example, would take just over 4 hours instead of 10 hours on subsonic aeroplanes. CMCs are the current material of choice for the combustor and acoustic liners for the proposed low NO_x propulsion system.

What the Future May Hold for Advanced Ceramics

Imagine a car that has a fuel efficiency of 80 mpg, a range of 500 miles, emits no pollutants, and runs on many different fuels such as gasoline, diesel, kerosene, or alcohol. Car manufacturer hopes to have a family car with this technology available by 2010, and the cost will be the same as that of a standard petrol-engined car. This type of vehicle is made possible by fuel cell technology. Fuel cells work like batteries, but are better because they won't run down. These fuels cell would not be possible however if not with the use of ceramic materials.

Another interesting area of research is the so called "smart" ceramics. These ceramic systems provide the necessary life functions of sensing, actuating, control, and intelligence. Some examples of smart systems include: medical systems that treat diabetes with blood sugar sensors and insulin-delivery pumps; water purification systems that sense and remove toxic pollutants; and houses that have electrochromic windows that control the flow of heat and light in response to weather changes and human activity. [5] A major ski manufacturer now offers a "smart" ski that makes use of ceramics piezoelectric properties. When skiing at high speeds, skis tend to vibrate, lessening the contact area between the ski edge and snow surface. This results in reduced stability and control and decreases the skiers speed. The piezoceramic embedded in the ski converts the unwanted vibrations into electrical energy, thus keeping the skis on the snow.

Ceramic or high-temperature superconductors are now being developed for commercial applications and appear to be a sure bet to enter more commercial markets over the next few years. Electric wires made from these materials carry electricity with little or no resistance losses. In the utility power industry, these wires can be used to produce super efficient coils, magnets, conductors, and machines and power components. The use of high temperature superconductors in these applications could save billions of dollars in energy costs and help the environment at the same time.

Circuits using high-temperature superconducting materials could boost the processing speed of computers, reduce resistance losses in motor controllers, and enhance the ability of magnetic resonance imaging scanners and other non-destructive examination devices to sense minute changes in magnetic fields. [6] Even the processes of getting to work and travelling between major cities could be changed by high-temperature superconductors. Research is being conducted to use this material for magnetic levitation (maglev) trains.

Another growth area for advanced ceramics is in the medical field. Surgeons are already using bioceramic materials for repair and replacement of human hips, knees, shoulders, elbows, fingers, eyes and wrists. Ceramics are also being used to replace diseased heart valves. Dentists are using ceramics for tooth replacement implants and for brackets.

New Words and Expressions

pottery [ˈpɔtəri] n. 陶器，陶瓷
Sanskrit [ˈsænskrit] n. 梵语，梵文
composite [ˈkɔmpəzit] n. 复合材料，混合物
dinnerware [ˈdinəweə(r)] n. 餐具
tile [tail] n. 瓦片，瓷砖
silicate [ˈsilikeit] n. 硅酸盐，硅酸盐矿物
archaeologist [ˌɑːkiˈɔlədʒist] n. 考古学家
refractory [riˈfræktəri] adj. 难熔的，耐火的
line [lain] n. 直线；v. 排队，衬里，填塞
furnace [ˈfəːnis] n. 熔炉，高炉
trough [trɔf] n. 槽，低谷，低压槽
incandescent [ˌinkænˈdes(ə)nt] adj. 白热的，白炽的
transparency [trænsˈpærənsi] n. 透明，透明度
ignite [igˈnait] v. 点火，点燃
insulator [ˈinsjuleitə] n. 绝缘体，绝热器
encapsulate [inˈkæpsjuleit] v. 封装，装入胶囊，密封
capacitor [kəˈpæsitə] n. 电容器
substrate [ˈsʌbstreit] n. 底物，基底，基质

piezoelectric [paiˌiːzəuiˈlektrik] adj. 压电的
sheer [ʃi(ə)r] adj. 纯粹的，全然的，陡峭的
acoustic [əˈkuːstik] adj. 声音的，音响的，听觉的
liner [ˈlainər] n. 衬里，内衬，邮轮，班机
kerosene [ˈkerəsiːn] n. 煤油，柴油
actuate [ˈæktʃueit] v. 激励，驱使，驱动
insulin [ˈinsjulin] n. 胰岛素
electrochromic [elektrəukˈrəumik] n. 电致变色
ski [skiː] n. 滑雪橇；vi. 滑雪
piezoceramic [paiˌiːzəusiˈræmik] n. 压电陶瓷
embed [imˈbed] vt. 使嵌入，深留，嵌入
levitation [ˌleviˈteiʃən] n. 悬浮，浮起，漂浮
surgeon [ˈsəːdʒən] n. 外科医生
implant [ˈimplɑːnt] n. 植入物
bracket [ˈbrækit] n. 支架，托架

Phrases

be derived from... 来源于……
make up... 构成……
be referred to as 被称作，被称为
spark plug 火花塞
internal combustion engine 内燃机
integrated circuit package 集成电路块(组件)
ceramic matrix composite (CMC) 陶瓷基复合材料
run down 用完，停止
magnetic resonance imaging 磁共振成像

Affixes

piezo- [paiˌiːzəu] 表示"压力"；如 piezoelectricity 压电（现象），piezodialysis 加压渗析，piezochemistry 高压化学

Notes

1. The combination of two or more of these materials together to produce a new material whose properties would not be attainable by conventional means is called a compos-

ite. "these materials"指上文提到的陶瓷、金属和高分子三大固体材料,"whose"引导的从句修饰"new material"。参考译文:将这些材料中的两种或多种结合在一起可以制造出其性能用传统方法无法得到的新材料,这种材料叫做复合材料。

2. Ceramics can be defined as inorganic, non-metallic materials that are typically produced using clays and other minerals from the earth or chemically processed powders. "that"引导定语从句修饰"materials"。参考译文:陶瓷可以定义为无机非金属材料,一般由土壤中的黏土和其他矿物或者化学方法加工得到的粉末制得。

3. These advanced or technical ceramics are being used for applications such as space shuttle tile, engine components, artificial bones and teeth, computers and other electronic components, and cutting tools, just to name a few. 参考译文:这些高级或工艺陶瓷可用作航天飞机的隔热板、发动机组件、人造骨头和牙齿、计算机和其他电子组件、切割工具,这里只列举了一部分。

4. Advanced ceramics, also known as engineering or technical ceramics, refer to materials which exhibit superior mechanical properties, corrosion/oxidation resistance, and thermal, electrical, optical or magnetic properties. "which"引导的从句修饰"materials","materials"指"advanced ceramics"。参考译文:先进陶瓷,也叫工程或工艺陶瓷,指具有优异的机械性能、耐腐蚀/耐氧化性能,和优异的热、电、光学或磁性能的材料。

5. Some examples of smart systems include: medical systems that treat diabetes with blood sugar sensors and insulin-delivery pumps; water purification systems that sense and remove noxious pollutants; and houses that have electrochromic windows that control the flow of heat and light in response to weather changes and human activity. 参考译文:几个智能系统的例子包括:用血糖传感器和胰岛素输送泵治疗糖尿病的医疗系统;感应和消除有毒污染物的净化水系统;安装有光致变色玻璃的房屋,这种玻璃能响应天气变化和人类活动来控制热和光的流量。

6. Circuits using high-temperature superconducting materials could boost the processing speed of computers, reduce resistance losses in motor controllers, and enhance the ability of magnetic resonance imaging scanners and other non-destructive examination devices to sense minute changes in magnetic fields. 参考译文:使用高温超导材料电路能提高计算机的处理速度,减少马达控制器的阻抗损耗,增强磁共振扫描仪和其他非破坏性检测设备的能力以感应磁场的微小变化。

17. Biomaterials: Body Parts of the Future

During the last 90 years, man-made materials and devices have been developed to the point at which they can be used successfully to replace parts of living systems in the human body. These special materials—able to function in intimate contact with living tissue, with minimal adverse reaction or rejection by the body—are called biomaterials. Devices engineered from biomaterials and designed to perform specific functions in the body are generally referred to as biomedical devices or implants.

The earliest successful implants were bone plates, introduced in the early 1900s to stabilize bone fractures and accelerate their healing. Advances in materials engineering and surgical techniques led to blood vessel replacement experiments in the 1950s, and artificial heart valves and hip joints were under development in the 1960s. As early as the first bone plate implants, surgeons identified material and design problems that resulted in premature loss of implant function, as evidenced by mechanical failure, corrosion, and poor biocompatibility.[1] Design, material selection, and biocompatibility remain the three critical issues in today's biomedical implants and devices.

As advances have been made in the medical sciences, and with the advent of antibiotics, infectious diseases have become a much smaller health threat. Because average life expectancy has increased, degenerative diseases are a critical issue, particularly in the aging population. More organs, joints, and other critical body parts will wear out and must be replaced if people are to maintain a good quality of life. Biomaterials now play a major role in replacing or improving the function of every major body system (skeletal, circulatory, nervous, etc.). Some common implants include orthopedic devices such as total knee and hip joint replacements, spinal implants, and bone fixators; cardiac implants such as artificial heart valves and pacemakers; soft tissue implants such as breast implants and injectable collagen for soft tissue augmentation; and dental implants to replace teeth/root systems and bony tissue in the oral cavity.[2]

It was estimated in 1988 that 674000 adults in the U. S. were using 811000 artificial hips. It was also estimated that 170000 people worldwide received artificial heart valves in 1994.

The biomaterials program includes such diverse activities as biomaterials development and testing, bioengineering and device design, and drug delivery. This article highlights some emerging technologies in the field of biomaterials.

Orthopedic Biomaterials

Imagine that you are a 65-year-old woman who has suffered from chronic hip pain for the last 10 years because of degenerative arthritis. Able to walk only with difficulty and losing your independence, you turn to an orthopedic surgeon for help. In cases such as this, when improvement cannot be gained through physical therapy, nonsurgical treatments, or surgical repairs, orthopedic surgeons often advised joint replacement surgery in which the deteriorated joint is removed and replaced with a man-made device.[3]

Artificial joints consist of a plastic cup made of ultrahigh molecular weight polyethylene (UHMWPE), placed in the joint socket, and a metal (titanium or cobalt chromium alloy) or ceramic (aluminum oxide or zirconium oxide) ball affixed to a metal stem. This type of artificial joint is used to replace hip, knee, shoulder, wrist, finger, or toe joints to restore function that has been impaired as a result of arthritis or other degenerative joint diseases or trauma from sports injuries or other accidents. Joint replacement surgery is performed on an estimated 300000 patients per year in the U.S. In most cases, it brings welcome relief and mobility after years of pain.

One might think that only surgeons and bioengineers would be involved in improving the design and performance of these implants. Not so. Materials and design engineers must consider the physiologic loads to be placed on the implants, so they can design for sufficient structural integrity. Material choices also must take into account biocompatibility with surrounding tissues, the environment and corrosion issues, friction and wear of the articulating surfaces, and implant fixation either through osseointegration (the degree to which bone will grow next to or integrate into the implant) or bone cement.[4] In fact, the orthopedic implant community agrees that one of the major problems plaguing these devices is purely materials-related: wear of the polymer cup in total joint replacements.

Although the wear problem is one of materials, it plays out as a biological disaster in the body. Any use of the joint, such as walking in the case of knees or hips, results in cyclic articulation of the polymer cup against the metal or ceramic ball. Due to significant localized contact stresses at the ball/socket interface, small regions of UHMWPE tend to adhere to the metal or ceramic ball. During the reciprocating motion of normal joint use, fibrils will be drawn from the adherent regions on the polymer surface and break off to form submicrometer-sized wear debris. This adhesive wear mechanism, coupled with fatigue-related delamination of the UHMWPE (most prevalent in knee joints), results in billions of tiny polymer particles being shed into the surrounding synovial fluid and tissues.[5] The biological interaction with small particles in the body then becomes critical. The body's immune system attempts, unsuccessfully, to digest the wear particles (as it would a bacterium or virus). Enzymes are released that eventually result in the death of adjacent bone cells, or osteolysis. Over time, sufficient bone is resorbed around the implant to cause mechanical loosening, which necessitates a costly and painful implant replacement, or revision.

The average life of a total joint replacement is 8~12 years—even less in more active or younger patients.

Bioactive Materials

When a man-made material is placed in the human body, tissue reacts to the implant in a variety of ways depending on the material type. Therefore, the mechanism of tissue attachment (if any) depends on the tissue response to the implant surface. In general, materials can be placed into three classes that represent the tissue response they elicit: inert, bioresorbable, and bioactive. Inert materials such as titanium, UHMWPE, and alumina (Al_2O_3) are nearly chemically inert in the body and exhibit minimal chemical interaction with adjacent tissue. A fibrous tissue capsule will normally form around inert implants. Tissue attachment with inert materials can be through tissue growth into surface irregularities, by bone cement, or by press fitting into a defect. This morphological fixation is not ideal for the long-term stability of permanent implants and often becomes a problem with orthopedic and dental implant applications.[6] Bioresorbable materials, such as tricalcium phosphate and polylactic-polyglycolic acid copolymers, are designed to be slowly replaced by tissue (such as bone) or for use in drug-delivery applications.

Certain glasses, ceramics, and glass-ceramics that contain oxides of silicon, sodium, calcium, and phosphorus (SiO_2, Na_2O, CaO, and P_2O_5) have been shown to be the only materials known to form a chemical bond with bone, resulting in a strong mechanical implant/bone bond.[7] These materials are referred to as bioactive because they bond to bone (and in some cases to soft tissue) through a time-dependent, kinetic modification of the surface triggered by their implantation within living bone. In particular, an ion-exchange reaction between the bioactive implant and surrounding body fluids results in the formation of a biologically active hydrocarbonate apatite (calcium phosphate) layer on the implant that is chemically and crystallographically equivalent to the mineral phase in bone. This equivalence is responsible for the relatively strong interfacial bonding.

Heart Valve Materials

An example of the successful development of a critical implant technology is the artificial heart valve. Although poor heart valve designs resulted in clinical failures in the past, the current limiting factor for long-term success is the materials themselves.

Two types of materials are used for artificial heart valves: "soft" bioprosthetic materials such as denatured porcine aortic valves or bovine pericardium, and "hard" man-made materials used in mechanical heart valves, the most successful being pyrolytic carbon. Both categories of material exhibit problems when implanted.

Bioprosthetic valves, which must be used in children, often fail due to calcification (calcium from the blood stream forms deposits on the implant), which can result in mechanical dysfunction, vascular obstruction, or embolization of calcific deposits.[8] Bioprosthetic valves are also susceptible to mechanical fatigue. The cyclic loading of the valves can facilitate fatigue crack growth, often resulting in catastrophic failure. The principal problem with mechanical heart valves is thrombosis, which may be revealed as a thromboembolism or anticoagulation-related hemorrhaging. Graphite coated with pyrolytic carbon has become the material of choice for mechanical heart valves, because of its excellent thromboresistance. Pyrolytic carbon is also being studied to assess its susceptibility to fatigue damage.

Researchers have investigated the calcification process in heart valves by using molecular modeling and have developed improved lifetime assurance technology for pyrolytic carbon valves. It has been suggested that the service lives of pyrolytic carbon heart valves may be limited by cyclic fatigue, because cyclic crack growth is possible in this material. Thus, predicting the lifetime of pyrolytic carbon heart valves has been a topic of great interest to a number of parties, including the FDA, heart valve manufacturers, attorneys, scientists, and, of course, implant recipients.[9] Proof testing to evaluate the structural integrity of heart valves is an appropriate next step.

The Future of Biomaterials

Biomaterials research is an exciting and rapidly growing field. Future biomaterials will incorporate biological factors (such as bone growth) directly into an implant's surface to improve biocompatibility and bioactivity. New projects will be directed at materials development for improved mechanical integrity, corrosion resistance, and biocompatibility.

New Words and Expressions

biomaterial [,baiəumə'tiəriəl] n. 生物材料   implant [im'plɑːnt] v. 植入

fracture ['fræktʃə] n. 破裂，骨折
premature ['premətʃə(r)] adj. 早熟的，不成熟的
biocompatibility [,baiəukəm,pætə'biliti] n. 生物适应性，生物相容性，生物兼容性
advent ['ædvənt] n. 出现，到来
infectious [in'fekʃəs] adj. 传染性的，传染的
expectancy [ik'spektənsi] n. 预期，预料，期望，期望值
degenerative [di'dʒenərətiv] adj. 退步的，变质的，退化的
circulatory [sə:kju'leitəri] adj. 循环的
orthopedic [,ɔ:θəu'pi:dik] adj. 整形外科的，整形手术的
spinal ['spainl] adj. 脊柱的，脊髓的
cardiac ['kɑ:(r)diæk] adj. 心脏的，心脏病的
pacemaker ['peismeikə] n. 起搏器
collagen ['kɔlədʒ(ə)n] n. 胶原蛋白，骨胶原
augmentation [,ɔ:gmen'teiʃən] n. 增加，增加物，增大，增值，增强
cavity ['kæviti] n. 腔，窝
arthritis [ɑ:'θraitis] n. 关节炎，风湿病
socket ['sɔkit] n. 窝，穴，牙槽
titanium [tai'teiniəm] n. 钛
chromium ['krəumiəm] n. 铬
zirconium [zə:'kəuniəm] n. 锆
affix [ə'fiks] v. 使附于，粘贴
impair [im'peə(r)] v. 损害，损伤，伤害
trauma ['trɔ:mə] n. 外伤，损伤
physiologic [,fiziə'lɔdʒik] adj. 生理的
osseointegration [ɔziəuintig'reiʃn] n. 骨整合，骨结合，骨融合
cement [sə'ment] n. 水泥，胶合剂，胶接剂
plague [pleig] n. 瘟疫，传染病，祸患；v. 困扰，折磨，使受煎熬
articulation [ɑ:(r),tikju'leiʃ(ə)n] n. 关节，接合，连接
reciprocating [ri'siprəkeitiŋ] adj. 往复的，来回的，摆动的
fibril ['faibril] n. 小纤维，微纤维，细纤维
debris ['debri:] n. 碎片，残骸

fatigue [fə'ti:g] n. 疲乏，疲劳；v.（使）疲劳
delamination [di:,læmi'neiʃən] n. 分层，脱层
prevalent ['prevələnt] adj. 流行的，盛行的，普遍的
synovial [sai'nəuviəl] adj. 滑液的，含有滑液的，分泌滑液的
immune [i'mju:n] adj. 免疫的
osteolysis [,ɔsti'ɔlisis] n. 骨质溶解
resorb [ri'sɔ:b] v. 再吸收，消溶
elicit [i'lisit] v. 引出，探出，诱出
bioresorbable adj. 生物可吸收的
fibrous ['faibrəs] adj. 纤维状的，纤维的
capsule ['kæpsju:l] n. 太空舱，荚，胶囊
apatite ['æpətait] n. 磷灰石
crystallographically adv. 结晶学地
prosthetic [prɔs'θetik] adj. 修复术的，假体的，修复的，义肢的
denatured [di:'neitʃəd] adj. 变性的
porcine ['pɔ:sain] adj. 猪的
aortic [ei'ɔ:tik] adj. 大动脉的
bovine ['bəuvain] adj. 牛的，似牛的
pericardium [,peri'kɑ:diəm] n. 心包，心包膜
pyrolytic [,pai'rəlitik] adj. 高温的，热解的
calcification [,kælsifi'keiʃən] n. 钙化
dysfunction [dis'fʌnkʃən] n. 机能不良，功能紊乱，官能障碍
vascular ['væskjulə] adj. 脉管的，血管的
obstruction [əb'strʌkʃən] n. 阻塞，妨碍，障碍物
embolization [embəlai'zeiʃən] n. 栓塞
calcific [kæl'sifik] adj. 石灰质的，钙化的
catastrophic [,kætə'strɔfik] adj. 灾难的，悲惨的
thrombosis [θrɔm'bəusis] n. 血栓症，栓塞
thromboembolism [θrɔmbəu'embəlizəm] n. 血栓栓塞
anticoagulate [æntikə'uægjuleit] v.（尤指用抗凝血剂）防止……凝血
hemorrhage ['heməridʒ] v. 出血
attorney [ə'tə:ni] n. 律师

acoustic [əˈkuːstik] *adj.* 声音的，音响的，听觉的

Phrases

be referred to as… 被称为……，被认为是……
heart valve 心脏瓣膜
be involved in… 涉及……，包含有……
in vitro 在生物体外，在试管中

Affixes

dys- [dis] 表示"困难的，有病的"；如 dysfunction 机能失调, dysphonia 发音困难, dyspepsia 消化不良

Notes

1. As early as the first bone plate implants, surgeons identified material and design problems that resulted in premature loss of implant function, as evidenced by mechanical failure, corrosion, and poor biocompatibility. "as early as" 意思是 "早在……"，"that" 引导的定语从句修饰 "problems"。参考译文：早在第一块骨板植入时，外科医生就发现材料和设计问题是导致植入功能过早丧失的原因，证据是机械故障、腐蚀和生物兼容性差。

2. Some common implants include orthopedic devices such as total knee and hip joint replacements, spinal implants, and bone fixators; cardiac implants such as artificial heart valves and pacemakers; soft tissue implants such as breast implants and injectable collagen for soft tissue augmentation; and dental implants to replace teeth/root systems and bony tissue in the oral cavity. 参考译文：普通的植入包括整形外科植入，例如整个膝盖和髋关节替换、脊柱移植以及骨固定器；心脏移植，例如人造心脏瓣膜和起搏器；软组织移植，例如胸部移植和用于增加软组织的注射用胶原蛋白；以及更换牙/牙根系统和口腔中类骨组织的牙移植。

3. In cases such as this, when improvement cannot be gained through physical therapy, nonsurgical treatments, or surgical repairs, orthopedic surgeons often advised joint replacement surgery in which the deteriorated joint is removed and replaced with a man-made device. 参考译文：在这种情况下，当通过物理治疗、非手术处理或者外科修复不能使病情得到改善时，整形外科医生常常建议进行关节替换手术，移除退化的关节，用人造关节来替换。

4. Material choices also must take into account biocompatibility with surrounding tissues, the environment and corrosion issues, friction and wear of the articulating surfaces, and implant fixation either through osseointegration (the degree to which bone will grow next to or integrate into the implant) or bone cement. "take into account" 意思是 "考虑"。参考译文：材料的选择还必须考虑它与周围组织的生物兼容性，环境及腐蚀问题，结合表面的摩擦和磨损，以及通过骨整合（骨头将挨着植入体生长或与植入体成一整体）或骨接合剂的植入体固定。

5. This adhesive wear mechanism, coupled with fatigue-related delamination of the UHMWPE (most prevalent in knee joints), results in billions of tiny polymer particles being shed into the surrounding synovial fluid and tissues. "coupled with" 意思是 "与……一起"。参考译文：这种黏附磨损机理结合超高分子量聚乙烯的疲劳相关的脱层（在膝关节中普遍存在），导致大量高分子粒子分散在周围的滑液和组织中。

6. This morphological fixation is not ideal for the long-term stability of permanent im-

plants and often becomes a problem with orthopedic and dental implant applications. 参考译文：这种形态固定不利于永久植入体的长期稳定，常常成为外科整形和牙植入应用的一个麻烦。

7. Certain glasses, ceramics, and glass-ceramics that contain oxides of silicon, sodium, calcium, and phosphorus (SiO_2, Na_2O, CaO, and P_2O_5) have been shown to be the only materials known to form a chemical bond with bone, resulting in a strong mechanical implant/bone bond. "that"引导的主语从句修饰"certain glasses, ceramics, and glass-ceramics"。参考译文：研究表明，某些玻璃、陶瓷及以及含有硅、钠、钙和磷的氧化物（SiO_2，Na_2O，CaO，P_2O_5）的玻璃-陶瓷是仅有的一些已知可以和骨头形成化学键的材料，会在机械植入体和骨头之间形成强键合作用。

8. Bioprosthetic valves, which must be used in children, often fail due to calcification (calcium from the blood stream forms deposits on the implant), which can result in mechanical dysfunction, vascular obstruction, or embolization of calcific deposits. 第一个"which"修饰"Bioprosthetic valves"，第二个"which"修饰"calcification"。参考译文：生物修复瓣膜，只能用于儿童，经常由于钙化（血液中的钙在移植器官表面沉积）而失败，钙化可以导致机械功能障碍、血管阻塞，或者钙化沉积物的栓塞。

9. Thus, predicting the lifetime of pyrolytic carbon heart valves has been a topic of great interest to a number of parties, including the FDA, heart valve manufacturers, attorneys, scientists, and, of course, implant recipients. 参考译文：因而，预测热解碳心脏瓣膜的寿命成为大众感兴趣的话题，包括FDA（美国食品药品管理局）、心脏瓣膜生产商、律师和科学家，当然还有移植对象。

18. The Future of Pharmaceutical Engineering

The healthcare industry is changing. Unmet medical needs, an aging population, rising healthcare costs, and sparse pharmaceutical pipelines are forcing healthcare companies to reevaluate their competitive strategies.[1] Also, consumers are playing a larger role in healthcare. Patients are more knowledgeable and assertive regarding their individual healthcare decisions and are putting additional pressure on the industry to lower cost through innovation. The healthcare sector, comprised of pharmaceutical, biotechnology, medical device companies, government agencies such as the Food and Drug Administration (FDA), healthcare providers, insurers, and consumers, is a dynamic and unique entity, rapidly moving towards highly automated and electronic environments in which the storage, management, and use of complex information is essential for success.

Pharmaceutical companies lie at the center of America's healthcare debate. In response to market and regulatory forces, the industry is restructuring, consolidating, and reevaluating their competitive strategies. The cost to bring a single new drug product to market has steadily increased to $500-$800 million. As much as 75% of the total cost of each marketed drug is attributed to high failure rates of other candidates due to efficacy and safety problems. The high risk of drug development places increased pressure on all levels of the organization to reduce cost and increase productivity. From identifying candidate failures sooner in the research and development (R&D) process to maintaining manufacturing compliance with federal regulations and improving efficiency, pharmaceutical companies are actively searching for innovative solutions to these complex problems. Decreasing a promising candidate's time to market in drug development is especially important due to dwindling patent protection, increased generic competition, and early introduction of competitor's "me-too" products. Increasingly, technical and scientific decisions are coupled with business, legal, and marketing priorities.[2] Corporate strategy, generally aimed at identifying and producing blockbuster drugs, may be shifting toward strategies targeting smaller patient populations with safer and more effective medicines through pharmacogenomics. Genomics and other biotechnology tools are beginning to find their way into large pharmaceutical companies as biotech products start to compose a significant portion of many companies' pipelines. However, the integration of biotechnology with the pharmaceutical industry will require significant changes in R&D and manufacturing strategies.

Industry experts cite the need for quality and efficiency to be built into each area of drug discovery, development, and manufacturing. New FDA initiatives are promoting quality and efficiency by implementing a risk approach through continuous assurance programs. To help prevent the production of poor quality products, programs such as quality manufacturing operations, risk assessment, and risk management are being implemented. The integration of discovery, development, and manufacturing and increased interaction among industry, academia, and government are avenues to improve efficiency within the healthcare sector. This drive for improved product quality and process efficiency within the industry is increasing the demand for new crossfunctional scientists and engineers to tackle difficult and complex problems. Today's pharmaceutical scientists and engineers are found working in the pharmaceutical, biotechnology, and medical device industries. Informatics, high-throughput screening, simulations, and process analytical technologies (PATs) are some examples of current and new science and technology tools that are affecting the way in which discovery, development, and manufacturing of therapies, diagnostics, and devices are performed.[3]

Developing new and innovative graduate research and training programs in Pharmaceutical Engineering is necessary to educate and train the healthcare industry's future technical leaders. Such programs are a means to provide the foundation for developing crossfunctional skills in engineering, life sciences, regulations, and management as applied to the pharmaceutical, biotechnology, and medical device industries. Through academic and practical training, students should be exposed to different aspects of the healthcare industry early in their careers by providing them the opportunity to learn from members of industry, academia, and government. This exposure will allow students to better understand the complexities involved in this constantly changing, technology-driven environment. Students can enhance their technical knowledge within pharmaceutical and biotechnology industries through practical training in discovery, process development, formulation, and manufacturing. Additionally, they can gain knowledge in social, regulatory, legal, and business aspects of the healthcare industry through formal and informal active participation in frequently held discussions. Interdisciplinary programs emphasizing the development of crossfunctional skills will give students the education and training needed to succeed in bringing innovative and practical solutions to the future healthcare industry.

In the true spirit of crossfunctional training and learning, programs should be available to eligible students from a variety of undergraduate backgrounds with solid fundamental engineering and science training. In a properly structured and demanding environment, diverse backgrounds foster innovative and "out-of-the-box" thinking among students. For the successful implementation of a strong, interdisciplinary degree program in Pharmaceutical Engineering, a three-tiered approach may be used. First, a strong engineering and scientific foundation will provide the backbone to each individual student's course of study. Second, additional academic courses in statistical analysis, risk assessment, intellectual property, corporate business strategy, and technology development will elaborate on the student's academic core. Knowledge gained from these courses will be crucial components for decision making at all levels of an organization. These classes, coupled with several seminar/lecture series on current health science and engineering-related topics will create a solid platform from which the student can advance into the third and final component of practical training. Hands-on industry experience will pull together the students' prior studies and experiences to instill the foundation for advanced crossfunctional thinking. To develop the future technical leaders for the pharmaceutical and life science industries, new Pharmaceutical Engineering programs should emphasize the development of both technical and "soft" skills to prepare the students for a competitive and teamwork-driven environment. Universities with strong engineering, pharmacy, medical, business, and law colleges are ideal institutions to administer such strong interdisciplinary graduate training and life-long learning programs. Successful programs should incorporate collaboration with industrial partners who are willing to provide technical and financial resources along with practical training opportunities for students. Recruitment of students should come from both undergraduate science and engineering programs and industry. Recent graduates will benefit significantly from a learning environment that includes working professionals with varied educational backgrounds and experiences.

In the past, more traditional curricula in Pharmaceutical Engineering, or Industrial Pharmacy, have been narrowly defined, focusing education and training on the late-stage development and manufacturing processes. Future pharmaceutical engineers should be trained more broadly, learning the roles they can play as crossfunctional technical leaders and managers in a variety of job functions. This includes pharmaceutical/clinical development and manufacturing, as well as discovery and early-stage development operations. The need for well-trained engineers in all disciplines of pharmaceutical discovery and development is increasing as the scope of therapeutics expands beyond small molecular weight compounds to new and more complex biopharmaceuticals and combination therapies.[4] The convergence of the biomedical device and drug markets has led to the development and manufacture of innovative products such as drug eluting stents for cardiovascular disease treatment. The possibilities of combination products and therapies are endless as healthcare companies move from disease treatment toward disease management. The increased complexity in healthcare products has further emphasized the demand for crossfunctionally trained and technology-driven professionals.

Upon graduation, new pharmaceutical engineers may find themselves supporting drug discovery and/or development with high throughput screening (HTS) procedures, total quality management (TQM) to reduce false positive and false negative results, and developing computational tools in bioinformatics or cheminformatics.[5] Examples of specific projects in pharmaceutical/biopharmaceutical development that may be led by pharmaceutical engineers include the development of experimental and computational tools for biopharmaceutical and pharmacokinetic parameters (ADME) and toxicology evaluation to reduce drug candidate failure.[6] These pharmaceutical engineers may also be involved in developing quantitative models and process analytical technology tools for evaluation and scale-up of pharmaceutical solids and semisolids unit operations. In the areas of pharmaceutical and biopharmaceutical manufacturing, pharmaceutical engineers will be concerned with current Good Manufacturing Practice (cGMP) compliant operations, as well as the introduction and implementation of robust PAT tools for process and product validation and continuous improvement. In addition to quality management, Pharmaceutical Engineering graduates may also use their knowledge and expertise to participate with policymaking and regulatory agencies such as the FDA.

As the healthcare industry continues to face significant challenges, pharmaceutical companies in particular have an increased demand for technically competent leaders throughout the entire discovery, development, and manufacturing processes. This complex and evolving industry requires innovative technologies and improved knowledge of cutting-edge science to overcome the challenges ahead. New interdisciplinary Pharmaceutical Engineering graduate education and training programs have the potential to produce tomorrow's leaders with the technical knowledge and skills needed to meet the challenges presented by the evolving healthcare industry. It is these leaders who will define the Pharmaceutical Engineering discipline and ultimately help to shape the future of the healthcare industry.

New Words and Expressions

pharmaceutical [,fɑː(r)məˈsjuːtik(ə)l] *adj.* 制药的

healthcare [ˈhelθkeə] *n.* 医疗保健, 医疗卫生

sparse [spɑː(r)s] *adj.* 稀少的, 稀疏的

assertive [əˈsɜː(r)tiv] *adj.* 坚定自信的, 坚

决主张的
consolidate [kənˈsɔlideit] v. 使加强，使巩固
efficacy [ˈefikəsi] n. 效力，功效，效能
dwindle [ˈdwind(ə)l] v. 变小，缩小，减少
blockbuster [ˈblɔkˌbʌstə(r)] n. 一鸣惊人的事物，（尤指）非常成功的书（或电影）
pharmacogenomics [fɑməkədʒeˈnɔmiks] n. 药物基因组学
informatics [ˌinfəˈmætiks] n. 信息学，情报学
crossfunctional adj. 跨职能的，多功能的
out-of-the-box adj. 拆盒即可使用的，开箱即用的
three-tiered 三层式，三阶式的
elaborate [iˈlæbəreit] v. 精心制作，详尽阐述，详细描述，详细制订
instill [inˈstil] v. 滴注，慢慢灌输

curricula [kəˈrikjələ] n. 课程，总课程（curriculum 的名词复数）
therapeutics [ˌθerəˈpju:tiks] n. 治疗学，疗法
convergence [kənˈvə:(r)dʒ(ə)ns] n. 会聚，收敛
stent [stent] n. 血管支架
cardiovascular [ˌkɑ:(r)diəuˈvæskjulə(r)] adj. 心血管的
bioinformatics [bi:əuinˈfɔ:mətiks] n. 生物信息学
cheminformatics n. 化学信息学
pharmacokinetic adj. 药动学的，药物动力的，药代动力学的
cutting-edge adj. 先进的，前沿的，尖端的
interdisciplinary adj. [ˌintə(r)disiˈplinəri] 多学科的，跨学科的，跨领域的

Phrases

comprise of   包括，由……构成；由……组成
Food and Drug Administration (FDA)   美国食品与药物管理局
be attributed to   被认为是……所为，归因于
couple with   与……相结合；与……结合
process analytical technology   加工分析技术，过程分析技术，工艺分析技术
be exposed to   暴露于，面临，暴露在
intellectual property   知识产权

drug eluting stent   药物洗脱支架
high throughput screening   高通量筛选
total quality management   全面质量管理
ADME   即"药代动力学"，指机体对外源化学物的吸收、分布、代谢及排泄过程。
be concerned with   关心，与……有关，参与
Good Manufacturing Practice   缩写 GMP，中文含义是"良好生产规范"。世界卫生组织将 GMP 定义为指导食物、药品、医疗产品生产和质量管理的法规。

Affixes

pharmaco- [ˈfɑməkəu] 药的；如 pharmacodynamics 药效学，药效动力学，药物效力学，pharmacogenetics 药物基因学，pharmacogenomics 药物基因组学
cross- 交叉的，跨的；如 cross-fertilize 异花受精，cross-refer 交相参照，crosstalk 串扰
cardio- [kɑ:(r)diəu] 心脏的；如 cardiovascular 心血管的，electrocardiogram 心电图，cardiologist 心脏科医师，心脏学家

Notes

1. Unmet medical needs, an aging population, rising healthcare costs, and sparse pharmaceutical pipelines are forcing healthcare companies to reevaluate their competitive strategies. 参考译文：医疗需求无法满足、人口老龄化、日益增加的医疗卫生成本和稀少的制药管

线，正在迫使医疗卫生企业重新评估他们的竞争策略。

2. Decreasing a promising candidate's time to market in drug development is especially important due to dwindling patent protection, increased generic competition, and early introduction of competitor's "me-too" products. "me-too", 仿效别人（成功之事）的。参考译文：由于专利保护的缩小，普通竞争的增加和竞争对手仿制品的早期引入，在药物开发中，缩短有希望的候选药物进入市场的时间尤其重要。

3. Informatics, high-throughput screening, simulations, and process analytical technologies (PATs) are some examples of current and new science and technology tools that are affecting the way in which discovery, development, and manufacturing of therapies, diagnostics, and devices are performed. "that are affecting…"为定语，用来修饰"tools"，"in which…"为定语中的定语，用来修饰"the way"。参考译文：信息学、高通量筛选、模拟和工艺分析技术是目前新科技手段的一些例子，这些科技手段影响了药物发现和开发的方法，也影响了治疗、诊断和设备制造的方法。

4. The need for well-trained engineers in all disciplines of pharmaceutical discovery and development is increasing as the scope of therapeutics expands beyond small molecular weight compounds to new and more complex biopharmaceuticals and combination therapies. 句中"as"引导时间状语从句。参考译文：随着治疗范围从小分子化合物扩展到新的更加复杂的生物制药和联合疗法，在药物发现和开发的所有领域中，对训练有素工程师的需求日益增加。

5. Upon graduation, new pharmaceutical engineers may find themselves supporting drug discovery and/or development with high throughput screening (HTS) procedures, total quality management (TQM) to reduce false positive and false negative results, and developing computational tools in bioinformatics or cheminformatics. 参考译文：一毕业，作为一位新制药工程师，他们会发现自己能通过使用高通量筛选方法与以减少假阳性和假阴性结果的全面质量管理为药物发现和/或开发提供支持，能开发生物信息学或化学信息学中的计算工具。

6. Examples of specific projects in pharmaceutical/biopharmaceutical development that may be led by pharmaceutical engineers include the development of experimental and computational tools for biopharmaceutical and pharmacokinetic parameters (ADME) and toxicology evaluation to reduce drug candidate failure. 主语为"examples"，谓语为"include"，宾语"the development"。参考译文：在制药/生物制药开发中，制药工程师领导项目的实例包括开发实验和计算方法用于生物制药和药代动力学的参数以及毒理学评估，以减少药物候选的失败。

Part D

Chemistry Glossaries

1. General Chemistry

1.1 Atoms, Elements and Ions

atom ['ætəm] *n.* 原子　　Compare with molecule and ion.

An atom is the smallest particle of an element that retains the chemical properties of the element. Atoms are electrically neutral, with a positively charged nucleus that binds one or more electrons in motion around it.

element ['elimənt] *n.* 元素

An element is a substance composed of atoms with identical atomic number. The older definition of element (an element is a pure substance that can't be decomposed chemically) was made obsolete by the discovery of isotopes.

ion ['aiən] *n.* 离子

An atom or molecule that has acquired a charge by either gaining or losing electrons. An atom or molecule with missing electrons has a net positive charge and is called a cation; one with extra electrons has a net negative charge and is called an anion.

anion ['ænaiən] *n.* 阴离子　　Compare with cation.

An anion is a negatively charged ion. Nonmetals typically form anions.

cation ['kætaiən] *n.* 阳离子

A cation is a positively charged ion. Metals typically form cations.

electron [i'lektrɔn] *n.* 电子　(e)　　Compare with proton and neutron.

A fundamental constituent of matter, having a negative charge of $1.602176462 \times 10^{-19}$ coulombs $\pm 0.000000063 \times 10^{-19}$ coulombs and a mass of $9.10938188 \times 10^{-31}$ kg $\pm 0.00000072 \times 10^{-31}$ kg [1998 CODATA values].

neutral ['njuːtrəl] *adj.* 中性的

(1) Having no net electrical charge. Atoms are electrically neutral; ions are not.

(2) A solution containing equal concentrations of H^+ and OH^-.

proton ['prəutɔn] *n.* 质子　(p)

An elementary particle found in the atomic nucleus with a positive charge equal and opposite that of the electron. Protons have a mass of 1.007276 daltons.

atomic nucleus [ə'tɔmik] ['nju:kliəs] 原子核

A tiny, incredibly dense positively charged mass at the heart of the atom. The nucleus is composed of protons and neutrons (and other particles). It contains almost all of the mass of the atom but occupies only a tiny fraction of the atom's volume.

nucleon ['nju:kliɔn] *n*. 核子　　Compare with proton, neutron and atomic nucleus.

A proton or a neutron in the atomic nucleus.

nuclide symbol ['nju:klaid] ['simbəl] *n*. 核素符号　　Compare with atomic nucleus, nuclide and element symbol.

A symbol for a nuclide that contains the mass number as a leading superscript and the atomic number as a leading subscript. For ions, the ionic charge is given as a trailing superscript. For example, the nuclide symbol for the most common form of the chloride ion is $^{35}_{17}Cl^-$, where 35 is the mass number, 17 is the atomic number, and the charge on the ion is -1. The atomic number is sometimes omitted from nuclide symbols.

nuclide ['nju:klaid] *n*. 核素　　Compare with atomic nucleus and nuclide symbol.

An atom or ion with a specified mass number and atomic number. For example, uranium-235 and carbon-14 are nuclides.

isotope ['aisəutəup] *n*. 同位素 isotopic; isotopy.　　Compare with isomer, allotrope, isobar, and isotone.

Atoms or ions of an element with different numbers of neutrons in their atomic nucleus. Isotopes have the same atomic number but different mass number. Isotopes have very similar chemical properties but sometimes differ greatly in nuclear stability.

alpha particle ['ælfə] ['pɑ:tikl] *n*. α粒子　(^4_2He)

A particle that is commonly ejected from radioactive nuclei, consisting of two protons and two neutrons. Alpha particles are helium nuclei. Alpha particles have a mass of $6.64465598 \times 10^{-27}$ kg or 4.0015061747 atomic mass units. [1998 CODATA values]

alpha ray ['ælfə] [rei]　α射线（α-ray） alpha radiation.

A stream of alpha particles. Alpha rays rapidly dissipate their energy as they pass through materials, and are far less penetrating than beta particles and gamma rays.

beta particle ['bi:tə,'beitə] ['pɑ:tikl] β粒子（β⁻）

An electron emitted by an unstable nucleus, when a neutron decays into a proton and an electron. In some cases, beta radiation consists of positrons ("antielectrons which are identical to electrons but carry a $+1$ charge.") Note that beta particles are created in nuclear decay; they do not exist as independent particles within the nucleus.

anode ['ænəud] *n*. 阳极，正极　　Compare with cathode.

The electrode at which oxidation occurs in a cell. Anions migrate to the anode.

cathode ['kæθəud] *n*. 阴极

The electrode at which reduction occurs.

atomic mass unit 原子质量单位

A unit of mass equal to 1/12 the mass of a carbon-12 nucleus, which is $1.66053873 \times 10^{-27}$ kg $\pm 0.00000013 \times 10^{-27}$ kg [1998 CODATA values]. Abbreviated as amu or u. Sometimes called the dalton, after John Dalton, architect of the first modern atomic theory.

element symbol 元素符号

An international abbreviation for element names, usually consisting of the first one or two distinctive letters in element name. Some symbols are abbreviations for ancient names.

atomic number   *n*. 原子序数（Z）
　　The number of protons in an atomic nucleus. The atomic number and the element symbol are two alternate ways to label an element. In nuclide symbols, the atomic number is a leading subscript; for example, in $_6^{12}C$, the "6" is the atomic number.

atomic weight   [ə'tɔmik] [weit] *n*. 原子量 atomic mass.
　　The average mass of an atom of an element, usually expressed in atomic mass units. The terms mass and weight are used interchangeably in this case. The atomic weight given on the periodic table is a weighted average of isotopic masses found in a typical terrestrial sample of the element.

mass number   质量数   Compare with atomic number and atomic weight.
　　The total number of protons and neutrons in an atom or ion. In nuclide symbols the mass number is given as a leading superscript. In isotope names (e. g., carbon-14, sodium-23) the mass number is the number following the element name.

atomic theory   [ə'tɔmik] ['θiəri] *n*. 原子理论
　　An explanation of chemical properties and processes that assumes that tiny particles called atoms are the ultimate building blocks of matter.

Brownian motion   ['brauniən] ['məuʃən] *n*. 布朗运动   Brownian movement.
　　Small particles suspended in liquid move spontaneously in a random fashion. The motion is caused by unbalanced impacts of molecules on the particle. Brownian motion provided strong circumstantial evidence for the existence of molecules.

cathode ray   ['kæθəud] [rei] *n*. 阴极射线
　　A negatively charged beam that emanates from the cathode of a discharge tube. Cathode rays are streams of electrons.

chemical change   化学变化，化学反应   Compare with physical change.
　　A chemical change is a dissociation, recombination, or rearrangement of atoms.

compound   ['kɔmpaund] *n*. 化合物   Compare with element and mixture.
　　A compound is a material formed from elements chemically combined in definite proportions by mass. For example, water is formed from chemically bound hydrogen and oxygen. Any pure water sample contains 2 g of hydrogen for every 16 g of oxygen.

deuterium   [djuː'tiəriəm] *n*. 氘 （D, $_1^2H$）
　　An isotope of hydrogen that contains one neutron and one proton in its nucleus.

electric charge   *n*. 电荷
　　A property used to explain attractions and repulsions between certain objects. Two types of charge are possible: negative and positive. Objects with different charge attract; objects with the same charge repel each other.

heavy water   重水（D_2O）
　　Water that contains ^2H, rather than ^1H. Heavy water is about 11% denser than ordinary water.

isotopic abundance   [ˌaisəu'tɔpik] [ə'bʌndəns] *n*. 同位素的丰度   Compare with natural abundance.
　　The fraction of atoms of a given isotope in a sample of an element.

natural abundance   自然丰度
　　The average fraction of atoms of a given isotope of an element on Earth.

isotopic mass   同位素质量 isotopic masses.
　　The mass of a single atom of a given isotope, usually given in daltons.

law of conservation of mass 物质守恒定律，物质不灭定律

There is no change in total mass during a chemical change. The demonstration of conservation of mass by Antoine Lavoisier in the late 18th century was a milestone in the development of modern chemistry.

law of definite proportions [ˈdefinit] [prəˈpɔːʃən] 定比定律

When two pure substances react to form a compound, they do so in a definite proportion by mass. For example, when water is formed from the reaction between hydrogen and oxygen, the "definite proportion" is 1 g of H for every 8 g of O.

law of multiple proportions [ˈmʌltipl] [prəˈpɔːʃən] 倍比定律

When one element can combine with another to form more than one compound, the mass ratios of the elements in the compounds are simple whole-number ratios of each other. For example, in CO and in CO_2, the oxygen-to-carbon ratios are 16 : 12 and 32 : 12, respectively. Note that the second ratio is exactly twice the first, because there are exactly twice as many oxygens in CO_2 per carbon as there are in CO.

mass spectrometer [spekˈtrɔmitə] 质谱仪

An instrument that measures the masses and relative abundances of a sample that has been vaporized and ionized.

mass spectrometry [spekˈtrɔmitri] 质谱学，质谱测量，质谱分析 mass spectroscopy.

A method for experimentally determining isotopic masses and isotopic abundances. A sample of an element is converted into a stream of ions and passed through an electromagnetic field. Ions with different charge-to-mass ratios are deflected by different amounts, and strike different spots on a film plate or other detector. From the position of the spots, the mass of the ions can be determined; from the intensity of the spot, the relative number of ions (the isotopic abundance) can be determined.

mass spectrum [ˈspektrəm] 质谱 mass spectra.

A plot showing the results of a mass spectrometry experiment, which shows the presence of particles with different masses as a series of sharp, separate peaks. The position of the peaks on the x-axis indicates the mass of the particles; the peak heights indicate the relative abundance of the particles.

nuclear binding energy [ˈnjuːkliə] [ˈbaindiŋ] [ˈenədʒi] 核结合能

Energy needed to break an atomic nucleus into separate protons and neutrons.

radioactivity [ˌreidiəuækˈtiviti] n. 放射性 radiation; radioactive.

Spontaneous emission of particles or high-energy electromagnetic radiation from the nuclei of unstable atoms. "Radiation" refers to the emissions, and "radioactive source" refers to the source of the radiation.

1.2 Electrons in Atoms

absorption spectrum [əbˈsɔːpʃən] [ˈspektrəm] 吸收光谱，吸收频谱 absorption spectra.

Compare with absorption spectroscopy.

A plot that shows how much radiation a substance absorbs at different wavelengths. Absorption spectra are unique for each element and compound and they are often used as chemical "fingerprints" in analytical chemistry. The spectrum can be represented by a plot of either absorbance or transmittance versus wavelength, frequency, or wavenumber.

emission spectrum [iˈmiʃən] 发射光谱 emission spectra. Compare with absorption spectrum.

A plot of relative intensity of emitted radiation as a function of wavelength or frequency.

angular momentum quantum number [ˈæŋgjulə] [məuˈmentəm] [ˈkwɔntəm] 角量子数 (l) azimuthal quantum number; orbital angular momentum quantum number.

A quantum number that labels the subshells of an atom. Sometimes called the orbital angular momentum quantum number, this quantum number dictates orbital shape. l can take on values from 0 to $n-1$ within a shell with principal quantum number n.

atomic orbital [əˈtɔmik] [ˈɔːbitl] 原子轨道

A wavefunction that describes the behavior of an electron in an atom.

band spectrum 谱带，带（状）光谱 band spectra. Compare with line spectrum and continuous spectrum.

An emission spectrum that contains groups of sharp peaks that are so close together that they are not distinguishable separately, but only as a "band".

line spectrum 线（状）光谱，（光）谱线 line spectra; line emission spectrum. Compare with band spectrum and continuous spectrum.

An emission spectrum that contains very sharp peaks, corresponding to transitions between states in free atoms. For example, the line spectrum of hydrogen contains 4 sharp lines in the visible part of the spectrum.

continuous spectrum 连续光谱 Compare with line spectrum and band spectrum.

A plot of the relative absorbance or intensity of emitted light vs. wavelength or frequency that shows a smooth variation, rather than a series of sharp peaks or bands.

basis function 基函数

A mathematical function that can be used to build a description of wavefunctions for electrons in atoms or molecules.

basis set 基组

A set of mathematical functions that are combined to approximate the wavefunctions for electrons in atoms and molecules.

Bohr atom 玻尔原子 Bohr's theory; Bohr's atomic theory; Bohr model.

A model of the atom that explains emission and absorption of radiation as transitions between stationary electronic states in which the electron orbits the nucleus at a definite distance. The Bohr model violates the Heisenberg uncertainty principle, since it postulates definite paths and momenta for electrons as they move around the nucleus. Modern theories usually use atomic orbitals to describe the behavior of electrons in atoms.

core electron [kɔː] [iˈlektrɔn] 内核电子 Compare with valence electron.

Electrons occupying completely filled shells under the valence shell.

degenerate [diˈdʒenəreit] *adj*. 等价的，简并的 degenerate orbital（简并轨道）.

A set of orbitals are said to be degenerate if they all have the same energy. This degeneracy can sometimes be "lifted" by external electric or magnetic fields.

diamagnetism [ˈdaiəˈmægnitizəm] *n*. 反磁性，逆磁性，反磁性学 diamagnetic. Compare with paramagnetism.

Diamagnetic materials are very weakly repelled by magnetic fields. The atoms or molecules of diamagnetic materials contain no unpaired spins.

paramagnetism [pærəˈmægnitizəm] *n*. 顺磁性 paramagnetic. Compare with diamagnetism and ferromagnetism.

Paramagnetic materials are attracted to a magnetic field due to the presence of at least one unpaired spin in their atoms or molecules.

effective nuclear charge 有效电荷数 (Z_{eff})　　Compare with atomic number.
　　The nuclear charge experienced by an electron when other electrons are shielding the nucleus.

electron configuration [kən,figju'reiʃən] 电子排布（构型） electronic configuration.
　　A list showing how many electrons are in each orbital or subshell. There are several notations. The subshell notation lists subshells in order of increasing energy, with the number of electrons in each subshell indicated as a superscript. For example, $1s^2\ 2s^2\ 2p^3$ means "2 electrons in the 1s subshell, 2 electrons in the 2s subshell, and 3 electrons in the 2p subshell".

excited state 激发态　　Compare with ground state.
　　An atom or molecule which has absorbed energy is said to be in an excited state. Excited states tend to have short lifetimes; they lose energy either through collisions or by emitting photons to "relax" back down to their ground states.

ground state 基态　　Compare with excited state.
　　The lowest energy state for an atom or molecule. When an atom is in its ground state, its electrons fill the lowest energy orbitals completely before they begin to occupy higher energy orbitals, and they fill subshells in accordance with Hund's rule.

f orbital　f 轨道
　　An orbital with angular momentum quantum number $l=3$. The f orbitals generally have 3 nuclear nodes and rather complex shapes.

Hund's rule 洪特规则　　rule of maximum multiplicity.
　　A rule of thumb stating that subshells fill so that the number of unpaired spins is maximized, or "spread them out and line them up".

isoelectronic [,aisəuilek'trɔnik] *adj*. 等电子的（with）
　　Refers to a group of atoms or ions having the same number of electrons. For example, F^-, Ne, and Na^+ are isoelectronic.

magnetic quantum number [mæg'netik] ['kwɔntəm] ['nʌmbə] 磁量子数 (m)
　　Quantum number that labels different orbitals within a subshell. m can take on values from $-l$ to $+l$. The number of orbitals in a subshell is the same as the number of possible m values.

noble gas core 惰性电子内层　　Compare with valence shell.
　　All completely filled shells underneath the valence shell.

orbital ['ɔːbitl] *n*. 轨道
　　A wavefunction that describes what an electron with a given energy is doing inside an atom or molecule.

Pauli principle 泡利原理　　exclusion principle; Pauli exclusion; Pauli exclusion principle.
　　No two electrons in an atom can have the same set of 4 quantum numbers. Because the n, l, and m_l quantum numbers address a particular orbital, and because the m_s quantum number has only two possible values, the Pauli principle says that a maximum of two electrons can occupy an atomic orbital — and these electrons must have opposite spins.

penetration [peni'treiʃən] *n*. 穿透（效应）　　Compare with shielding.
　　Electrons in penetrating orbitals can reach the nucleus. The n and l quantum numbers determine how well an orbital penetrates. Lower n and lower l values mean better penetration. A low n value means the orbital is small. A low l value means the orbital has fewer nuclear nodes (planes that pass through the nucleus where the probability of locating the electron is zero).

In order of decreasing penetration, the subshells are s>p>d>f. A 1s orbital penetrates better than a 2s orbital.

shielding ['ʃi:ldiŋ] *n*. 屏蔽（效应）

Electrons in orbitals with high penetration can shield the nucleus from less penetrating electrons. Because they are closer to the nucleus on average, they repel those farther away and lessen the effective nuclear charge for the more distant electrons.

principal quantum number ['prinsəp(ə)l] ['kwɔntəm] ['nʌmbə] 主量子数

The quantum number that determines the size and (in hydrogen atoms) the energy of an orbital. *n* is used to label electron shells. *n* may take on integer values from 1 to infinity.

shell [ʃel] *n*. 电子层   Compare with subshell.

A set of electrons with the same principal quantum number. The number of electrons permitted in a shell is equal to $2n^2$. A shell contains n^2 orbitals, and n subshells.

subshell ['sʌbʃel] *n*. 亚层

A set of electrons with the same azimuthal quantum number. The number of electrons permitted in a subshell is equal to $2l+1$.

spectrophotometry [ˌspektrəufəu'tɔmitri]   分光光度测定法，分光光度学   spectrophotometric.

Determination of the concentration of a material in a sample by measurement of the amount of light the sample absorbs.

spectroscopy [spek'trɔskəpi] *n*. 光谱学，波谱学   spectrometry; spectroscopic.

Spectroscopy is analysis of the interaction between electromagnetic radiation and matter. Different types of radiation interact in characteristic ways with different samples of matter; the interaction is often unique and serves as a diagnostic "fingerprint" for the presence of a particular material in a sample. Spectroscopy is also a sensitive quantitative technique that can determine trace concentrations of substances.

spin [spin] *n*. 旋转

Electrons have an intrinsic angular momentum that is similar to what would be observed if they were spinning. Electron spin is sometimes called a "twoness" property because it can have two values, referred to as "spin up" and "spin down". Nuclei can have spins of their own.

spin pair (↓↑) 自旋配对, electron pair; paired electrons.   Compare with unpaired spin.

Two electrons with opposite spins, usually occupying the same orbital.

unpaired spin (↑) 未配对（电子）unpaired electron.

A single electron occupying an orbital.

1.3 Gases, Liquids and Solids

1.3.1 Gases

atmosphere ['ætməsfiə] *n*. 大气压

A unit of pressure, equal to a barometer reading of 760 mm Hg. 1 atmosphere is 101325 Pascals and 1.01325 bar.

Avogadro's law   阿伏伽德罗定律

Equal volumes of an ideal gas contain equal numbers of molecules, if both volumes are at the same temperature and pressure. For example, 1 L of ideal gas contains twice as many molecules as 0.5 L of ideal gas at the same temperature and pressure.

bar [bɑː(r)] *n.* 巴（压力单位）

Unit of pressure. 1 bar = 10^5 Pascals = 1.01325 atmospheres.

manometer [məˈnɔmitə] *n.* 压力计　　Compare with barometer.

An instrument for measuring gas pressures. A mercury or oil manometer measures gas pressure as the height of a fluid column the gas sample is able to support. Open manometers measure gas pressure relative to atmospheric pressure.

barometer [bəˈrɔmitə] *n.* 气压计　　Compare with manometer.

An instrument that measures atmospheric pressure. A mercury barometer is a closed tube filled with mercury inverted in a mercury reservoir. The height of the mercury column indicates atmospheric pressure （with 1 atm = 760 mm of mercury）. An aneroid barometer consists of an evacuated container with a flexible wall. When atmospheric pressure changes, the wall flexes and moves a pointer which indicates the changing pressure on a scale.

Torr [tɔː] *n.* 托（压力单位）　　Compare with barometer and pressure.

A unit of pressure, defined so that 760 Torr is exactly 1 atmosphere. A Torr is equivalent to 1mmHg on barometer readings taken at 0℃; at other temperatures, the conversion from mmHg to Torr is approximately $p(\text{Torr}) = p(\text{mmHg}) \times (1 - 1.8 \times 10^{-4} t)$, where t is in ℃.

pressure [ˈpreʃə(r)] *n.* 压力（p）

Force per unit area. The SI unit of pressure is the Pascal, defined as one newton per square meter. Other common pressure units are the atmosphere, the bar, and the Torr.

Boyle's law　波义耳定律

The pressure of an ideal gas is inversely proportional to its volume, if the temperature and amount of gas is held constant. Doubling gas pressure halves gas volume, if temperature and amount of gas don't change. If the initial pressure and volume are p_1 and V_1 and the final pressure and volume are $p_2 V_2$, then $p_1 V_1 = p_2 V_2$ at fixed temperature and gas amount.

Charles' law　查理定律

The volume of a gas is directly proportional to its temperature in Kelvins, if pressure and amount of gas remain constant. Doubling the Kelvin temperature of a gas at constant pressure will double its volume. If V_1 and T_1 are the initial volume and temperature, the final volume and temperature ratio $V_2/T_2 = V_1/T_1$ if pressure and moles of gas are unchanged.

Dalton's law　道尔顿分压定律　　Dalton's law of partial pressure.

The total pressure exerted by a mixture of gases is the sum of the pressures that each gas would exert if it were alone. For example, if dry oxygen gas at 713 Torr is saturated with water vapor at 25 Torr, the pressure of the wet gas is 738 Torr.

diffusion [diˈfjuːʒən] *n.* 扩散，传播　　Compare with effusion.

The mixing of two substances caused by random molecular motions. Gases diffuse very quickly; liquids diffuse much more slowly, and solids diffuse at very slow (but often measurable) rates. Molecular collisions make diffusion slower in liquids and solids.

effusion [iˈfjuːʒ(ə)n] *n.* 逸出　　Compare with diffusion and diffraction.

Gas molecules in a container escape from tiny pinholes into a vacuum with the same average velocity they have inside the container. They also move in straight-line trajectories through the pinhole.

diffusion rate [diˈfjuːʒən] [reit]　扩散速率　　rate of diffusion.

The number of randomly moving molecules that pass through a unit area per second. Diffusion rates are fastest when a large concentration difference exists on either side of the unit area. Diffusion rates increase with temperature, and decrease with increasing pressure, molecular weight, and molecular size.

ideal gas 理想气体 ideal gases; perfect gas; ideal gas law.

A gas whose pressure p, volume V, and temperature T are related by $pV=nRT$, where n is the number of moles of gas and R is the ideal gas law constant. Ideal gases have molecules with negligible size, and the average molar kinetic energy of an ideal gas depends only on its temperature. Most gases behave ideally at sufficiently low pressures.

ideal gas law constant 理想气体常数 ideal gas constant; universal gas constant.

A constant R equal to $pV/(nT)$ for ideal gases, where the pressure, volume, moles, and temperature of the gas are p, V, n, and T, respectively. The value and units of R depend on the units of p, V, and T. Commonly used values and units of R include: 82.055 cm^3·atm·K^{-1}·mol^{-1}; 0.082055L·atm·mol^{-1}·K^{-1}; 8.31434J·mol^{-1}·K^{-1}; 1.9872cal·K^{-1}·mol^{-1}; 8314.34L·Pa·mol^{-1}·K^{-1}; 8.31434Pa·m^3·mol^{-1}·K^{-1}.

law of combining volumes 化合体积定律，盖·吕萨克定律 Gay-Lussac's law.

When gases react, they do so in a definite proportion by volume, if the volumes are measured at the same pressure and temperature. For example, in the reaction $N_2(g)+3H_2(g) \Longrightarrow 2NH_3(g)$, 3 liters of hydrogen will react with 1 liter of nitrogen to give 2 liters of ammonia if all volumes are measured at the same temperature and pressure.

Pascal [ˈpæskəl] 帕斯卡 (Blaise, 1623—1662, 法国数学家、物理学家、哲学家) (Pa)

The SI unit of pressure, equal to a force of one newton per square meter. 101325 Pascals=1 atmosphere; 10^5 Pascals=1bar.

standard molar volume 标准摩尔体积

The volume of 1 mole of an ideal gas at STP, equal to 22.414 liters.

standard pressure 标准压力 Standard pressure is a pressure of 1 bar. Before 1982, the standard pressure was 1atm (1atm=1.01325bar).

van der Waals equation 范德华方程

A semiempirical equation that describes the relationship between pressure (p), volume (V), temperature (T), and moles of gas (n) for a real gas. The equation is $(p+n^2a/V^2)(V-nb)=nRT$, where a and b are constants that include the effects of molecular attractions and molecular volume. a and b are usually fitted to experimental data for a particular gas.

1.3.2 Liquids

adhesion [ədˈhiːʒən] $n.$ 黏附

Attraction between different substances on either side of a phase boundary.

cohesion [kouˈhiːʒən] $n.$ 凝聚，内聚力 Compare with adhesion.

Attraction between like molecules.

boiling point 沸点 (b.p.) standard boiling point; normal boiling point.

The temperature at which the vapor pressure of a liquid is equal to the external pressure on the liquid. The standard boiling point is the temperature at which the vapor pressure of a liquid equals standard pressure.

critical point 临界点 critical state.

State at which two phases of a substance first become indistinguishable. For example, at pressures higher than 217.6 atm and temperatures above 374℃, the meniscus between steam and liquid water will vanish; the two phases become indistinguishable and are referred to as a supercritical fluid.

critical molar volume　临界摩尔体积（V_c）
The molar volume at the critical point.

critical pressure　临界压力（p_c）
The pressure at the critical point.

critical temperature　临界温度（T_c）
The temperature at the critical point. A gas above the critical temperature will never condense into a liquid, no matter how much pressure is applied. Most substances have a critical temperature that is about 1.5 to 1.7 times the standard boiling point, in Kelvin.

dipole-dipole interaction [ˌintərˈækʃən]　偶极相互作用 dipole-dipole force.
Electrostatic attraction between oppositely charged poles of two or more dipoles.

dynamic equilibrium [daiˈnæmik] [ˌiːkwiˈlibriəm]　动态平衡　Compare with position of equilibrium.
Dynamic equilibrium is established when two opposing processes are occurring at precisely the same rate, so that there is no apparent change in the system over long periods of time.

enthalpy of vaporization [ˌveipəraiˈzeiʃən]　汽化热（焓）（ΔH_{vap}）　heat of vaporization.
The change in enthalpy when one mole of liquid evaporates to form one mole of gas. Enthalpies of vaporization are always positive because vaporization involves overcoming most of the intermolecular attractions in the liquid.

flash point　闪点　Compare with auto-ignition temperature.
The temperature when vapor pressure of a substance becomes high enough to allow the air/vapor layer over the substance to be ignited. Ether and acetone have flash points below room temperature, which makes them very dangerous.

immiscible [iˈmisəbl] *adj*. 不相溶的　immiscibility.　Compare with miscible and partial miscibility.
Two liquids are considered "immiscible" or unmixable if shaking equal volumes of the liquids together results in a meniscus visible between two layers of liquid. If the liquids are completely immiscible, the volumes of the liquid layers are the same as the volumes of liquids originally added to the mixture.

miscible [ˈmisəbl] *adj*. 易混合的　miscibility; liquid miscibility.
Two liquids are considered "miscible" or mixable if shaking them together results in a single liquid phase, with no meniscus visible between layers of liquid.

partial miscibility [ˈpɑːʃəl] [ˌmisiˈbiliti]　部分相溶的　partially miscible.　Compare with miscible and immiscible.
Two liquids are considered partially miscible if shaking equal volumes of the liquids together results in a meniscus visible between two layers of liquid, but the volumes of the layers are not identical to the volumes of the liquids originally added.

intermolecular force　分子间力
An attraction or repulsion between molecules. Intermolecular forces are much weaker than chemical bonds. Hydrogen bonds, dipole-dipole interactions, and London forces are examples of intermolecular forces.

liquid [ˈlikwid] *n*. 液体，流体

A state of matter that has a high density and is incompressible compared to a gas. Liquids take the shape of their container but do not expand to fill the container as gases do. Liquids diffuse much more slowly than gases.

London force 色散力 dispersion force.

An intermolecular attractive force that arises from a cooperative oscillation of electron clouds on a collection of molecules at close range.

meniscus [mi'niskəs] *n.* 弯月面，弯液面 meniscuses; menisci.

A phase boundary that is curved because of surface tension.

Newtonian fluid 牛顿流体 Compare with non-Newtonian fluid.

A fluid whose viscosity doesn't depend on gradients in flow speed. Gases and low-molecular weight liquids are usually Newtonian fluids.

non-Newtonian fluid 非牛顿流体

A fluid whose viscosity changes when the gradient in flow speed changes. Colloidal suspensions and polymer solutions like ketchup and starch/water paste are non-Newtonian fluids.

nucleation [ˌnju:kli'eiʃən] *n.* 成核（现象），晶核形成

The process of providing sites for 1) new bubbles to form in a liquid that is boiling or supersaturated with gas; 2) new droplets to condense from a supersaturated vapor, or 3) new crystals to form in a supersaturated solution. Nucleation sites can be scratches in a surface, dust particles, seed crystals, and so on.

phase diagram ['daiəgræm] 相图 phase map.

A map that shows which phases of a sample are most stable for a given set of conditions. Phases are depicted as regions on the map; the borderlines between regions correspond to conditions where the phases can coexist in equilibrium.

supercritical fluid [ˌsju:pə'kritikəl] ['flu(:)id] 超临界流体

A fluid state that occurs when the pressure and temperature exceed the substance's critical pressure and critical temperature. Supercritical fluids fill their containers like gases but dissolve substances like liquids, which makes them very useful as solvents. Their density and other properties are intermediate between gases and liquids.

supercooling [ˌsju:pə'ku:liŋ] 过冷（现象） supercooled, supercool.

Liquids at temperatures below their normal freezing points are said to be "supercooled".

surface tension ['tenʃən] 表面张力

The work required to expand the surface of a liquid by unit area.

surfactant [sə:'fæktənt] *n.* 表面活性剂

A material that spreads along a surface, changing the properties of the surface. For example, soap spreads over a water surface and lowers its surface tension.

viscosity [vis'kɔsiti] *n.* 黏质，黏度（η） coefficient of viscosity.

The resistance a liquid exhibits to flow. Experimentally, the frictional force between two liquid layers moving past each other is proportional to area of the layers and the difference in flow speed between them. The constant of proportionality is called "viscosity" or "coefficient of viscosity", and is given the symbol η. The time required for a liquid to drain out of a capillary tube is directly proportional to its viscosity. The poise is a non-SI unit frequently used to express viscosities.

wetting ['wetiŋ] *n.* 润湿

Covering with a surface with thin film of liquid. Liquid beads up on a surface if it cannot wet it.

1.3.3 Solids

crystalline solid [ˈkristəlain] [ˈsɔlid]　晶状固体　　Compare with amorphous.

A solid that has a repeating, regular three-dimensional arrangement of atoms, molecules, or ions.

amorphous [əˈmɔːfəs] *adj.* 无定形的，无组织的　amorphous solid.　　Compare with crystal.

A solid that does not have a repeating, regular three-dimensional arrangement of atoms, molecules, or ions.

crystal [ˈkristl]　晶体

A sample of a crystalline solid that has a regular shape bound by plane surfaces (*facets*) that intersect at characteristic angles. The shape results from the arrangement of the substances atoms, ions, or molecules. Most crystals contain defects that can strongly affect their optical and electrical properties.

freezing point　凝固点（m. p.）

The temperature at which the vapor pressure of a liquid is equal to the vapor pressure of the corresponding solid form. The liquid and solid forms can coexist at equilibrium at the freezing point. The standard melting point is the melting point at standard pressure.

lattice [ˈlætis] *n.* 点阵，晶格

A regular array of ions or atoms.

perfect crystal　完美晶体

A crystal with no defects or impurities, made of completely identical repeating subunits. Further, a perfect crystal has only one possible arrangement of subunits, with every subunit making exactly the same contribution to the total energy of the crystal.

van der Waals radius [ˈreidiəs]　范德华半径

One half the distance between two nonbonded atoms, when attractive and repulsive forces between the atoms are balanced.

1.4 Solution

solution [səˈluːʃ(ə)n] *n.* 溶液　homogeneous mixture.　　Compare with heterogeneous mixture.

A sample of matter consisting of more than one pure substance with properties that do not vary within the sample. Also called a homogeneous mixture.

ideal solution　理想溶液

All molecules in an "ideal solution" interact in exactly the same way; the solvent-solvent, solvent-solute, and solute-solute intermolecular forces are all equivalent. Ideal solutions obey Raoult's law exactly. Real solutions behave ideally only when they are very dilute.

standard solution　标准溶液

A solution of precisely known concentration.

solute [ˈsɔljuːt] *n.* 溶解物，溶质

A substance dissolved in a solvent to make a solution.

solvent [ˈsɔlvənt] *n.* 溶剂

The most abundant component in a solution.

sol [səul] *n.* 溶胶，胶体溶液

A colloid with solid particles suspended in a liquid. Examples are protoplasm, starch in water, and gels.

solubility [ˌsɔljuˈbiliti] *n.* 可溶性，溶解性   solubilities; equilibrium solubility.

The solubility of a substance is its concentration in a saturated solution. Substances with solubilities much less than 1 g/100 mL of solvent are usually considered insoluble. The solubility is sometimes called "equilibrium solubility" because the rates at which solute dissolves and is deposited out of solution are equal at this concentration.

solubilizing group   增溶基团

A group or substructure on a molecule that increases the molecule's solubility. Solubilizing groups usually make the molecule they are attached to ionic or polar. For example, hydrocarbon chains can be made water-soluble by attaching a carboxylic acid group to the molecule.

Raoult's law   拉乌尔定律

The vapor pressure of a solvent in an ideal solution equals the mole fraction of the solvent times the vapor pressure of the pure solvent.

aeration [ˌeiəˈreiʃən] *n.* 充气，通气

Preparation of a saturated solution of air gases by either spraying the solution in air or by bubbling air through it.

aerosol [ˈeərəsɔl] *n.* 气溶胶   Compare with colloid.

A colloid in which solid particles or liquid droplets are suspended in a gas. Smoke is an example of a solid aerosol; fog is an example of a liquid aerosol.

colloid [ˈkɔlɔid] *n.* 胶体

A colloid is a heterogeneous mixture composed of tiny particles suspended in another material. The particles are larger than molecules but less than 1 μm in diameter. Particles this small do not settle out and pass right through filter paper. Milk is an example of a colloid. The particles can be solid, tiny droplets of liquid, or tiny bubbles of gas; the suspending medium can be a solid, liquid, or gas (although gas-gas colloids aren't possible).

gel [dʒel] *n.* 凝胶

A gel is a sol in which the solid particles fuse or entangle to produce a rigid or semirigid mixture. For example, gelatin dissolved in water produces a sol of protein molecules. When the gelatin is cooked, the protein chains entangle and crosslink, forming a gel which is a mesh of solid protein with trapped pockets of liquid inside. Fruit jellies are also gels.

aqueous [ˈeikwiəs] *adj.* 水的，水状的 （aq.）   aqueous solution.

A substance dissolved in water.

emulsion [iˈmʌlʃən] *n.* 乳状液   Compare with colloid.

A colloid formed from tiny liquid droplets suspended in another, immiscible liquid. Milk is an example of an emulsion.

foam [fəum] *n.* 泡沫   Compare with colloid.

A colloid in which bubbles of gas are suspended in a solid or liquid. Aerogel (solid smoke) and styrafoam are examples of solid foams; whipped cream is an example of a liquid foam.

azeotrope [əˈziːətrəup] *n.* 共沸混合物，恒沸物   azeotropic mixture; azeotropy.

A solution that does not change composition when distilled. For example, if a 95% (W/W) ethanol solution in water is boiled, the vapor produced also is 95% ethanol — and it is not possible to obtain higher percentages of ethanol by distillation.

boiling point elevation *n.* 沸点升高

The boiling point of a solution is higher than the boiling point of the pure solvent. Boiling point elevation is a colligative property.

colligative property ['kɔligətiv] ['prɔpəti] 依数性 colligative; colligative properties.

Properties of a solution that depend on the number of solute molecules present, but not on the nature of the solute. Osmotic pressure, vapor pressure, freezing point depression, and boiling point elevation are examples of colligative properties.

dilution [dai'lju:ʃən,di'l-] n. 稀释,稀释法

Adding solvent to a solution to lower its concentration.

ebulliometry [i,bʌli'ɔmitri] n. 沸点升高测定法 ebulliometric.

Determination of average molecular weight of a dissolved substance from the boiling point elevation of the solution.

equivalent [i'kwivələnt] n. 当量,等价物,相等物 Compare with normality.

(1) The amount of substance that gains or loses one mole of electrons in a redox reaction.

(2) The amount of substances that releases or accepts one mole of hydrogen ions in a neutralization reaction.

(3) The amount of electrolyte that carries one mole of positive or negative charge, for example, 1 mole of Ba^{2+} (aq) is 2 equivalents of Ba^{2+} (aq).

normality [nɔ:'mæliti] n. 当量浓度 Compare with molarity and equivalent.

A measure of solution concentration, defined as the number of equivalents of solute per liter of solution.

molarity [məu'læriti] n. 摩尔浓度 molar concentration.

Concentration of a solution measured as the number of moles of solute per liter of solution. For example, a 6 M HCl solution contains 6 moles of HCl per liter of solution.

molality [məu'læliti] n. 质量摩尔浓度 Compare with molarity.

Concentration measured as moles of solute per kilogram of solvent. For example, a 1 m NaCl solution contains 1 mole of NaCl per kilogram of water. Molalities are preferred over molarities in experiments that involve temperature changes of solutions, e. g. calorimetry and freezing point depression experiments.

eutectic mixture [ju:'tektik] ['mikstʃə] 低熔混合物

A mixture of two or more substances with melting point lower than that for any other mixture of the same substances.

freezing point depression [di'preʃən] 凝固点下降 (ΔT_{fp})

The freezing point of a solution is always lower than the freezing point of the pure solvent. The freezing point depression is roughly proportional to the molality of solute particles in the solution. Freezing point depression is an example of a colligative property of a solution.

Henry's Law 亨利定律 Henry's law constant.

Henry's law predicts that the solubility (c) of a gas or volatile substance in a liquid is proportional to the partial pressure (p) of the substance over the liquid:

$$p = kc$$

where k is called the Henry's law constant and is characteristic of the solvent and the solute.

hydrophilic [,haidrəu'filik] adj. 亲水的,吸水的 hydrophilicity; hydrophilic group.

A polar molecule or group that can form strong hydrogen bonds with water.

hydrophobic [,haidrəu'fəubik] adj. 疏水的,憎水的, hydrophobicity; hydrophobic group.

A nonpolar molecule or group that has little affinity for water. Hydrophobic groups on molecules in solution tend to turn in on themselves or clump together with other hydrophobic groups because they are unable to disrupt the network of strong hydrogen bonds in the water around them.

hypertonic [ˌhaipə(ː)'tɔnik] *adj.* 高渗的   Compare with osmotic pressure.

Describes a solution which has higher osmotic pressure than some other solution (usually, higher osmotic pressure than cell or body fluids). Freshwater fish die if placed in seawater because the seawater is hypertonic, and causes water to leave the cells in fish's body.

hypotonic [ˌhaipəu'tɔnik] *adj.* 低渗的   Compare with osmotic pressure.

Describes a solution which has lower osmotic pressure than some other solution (usually, lower osmotic pressure than cell or body fluids). Washing your contact lenses with distilled water rather than saline is painful because distilled water is hypotonic; it causes water to move into cells, and they swell and burst.

osmotic pressure [ɔz'mɔtik] ['preʃə(r)] 渗透压

Pressure which must be applied to a solution to prevent water from flowing in via a semipermeable membrane.

semipermeable membrane ['semi'pəːmiəb(ə)l] ['membrein] 半透膜

A membrane that allows some but not all of the components in a mixture to pass through it. Semipermeable membranes are used in dialysis.

sorption ['sɔːpʃən] *n.* 吸附作用，吸着作用   Compare with adsorption.

Assimilation of molecules of one substance by a material in a different phase. Adsorption (sorption on a surface) and absorption (sorption into bulk material) are two types of sorption phenomena.

Tyndall effect 丁铎尔效应

Light passing through a colloid is scattered by suspended particles. The light beam becomes clearly visible; this phenomenon is called the Tyndall effect. For example, car headlight beams can be seen in fog, but the beams are invisible in clear air.

vapor pressure lowering ['veipə] ['preʃə(r)] ['ləuəriŋ] 蒸气压降低   vapour pressure depression.

A colligative property of solutions. The vapor pressure of a solution is always lower than the vapor pressure of the pure solvent; the ratio of solution to pure solvent vapor pressures is approximately equal to the mole fraction of solvent in the solution.

1.5 Reactions in Solution

balanced equation 平衡方程式

A description of a chemical reaction that gives the chemical formulas of the reactants and the products of the reaction, with coefficients introduced so that the number of each type of atom and the total charge is unchanged by the reaction. For example, a balanced equation for the reaction of sodium metal [$Na(s)$] with chlorine gas [$Cl_2(g)$] to form table salt [$NaCl(s)$] would be $2Na(s)+Cl_2(g) = 2NaCl(s)$, NOT $Na(s)+Cl_2(g) = NaCl(s)$.

chemical equation 化学方程式

A compact notation for describing a chemical change. The formulas of the reactants are added together on the left hand side of the equation; the formulas of the products are added together on the right side. Coefficients are inserted before the formulas to ensure that the equation is balanced. The phase in which each substance is found is usually indicated in parentheses after each formula. For example, $2H_2(g) + O_2(g) \Longrightarrow 2H_2O(g)$ indicates that 2 moles of hydrogen gas combine with one mole of oxygen gas to produce two moles of steam.

combination reaction　化合反应

A reaction in which two or more substances are chemically bonded together to produce a product. For example, $2Na(s) + Cl_2(g) \longrightarrow 2NaCl(s)$ is a combination reaction.

combustion [kəm'bʌstʃən] *n.* 燃烧　combustion reaction.

A chemical reaction between a fuel and an oxidizing agent that produces heat (and usually, light). For example, the combustion of methane is represented as $CH_4(g) + 2O_2(g) \Longrightarrow CO_2(g) + 2H_2O(l)$.

complete ionic equation　完全离子方程式　total ionic equation.　Compare with net ionic equation.

A balanced equation that describes a reaction occurring in solution, in which all strong electrolytes are written as dissociated ions.

net ionic equation　净离子方程式　Compare with net ionic equation and molecular equation.

A net ionic equation is an ionic equation with all define spectator ions eliminated. For example, $Ag^+(aq) + NO_3^-(aq) + Na^+(aq) + Cl^-(aq) \Longrightarrow AgCl(s) + Na^+(aq) + NO_3^-(aq)$ is an ionic equation; the net ionic equation would be $Ag^+(aq) + Cl^-(aq) \Longrightarrow AgCl(s)$ because the sodium and nitrate ions are spectators (they appear on both sides of the ionic equation).

molecular equation　分子方程式　Compare with ionic equation.

A molecular equation is a balanced chemical equation in which ionic compounds are written as neutral formulas rather than as ions. For example, $AgNO_3(aq) + NaCl(aq) \Longrightarrow AgCl(s) + NaNO_3(aq)$ is a molecular equation; $Ag^+(aq) + NO_3^-(aq) + Na^+(aq) + Cl^-(aq) \Longrightarrow AgCl(s) + Na^+(aq) + NO_3^-(aq)$ is not.

ionic equation　离子方程式　complete ionic equation.　Compare with net ionic equation and molecular equation.

An ionic equation is a balanced chemical equation in which strong electrolytes are written as dissociated ions. For example, $Ag^+(aq) + NO_3^-(aq) + Na^+(aq) + Cl^-(aq) \Longrightarrow AgCl(s) + Na^+(aq) + NO_3^-(aq)$ is an ionic equation; $AgNO_3(aq) + NaCl(aq) \Longrightarrow AgCl(s) + NaNO_3(aq)$ is not.

decomposition reaction *n.* 分解反应　Compare with synthesis.

A reaction in which a compound is broken down into simpler compounds or elements. Compounds sometimes decompose if heated strongly or if subjected to a strong electric current (electrolysis).

synthesis ['sinθisis] *n.* 合成　synthesize; synthetic reaction.　Compare with decomposition.

Formation of a complex product from simpler reactants. For example, water can be synthesized from oxygen and hydrogen gas: $H_2(g) + 1/2 O_2(g) \longrightarrow H_2O(l)$.

displacement [dis'pleismənt] *n.* 置换, 取代　displacement reaction; replacement reaction.

A reaction in which a fragment of one reactant is replaced by another reactant (or by a fragent of another reactant). Displacement reactions have the same number of products as reactants, and are described by equations of the form A+BC ⟶ AB +C (single displacement) or AB+CD ⟶ AC+BD (double displacement).

double displacement ['dʌbl] [dis'pleismənt] 复分解反应

A double displacement or metathesis is a reaction in which two reactants trade fragments:

$$AB+CD = AC+BD$$

Most commonly, the fragments are ions, e.g. $AgNO_3(aq) + NaCl(aq) = AgCl(s) + NaNO_3(aq)$

endpoint ['endpɔint] *n*. 终点   end point.   Compare with equivalence point.

The experimental estimate of the equivalence point in a titration.

equivalence point   化学计量点   Compare with end point.

The equivalence point is the point in a titration when enough titrant has been added to react completely with the analyte.

insoluble [in'sɔljubl] *adj*. 不能溶解的   insolubility.

Refers to a substance that does not dissolve in a solvent to any significant degree. Compounds with solubilities of less than 1 g per liter of water are often referred to as "insoluble", even though they *do* dissolve to a small extent.

limiting reactant   起限定作用的反应物

The reactant that limits the amount of product produced in a chemical reaction. For example, mixing one mole of $H_2(g)$ with one mole of O_2 produces one mole of steam [$H_2O(g)$], with half a mole of $O_2(g)$ remaining. The hydrogen gas limits the amount of steam produced in this case.

nonelectrolyte ['nɔni'lektrəulait] *n*. 非电解质

A nonelectrolyte is a substance which does not ionize in solution.

precipitate [pri'sipiteit] *n*. 沉淀物

An insoluble substance that has been formed from substances dissolved in a solution. For example, mixing silver nitrate and sodium chloride solutions produces a precipitate, insoluble silver chloride (along with soluble sodium nitrate).

precipitation [pri,sipi'teiʃən] *n*. 沉淀

Precipitation is the conversion of a dissolved substance into insoluble form by chemical or physical means.

product ['prɔdəkt] *n*. 产物   Compare with reactant.

A substance that is produced during a chemical change.

reactant [ri:'æktənt] *n*. 反应物

A substance that is consumed during a chemical change.

rearrangement reaction [,ri:ə'reindʒmənt] [ri(:)'ækʃən] 重排反应   isomerization; isomerize.

A reaction in which a reactant and product are isomers of each other. Chemical bonds within the reactant are broken and reformed to produce the product.

saturated solution   饱和溶液   Compare with supersaturated solution.

A solution which does not dissolve any more solute. When a saturated solution is placed in contact with additional solute, solute neither dissolves nor is deposited from a saturated solution.

supersaturated solution [sju:pə'sætʃəreit] 过饱和溶液   supersaturated.

A supersaturated solution has concentration of solute that is higher than its solubility. A crystal of solute dropped into a supersaturated solution grows; excess solute is deposited out of the solution until the concentration falls to the equilibrium solubility.

spectator ion　表观离子

A spectator ion is an ion that appears as both a reactant and a product in an ionic equation. For example, in the ionic equation

$$Ag^+(aq) + NO_3^-(aq) + Na^+(aq) + Cl^-(aq) \Longrightarrow AgCl(s) + Na^+(aq) + NO_3^-(aq)$$

The sodium and nitrate ions are spectator ions.

titrant ['taitrənt] $n.$ 滴定剂，滴定（用）标准液

The substance that quantitatively reacts with the analyte in a titration. The titrant is usually a standard solution added carefully to the analyte until the reaction is complete. The amount of analyte is calculated from the volume of titrant required for complete reaction.

titration curve　滴定曲线

A plot that summarizes data collected in a titration. A linear titration curve plots moles of analyte (or, some quantity proportional to moles of analyte) on the Y axis, and the volume of titrant added on the X axis. Nonlinear plots use the log of the concentration of the analyte instead. Nonlinear titration curves are often used for neutralization titrations (pH vs. mL NaOH solution). Logs are used to exaggerate the rate of change of concentration on the plot, so that the endpoint can be determined from the point of maximal slope.

titration [tai'treiʃən] $n.$ 滴定

A procedure for determining the amount of some unknown substance (the analyte) by quantitative reaction with a measured volume of a solution of precisely known concentration (the titrant).

strong electrolyte [i'lektrəulait]　强电解质　　Compare with weak electrolyte.

A strong electrolyte is a solute that completely dissociates into ions in solution. Solutions of strong electrolytes conduct electricity. Most soluble ionic compounds are strong electrolytes.

weak electrolyte　弱电解质

A weak electrolyte is a solute that incompletely dissociates into ions in solution. For example, acetic acid partially dissociates into acetate ions and hydrogen ions, so that an acetic acid solution contains both molecules and ions. A solution of a weak electrolyte can conduct electricity, but usually not as well as a strong electrolyte because there are fewer ions to carry the charge from one electrode to the other.

2. Inorganic Chemistry

2.1 The Periodic Table

inorganic chemistry 无机化学

The study of inorganic compounds, specifically their structure, reactions, catalysis, and mechanism of action.

inorganic compound 无机化合物

A compound that does not contain carbon chemically bound to hydrogen. Carbonates, bicarbonates, carbides, and carbon oxides are considered inorganic compounds, even though they contain carbon.

alkaline metal [ˈælkəlain] [ˈmet(ə)l] 碱金属

The Group 1 elements, lithium (Li), sodium (Na), potassium (K), rubidium (Rb), cesium (Cs), and francium (Fr) react with cold water for form strongly alkaline hydroxide solutions, and are referred to as "alkali metals". Hydrogen is not considered an alkali metal, despite its position on some periodic tables.

alkaline earth [ˌælkəlain] 碱土

An oxide of an alkaline earth metal, which produces an alkaline solution in reaction with water.

alkaline earth metal 碱土金属 (alkali metal)

The Group 2 elements, beryllium (Be), magnesium (Mg), calcium (Ca), strontium (Sr), barium (Ba), and radium (Ra) form alkaline oxides and hydroxides and are called "alkaline earth metals".

amphoteric [ˌæmfəˈterik] *adj.* 两性的 ampholyte.

A substance that can act as either an acid or a base in a reaction. For example, aluminum hydroxide can neutralize mineral acids [$Al(OH)_3 + 3HCl = AlCl_3 + 3H_2O$] or strong bases [$Al(OH)_3 + 3NaOH = Na_3AlO_3 + 3H_2O$].

block [blɔk] *n.* 区

A region of the periodic table that corresponds to the type of subshell (s, p, d, or f) being filled during the aufbau construction of electron configurations.

congener [ˈkɔndʒinə] *n.* 同族元素，同系物

(1) Elements belonging to the same group on the periodic table. For example, sodium and potassium are congeners.

(2) Compounds produced by identical synthesis reactions and procedures.

first ionization energy [ˌaiənaiˈzeiʃən] 第一电离能 (IE, IP) first ionization potential.

Compare with second ionization energy, adiabatic ionization energy, vertical ionization energy, electronegativity, and electron affinity.

The energy needed to remove an electron from an isolated, neutral atom.

ionization energy 电离能 ionization potential. Compare with adiabatic ionization energy, vertical ionization energy, electronegativity, and electron affinity.

The energy needed to remove an electron from a gaseous atom or ion.

second ionization energy 第二电离能 second ionization potential. Compare with first ionization energy, adiabatic ionization energy, vertical ionization energy, electronegativity, and electron affinity.

The energy needed to remove an electron from an isolated +1 ion. The third ionization energy would be the energy required to remove an electron from an isolated $+2$ ion, and so on.

group [gru:p] *n.* 官能团，族

(1) A substructure that imparts characteristic chemical behaviors to a molecule, for example, a carboxylic acid group (also: functional group).

(2) A vertical column on the periodic table, for example, the halogens. Elements that belong to the same group usually show chemical similarities, although the element at the top of the group is usually atypical.

halogen [ˈhælədʒən] *n.* 卤素　　group ⅦA; group 18.

An element of group ⅦA. The name means "salt former"; halogens react with metals to form binary ionic compounds. Fluorine (F), chlorine (Cl), bromine (Br), iodine (I), and astatine (At) are known at this time.

lanthanide contraction [lænθəˈnid, -ˈnaid] [kənˈtrækʃən] 镧系收缩

An effect that causes sixth period elements with filled 4f subshells to be smaller than otherwise expected. The intervention of the lanthanides increases the effective nuclear charge, which offsets the size increase expected from filling the $n=6$ valence shell. As a consequence, sixth period transition metals are about the same size as their fifth period counterparts.

lanthanide [lænθəˈnid, -ˈnaid] *n.* 镧系元素　　Compare with actinide and inner transition metals.

Elements 57~71 are called lanthanides. Electrons added during the Aufbau construction of lanthanide atoms go into the 4f subshell.

actinide [ˈæktinaid] *n.* 锕系元素

Elements 89~103 are called actinides. Electrons added during the Aufbau construction of actinide atoms go into the 5f subshell. Actinides are unstable and undergo radioactive decay. The most common actinides on Earth are uranium and thorium.

main elements　主族元素

Elements of the s and p blocks.

metal *n.* 金属　　metallic.　　Compare with nonmetal and metalloid.

A metal is a substance that conducts heat and electricity, is shiny and reflects many colors of light, and can be hammered into sheets or drawn into wire. Metals lose electrons easily to form cations. About 80% of the known chemical elements are metals.

nonmetal [ˈnɔnˈmetl] *n.* 非金属（元素）(metal, metalloid) non-metal.

A nonmetal is a substance that conducts heat and electricity poorly, is brittle or waxy or gaseous, and cannot be hammered into sheets or drawn into wire. Nonmetals gain electrons easily to form anions. About 20% of the known chemical elements are nonmetals.

periodic law [piəriˈɔdik] [lɔː]（元素）周期律

The periodic law states that physical and chemical properties of the elements recur in a regular way when the elements are arranged in order of increasing atomic number.

periodic table　（元素）周期表

An arrangement of the elements according to increasing atomic number that shows relationships between element properties.

periodic trend　周期趋势

A regular variation in element properties with increasing atomic number that is ultimately due to regular variations in atomic structure.

period ['piəriəd] *n.* 周期

Rows in the periodic table are called periods. For example, all of the elements in the second row are referred to as 'second period elements'. All elements currently known fall in the first seven periods.

transition metal 过渡金属元素　transition element

An element with an incomplete d subshell. Elements which have common cations with incomplete d subshells are also considered transition metals. Elements with incomplete f subshells are sometimes called "inner transition elements".

atomic radius 原子半径　metallic radius; covalent radius; atomic radii.　Compare with ionic radius.

One half the distance between nuclei of atoms of the same element, when the atoms are bound by a single covalent bond or are in a metallic crystal. The radius of atoms obtained from covalent bond lengths is called the covalent radius; the radius from interatomic distances in metallic crystals is called the metallic radius.

ionic radius 离子半径

The radii of anions and cations in crystalline ionic compounds, as determined by consistently partitioning the center-to-center distance of ions in those compounds.

2.2　Chemical Bonds

antibonding orbital ['ænti,bɔndiŋ] ['ɔːbitl] 反键轨道　antibonding; antibonding molecular orbital.

A molecular orbital that can be described as the result of destructive interference of atomic orbitals on bonded atoms. Antibonding orbitals have energies higher than the energies its constituent atomic orbitals would have if the atoms were separate.

average bond enthalpy ['enθælpi, en'θælpi] 平均键焓　Compare with bond enthalpy.

Average enthalpy change per mole when the same type of bond is broken in the gas phase for many similar substances.

bond enthalpy 键焓　Compare with average bond enthalpy.

Enthalpy change per mole when a bond is broken in the gas phase for a particular substance.

bond energy 键能　Compare with bond enthalpy.

Energy change per mole when a bond is broken in the gas phase for a particular substance.

bond length 键长

The average distance between the nuclei of two bonded atoms in a stable molecule.

bond order 键级

(1) In Lewis structures, the number of electron pairs shared by two atoms.

(2) In molecular orbital theory, the net number of electron pairs in bonding orbitals (calculated as half the difference between the number of electrons in bonding orbitals and the number of electrons in antibonding orbitals).

chemical bond 化学键　bond; bonding; chemical bonding.

A chemical bond is a strong attraction between two or more atoms. Bonds hold atoms in molecules and crystals together. There are many types of chemical bonds, but all involve electrons which are either shared or transferred between the bonded atoms.

covalent bond 共价键   covalent; covalently bound.   Compare with covalent compound and ionic bond.

A covalent bond is a very strong attraction between two or more atoms that are sharing their electrons. In structural formulas, covalent bonds are represented by a line drawn between the symbols of the bonded atoms.

electric dipole 电偶极   dipole.

An object whose centers of positive and negative charge do not coincide. For example, a hydrogen chloride (HCl) molecule is an electric dipole because bonding electrons are on average closer to the chlorine atom than the hydrogen, producing a partial positive charge on the H end and a partial negative charge on the Cl end.

electric dipole moment 电偶极矩 (μ) dipole moment.

A measure of the degree of polarity of a polar molecule. Dipole moment is a vector with magnitude equal to charge separation times the distance between the centers of positive and negative charges. Chemists point the vector from the positive to the negative pole; physicists point it the opposite way. Dipole moments are often expressed in units called Debyes.

electronegativity [ˌilektrəuneɡəˈtivɪti] *n.* 电负性   Compare with ionization energy and electron affinity.

Electronegativity is a measure of the attraction an atom has for bonding electrons. Bonds between atoms with different electronegativities are polar, with the bonding electrons spen-ding more time on average around the atom with higher electronegativity.

free radical 自由基

A free radical is a molecule with an odd number of electrons. Free radicals do not have a completed octet and often undergo vigorous redox reactions. Free radicals produced within cells can react with membranes, enzymes, and genetic material, damaging or even killing the cell. Free radicals have been implicated in a number of degenerative conditions, from natural aging to Alzheimer's disease.

geometric isomer 几何异构体

Geometric isomers are molecules that have the same molecular formula and bond connections, but distinctly different shapes.

hydrogen bond 氢键   hydrogen bonding.

An especially strong dipole-dipole force between molecules X—H⋯Y, where X and Y are small electronegative atoms (usually F, N, or O) and "⋯" denotes the hydrogen bond. Hydrogen bonds are responsible for the unique properties of water and they loosely pin biological polymers like proteins and DNA into their characteristic shapes.

incomplete octet 不完全八隅体

(1) An atom with less than eight electrons in its valence shell.

(2) An atom with less than eight total bonding and nonbonding electrons in a Lewis structure, for example, B in BH_3 has an incomplete octet.

inductive effect 诱导效应   inductance effect.

An inductive effect is the polarization of a chemical bond caused by the polarization of an adjacent bond. (Field effects are polarization caused by nonadjacent bonds).

inert pair 惰性电子对   inert pair effect.

Valence electrons in an s orbital penetrate to the nucleus better than electrons in p orbitals, and as a result they're more tightly bound to the nucleus and less able to participate in bond formation. A pair of such electrons is called an "inert pair". The inert pair effect explains why common ions of Pb are Pb^{4+} and Pb^{2+}, and not just Pb^{4+} as we might expect from the octet rule.

infrared spectroscopy 红外光谱学　IR spectroscopy.

A technique for determining the structure (and sometimes concentration) of molecules by observing how infrared radiation is absorbed by a sample.

ionic bond 离子键　ionically bound; ionic bonding.　Compare with covalent bond.

An attraction between ions of opposite charge. Potassium bromide consists of potassium ions (K^+) ionically bound to bromide ions (Br^-). Unlike covalent bonds, ionic bond formation involves transfer of electrons, and ionic bonding is not directional.

ionic compound 离子化合物　salt.　Compare with covalent compound and ionic bond.

A compound made of distinguishable cations and anions, held together by electrostatic forces.

polar bond 极性键　Compare with covalent bond and ionic bond.

A bond involving electrons that are unequally shared. Polar bonds can be thought of as intermediate between the extremes represented by covalent bonds and ionic bonds.

polar molecule 极性分子　Compare with covalent compound, ionic compound and polar bond.

An asymmetric molecule containing polar bonds. H_2O, NH_3, and HCl are examples of polar molecules. Non-examples are CO_2, CCl_4, and BCl_3 which contain polar bonds but are nonpolar because they have symmetric shapes. Alkanes are usually asymmetric but are nonpolar because they contain no polar bonds. Polar molecules are electric dipoles and they attract each other via dipole-dipole forces.

lone pair 孤电子对　nonbonding pair; unshared pair.

Electrons that are not involved in bonding.

molecular geometry 分子构型

(1) The three-dimensional shape of a molecule. For example, methane (CH_4) has a tetrahedral molecular geometry.

(2) The study of molecular shapes.

molecular orbital 分子轨道　Compare with atomic orbital and orbital.

A wavefunction that describes the behavior of an electron in a molecule. Molecular orbitals are usually spread across many atoms in the molecule, and they are often described as a combination of atomic orbitals on those atoms.

multiple bond 多键，重键

Sharing of more than one electron pair between bonded atoms. A double bond consists of two shared pairs of electrons; a triple bond consists of three shared pairs.

octet rule 八隅律，八电子规则

A guideline for building Lewis structures that states that atoms tend to gain, lose, or share valence electrons with other atoms in a molecule until they hold or share eight valence electrons. The octet rule almost always holds for carbon, nitrogen, oxygen, and fluorine; it is regularly violated for other elements.

pi bond π键 (π bond)　Compare with sigma bond.

In the valence bond theory, a pi bond is a valence bond formed by side-by-side overlap of p orbitals on two bonded atoms. In most multiple bonds, the first bond is a sigma bond and all of the others are pi bonds.

sigma bond σ键 (σ bond)

In the valence bond theory, a sigma bond is a valence bond that is symmetrical around the imaginary line between the bonded atoms. Most single bonds are sigma bonds.

resonance ['rezənəns] *n*. 共振

Description of the ground state of a molecule with delocalized electrons as an average of several Lewis structures. The actual ground state doesn't switch rapidly between the separate structures; it is an average.

resonance effect 共振效应 mesomeric effect.

If electron density at a particular point in a molecule is higher or lower than what you'd expect from a single Lewis structure, and various canonical structures can be drawn to show how electron delocalization will explain the discrepancy, the difference in electron density is called a "resonance effect" or "mesomeric effect".

triple bond 三键

A covalent bond that involves 3 bonding pairs. In the valence bond theory, one of the bonds in a triple bond is a sigma bond and the other two are pi bonds. For example, the central bond in acetylene is a triple bond: H—C≡C—H.

valence ['veiləns] *n*. （化合）价，原子价

The number of hydrogen atoms that typically bond to an atom of an element. For example, in H_2O, oxygen has a valence of -2; carbon in CH_4 has a valence of -4.

valence bond 共价键

In the valence bond theory, a valence bond is a chemical bond formed by overlap of half-filled atomic orbitals on two different atoms.

valence electron 价电子

Electrons that can be actively involved in chemical change; usually electrons in the shell with the highest value of n. For example, sodium's ground state electron configuration is $1s^2 2s^2 2p^6 3s^1$; the 3s electron is the only valence electron in the atom. Germanium (Ge) has the ground state electron configuration $1s^2 2s^2 2p^6 3s^2 3p^6 3d^{10} 4s^2 4p^2$; the 4s and 4p electrons are the valence electrons.

valence shell 价电子层

The shell corresponding to the highest value of principal quantum number in the atom. The valence electrons in this shell are on average farther from the nucleus than other electrons; they are often directly involved in chemical reaction.

acid-base indicator 酸碱指示剂

A weak acid that has acid and base forms with sharply different colors. Changes in pH around the acid's pK_a are "indicated" by color changes.

base hydrolysis constant 碱电离平衡常数，碱离解常数 (K_b) base ionization constant; basic hydrolysis constant. Compare with acid dissociation constant.

The equilibrium constant for the hydrolysis reaction associated with a base. For example, K_b for ammonia is the equilibrium constant for $NH_3(aq) + H_2O(l) \rightleftharpoons NH_4^+ (aq) + OH^- (aq)$, or $K_b = [NH_4^+][OH^-]/[NH_3]$.

acid dissociation constant 酸电离平衡常数，酸离解常数 (K_a) acid ionization constant. Compare with base hydrolysis constant.

The equilibrium constant for the dissociation of an acid into a hydrogen ion and an anion. For example, the acid dissociation constant for acetic acid is the equilibrium constant for $CH_3COOH(aq) \rightleftharpoons H^+(aq) + CH_3COO^-(aq)$, which is $K_a = [H^+][CH_3COO^-]/[CH_3COOH]$.

alkaline ['ælkəlain] *adj*. 碱的，碱性的

Having a pH greater than 7.

amphiprotic solvent　两性溶剂　Compare with aprotic solvent.

Solvents that exhibit both acidic and basic properties; amphiprotic solvents undergo autoprotolysis. Examples are water, ammonia, and ethanol.

aprotic solvent　非质子溶剂　Compare with amphiprotic solvent.

A solvent that does not act as an acid or as a base; aprotic solvents don't undergo autoprotolysis. Examples are pentane, pet ether, and toluene.

aqua regia　王水

A mixture of nitric and hydrochloric acids, usually 1 : 3 or 1 : 4 parts HNO_3 to HCl, used to dissolve gold.

autoprotolysis [ˌɔːtəprəuˈtɔlisis]　质子自递作用　autoionization; autoionization constant; autoprotolysis constant.

Transfer of a hydrogen ion between molecules of the same substance, e. g. the autoprotolysis of methanol

buffer [ˈbʌfə] *n*. 缓冲液，缓冲剂　pH buffer; buffer solution.

A solution that can maintain its pH value with little change when acids or bases are added to it. Buffer solutions are usually prepared as mixtures of a weak acid with its own salt or mixtures of salts of weak acids. For example, a 50 : 50 mixture of 1mol/L acetic acid and 1mol/L sodium acetate buffers pH around 4.7.

ionic dissociation　离子离解，电离　ionize; ionization.

When ionic substances dissolve, their ions are surrounded by solvent molecules and separated from each other. This phenomena is also called ionization.

K_w　水的离子积常数

Symbol for the autoprotolysis constant for water, equal to 1.01×10^{-14} at 25℃.

litmus [ˈlitməs] *n*. 石蕊

A mixture of pigments extracted from certain lichens that turns blue in basic solution and red in acidic solution.

litmus paper　石蕊试纸　litmus test.

Paper impregnated with litmus, usually cut in narrow strips. Dipping red litmus paper into a basic solution turns it blue; dipping blue litmus paper into an acidic solution turns it red.

neutral [ˈnjuːtrəl] *adj*. 中性的

(1) Having no net electrical charge. Atoms are electrically neutral; ions are not.

(2) A solution containing equal concentrations of H^+ and OH^-.

neutralization reaction　中和反应　neutralization; acid-base reaction.

A chemical change in which one compound acquires H^+ from another. The compound that receives the hydrogen ion is the base; the compound that surrenders it is an acid.

nitric acid　硝酸

A corrosive liquid with a sharp odor that acts as a strong acid when dissolved in water. Nitric acid is used to synthesize ammonium nitrate for fertilizers, and is also used in the manufacture of explosives, dyes, and pharmaceuticals. Salts of nitric acid are called nitrates.

pH

pH is a measure of effective concentration of hydrogen ions in a solution. It is approximately related to the molarity of H^+ by $pH = -\lg[H^+]$

phenolphthalein [ˌfinəlˈfθæliːn]　酚酞

An organic compound used as an acid-base indicator. The compound is colorless in acidic solution and pink in basic solution (with the transition occuring around pH 8.3). Phenolpthalein was used for many years as a laxative in very low concentrations—high concentrations are toxic!

proton donor 质子给（予）体，质子供体，酸 acid.   Compare with base.

Because a free H^+ ion is technically a bare proton, acids are sometimes referred to as "proton donors" because they release hydrogen ions in solution. The term "proton donor" is misleading, since in aqueous solution, the hydrogen ion is never a bare proton—it's covalently bound to a water molecule as an H_3O^+ ion. Further, acids don't "donate" protons; they yield them to bases with a stronger affinity for them.

strong acid 强酸

A strong acid is an acid that completely dissociates into hydrogen ions and anions in solution. Strong acids are strong electrolytes. There are only six common strong acids: HCl (hydrochloric acid), HBr (hydrobromic acid), HI (hydroiodic acid), H_2SO_4 (sulfuric acid), $HClO_4$ (perchloric acid), and HNO_3 (nitric acid).

weak acid 弱酸

An acid that only partially dissociates into hydrogen ions and anions in solution. Weak acids are weak electrolytes. Recognize weak acids by learning the six common strong acids; any acid that doesn't appear on the list of strong acids is usually a weak acid.

strong base 强碱

A strong base is a base that completely dissociates into ions in solution. Strong bases are strong electrolytes. The most common strong bases are alkali metal and alkaline earth metal hydroxides.

weak base 弱碱

A base that only partially dissociates into ions in solution. Weak bases are weak electrolytes. Ammonia is an example of a weak base; the reaction $NH_3(aq) + H_2O(l) \rightleftharpoons NH_4^+(aq) + OH^-(aq)$ is reversible.

EDTA   乙二胺四乙酸   ethylenediaminetetracetic acid; versine.

A polydentate ligand that tightly complexes certain metal ions. EDTA is used as a blood preservative by complexing free calcium ion (which promotes blood clotting). EDTA's ability to bind to lead ions makes it useful as an antidote for lead poisoning.

2.3 Redox Reactions

agar ['eigɑ:] *n*.   琼脂（一种植物胶）

A gel made from seaweed used to make salt bridges.

anodize ['ænəudaiz] *v*.   阳极电镀，作阳极化处理

To coat a metal with a protective film by electrolysis.

battery acid 电池酸

A solution of approximately 6M sulfuric acid used in the lead storage battery.

corrosion [kə'rəuʒən] *n*.   侵蚀，腐蚀   corrode.

Corrosion is a reaction that involves action of an oxidizing agent on a metal. The oxidizing agent is often oxygen dissolved in water.

disproportionation [,disprə,pɔ:ʃə'neiʃən] *n*.   歧化反应   disproportionate; disproportionating.

A reaction involving a substance that produces two different forms of the substance, one more oxidized and the other more reduced than the original.

dry cell 干电池

A electrolytic cell that uses a moist paste rather than a liquid as an electrolyte. Flashlight batteries are dry cells with a zinc cup for an anode, a carbon rod for a cathode, and a paste made of powdered carbon, NH_4Cl, $ZnCl_2$, and MnO_2 for an electrolyte.

electrochemical cell 电化学电池 electric cell.

A device that uses a redox reaction to produce electricity, or a device that uses electricity to drive a redox reaction in the desired direction.

electrolytic cell [i,lektrəu'litik] *n.* 电解池

A device that uses electricity from an external source to drive a redox reaction.

electrolysis [ilek'trɔlisis] *n.* 电解

The process of driving a redox reaction in the reverse direction by passage of an electric current through the reaction mixture.

ferroin ['ferə,in] *n.* 邻二氮菲亚铁离子，邻菲咯啉亚铁离子

A blood-red complex of Fe^{2+} ion with 1,10-phenanthroline, used as a redox indicator. Ferroin changes from red to pale blue when oxidized.

oxidation [ɔksi'deiʃən] *n.* 氧化 oxidize; oxidizing; oxidized.   Compare with reduction.

Oxidation is the loss of one or more electrons by an atom, molecule, or ion. Oxidation is accompanied by an increase in oxidation number on the atoms, molecules, or ions that lose electrons.

reduction [ri'dʌkʃən] *n.* 还原   reduce; reduced; reducing.

Reduction is gain of one or more electrons by an atom, molecule, or ion. Reduction is accompanied by a decrease in oxidation number.

oxidizing agent 氧化剂 oxidant; oxidizer.   Compare with reducing agent.

A reactant that removing electrons from other reactants in a chemical reaction. Oxidizing agents cause other substances to be oxidized in chemical reactions while they themselves are reduced. For example, nitrate ion is an oxidizing agent in the following reaction:
$$Cu(s)+4H^+(aq)+2NO_3^-(aq) \longrightarrow Cu^{2+}(aq)+2H_2O(l)+2NO_2(g)$$
Copper gets oxidized (its oxidation number goes from 0 to $+2$) while the nitrogen gets reduced (from $+5$ in nitrate to $+4$ in nitrogen dioxide).

reducing agent 还原剂 reductant.   Compare with oxidizing agent.

A reducing agent is a substance that reduce another substance by supplying electrons to it. Reducing agents cause other substances to be reduced in chemical reactions while they themselves are oxidized. For example, tin(Ⅱ) is a reducing agent in the following reaction:
$$Sn^{2+}(aq)+2Fe^{3+}(aq) \longrightarrow Sn^{4+}(aq)+2Fe^{2+}(aq)$$

oxidation number 氧化数 oxidation state; positive valence.

A convention for representing a charge of an atom embedded within a compound, if the compound were purely ionic. For example, H_2O is a covalent compound; if it were ionic, the hydrogens would be H^+ (oxidation number $+1$) and the oxygen would be O_2^- (oxidation number -2). Oxidation number rises for at least one atom in a compound that is oxidized; oxidation number becomes smaller if the compound is reduced.

potential difference 电势差 electrical potential difference.

Work that must be done to move an electric charge between specified points. Electric potential differences are measured in volts.

redox indicator 氧化还原指示剂 oxidation-reduction indicator.

An organic molecule that has reduced and oxidized forms with different colors; interconversion of the reduced and oxidized forms of the indicator must be reversible. Ferroin is an example.

redox reaction　氧化还原反应　electrochemical reaction; oxidation-reduction reaction; redox.

A reaction that involves transfer of electrons from one substance to another. Redox reactions always involve a change in oxidation number for at least two elements in the reactants.

redox titration　氧化还原滴定　oxidation-reduction titration.

A titration based on a redox reaction. For example, iron in water can be determined by converting dissolved iron to Fe^{2+} and titrating the solution with potassium permanganate ($KMnO_4$), a powerful oxidizing agent.

salt bridge　盐桥

A tube (often filled with ion-laced agar) that allows two solutions to be in electrical contact without mixing in an electrochemical cell.

voltaic cell　原电池　galvanic cell.

An electrochemical cell that spontaneously generates electrical energy.

voltaic pile　原电池

An early battery consisting of disks of dissimilar metals (usually zinc and copper) separated by moist paper or cloth soaked in an electrolyte solution.

voltammeter [vɔlˈtæmitə] *n*. 伏特安培计，电压电流两用表

An instrument for measuring voltages and amperages.

coordination number　配位数

The number of bonds formed by the central atom in a metal-ligand complex.

crystal field splitting energy　晶体场分裂能（Δ）

Ligands complexed to a metal ion will raise the energy of some of its d orbitals and lower the energy of others. The difference in energy is called the crystal field splitting energy.

crystal field theory　晶体场理论　crystal field.

The color, spectra, and magnetic properties of metal-ligand complexes can be explained by modeling the effect of ligands on metal's d orbital energies.

high spin complex　高自旋体，高自旋配合物

A metal-ligand complex with the same number of unpaired electrons as the uncomplexed metal ion. When a weak ligand complexes the metal ion, the crystal field splitting is small and the electrons can still occupy all of the d orbitals without pairing.

low spin complex　低自旋体，低自旋配合物

Compare with high spin complex.

A metal-ligand complex with fewer unpaired electrons than the uncomplexed metal ion. When a strong ligand complexes the metal ion, the crystal field splitting is large and some electrons pair rather than occupying the higher energy d orbitals.

ligand [ˈligənd, ˈlaigənd] *n*. 配体

(1) In inorganic chemistry, a molecule or ion that binds to a metal cation to form a complex.

(2) In biochemistry, a molecule that binds to a receptor, having a biological effect.

2.4　Simple Compounds

acid [ˈæsid] *n*. 酸　Compare with base.

(1) A compound which releases hydrogen ions (H$^+$) in solution (*Arrhenius*).
(2) A compound containing detachable hydrogen ions (*Brønsted-Lowry*).
(3) A compound that can accept a pair of electrons from a base (*Lewis*).

base [beis] 碱 alkali; alkaline; basic.
(1) A compound that reacts with an acid to form a salt.
(2) A compound that produces hydroxide ions in aqueous solution (*Arrhenius*).
(3) A molecule or ion that captures hydrogen ions. (*Bronsted-Lowry*).
(4) A molecule or ion that donates an electron pair to form a chemical bond. (*Lewis*).

Brøsted acid
A material that gives up hydrogen ions in a chemical reaction.

Brøsted base
A material that accepts hydrogen ions in a chemical reaction.

acetate ['æsɪˌteit] *n.* 醋酸盐，醋酸纤维素及其制成的产品（CH_3COO^-，$C_2H_3O_2^-$）acetate ion.
(1) An ion formed by removing the acidic hydrogen of acetic acid，$HC_2H_3O_2$.
(2) A compound derived by replacing the acidic hydrogen in acetic acid.
(3) A fiber made of cellulose.

acetic acid [ə'siːtɪk] ['æsid] *n.* 醋酸，乙酸 vinegar acid; methanecarboxylic acid.
A simple organic acid that gives vinegar its characteristic odor and flavor. Glacial acetic acid is pure acetic acid.

addition compound 复合化合物 complex compound.   Compare with hydrate.
An addition compound contains two or more simpler compounds that can be packed in a definite ratio into a crystal. A dot is used to separate the compounds in the formula. For example，$ZnSO_4 \cdot 7H_2O$ is an addition compound of zinc sulfate and water. This represents a compound，and not a mixture，because there is a definite 1∶7 ratio of zinc sulfate to water in the compound. Hydrates are a common type of addition compound.

hydrate ['haidreit] *n.* 水合物
A hydrate is an addition compound that contains water in weak chemical combination with another compound. For example，crystals of $CuSO_4 \cdot 5H_2O$（copper sulfate pentahydrate）are made of regularly repeating units，each containing 5 molecules of water weakly bound to a copper(Ⅱ) ion and a sulfate ion.

ammonia [ə'məuniə] *n.* 氨，氨水   Compare with ammonium.
Pure NH_3 is a colorless gas with a sharp，characteristic odor. It is easily liquified by pressure，and is very soluble in water. Ammonia acts as a weak base. Aqueous solutions of ammonia are (incorrectly) referred to as "ammonium hydroxide".

ammonium ion 铵离子（NH_4^+） ammonium.
NH_4^+ is a cation formed by neutralization of ammonia，which acts as a weak base.

anhydrous [æn'haidrəs] *adj.* 无水的 anhydrous compound; anhydride.   Compare with hydrate.
A compound with all water removed，especially water of hydration. For example，strongly heating copper(Ⅱ) sulfate pentahydrate（$CuSO_4 \cdot 5H_2O$）produces anhydrous copper(Ⅱ) sulfate（$CuSO_4$）.

covalent compound 共价化合物   Compare with ionic bond and ionic compound.
A compound made of molecules—not ions. The atoms in the compound are bound together by shared electrons. Also called a molecular compound.

hygroscopic [haigrəu'skɔpik] *adj.* 吸湿的

Able to absorb moisture from air. For example, sodium hydroxide pellets are so hygroscopic that they dissolve in the water they absorb from the air.

hygroscopicity [haigrəuskə'pisiti] *n.* 吸湿性

The ability of a substance to absorb moisture from air. For example, sodium hydroxide pellets are so hygroscopic that they dissolve in the water they absorb from the air.

empirical formula [im'pirikl] ['fɔ:mjulə] 经验式　　Compare with molecular formula.

Empirical formulas show which elements are present in a compound, with their mole ratios indicated as subscripts. For example, the empirical formula of glucose is CH_2O, which means that for every mole of carbon in the compound, there are 2 moles of hydrogen and one mole of oxygen.

molecular formula　分子式　chemical formula.

A notation that indicates the type and number of atoms in a molecule. The molecular formula of glucose is $C_6H_{12}O_6$, which indicates that a molecule of glucose contains 6 atoms of carbon, 12 atoms of hydrogen, and 6 atoms of oxygen.

structural formula　结构式　Compare with molecular formula and empirical formula.

A structural formula is a diagram that shows how the atoms in a molecule are bonded together. Atoms are represented by their element symbols and covalent bonds are represented by lines. The symbol for carbon is often not drawn. Most structural formulas don't show the actual shape of the molecule.

hydrazine ['haidrəzi:n, -zin] *n.* 肼, 联氨 (NH_2NH_2)

A colorless, fuming, corrosive liquid that is a powerful reducing agent. NH_2NH_2 is used in jet and rocket fuels, and as an intermediate in the manufacture of agricultural, textile, photographic, and industrial chemicals.

hydronium ion [hai'drəuniəm] ['aiən]　水合氢离子 (H_3O^+)　hydronium.

The H_3O^+ ion, formed by capture of a hydrogen ion by a water molecule. A strong covalent bond is formed between the hydrogen ion and water oxygen; all hydrogen ions in aqueous solution are bound inside hydronium ions.

hydroxide [hai'drɔksaid, -sid] *n.* 氢氧化物, 氢氧根 (OH^-)

(1) The OH^- ion.

(2) Compounds containing the OH^- ion.

molecular model　分子模型　stick model; ball and stick model; space-filling model.

A representation of a molecule. The model can be purely computational or it can be an actual physical object. Stick models show bonds, ball-and-stick models show bonds and atoms, and space-filling models show relative atomic sizes.

nomenclature [nəu'menklətʃə] *n.* 命名法

A system for naming things. For example, "organic nomenclature" is the system used to name organic compounds.

polyatomic ion　多原子离子　Compare with molecule, ion and polyatomic molecule.

A polyatomic ion is a charged particle that contains more than two covalently bound atoms.

polyatomic molecule　多原子分子　Compare with polyatomic ion and diatomic molecule.

A polyatomic molecule is an uncharged particle that contains more than two atoms.

diatomic molecule　双原子分子　Compare with binary compound and polyatomic molecule.

A molecule that contains only two atoms. All of the noninert gases occur as diatomic molecules; e. g. hydrogen, oxygen, nitrogen, fluorine, and chlorine are H_2, O_2, N_2, F_2, and Cl_2, respectively.

binary compound　二元化合物

A compound that contains two different elements. NaCl is a binary compound; NaClO is not.

sugar [ˈʃugə] *n.* 糖

A carbohydrate with a characteristically sweet taste. Sugars are classified as monosaccharides, disaccharides, or trisaccharides.

superoxide [ˌsjuːpəˈɔksaid] *n.* 过氧化物，超氧化物　superoxide ion.

A binary compound containing oxygen in the $-1/2$ oxidation state. For example, KO_2 is potassium superoxide, an ionic compound containing the superoxide ion, O_2^-.

3. Organic Chemistry

3.1 Organic Chemistry

organic chemistry 有机化学
The study of compounds that contain carbon chemically bound to hydrogen, including synthesis, identification, modelling, and reactions of those compounds.

organic compound 有机化合物 Compare with inorganic compound.
Compounds that contain carbon chemically bound to hydrogen. They often contain other elements (particularly O, N, halogens, or S). Organic compounds were once thought to be produced only by living things. We now know that any organic compound can be synthesized in the laboratory (although this can be extremely difficult in practice!)

acid anhydride [æn'haidraid] *n.* 酸酐
Nonmetallic oxides or organic compounds that react with water to form acids. For example, SO_2, CO_2, P_2O_5, and SO_3 are the acid anhydrides of sulfurous, carbonic, phosphoric, and sulfuric acids, respectively. Acetic anhydride [$(CH_3CO)_2O$] reacts with water to form acetic acid.

acyl halide ['hælaid] 酰卤
Compounds containing a carbonyl group bound to a halogen atom.

alcohol ['ælkəhɔl] *n.* 醇 (ROH) Compare with phenol and hydroxide.
An alcohol is an organic compound with a carbon bound to a hydroxyl group. Examples are methanol, CH_3OH; ethanol, CH_3CH_2OH; propanol, $CH_3CH_2CH_2OH$. Compounds with —OH attached to an aromatic ring are called phenols rather than alcohols.

phenol ['fi:nəl] *n.* 苯酚，石炭酸
A group or molecule containing a benzene ring that has a hydroxyl group substituted for a ring hydrogen.

aldehyde ['ældihaid] *n.* 醛 (RCHO)
An aldehyde is an organic compound with a carbon bound to a —CHO group. Examples are formaldehyde (HCHO), acetaldehyde, CH_3CHO, and benzaldehyde, C_6H_6CHO.

aliphatic [,æli'fætik] *adj.* 脂肪族的 Compare with aromatic.
An organic compound that does not contain ring structures.

alkane ['ælkein] *n.* 链烷，烷烃 Compare with hydrocarbon and alkene.
A series of organic compounds with general formula C_nH_{2n+2}. Alkane names end with **-ane**. Examples are propane (with $n=3$) and octane (with $n=8$).

alkene ['ælki:n] *n.* 烯烃，链烯
A compound that consists of only carbon and hydrogen, that contains at least one carbon-carbon double bond. Alkene names end with **-ene**. Examples are ethylene (CH_2=CH_2); 1-propene (CH_2=$CHCH_3$), and 2-octene [CH_3CH=$CH(CH_2)_4CH_3$].

hydrocarbon [,haidrəu'kɑ:bən] *n.* 烃，碳氢化合物 Compare with alkane, alkene, alkyne, and organic.
Hydrocarbons are organic compounds that contain only hydrogen and carbon. The simplest hydrocarbons are the alkanes.

alkyne ['ælkain] *n.* 炔
A compound that consists of only carbon and hydrogen, that contains at least one carbon-carbon triple bond. Alkyne names end with **-yne**. Examples are acetylene (HC≡

CH); 1-propyne (HC≡CCH$_3$), and 2-octyne [CH$_3$C≡C(CH$_2$)$_4$CH$_3$].

octane ['ɔktein] *n.* 辛烷（C$_8$H$_{18}$） Compare with alkane and hydrocarbon.

Flammable liquid compounds found in petroleum and natural gas. There are 18 different octanes—they have different structural formulas but share the molecular formula C$_8$H$_{18}$. Octane is used as a fuel and as a raw material for building more complex organic molecules. It is the eighth member of the alkane series.

propane ['prəupein] *n.* 丙烷（C$_3$H$_8$） Compare with alkane and hydrocarbon.

A colorless, odorless, flammable gas, found in petroleum and natural gas. It is used as a fuel and as a raw material for building more complex organic molecules. Propane is the third member of the alkane series.

alkoxide [æl'kɔksaid] 醇盐（RO$^-$M$^+$） alkoxide ion.

An ionic compound formed by removal of hydrogen ions from the hydroxyl group in an alcohol using reactive metals, e.g. sodium. For example, potassium metal reacts with methanol (CH$_3$OH) to produce potassium methoxide (KOCH$_3$).

alkyl ['ælkil] *n.* 烷基，烃基（—C$_n$H$_{2n+1}$） alkyl group.

A molecular fragment derived from an alkane by dropping a hydrogen atom from the formula. Examples are methyl (—CH$_3$) and ethyl (—CH$_2$CH$_3$).

allyl ['ælil] *n.* 烯丙基 allylic; allyl group; allyl radical.

A molecular fragment derived by removing a methyl hydrogen from propene (—CH$_2$—CH=CH$_2$). For example, "allyl chloride" is 3-chloropropene, Cl—CH$_2$—CH=CH$_2$.

amide ['æmaid] *n.* 氨基化合物

An amide is an organic compound that contains a carbonyl group bound to nitrogen:
$$-\overset{\overset{O}{\|}}{C}-N\diagup$$
. The simplest amides are formamide (HCONH$_2$) and acetamide (CH$_3$CONH$_2$).

amine ['æmi:n] *n.* 胺 Compare with ammine.

An amine is an organic compound that contains a nitrogen atom bound only to carbon and possibly hydrogen atoms. Examples are methylamine, CH$_3$NH$_2$; dimethylamine, CH$_3$NHCH$_3$; and trimethylamine, (CH$_3$)$_3$N.

ammine ['æmi:n] *n.* 氨络物

A metal ion complex containing ammonia as a ligand. The ammonia nitrogen is bound directly to a metal ion in ammines; amines differ in that the ammonia nitrogen is directly bound to a carbon atom.

amino acid 氨基酸

Amino acids are molecules that contain at least one amine group (—NH$_2$) and at least one carboxylic acid group (—COOH). When these groups are both attached to the same carbon, the acid is an α-amino acid. α-amino acids are the basic building blocks of proteins.

arene [ə'ri:n] *n.* 芳烃

A hydrocarbon that contains at least one aromatic ring.

aromatic ring [ˌærəu'mætik] [riŋ] 芳环，苯环（Ar）

An exceptionally stable planar ring of atoms with resonance structures that consist of alternating double and single bonds, e.g. benzene.

aromatic compound 芳香化合物

A compound containing an aromatic ring. Aromatic compounds have strong, characteristic odors.

azo ['æzəu] *adj.* 偶氮的　azo compound; azo group; azo dye.

The azo group has the general structure Ar—N=N—Ar′, where Ar and Ar′ indicate substituted aromatic rings. Compounds containing the azo compounds are often intensely colored and are economically important as dyes. Methyl orange is an example of an azo dye.

carbonyl ['kɑːbənil] *n.* 碳酰基，羰基　carbonyl group.

A divalent group consisting of a carbon atom with a double-bond to oxygen. For example, acetone (CH_3COCH_3) is a carbonyl group linking two methyl groups. Also refers to a compound of a metal with carbon monoxide, such as iron carbonyl, $Fe(CO)_5$.

carboxylic acid [,kɑːbɔk'silik] ['æsid] 羧基酸　carboxyl; carboxyl group.

A carboxylic acid is an organic molecule with a —COOH group. The group is also written as —COOH and is called a carboxyl group. The hydrogen on the —COOH group ionizes in water; carboxylic acids are weak acids. The simplest carboxylic acids are formic acid (H—COOH) and acetic acid (CH_3—COOH).

carotene ['kærətiːn] *n.* 胡萝卜素

Carotene is an unsaturated hydrocarbon pigment found in many plants. Carotene is the basic building block of vitamin A.

chelate ['kiːleit] *n.* 螯合物

A stable complex of a metal with one or more polydentate ligands. For example, calcium complexes with EDTA to form a chelate.

chiral ['tʃirəl] *adj.* 手（征）性的　chirality.

Having nonsuperimposable mirror images. For example, a shoe or a glove is chiral.

chiral center　手性中心　asymmetric center.

An atom in a molecule that causes chirality, usually an atom that is bound to four different groups. A molecule can have chirality without having a chiral center, and a molecule may also have more than one chiral centers.

conformer [kən'fɔːmə] *n.* 构象

Molecular arrangements that differ only by rotations around single bonds. For example, the "boat" and "chair" forms of cyclohexane are conformers.

D-. D-isomer，D-异构体　　Compare with L-.

Prefix used to designate a dextrorotatory enantiomer.

L-. L-isomer，L-异构体

Prefix used to designate a levorotatory enantiomer.

dextrorotatory ['dekstrəu'rəutətəri] *n.* 右旋性的　dextrorotary.　　Compare with levorotatory.

Having the property of rotating plane-polarized light clockwise.

levorotatory [liːvəu'rəutə,təri] *adj.* 左旋性的

Having the property of rotating plane-polarized light counterclockwise.

diazonium salt [,daiə'zəuniəm] [sɔːlt] *adj.* 重氮盐，偶氮盐

A diazonium salt is a compound with general form Ar—N≡N$^+$ X$^-$, where Ar represents a substituted benzene ring and X$^-$ is a halide ion such as chloride. Diazonium salts are unstable and explosive in dry form. They are used to manufacture many different organic compounds, including azo dyes. See also diazotization.

diazotization [dai,æzətai'zeiʃən; -ti'z-] *n.* 重氮化作用

Diazotization is a reaction that converts an —NH_2 group connected to a phenyl ring to a diazonium salt. For example:

$$\underset{\text{sulfanilic acid}}{\text{HSO}_3\text{-C}_6\text{H}_4\text{-NH}_3^+\text{Cl}^-} + \text{HONO} \longrightarrow \underset{\text{diazonium salt}}{\text{HSO}_3\text{-C}_6\text{H}_4\text{-N}_2^+\text{Cl}^-} + 2\text{H}_2\text{O}$$

Diazotization reactions are extremely useful in organic synthesis. The nitrous acid provides NO^+ which replaces a hydrogen on the $-NH_3^+$ group to produce $-NH_2NO^+$ and water; a second water is eliminated to produce the $-N_2^+$ group.

dichloromethane [dai,klɔːrəˈmeθein] *n.* 二氯甲烷（CH_2Cl_2）

Dichloromethane (CH_2Cl_2) is an organic solvent often use to extract organic substances from samples. It is toxic but much less so than chloroform or carbon tetrachloride, which were previously used for this purpose.

ester [ˈestə] *n.* 酯

An ester is a compound formed from an acid and an alcohol. In esters of carboxylic acids, the $-COOH$ group and the $-OH$ group lose a water and become a $-COO-$ linkage:

$$R-COOH + R'-OH \Longleftrightarrow R-COO-R' + H_2O$$

where R and R′ represent organic groups.

fatty acid 脂肪酸

Fatty acids are carboxylic acids with long hydrocarbon side chains. Most natural fatty acids have hydrocarbon chains that don't branch; any double bonds occuring in the chain are *cis* isomers (side chains are attached on the same side of the double bond).

cis *trans*

functional group 官能团

A substructure that imparts characteristic chemical behaviors to a molecule, for example, a carboxylic acid group.

glycerol [ˈglisəˌrɔl] *n.* 甘油，丙三醇 [$HOCH_2CH(OH)CH_2OH$]

Glycerol is a small molecule with three alcohol groups. It is a basic building block of fats and oils.

heterocyclic [ˌhetərəuˈsaiklik] *adj.* 杂环的 heterocycle; heterocyclic ring.

An organic group or molecule containing rings with at least one noncarbon atom on the ring.

homolog [ˈhɔmələg] *n.* 同系物 homologue; homologous; homologous series.

A compound belonging to a series of compounds that differ by a repeating group. For example, propanol ($CH_3CH_2CH_2OH$), *n*-butanol ($CH_3CH_2CH_2CH_2OH$), and *n*-pentanol ($CH_3CH_2CH_2CH_2CH_2OH$) are homologs; they belong to a homologous series $CH_3(CH_2)_nOH$.

ketone [ˈkiːtəun] *n.* 酮（$R-CO-R'$）

An organic compound that contains a carbonyl group. For example, methyl ethyl ketone ($CH_3COCH_2CH_3$) is used in some adhesives.

methyl [ˈmeθil, ˈmiːθail] *n.* 甲基，木精（$-CH_3$）

A group derived from methane. For example, CH_3Cl is "methyl chloride" (systematic name: chloromethane); CH_3OH is "methyl alcohol" (systematic name: methanol).

monodentate 单齿（基）配体

A ligand that has only one atom that coordinates directly to the central atom in a complex. For example, ammonia and chloride ion are monodentate ligands of copper in the complexes $[Cu(NH_3)_6]^{2+}$ and $[CuCl_6]^{2+}$.

polydentate [,pɔli'denteit] 多齿（基）配体　polydentate ligand.

A ligand that has more than one atom that coordinates directly to the central atom in a complex. Polydentate ligands are called chelating agents when two or more coordinating atoms are attached to the same metal ion in a complex. For example, EDTA or ethylenediaminotetracetic acid is a hexadentate ligand of calcium ion.

optical activity　旋光性（度）　optically active.

A substance that is capable of rotating plane-polarized light. Molecules of an optically active substance cannot be superimposed on their own mirror images, just as your left hand cannot be superimposed on your right when both are held palm-down.

paraffin ['pærəfin, -fiːn] n. 石蜡　paraffin wax.

(1) A waxy substance that is a mixture of alkanes with chains containing 18 to 36 carbon atoms.

(2) An alkane.

phenyl ['fenəl, 'fiːnəl, 'fiːnil] n. 苯基

A molecular group or fragment formed by abstracting or substituting one of the hydrogen atoms attached to a benzene ring.

polymer ['pɔlimə] n. 聚合物

A large molecule made by linking smaller molecules ("monomers") together.

racemic [rə'siːmik] adj. 外消旋的　racemic mixture.

A mixture of equal parts of the levorotatory and dextrorotatory isomers of the the same substance. Racemic mixtures are not optically active.

strong ligand　强配体　Compare with weak ligand.

A ligand that causes a large crystal field splitting which results in a low-spin complex.

weak ligand　weak field ligand.

A ligand that causes a small crystal field splitting which results in a high-spin complex.

tautomer ['tɔːtəmə] n. 互变（异构）体

A structure formed by facile motion of a hydrogen from one site to another within the same molecule.

thin layer chromatography　薄层色谱（TLC）　Compare with chromatography.

A technique for separating components in a mixture on the basis of their differing polarities. A spot of sample is placed on a flat sheet coated with silica and then carried along by a solvent that soaks the sheet. Different components will move different distances over the surface. TLC is a useful screening technique in clinical chemistry; for example, it can be used to detect the presence of drugs in urine.

triglyceride [trai'glisə,raid] n. 甘油三酸酯

A triglyceride is an ester of glycerol and three fatty acids. Most animal fats are composed primarily of triglycerides. In the structures below, the fatty acids attached to the

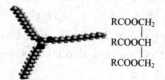

glycerol are represented by 'R'. The fatty acids can be the same or different.

unsaturated compound 不饱和化合物

An organic compound with molecules containing one or more double bonds.

water gas *n*. 水煤气   blue gas; synthesis gas.

A fuel gas used in industrial synthesis of organic chemicals, and in welding, glassmaking, and other high-temperature industrial applications. Water gas made by passing steam over a bed of hot coal or coke. It consists mainly of carbon monoxide (CO) and hydrogen (H_2), contaminated with small amounts of CO_2, N_2, CH_4, and O_2.

wax [wæks] *n*. 蜡

An ester formed from long-chain fatty acids and alcohols that is usually solid at room temperature.

zwitterions ['tsvitəraiən] *n*. 两性离子

A particle that contains both positively charged and negatively charged groups. For example, amino acids (NH_2—CHR—COOH) can form zwitterions ($^+NH_3$—CHR—COO^-).

3.2 Polymer

copolymer [kəu'pɔlimə] *n*. 共聚物

A polymer composed of two or more different monomers. The different monomers can be linked randomly, or in repeating sequences, or in blocks, or as side chains off the main chain.

monomer ['mɔnəmə] *n*. 单体

A small molecule that is linked with large numbers of other small molecules to form a chain or a network (polymer).

osmometry 渗透压测定法   Compare with osmosis.

Determination of the average molecular weight of a dissolved substance from measurements of osmotic pressure.

polymerization [,pɔlimərai'zeiʃən] *n*. 聚合

A process that links smaller molecules together to form a larger molecule.

polymerize ['pɔliməraiz] *v*. （使）聚合

To link smaller molecules together to form a larger molecule.

thermoplastic [,θə:mə'plæstik] *n*. 热塑性塑料   Compare with thermosetting.

A polymer that softens or melts on heating, and becomes rigid again on cooling. Thermoplastic polymer chains are not cross-linked. Polystyrene is a thermoplastic.

thermosetting [,θə:məu'setiŋ] *n*. 热固性塑料   thermosetting plastic.   Compare with thermoplastic.

A polymer that solidifies on heating and cannot be remelted. The setting action results from crosslinking of the polymer chains at high temperature—a process that is not reversed by cooling and reheating.

auto-ignition temperature [,ɔ:təuig'niʃən] 自燃温度   Compare with flash point.

Minimum temperature at which the vapor/air mixture over a liquid spontaneously catches fire.

autoxidation [ɔ:,tɔksi'deiʃən] *n*. 自氧化   autooxidation; autoxidize; autoxidizing.

Oxidation caused by exposure to air. Rust is an example of autoxidation. Autoxidation makes ether taken from half-filled bottles very dangerous, because air oxidizes ether to highly explosive organic peroxides.

4. Analytical Chemistry

The following list of definitions, though by no means exhaustive, will help both in the study and practice of analytical chemistry.

4.1 Basic Terms

absolute error [ˈæbsəluːt] [ˈerə] 绝对误差 absolute uncertainty. Compare with relative error.

The uncertainty in a measurement, expressed with appropriate units. For example, if three replicate weights for an object are 1.00g, 1.05g, and 0.95g, the absolute error can be expressed as ±0.05g. Absolute error is also used to express inaccuracies; for example, if the "true value" is 1.11g and the measured value is 1.00g, the absolute error could be written as 1.00g − 1.11g = −0.11g. Note that when absolute errors are associated with indeterminate errors, they are preceded with "±"; when they are associated with determinate errors, they are preceded by their sign.

accuracy [ˈækjurəsi] *n.* 准确度 Compare with precision and trueness.

(1) Accuracy is the correctness of a single measurement. The accuracy of a measurement is assessed by comparing the measurement with the true or accepted value, based on evidence independent of the measurement. The closeness of an average to a true value is referred to as "trueness".

(2) The closeness of an experimental measurement or result to the true or accepted value.

analyte [ˈænəlait] （被）分析物

Constituent of the sample which is to be studied by quantitative measurements or identified qualitatively.

assay [əˈsei] *n.* 含量测定

A highly accurate determination, usually of a valuable constituent in a material of large bulk, e.g. minerals and ores. Also used in the assessment of the purity of a material, e.g. the physiologically active constituent of a pharmaceutical product.

background [ˈbækgraund] *n.* 背景

That proportion of a measurement which arises from sources other than the analyte itself. Individual contributions from instrumental sources, added reagents and the matrix can, if desired, be evaluated separately.

blank [blæŋk] *n.* 空白

A measurement or observation in which the sample is replaced by a simulated matrix, the conditions otherwise being identical to those under which a sample would be analysed. Thus, the blank can be used to correct for background effects and to take account of analyte other than that present in the sample which may be introduced during the analysis, e.g. from reagents.

calibration [ˌkæliˈbreiʃən] *n.* 校准，校正，标度

(1) A procedure which enables the response of an instrument to be related to the mass, volume or concentration of an analyte in a sample by first measuring the response from a sample of known composition or from a known amount of the analyte, i.e. a standard. Often, a series of standards is used to prepare a calibration curve in which instrument

response is plotted as a function of mass, volume or concentration of the analyte over a given range. If the plot is linear, a calibration factor without reference to the original curve.

(2) Determination of the accuracy of graduation marks on volumetric apparatus by weighing measured volumes of water, or determinations of the accuracy of weights by comparison with weights whose value is known with a high degree of accuracy.

(3) Calibration is correcting a measuring instrument by measuring values whose true values are known. Calibration minimizes systematic error.

constituent [kən'stitjuənt] *n.* 成分 element.

A component of a sample; it may be further classified as: major $>10\%$; minor $0.01\%\sim10\%$; trace $0.0001\%\sim0.01\%$; ultratrace $<0.0001\%$.

detection limit 检出限

The smallest amount or concentration of an analyte that can be detected by a given procedure and with a given degree of confidence.

determination [ditə:mi'neiʃən] 测定

A quantitative measure of an analyte with an accuracy of considerably better than 10% of the amount present.

equivalent [i'kwivələnt] 当量

That amount of a substance which, in a specified chemical reaction, produces, reacts with or can be indirectly equated with one mole (6.023×10^{23}) of hydrogen ions. This confusing term is obsolete but its use is still to be found in some analytical laboratories.

estimation [esti'meiʃən] 估算，估定

A semi-quantitative measure of the amount of an analyte present in a sample, i.e. an approximate measurement having an accuracy no better than about 10% of the amount present.

limit of quantitation 定量限 (LOD) quantitative detection limit; limit of determination.

The smallest detectable concentration an analytical instrument can determine at a given confidence level. IUPAC defines the quantitative detection limit as $C_{ld}=ks/m$, where k is 10, s is the standard deviation of instrument readings taken on a "blank" (a solution with zero concentration of analyte), and m is the slope of a plot of instrument response vs. concentration, as calculated by linear regression.

gross error [grəus] ['erə] 过失误差 Compare with systematic error, random error and mistake.

Gross errors are undetected mistakes that cause a measurement to be very much farther from the mean measurement than other measurements.

interference [,intə'fiərəns] 干扰

An effect which alters or obscures the behavior of an analyte in an analytical procedure. It may arise from the sample itself, from contaminants or reagents introduced during the procedure or from the instrumentation used for the measurements.

internal standard 内标

A compound or element added to all calibration standards and samples in a constant known amount. Sometimes a major constituent of the samples to be analysed can be used for this purpose. Instead of preparing a conventional calibration curve of instrument response as a function of analyte mass, volume or concentration, a response ratio is computed for each calibration standard and sample, i.e. the instrument response for the analyte is divided by the corresponding response for the fixed amount of added internal standard. Ideally, the latter will be the same for each pair of measurements but variations in experimental conditions may alter the responses of both analyte and internal standard. However, their ratio should be unaffected and should therefore be a more reliable function of the mass, volume or concentration of the analyte than its response alone. The analyte in a sample is determined from its response ratio using the calibration graph and should be independent of sample size.

masking [ˈmɑːskiŋ] 掩蔽

Treatment of a sample with a reagent to prevent interference with the response of the analyte by other constituents of the sample.

matrix [ˈmeitriks] 基体

The remainder of the sample of which the analyte forms a part.

mistake [misˈteik] *n*. 错误，过失　　Compare with systematic error, random error and gross error.

A mistake is a measurement which is known to be incorrect due to carelessness, accidents, or the ineptitude of the experimenter. It's important to distinguish mistakes from errors: mistakes can be avoided. Errors can be minimized but not entirely avoided, because they are part of the process of measurement. Data that is mistaken should be discarded. Data that contains errors can be useful, if the sizes of the errors can be estimated.

precision [priˈsiʒən] *n*. 精密度，精度　　Compare with accuracy, reproducibility.

(1) Precision is reproducibility. Saying "These measurements are precise" is the same as saying, "The same measurement was repeated several times, and the measurements were all very close to one another". Don't confuse precision with accuracy.

(2) The random or indeterminate error associated with a measurement or result. Sometimes called the variability, it can be represented statistically by the standard deviation or relative standard deviation (coefficient of variation).

primary standard 原始标准物

A substance whose purity and stability are particularly well established and with which other standards may be compared.

reagent [ri(ː)ˈeidʒənt] 试剂

A chemical used to produce a specified reaction in relation to an analytical procedure.

random error [ˈrændəm] [ˈerə] 偶然误差　　indeterminate error.　　Compare with systematic error, gross error and mistake.

Random errors are errors that affect the precision of a set of measurements. Random error scatters measurements above and below the mean, with small random errors being more likely than large ones.

relative error 相对误差　　relative uncertainty.　　Compare with absolute error.

The uncertainty in a measurement compared to the size of the measurement. For example, if three replicate weights for an object are 2.00g, 2.05g, and 1.95g, the absolute error can be expressed as ±0.05g and the relative error is ±0.05g/2.00g=0.025=2.5%.

relative standard deviation (RSD) 相对标准偏差　　Compare with standard deviation.

The relative standard deviation is a measure of precision, calculated by dividing the standard deviation for a series of measurements by the average measurement.

sample [ˈsæmpl] 样品

A substance or portion of a substance about which analytical information is required.

sensitivity [ˌsensəˈtivəti] 灵敏度

(1) The change in the response from an analyte relative to a small variation in the amount being determined. The sensitivity is equal to the slope of the calibration curve,

being constant if the curve is linear.

(2) The ability of a method to facilitate the detection or determination of an analyte.

standard ['stændəd] 标准

(1) A pure substance which reacts in a quantitative and known stoichiometric manner with the analyte or a reagent.

(2) The pure analyte or a substance containing an accurately known amount of it which is used to calibrate an instrument or to standardize a reagent solution.

standard deviation ['stændəd] [ˌdiːviˈeiʃən] 标准偏差(s, σ)

The standard deviation is a statistical measure of precision. The best estimate of the standard deviation s for small data sets is calculated using:

$$s = \sqrt{\frac{\sum(x_i - \overline{x})^2}{N-1}}$$

where x_i is the measurement from the i-th run, x-bar is the mean of all the measurements, and N is the number of measurements. For very large data sets, the standard deviation is the root-mean-square deviation from the true mean, and is usually written as to distinguish it from the best estimate standard deviation s used for small data sets.

standard addition 标准加入法

A method of quantitative analysis whereby the response from an analyte is measured before and after adding a known amount of that analyte to the sample. The amount of analyte originally in the sample is determined from a calibration curve or by simple proportion if the curve is linear. The main advantage of the method is that all measurements of the analyte are made in the same matrix which eliminates interference effects arising from differences in the overall composition of sample and standards.

standardization [ˌstændədaiˈzeiʃən] 标定

Determination of the concentration of an analyte or reagent solution from its reaction with a standard or primary standard.

systematic error [ˌsistiˈmætik] [ˈerə] 系统误差 determinate error. Compare with random error, gross error and mistake.

Systematic errors have an identifiable cause and affect the accuracy of results.

trueness [truːnis] n. 精确度 Compare with accuracy.

Trueness is the closeness of an average measurement to a "true" value, while accuracy is the the closeness of a single measurement to the true value.

validation of methods 方法的有效性

In order to ensure that results yielded by a method are as accurate as possible, it is essential to validate the method by analysing standards which have an accepted analyte content, and a matrix similar to that of the sample. The accepted values for these validated standards are obtained by extensive analysis, using a range of different methods. Internationally accepted standards are available.

4.2 Base Units

Base units are units that are fundamental building blocks in a system of measurement. There are seven base units in the SI system.

unit [ˈjuːnit] n. （计量）单位

A standard for comparison in measurements. For example, the meter is a standard length which may be compared to any object to describe its length.

derived unit ［di'raivd］［'juːnit］ 导出单位，衍生单位

Derived units are units constructed from the SI system's base units. For example, the SI unit for density is kg/m^3, derived from the base units kg and m.

SI. 国际（单位）制 International System ［of Units］.

SI is a system of units introduced to remove barriers to international trade, based on the older metric system. It is now used in science and technical communications worldwide.

measurement ['meʒəmənt] n. 测量，度量

Measurement is the collection of quantitative data. Measurement involves comparison of the quantity of interest with a standard called a unit. The comparison is never perfect. As a result, measurements always include error. You must consider the reliability of the measurement when using it to make decisions or estimate other quantities.

significant figure [sig'nifikənt]['figə] n. 有效数字 significant digit; significant.

A convention for recording measurements. Measurements are rounded so that they contain only the digits up to and including the first uncertain digit, when the number is written in scientific notation.

conversion factor [kən'vəːʃən]['fæktə] 转换因子，换算系数

A conversion factor is a fraction that relates one unit to another. Multiplying a measurement by a conversion factor changes the units of the measurement. For example, since 1 in＝2.54 cm, to convert 10 inches to centimeters, 10in＝25.4cm.

concentration [ˌkɔnsen'treiʃən] n. 浓度

The amount of a substance present in a given mass or volume of another substance. The abbreviations w/w, w/V and V/V are sometimes used to indicate whether the concentration quoted is based on the weights or volumes of the two substances.

ampere ['æmpeə(r)] n. 安培（A） amp.

The SI unit of electric current, equal to flow of 1 coulomb of charge per second. An ampere is the amount of current necessary to produce a force of 0.2 micronewtons per meter between two arbitrarily long, arbitrarily thin wires, placed parallel in a vacuum and exactly 1 m apart. Named for 19th century physicist André Marie Ampère.

coulomb ['kuːlɔm] n. 库仑（电量单位）（C）

The SI unit of electric charge, equal to the amount of charge delivered by a current of 1 ampere running for 1 second. One mole of electrons has a charge of about 96487 C.

power ['pauə] n. 功率

The rate at which energy is supplied. Power has define SI units of J/s, sometimes called "Watts" (W).

angstrom ['æŋstrəm] n. 埃（长度单位）（Å） Ångstrom; Ångstrom units.

A non-SI unit of length used to express wavelengths of light, bond lengths, and molecular sizes. 1Å＝10^{-10} m＝10^{-8} cm.

atto- 阿（托）（前缀）表示 "10^{-18}"

Prefix used in the SI system meaning "multiply by 10^{-18}". For example, 3 am means $3×10^{-18}$ meters.

celsius ['selsjəs] adj. 摄氏的（℃） celsius temperature scale; Celsius scale.

A common but non-SI unit of temperature, defined by assigning temperatures of 0℃ and 100℃ to the freezing and boiling points of water, respectively.

centi- ['senti] 表示 "厘，百分之一" 之义 (c)

Prefix used in the SI system meaning "one hundredth of". For example 1 cm means "one hundredth of a meter"; 2.3 cg could also be written "2.3×10^{-2} g" or "0.023g".

cgs. =centimeter-gram-second 厘米-克-秒制，cgs 制 Compare with SI.
An older metric system of units that uses centimeters, grams, and seconds as base units.

specific volume [spə'sifik] ['vɔlju:m] 比容 Compare with density.
The volume of a unit mass of substance. For example, the specific volume of water at 4℃ is 1.00000 mL/g. Specific volume is the reciprocal of density.

density ['densiti] *n.* 密度（ρ, d） Compare with specific gravity.
Mass of a substance per unit volume. Saying "the density of mercury is 13.55g/cm^3" is the same as saying "the mass of exactly 1 cm^3 of mercury is 13.55g".

dyne [dain] 达因（力的单位） large dyne, 大达因
The unit of force in the obsolete cgs system of units. A dyne is the force required to accelerate a 1 g mass by 1 cm/s per second.

femto- ['femtəu] 表示"飞，10^{-15}(f)"
Prefix used in the SI system meaning "multiply by 10^{-15}". For example 22 fg means 22×10^{-15} g.

gram [græm] *n.* 克
A metric unit of mass, equal to 1/1000 of a kilogram. Kilograms are the base SI units for mass, not grams.

hydrometer [hai'drɔmitə] *n.* 液体比重计，浮秤
An instrument for measuring the specific gravity of liquids. A hydrometer is a weight with a vertical scale attached. When placed into a liquid, the hydrometer bobs upright, and sinks to a certain level. The specific gravity or solution composition can be read from the liquid level on the vertical scale. Hydrometers are often calibrated in degrees Baumé.

Kelvin ['kelvin] *n.* 绝对温标，开氏温标（K）
The SI base unit of temperature, defined by assigning 273.15K to the temperature at which steam, ice, and water are at equilibrium (called the triple point of water). The freezing point of water is 273.15K.

absolute temperature 绝对温度
Temperature measured on a scale that sets absolute zero as zero. In the SI system, the Kelvin scale is used to measure absolute temperature.

absolute zero 绝对零度（0K）
The temperature at which the volume of an ideal gas becomes zero; a theoretical coldest temperature that can be approached but never reached. Absolute zero is zero on the Kelvin scale, -273.15℃ on the Celsius scale, and -459.67℉ on the Fahrenheit scale.

kilo- ['ki:ləu] 表示"千"（k）
Prefix used in the SI system meaning "one thousand of". For example 1km means "one thousand meters"; 2.8kg could also be written "2.8×10^3 g" or "2800g".

mass [mæs] *n.* 质量（m） Compare with weight.
Mass is a measure of the tendency of an object to resist acceleration. It's harder to roll a tractor trailer than a roller skate; the tractor trailer has a far greater mass.

weight [weit] *n.* 重力，重量，分量，砝码（W） Compare with mass.
Weight is the force exerted by an object in a gravitational field. The weight of an object (W) arises from its mass (m): $W = mg$, where g is the acceleration due to gravity (about 9.8m/s^2 on Earth).

mega- ['megə] 表示"兆，10^6(M)"
SI prefix meaning "multiply by 10^6". For example, 3.2 MJ is 3200000 J.

micro- ['maikrəu] 表示"微，10^{-6} (μ)".
Prefix used in the SI system meaning "one millionth of". For example 1μm means "one millionth of a meter"; 3.1 μL means "3.1×10^{-6} L".

milli- ['mili] 表示"毫，10^{-3} (m)
Prefix used in the SI system meaning "one thousandth of". For example 1mL means "one thousandth of a liter"; 1 mg means "one thousandth of a gram".

nano- ['nænəu, 'neinəu] 表示"纳，10^{-9}(n)"
Prefix used in the SI system meaning "multiply by 10^{-9}". For example 1nm means "0.000000001m"; 2.8ng could also be written "2.8×10^{-9}g".

pico- ['pi:kəu] 表示"皮，10^{-12}(p)"
Prefix used in the SI system meaning "multiply by 10^{-12}". For example, 3pm means 3×10^{-12} meters.

Avogadro number 阿伏伽德罗常数 Avogadro's number; Avogadro constant.
The number of particles in one mole, equal to 6.02214199×10^{23} mol^{-1} ($\pm0.00000047 mol^{-1}$) (1998 CODATA values).

mass percentage 质量百分比浓度，质量分数
Mass percentages express the concentration of a component in a mixture or an element in a compound. For example, household bleach is 5.25% NaOCl by mass, meaning that every 100g of bleach contains 5.25g of NaOCl. Mass percentage can be calculated as 100% times the mass of a component divided by the mass of the mixture containing the component.

molar ['məulə] 摩尔的
(1) Of or pertaining to moles.
(2) A synonym for molarity; for example, a "six molar solution of hydrochloric acid" contains 6 moles of HCl per liter of solution.

mole [məul] *n.* 摩尔 (mol)
SI unit for amount of substance, defined as the number of atoms in exactly 12 g of carbon-12. One mole of a molecular compound contains Avogadro's number molecules and has a mass equal to the substance's molecular weight, in grams.

volume percentage 体积百分比浓度，体积分数
Volume percentages express the concentration of a component in a mixture or an element in a compound. For example, 95% ethanol by volume contains 95 mL of ethanol in 100mL of solution (NOT in 100 mL of water!).

stoichiometry [ˌstɔiki'ɔmitri] 化学计量（法），化学计量学
(1) Ratios of atoms in a compound.
(2) Ratios of moles of compounds in a reaction.
(3) A branch of chemistry that quantitatively relates amounts of elements and compounds involved in chemical reactions, based on the law of conservation of mass and the law of definite proportions.

A notation that indicates the type and number of atoms in a molecule. The molecular formula of glucose is $C_6H_{12}O_6$, which indicates that a molecule of glucose contains 6 atoms of carbon, 12 atoms of hydrogen, and 6 atoms of oxygen.

experimental yield [ikˌsperi'mentl] [ji:ld] 实际收率 actual yield. Compare with theoretical yield and percent yield.

The measured amount of product produced in a chemical reaction.

theoretical yield [θiə'retikəl] [jiːld]　理论收率　maximum yield; stoichiometric yield.　Compare with actual yield and percent yield.

The amount of product obtained when all of the limiting reagent reacts.

percent yield　百分收率　percentage yield.　Compare with theoretical yield and actual yield.

Percent yield equals experimental yield divided by theoretical yield times 100%.

5. Physical Chemistry

5.1 Energy and Chemical Change

adiabat [ˈædiəbæt] *n.* 绝热线　adiabatic line.　Compare with adiabatic.

A line on an indicator diagram that represents an adiabatic process.

adiabatic [ˌædiəˈbætik] *adj.* 绝热的，隔热的　adiabatic process; isentropic process.

A process that neither absorbs nor releases energy into the surroundings. For example, a chemical reaction taking place in a closed thermos bottle can be considered adiabatic. Very fast processes can often be considered adiabatic with respect to heat exchange with the surroundings, because heat exchange is not instantaneous.

Boltzmann constant (k)　玻尔兹曼常数　Boltzmann's constant.

A fundamental constant equal to the ideal gas law constant divided by Avogadro's number, equal to $1.3805 \times 10^{-23} J \cdot K^{-1}$.

Boltzmann equation　玻尔兹曼方程

A statistical definition of entropy, given by $S = k \ln W$, where S and k are the entropy and Boltzmann's constant, respectively, and W is the probability of finding the system in a particular state.

calorie [ˈkæləri] *n.* 卡路里

The amount of heat required to raise the temperature of 1g of water at 14.5℃ to 15.5℃. One calorie is equivalent to exactly 4.184J.

calorimeter [ˌkæləˈrimitə] *n.* 量热计

An insulated vessel for measuring the amount of heat absorbed or released by a chemical or physical change.

calorimetry [ˌkæləˈrimitri] *n.* 量热法

Experimental determination of heat absorbed or released by a chemical or physical change.

empirical temperature [emˈpirikəl] [ˈtempritʃə(r)]　经验温度

A property that is the same for any two systems that are in thermodynamic equilibrium with each other.

endothermic [ˌendəuˈθɜːmik] *adj.* 吸热（性）的　Compare with exothermic.

A process that absorbs heat. The enthalpy change for an endothermic process has a positive sign.

exothermic [ˌeksəuˈθɜːmik] *adj.* 发热的，放热的　exothermic reaction.

A process that releases heat. The enthalpy change for an exothermic process is negative. Examples of exothermic processes are combustion reactions and neutralization reactions.

heat [hiːt] *n.* 热　Compare with work, energy, enthalpy, and temperature.

Heat is a transfer of energy that occurs when objects with different temperatures are placed into contact. Heat is a process, not a property of a material.

temperature [ˈtempritʃə(r)] *n.* 温度　Compare with heat and thermodynamic temperature.

Temperature is an intensive property associated with the hotness or coldness of an object. It determines the direction of spontaneous heat flow (always from hot to cold).

enthalpy [ˈenθælpi, enˈθælpi] *n.* 焓，热函 (H)　enthalpy change.

Enthalpy (H) is defined so that changes in enthalpy (ΔH) are equal to the heat absorbed or released by a process running at constant pressure. While changes in enthalpy can be measured using calorimetry, absolute values of enthalpy usually cannot be determined. Enthalpy is formally defined as $H = U + pV$, where U is the internal energy, p is the pressure, and V is the volume.

internal energy 内能 (U, E)　　Compare with enthalpy and energy.

Internal energy (U) is defined so that changes in internal energy (ΔU) are equal to the heat absorbed or released by a process running at constant volume. While changes in internal energy can be measured using calorimetry, absolute values of internal energy usually cannot be determined. Changes in internal energy are equal to the heat transferred plus the work done for any process.

enthalpy of combustion [kəmˈbʌstʃən] $n.$ 燃烧焓（热）(ΔH_c)　　heat of combustion.

The change in enthalpy when one mole of compound is completely combusted. All carbon in the compound is converted to $CO_2(g)$, all hydrogen to $H_2O(l)$, all sulfur to $SO_2(g)$, and all nitrogen to $N_2(g)$.

enthalpy of fusion [ˈfjuːʒən] $n.$ 熔化热(ΔH_{fus})　　heat of fusion; molar enthalpy of fusion.

The change in enthalpy when one mole of solid melts to form one mole of liquid. Enthalpies of fusion are always positive because melting involves overcoming some of the intermolecular attractions in the solid.

enthalpy of hydration [haiˈdreiʃən] $n.$ 水合热(ΔH_{hyd})　　hydration enthalpy.

The change in enthalpy for the process　$A(g) \rightarrow A(aq)$

where the concentration of A in the aqueous solution approaches zero. Enthalpies of hydration for ions are always negative because strong ion-water attractions are formed when the gas-phase ion is surrounded by water.

enthalpy of reaction　反应热（焓）(ΔH_{rea})　　heat of reaction.

The heat absorbed or released by a chemical reaction running at constant pressure.

enthalpy of sublimation [ˌsʌbliˈmeiʃən] $n.$ 升华热(ΔH_{sub})　　heat of sublimation.

The change in enthalpy when one mole of solid vaporizes to form one mole of gas. Enthalpies of sublimation are always positive because vaporization involves overcoming most of the intermolecular attractions in the sublimation.

enthalpy of vaporization [ˌveipəraiˈzeiʃən]　汽化热(ΔH_{vap})　　heat of vaporization.

The change in enthalpy when one mole of liquid evaporates to form one mole of gas. Enthalpies of vaporization are always positive because vaporization involves overcoming most of the intermolecular attractions in the liquid.

entropy [ˈentrəpi] $n.$ 熵(S)

Entropy is a measure of energy dispersal. Any spontaneous change disperses energy and increases entropy overall. For example, when water evaporates, the internal energy of the water is dispersed with the water vapor produced, corresponding to an increase in entropy.

first law of thermodynamics　热力学第一定律

The first law states that energy cannot be created or destroyed. Many equivalent statements are possible, including: Internal energy changes depend only on the initial and final states of the system, not on the path taken. The work done during an adiabatic process depends only on the initial and final states of the system, and not on the path taken. The internal energy change for any cyclic process is zero.

second law of thermodynamics 热力学第二定律

The second law states that every spontaneous process causes a net increase in the entropy of the universe. Many alternative statements are possible, including: Heat cannot be converted to work via an isothermal cycle. Heat cannot be converted to work with 100% efficiency. Heat cannot flow from a cold object to a warmer object without doing outside work.

free energy 自由能

Energy that is actually available to do useful work. A decrease in free energy accompanies any spontaneous process. Free energy does not change for systems that are at equilibrium.

Gibbs free energy (G) 吉布斯自由能 Gibbs' free energy.

A thermodynamic property devised by Josiah Willard Gibbs in 1876 to predict whether a process will occur spontaneously at constant pressure and temperature. Gibbs free energy G is defined as $G=H-TS$ where H, T and S are the enthalpy, temperature, and entropy. Changes in G correspond to changes in free energy for processes occurring at constant temperature and pressure; the Gibbs free energy change corresponds to the maximum nonexpansion work that can be obtained under these conditions. The sign of ΔG is negative for all spontaneous processes and zero for processes at equilibrium.

Gibbs free energy of formation (ΔG_f) 吉布斯生成自由能 Gibbs' free energy of formation.

The change in Gibbs free energy that accompanies the formation of one mole of a compound from its elements in their most stable form.

heat capacity 热容   Compare with molar heat capacity and specific heat.

The heat required to raise the temperature of an object by 1℃ is called the heat capacity of the object. Heat capacity is an extensive property with units of $J \cdot K^{-1}$.

molar heat capacity 摩尔热容   Compare with specific heat.

The heat required to raise the temperature of one mole of a substance by 1℃ is called the molar heat capacity of the substance. Molar heat capacity is an intensive property with SI system units of $J \cdot mol^{-1} \cdot K^{-1}$. The molar heat capacity of elements is sometimes called the "atomic heat capacity".

specific heat 比热   Compare with heat capacity.

The heat required to raise the temperature of 1g of a substance by 1℃ is called the specific heat of the substance. Specific heat is an intensive property with units of $J \cdot g^{-1} \cdot K^{-1}$.

Helmholtz free energy (A) 亥姆霍兹自由能

A thermodynamic property that can be used to predict whether a process will occur spontaneously at constant volume and temperature. Helmholtz free energy A is defined as $A=U-TS$ where U, T and S are the internal energy, temperature, and entropy. Changes in A correspond to changes in free energy for processes occurring at constant temperature and volume. The sign of ΔA is negative for spontaneous processes and zero for processes at equilibrium.

Hess's law 盖斯定律 law of constant heat summation; Hess's law of heat summation.

The heat released or absorbed by a process is the same no matter how many steps the process takes. For example, given a reaction A→B, Hess's law says that ΔH for the reaction is the same whether the reaction is written as A→C→B or as A→B. This is the same as writing that $\Delta H(A \rightarrow B) = \Delta H(A \rightarrow C) + \Delta H(C \rightarrow B)$.

isobar [ˈaisəubɑː] *n.* 等压线
(1) A contour line that corresponds to values measured at identical pressures. For example, curves on a plot of gas volumes measured at different temperatures in an open container are isobars.
(2) Nuclides that have the same isotopic mass but different atomic number.
isobaric [ˌaisəuˈbærik] *adj.* 等压的
Having constant pressure.
isochore [ˈaisəukɔː] *n.* 等容线，等体积线
A contour line that corresponds to values measured at identical volumes. For example, a curve on a plot of gas pressure measured at different temperatures in a rigid container is an isochore.
isochoric [ˌaisəuˈkɔːrik] *adj.* 等容的
Having constant volume.
isotherm [ˈaisəuθəːm] *n.* 等温线
A contour line that corresponds to values measured at identical temperatures. For example, curves on a plot of gas pressure measured at different volumes in a constant temperature bath are isotherms.
isothermal [ˌaisəuˈθəːməl] *adj.* 等温的
Having constant temperature.
joule [dʒuːl] *n.* 焦耳（J）
The SI unit of energy, equal to the work required to move a 1kg mass against an opposing force of 1 newton. $1 J = 1 kg \cdot m^2 \cdot s^{-2} = 4.184$ calories.
kinetic energy 动能   Compare with potential energy.
The energy an object possesses by virtue of its motion. An object of mass m moving at velocity v has a kinetic energy of $mv^2/2$.
potential energy 势能   Compare with kinetic energy.
Energy an object possesses by virtue of its position. For example, lifting a mass m by h meters increases its potential energy by mgh, where g is the acceleration due to gravity.
latent heat 潜热
Heat that is absorbed without causing a rise in temperature. For example, "latent heat of vaporization" refers to the amount of heat required to convert a liquid to vapor at a particular temperature.
spontaneous [spɔnˈteinjəs, -niəs] *adj.* 自发的   spontaneity; spontaneous process; spontaneous reaction.
A spontaneous process occurs because of internal forces; no external forces are required to keep the process going, although external forces may be required to get the process started. For example, the burning of wood is spontaneous once the fire is started. The combination of water and carbon dioxide to reform the wood and oxygen is NOT spontaneous!
standard entropy of reaction 标准反应熵（$\Delta S^{\ominus}_{rxn}$）   entropy of reaction.
A change in entropy associated with a reaction involving substances in their standard states. A superscript circle ($^{\ominus}$) distinguishes standard enthalpy changes from enthalpy changes which involve reactants and products that are not in their standard states.
standard enthalpy change 标准焓变（$\Delta H^{\ominus}$）   standard enthalpy.   Compare with enthalpy change.
A change in enthalpy associated with a reaction or transformation involving substances

in their standard states.

standard enthalpy of formation 标准生成焓($\Delta H_f^\ominus$) standard heat of formation; heat of formation; enthalpy of formation.

The change in enthalpy when one mole of compound is formed from its elements in their most stable form and in their standard states.

standard enthalpy of reaction 标准反应焓($\Delta H_{rxn}^\ominus$) standard heat of reaction.

A change in enthalpy associated with a reaction involving substances in their standard states.

standard molar entropy 标准摩尔熵($S^\ominus$)

The entropy of one mole of a substance in its standard state.

standard state 标准态

A set of conditions defined to allow convenient comparison of thermodynamic properties. The standard state for a gas is the the state of the pure substance in the gaseous phase at the standard pressure, with the gas behaving ideally. The standard state for liquids and solids is the state of the most stable form of the substance at the standard pressure. Temperature is not included in the definition of standard state and must be specified, but when not given a temperature of 25℃ is usually implied.

standard pressure 标准压力

Standard pressure is a pressure of 1bar. Before 1982, the standard pressure was 1 atm (1 atm=1.01325 bar).

state function 状态函数

A property that depends only on the condition or "state" of the system, and not on the path used to obtain the current conditions. Energy, enthalpy, temperature, volume, pressure, and temperature are examples of state functions; heat and work are examples of non-state functions.

thermal energy 热能

energy an object possesses by virtue of its temperature. For example, 1g of water at 15℃ has 4.184J more energy than 1g of water at 14℃.

thermochemical equation 热化学方程式

An compact equation representing a chemical reaction that describes both the stoichiometry and the energetics of the reaction. For example, the thermochemical equation $CH_4(g)+2O_2(g) \longrightarrow CO_2(g)+2H_2O(g)$, $\Delta H = -2220kJ$ means "When 1mol of gaseous CH_4 is burned in 2 moles of oxygen gas, 1mol of CO_2 gas and 2mol of steam are produced, and 2220kJ of heat are released".

thermodynamic equilibrium 热力学平衡

A system is at thermodynamic equilibrium if the energy it gains from its surroundings is exactly balanced by the energy it loses, no matter how much time is allowed to pass.

thermodynamics [θə:məudai'næmiks] *n.* 热力学 thermodynamic.

The study of energy transfers and transformations.

thermometry [θɔ:'mɔmitri] *n.* 温度测定法

The science of temperature measurement.

5.2 Reaction Rate

activated complex 活性络合物 transition state.

An intermediate structure formed in the conversion of reactants to products. The activated complex is the structure at the maximum energy point along the reaction path; the activation energy is the difference between the energies of the activated complex and the reactants.

activation energy 活化能（E_a）

The minimum energy required to convert reactants into products; the difference between the energies of the activated complex and the reactants.

catalyst 催化剂　catalyze; catalysis.

A substance that increases the rate of a chemical reaction, without being consumed or produced by the reaction. Catalysts speed both the forward and reverse reactions, without changing the position of equilibrium. Enzymes are catalysts for many biochemical reactions.

collision frequency [kəˈliʒən] [ˈfriːkwənsi] 碰撞频率　collision frequencies; frequency of collision.

The average number of collisions that a molecule undergoes each second.

collision theory 碰撞理论　collision model.

A theory that explains reaction rates in terms of collisions between reactant molecules.

elementary reaction 基元反应　Compare with net chemical reaction.

A reaction that occurs in a single step. Equations for elementary reactions show the actual molecules, atoms, and ions that react on a molecular level.

enzyme [ˈenzaim] $n.$ 酶

Protein or protein-based molecules that speed up chemical reactions occurring in living things. Enzymes act as catalysts for a single reaction, converting a specific set of reactants (called substrates) into specific products. Without enzymes life as we know it would be impossible.

first order reaction 一级反应　Compare with zero order reaction and second order reaction.

The sum of concentration exponents in the rate law for a first order reaction is one. Many radioactive decays are first order reactions.

second order reaction 二级反应　Compare with zero order reaction and first order reaction.

A reaction with a rate law that is proportional to either the concentration of a reactant squared, or the product of concentrations of two reactants.

zero order reaction 零级反应　Compare with first order reaction and second order reaction.

A reaction with a reaction rate that does not change when reactant concentrations change.

half life 半衰期

The half life of a reaction is the time required for the amount of reactant to drop to one half its initial value.

integrated rate law 积分速率方程

Rate laws like $d[A]/dt = -k[A]$ give instantaneous concentration changes. To find the change in concentration over time, the instantaneous changes must by added (integrated) over the desired time interval. The rate law $d[A]/dt = -k[A]$ can be integrated from time zero to time t to obtain the integrated rate law $\ln([A]/[A]_0) = -kt$, where $[A]_0$ is the initial concentration of A.

intermediate [ˌintəˈmiːdjət] 中间体　reactive intermediate; reaction intermediate.

A highly reactive substance that forms and then reacts further during the conversion of reactants to products in a chemical reaction. Intermediates never appear as products in the chemical equation for a net chemical reaction.

rate constant 速率常数（k）

A rate constant is a proportionality constant that appears in a rate law. For example, k is the rate constant in the rate law $d[A]/dt = -k[A]$. Rate constants are independent of concentration but depend on other factors, most notably temperature.

rate law 速率方程

A rate law or rate equation relates reaction rate with the concentrations of reactants, catalysts, and inhibitors. For example, the rate law for the one-step reaction $A+B \longrightarrow C$ is $d[C]/dt = k[A][B]$.

reaction mechanism [ˈmekənizəm] 反应机理

A list of all elementary reactions that occur in the course of an overall chemical reaction.

reaction rate 反应速率

A reaction rate is the speed at which reactants are converted into products in a chemical reaction. The reaction rate is given as the instantaneous rate of change for any reactant or product, and is usually written as a derivative (e.g., $d[A]/dt$) with units of concentration per unit time (e.g., $mol \cdot L^{-1} \cdot s^{-1}$).

unimolecular reaction [ˌjuːnɪməʊˈlekjulə] [ri(ː)ˈækʃən] 单分子反应

A reaction that involves isomerization or decomposition of a single molecule.

5.3 The Quantum Theory

amplitude [ˈæmplɪtjuːd] n. 振幅，幅度，波幅

The displacement of a wave from zero. The maximum amplitude for a wave is the height of a peak or the depth of a trough, relative to the zero displacement line.

interference [ˌɪntəˈfɪərəns] n. 干涉   Compare with constructive interference and destructive interference.

The amplitudes of waves moving into the same region of space add to produce a single resultant wave. The resultant wave can have higher or lower amplitude than the component waves. See constructive interference and destructive interference.

constructive interference （全息）结构干涉，相长干涉   Compare with destructive interference.

When the peaks and troughs of two interfering waves match, the amplitudes add to give the resultant wave a higher amplitude.

destructive interference 相消（性）干扰，破坏性干扰   Compare with constructive interference.

When the peaks of one wave match the troughs of another, the waves interfere destructively. The amplitudes of the interfering waves cancel to give the resultant wave a lower amplitude.

diffraction [dɪˈfrækʃən] n. 衍射   diffract.   Compare with effusion.

The ability of a wave to bend around the edges of obstacles or holes. The effect is most noticeable when the obstacle or hole is comparable to the size of the wavelength.

electromagnetic radiation 电磁辐射   electromagnetic wave.

A wave that involves perpendicular oscillations in the electric and magnetic fields, moving at a speed of 2.99792458×10^8 m/s in a vacuum away from the source. Gamma rays, X-rays, ultraviolet light, visible light, infrared radiation, and radio waves are all electromagnetic waves.

frequency (**v**) [ˈfriːkwənsi] *n*. 频率，频次   Compare with wavelength.
The number of cycles of a wave that move past a fixed observation point per second. The SI unit of frequency is the Hertz (Hz).

wavelength [ˈweivleŋθ] *n*. 波长
The distance between adjacent peaks (or adjacent troughs) on a wave. Varying the wavelength of light changes its color; varying the wavelength of sound changes its pitch.

microwave [ˈmaikrəuweiv] 微波   microwave radiation.
Electromagnetic radiation with wavelength between 3 mm and 30 cm.

gamma rays 伽马射线（γ-rays) gamma radiation.
A very high energy for m of electromagnetic radiation, typically with wavelengths of less than 3 pm. Gamma rays are produced by certain nuclear decay processes, and are used to sterilize food.

Hertz *n*. 赫，赫兹（Hz, s^{-1}）
The SI unit of frequency, equal to one cycle of the wave per second (s^{-1}).

infrared radiation [ˈinfrəˈred] [ˌreidiˈeiʃən] *n*. 红外辐射（IR） infrared.
Electromagnetic radiation with wavelength longer than visible light but shorter than that of microwaves. Infrared radiation is produced by hot objects; absorption of infrared radiation causes chemical bonds to vibrate.

momentum [məuˈmentəm] *n*. 动量（*p*）
Momentum is a property that measures the tendency of a moving object to keep moving in the same direction. Increasing the speed of an object increases its momentum, and a heavy object will have more momentum than a lighter one moving at the same speed. For a particle with mass *m* and velocity *v*, the momentum of the particle is *mv*.

node [nəud] *n*. 节点
A point, region, or surface where the amplitude of a standing wave is zero. The probability of finding an electron at an orbital node is zero.

phase [feiz] *n*. 相   in phase; out of phase; wave phase.
(1) A phase is a part of a sample of matter that is in contact with other parts but is separate from them. Properties within a phase are homogeneous (uniform). For example, oil and vinegar salad dressing contains two phases: an oil-rich liquid, and a vinegar-rich liquid. Shaking the bottle breaks the phases up into tiny droplets, but there are still two distinct phases.
(2) In wave motion, phase is the fraction of a complete cycle that has passed a fixed point since the current cycle began. The phase is often expressed as an angle, since a full cycle is 360 deg (2π). Two waves are "in phase" if the peaks of one wave align with the peaks of the other; they are "out of phase" if the peaks of one wave align with the troughs of the other.

photoelectric effect 光电效应
Ejection of electrons from an atom or molecule that has absorbed a photon of sufficient energy. The photoelectric effect is the operating principle behind "electric eyes"; it is experimental evidence for particle-like behavior of electromagnetic radiation.

photoelectron [ˌfəutəuiˈlektrɔn] *n*. 光电子
An electron ejected from an atom or molecule that has absorbed a photon.

photon [ˈfəutɔn] *n*. 光子 (*hv*) quantum; quanta.
A discrete packet of energy associated with electromagnetic radiation. Each photon

carries energy E proportional to the frequency ν of the radiation: $E=h\nu$, where h is Planck's constant.

Planck's constant 普朗克常数 (h)

A proportionality constant that relates the energy carried by a photon to its frequency. Planck's constant has a value of 6.6262×10^{-34} J·s.

quantum ['kwɔntəm] *n*. 量子 quanta.

A discrete packet of energy.

quantum mechanics *n*. 量子力学 quantum theory.

A branch of physics that describes the behavior of objects of atomic and subatomic size.

quantum number 量子数

Indices that label quantized energy states. Quantum numbers are used to describe the state of a confined electron, e. g., an electron in an atom.

ultraviolet light 紫外光 ultraviolet; ultraviolet radiation; ultraviolet region; UV.

Electromagnetic radiation with wavelength longer than that of X-rays but shorter than that of visible light. Ultraviolet light can break some chemical bonds and cause cell damage.

Uncertainty principle 测不准原理 Heisenberg's uncertainty principle; Heisenberg principle; indeterminancy; indeterminancy principle.

The exact momentum and exact location of a particle cannot be specified. Werner Heisenberg stated that the product of uncertainties in location and momentum measurements can never be smaller than $h/4\pi$, where h is Planck's constant.

visible light 可见光

Visible light is electromagnetic radiation with a wavelength between 400 and 750nm.

wavefunction 波函数 (Ψ)

A mathematical function that gives the amplitude of a wave as a function of position (and sometimes, as a function of time and/or electron spin). Wavefunctions are used in chemistry to represent the behavior of electrons bound in atoms or molecules.

wave [weiv] *n*. 波

An oscillating motion that moves outward from the source of some disturbance (ripples running away from a pebble tossed in a pond). Waves transmit the energy of the disturbance away from its source.

X-ray X 射线

A very high energy form of electromagnetic radiation (though not as high energy as gamma rays). X-rays typically have wavelengths from a few picometers up to 20 nanometers. X-rays easily penetrate soft tissue, which makes them useful in medical imaging and in radiation therapy.

X-ray diffraction pattern X 射线衍射图

Interference patterns created by X-rays as they pass through a solid material. Studying X-ray diffraction patterns gives detailed information on the three-dimensional structure of crystals, surfaces, and atoms.

X-ray tube X 射线管

A cathode ray tube that focuses energetic streams of electrons on a metal target, causing the metal to emit X-rays.

zero point energy zero energy 零点能

A minimum possible energy for an atom or molecule predicted by quantum mechanics. Electrons stay in motion and bonds continue to vibrate even at absolute zero because of zero point energy.

6. Other Related Chemistry

6.1 Consumer Chemistry

abrasive [ə'breisiv] *n.* 研磨剂

A very hard, brittle, heat-resistant substance that is used to grind the edges or rough surfaces of an object. boron carbide, diamond, and corundum are abrasives.

acidulant [ə'sidjulənt] *n.* 酸化剂

A substance added to food or beverages to lower pH and to impart a tart, acid taste. Phosphoric acid is an acidulant added to cola drinks.

activated charcoal ['æktiveitid] ['tʃɑːkəul] 活性炭 activated carbon; active carbon.

A porous form of carbon that acts as a powerful adsorbent, used to decolorize liquids, recover solvents, and remove toxins from water and air.

antichlor ['æntiklɔː(r)] *n.* 脱氯剂

A chemical compound that reacts with chlorine-based bleaches to stop the bleaching. Thiosulfate compounds are antichlors. A substance, such as sodium thiosulfate, used to neutralize the excess chlorine or hypochlorite left after bleaching textiles, fiber, or paper pulp.

antioxidant ['ænti'ɔksidənt] *n.* 抗氧化剂

Antioxidants are compounds that slow oxidation processes that degrade foods, fuels, rubber, plastic, and other materials. Antioxidants like butylated hydroxyanisole (BHA) are added to food to prevent fats from becoming rancid and to minimize decomposition of vitamins and essential fatty acids; they work by scavenging destructive free radicals from the food.

antiozonant ['ænti'əuzənənt] *n.* 抗臭氧剂 antiozidant.

Substances that reverse or prevent severe oxidation by ozone. Antiozonants are added to rubber to prevent them from becoming brittle as atmospheric ozone reacts with them over time. Aromatic amines are often used as antiozonants.

antipyretic ['æntipai'retik] *n.* 退热剂

A substance that can lessen or prevent fever.

bleach [bliːtʃ] *n.* 漂白剂

A dilute solution of sodium hypochlorite or calcium hypochlorite which kills bacteria and destroys colored organic materials by oxidizing them.

caffeine ['kæfiːn] *n.* 咖啡因（兴奋剂）($C_8H_{10}N_4O_2$） methyltheobromine; guaranine; 1,3,7-trimethylxanthine; 1,3,7-trimethyl-2,6-dioxopurine.

A substance found in tea, coffee, and cola that acts as a stimulant. It is extremely soluble in supercritical fluid carbon dioxide and somewhat soluble in water; aqueous solutions of caffeine quickly break down.

carbonate hardness ['kɑːbəneit] ['hɑːdnis] 碳酸盐硬度 carbonate water hardness.

Water hardness due to the presence of calcium and magnesium carbonates and bicarbonates. The "noncarbonate hardness" is due mostly to calcium and magnesium sulfates, chlorides, and nitrates.

water softening ['sɔfniŋ] 水软化 Compare with water softener and water hardness.

Removal of Ca^{2+} and Mg^{2+} from water to prevent undesirable precipitation reactions from occurring in plumbing, pools, washwater, and boilers.

water softener 水软化剂   soft water; water softening.   Compare with water hardness.

A material that lowers water hardness when dissolved in water. For example, sodium carbonate ("washing soda") softens water by precipitating Ca^{2+} ions as $CaCO_3$. Zeolites soften water by exchanging Ca^{2+} ions with Na^+ ions.

water hardness [ˈhɑːdnis] 水的硬度   hard water.

Hard water is water contaminated with compounds of calcium and magnesium. Dissolved iron, manganese, and strontium compounds can also contribute to the "total hardness" of the water, which is usually expressed as ppm $CaCO_3$. Water with a hardness over 80 ppm $CaCO_3$ is often treated with water softeners, since hard water produces scale in hot water pipes and boilers and lowers the effectiveness of detergents.

permanent hardness 永久硬度   permanent water hardness.   Compare with temporary hardness and water hardness.

Water hardness that remains after boiling the water, mainly due to dissolved calcium sulfate. Chlorides also contribute to permanent hardness.

temporary hardness 暂时硬度   temporary water hardness.

The component of total water hardness that can be removed by boiling the water. $Ca(HCO_3)_2$ and $Mg(HCO_3)_2$ are responsible for temporary.

emollient [iˈmɔliənt] n. 润肤剂，缓和剂

A substance added to a formulation that gives it softening ability. For example, oils that can soften skin are added as emollients in some skin creams.

humectant [hjuːˈmektənt] n. 湿润剂，保湿剂

A substance that absorbs or retains moisture, added to a product to keep it from drying out.

mixed glyceride [ˈglisəˌraid] 甘油复酸酯   Compare with glyceride.

A diglyceride or triglyceride that contains more than one type of fatty acid connected to glycerol via an ester linkage. Natrual oils and fats usually contain several different mixed glycerides.

glyceride [ˈglisəˌraid] n. 甘油酯，脂肪酸丙酯   monoglyceride; diglyceride; triglyceride.

Glycerides are fats and oils that are esters of glycerol with one or more fatty acids. Monoglycerides, diglycerides, and triglycerides contain one, two, and three fatty acids linked to the glycerol, respectively.

monosodium glutamate [ˈmɔnəuˈsəudjəm] [ˈgluːtəmeit] 谷氨酸单钠，味精（MSG）

MSG is monosodium glutamate, used as a flavor enhancer in many foods.

natural gas 天然气

A mixture of methane and other gases, found trapped over petroleum deposits under the earth.

propellant [prəˈpelənt] n. 推进剂

(1) A mixture of fuel and oxidizing agent that reacts to produce a high-energy stream of product gases that can produce thrust. For examples, see What makes a good rocket fuel?

(2) A compressed gas used to push a material through a nozzle, forming an aerosol or a foam. For example, nitrogen or propane are used as propellants for shaving cream; nitrous oxide is used as a propellant for whipped cream.

saturated fat [ˈsætʃəreitid] [fæt] 饱和脂肪   Compare with unsaturated fat.

A lipid that contains no carbon-carbon double bonds. Animal fats like butter and lard are composed of saturated fat. Saturated fats tend to be waxy or greasy solids.

unsaturated fat　不饱和脂肪

A lipid containing one or more carbon-carbon double bonds. Unsaturated fats tend to be oily liquids and are obtained from plants.

soap [səup] $n.$ 肥皂

A salt of a fatty acid. For example, sodium stearate is a soap made by neutralizing stearic acid. Commercial soaps are mixtures of fatty acid salts.

vitamin ['vaitəmin, 'vi-] $n.$ 维他命，维生素

A substance that is critical for proper functioning of a living organism that the organism is unable to produce in sufficient quantities for itself.

zeolite ['zi:əlait] $n.$ 沸石，与沸石类似的天然的或人工的硅酸盐

Addition compounds of the type $Na_2O \cdot Al_2O_3 \cdot nSiO_2 \cdot mH_2O$, with calcium sometimes replacing or present with the sodium. The sodium in the zeolite exchanges with calcium in water, making zeolites useful for water softening. The porous structure of zeolites also makes them effective molecular sieves used as gas adsorbents and drying agents. Artificial zeolites are used as ion exchange resins.

6.2　Environmental Chemistry

environmental chemistry　环境化学　chemical ecology.

The study of natural and man-made substances in the environment, including the detection, monitoring, transport, and chemical transformation of chemical substances in air, water, and soil.

cyanide process ['saiənaid] [prə'ses]　氰化处理

A method for separating a metal from an ore. Crushed ore is treated with cyanide ion to produce a soluble metal cyanide complex. The complex is washed out of the ore and reduced to metallic form using an active metal (usually zinc).

dissolved oxygen [di'zɔlv] ['ɔksidʒən]　溶解氧

The amount of oxygen dissolved in a solvent (usually water). Dissolved oxygen levels are used as a general indicator of water quality.

molecular sieve [məu'lekjulə] [siv]　分子筛

A material that contains many small cavities interconnected with pores of precisely uniform size. Zeolites are an example. Molecular sieves adsorb molecules that are small enough to pass through their pore systems—especially water. They are often used as drying agents, and to separate large molecules from smaller ones in preparatory work and in exclusion chromatography.

6.3　Biochemistry

chromosomes [,krəumə'səumə] $n.$ 染色体

(1) A threadlike linear strand of DNA and associated proteins in the nucleus of animal and plant cells that carries the genes and functions in the transmission of hereditary information.

(2) A circular strand of DNA in bacteria and cyanobacteria that contains the hereditary information necessary for cell life.

gene [dʒi:n] $n.$ 基因

The information unit in Deoxyribonucleic acid (DNA). A hereditary unit that occupies a specific location on a chromosome and determines a particular characteristic in an organism. Genes exist in a number of different forms and can undergo mutation.

metabolism [meˈtæbəlizəm] *n.* 新陈代谢

Metabolism is the sum of the chemical processes by which cells produce the material and energy necessary for life.

nucleotide [ˈnjuːklɪətaid] *n.* 核苷

Any of several compounds that consist of ribose or deoxyribose sugar joined to a purine or pyrimidine bare and to a phosphate group and that are basic structural units of nucleic acids.

nutrient [ˈnjuːtriənt] *n.* 营养素，养分

Nutrients are stuff such as carbohydrates, fats, proteins, and seven minerals needed every day in large amounts.

polynucleotide [ˌpɔliˈnjuːkljəˌtaid] *n.* 多（聚）核苷酸

(1) A polymeric chains of nucleotide.

(2) A polymeric compound consisting of a number of nucleotides.

(3) Any of various compounds consisting of a nucleoside combined with a phosphate group and forming the basic constituent of DNA and RNA. 核苷酸是由与磷原子团结合并形成 DNA 和 RNA 的基本成分的核苷构成的化合物。

vitamin A deficiency [diˈfiʃənsi] 维生素 A 不足

Vitamin A deficiency exists when the chronic failure to eat sufficient amounts of vitamin A or beta-carotene results in levels of bloodstream Vitamin A or that are below a defined range. Beta-carotene is a form of pre vitamin A, which is readily converted to a Vitamin A in the body.

glutamate [ˈgluːtəmeit] *n.* 谷氨酸盐

Ionic salts of glutamic acid used as flavor enhancers in many foods. Glutamate is usually manufactured by acid hydrolysis of vegetable proteins. Besides being a basic building block of proteins, glutamate functions as a neurotransmitter that helps neurons grow new connections; as such, glutamate plays an important role in learning and memory. At high concentrations, glutamate can function as an excitotoxin.

glutamate receptors [ˈgluːtəmeit] [riˈseptə] 谷氨酸受体

Glutamate receptors are protein molecules that helps gate the flow of ions across a nerve cell's membrane. They play a role in the formation of new connections between nerve cells (and so, in learning and memory). The receptors are normally activated by aspartate and glutamate. In amnesic shellfish poisoning, domoic acid acts as an excitotoxin that very strongly activates some of these receptors, preventing their proper functioning.

neurotransmitter [ˌnjuərətrænsˈmitə] *n.* 神经传递素

Neurotransmitters are molecules that are used to carry signals from one neuron to another. One neuron releases the neurotransmitter near another neuron's receptors. The neurotransmitter diffuses across the gap between the neurons and locks into a receptor site on the surface of the downstream neuron. This induces a change in the downstream neuron.

teratogen [ˈterətədʒən] *n.* 致畸剂，畸胎剂

A substance that can cause deformities in embryos. Dioxin is a teratogen.

Appendix

Appendix I IUPAC Names and Symbols of Elements

Name		Symbol	At. No.	汉语名
Actinium	[æk'tiniəm]	Ac	89	锕
Aluminum	[ə'ljuːminəm]	Al	13	铝
Americium	[ˌæmə'risjəm]	Am	95	镅
Antimony	['æntiməni]	Sb	51	锑
Argon	['ɑːgɔn]	Ar	18	氩
Arsenic	['ɑːsənik]	As	33	砷
Astatine	['æstətiːn]	At	85	砹
Barium	['bɛəriəm]	Ba	56	钡
Berkelium	['bəːkliəm]	Bk	97	锫
beryllium	[bə'riljəm]	Be	4	铍
Bismuth	['bizməθ]	Bi	83	铋
Boron	['bɔːrən]	B	5	硼
Bromine	['brəumiːn]	Br	35	溴
Cadmium	['kædmiəm]	Cd	48	镉
Calcium	['kælsiəm]	Ca	20	钙
Californium	[kæli'fɔːniəm]	Cf	98	锎
Carbon	['kɑːbən]	C	6	碳
Cerium	['siəriəm]	Ce	58	铈
Cesium	['siːzjəm]	Cs	55	铯
Chlorine	['klɔːriːn]	Cl	17	氯
Chromium	['krəumjəm]	Cr	24	铬
Cobalt	[kə'bɔːlt, 'kəubɔːlt]	Co	27	钴
Copper	['kɔpə]	Cu	29	铜
Curium	['kjuəriəm]	Cm	96	锔
Dysprosium	[dis'prəusiəm]	Dy	66	镝
Einsteinium	[ain'stainiəm]	Es	99	锿
Erbium	['əːbiəm]	Er	68	铒
Europium	[juə'rəupiəm]	Eu	63	铕

continued

Name		Symbol	At. No.	汉语名
Fermium	[ˈfəːmiəm]	Fm	100	镄
Fluorine	[ˈflu(ː)əriːn]	F	9	氟
Francium	[ˈfrænsiəm]	Fr	87	钫
Gadolinium	[ˌgædəˈliniəm]	Gd	64	钆
Gallium	[ˈgæliəm]	Ga	31	镓
Germanium	[dʒəːˈmeiniəm]	Ge	32	锗
Gold	[gəuld]	Au	79	金
Hafnium	[ˈhæfniəm]	Hf	72	铪
Helium	[ˈhiːljəm]	He	2	氦
Holmium	[ˈhɔlmiəm]	Ho	67	钬
Hydrogen	[ˈhaidrəudʒən]	H	1	氢
Indium	[ˈindiəm]	In	49	铟
Iodine	[ˈaiədiːn]	I	53	碘
Iridium	[iˈridiəm]	Ir	77	铱
Iron	[ˈaiən]	Fe	26	铁
Krypton	[ˈkriptɔn]	Kr	36	氪
Lanthanum	[ˈlænθənəm]	La	57	镧
Lawrencium	[ləːˈrensiəm, lɑː-]	Lr	103	铹
Lead	[led]	Pb	82	铅
Lithium	[ˈliθiəm]	Li	3	锂
Lutetium	[luːˈtiːʃiəm]	Lu	71	镥
Magnesium	[mægˈniːzjəm]	Mg	12	镁
Manganese	[ˈmæŋgəniːz]	Mn	25	锰
Mendelevium	[ˌmendəˈliːviəm]	Md	101	钔
Mercury	[ˈməːkjuri]	Hg	80	汞
Molybdenum	[məˈlibdinəm]	Mo	42	钼
Neodymium	[niː(ː)əˈdimiəm]	Nd	60	钕
Neon	[ˈniːən]	Ne	10	氖
Neptunium	[nepˈtjuːniəm]	Np	93	镎
Nickel	[ˈnikl]	Ni	28	镍
Niobium	[naiˈəubiəm]	Nb	41	铌
Nitrogen	[ˈnaitrədʒən]	N	7	氮
Nobelium	[nəuˈbeliəm]	No	102	锘
Osmium	[ˈɔzmiəm, -mjəm]	Os	76	锇
Oxygen	[ˈɔksidʒən]	O	8	氧
Palladium	[pəˈleidiəm]	Pd	46	钯
Phosphorus	[ˈfɔsfərəs]	P	15	磷
Platinum	[ˈplætinəm]	Pt	78	铂
Plutonium	[pluːˈtəuniəm]	Pu	94	钚
Polonium	[pəˈləuniəm]	Po	84	钋
Potassium	[pəˈtæsjəm]	K	19	钾
Praseodymium	[ˌpreiziəuˈdimiəm]	Pr	59	镨
Promethium	[prəˈmiːθiəm]	Pm	61	钷
Protactinium	[ˌprəutækˈtiniəm]	Pa	91	镤
Radium	[ˈreidjəm]	Ra	88	镭
Radon	[ˈreidɔn]	Rn	86	氡
Rhenium	[ˈriːniəm]	Re	75	铼
Rhodium	[ˈrəudiəm]	Rh	45	铑
Rubidium	[ruːˈbidiəm]	Rb	37	铷
Ruthenium	[ruːˈθiːniəm]	Ru	44	钌

continued

Name		Symbol	At. No.	汉语名
Samarium	[sə'meəriəm]	Sm	62	钐
Scandium	['kændiəm]	Sc	21	钪
Selenium	[si'li:niəm]	Se	34	硒
Silicon	['silikən]	Si	14	硅
Silver	['silvə]	Ag	47	银
Sodium	['səudjəm]	Na	11	钠
Strontium	['strɔnʃiəm]	Sr	38	锶
Sulfur	['sʌlfə]	S	16	硫
Tantalum	['tæntələm]	Ta	73	钽
Technetium	[tek'ni:ʃiəm]	Tc	43	锝
Tellurium	[te'ljuəriəm]	Te	52	碲
Terbium	['tə:biəm]	Tb	65	铽
Thallium	['θæliəm]	Tl	81	铊
Thorium	['θɔ:riəm]	Th	90	钍
Thulium	['θju:liəm]	Tm	69	铥
Tin	[tin]	Sn	50	锡
Titanium	[tai'teinjəm]	Ti	22	钛
Tungsten	['tʌŋstən]	W	74	钨
Uranium	[juə'reiniəm]	U	92	铀
Vanadium	[və'neidiəm]	V	23	钒
Xenon	['zenɔn]	Xe	54	氙
Ytterbium	[i'tə:biəm]	Yb	70	镱
Yttrium	['itriəm]	Y	39	钇
Zinc	[ziŋk]	Zn	30	锌
Zirconium	[zə:'kəuniəm]	Zr	40	锆

Appendix II Laboratory Equipments

adapter　接液管
air condenser　空气冷凝管
beaker　烧杯
boiling flask-3-neck　三颈烧瓶
burette clamp　滴定管夹
burette stand　滴定管架
burner　炉子，燃烧器，烧嘴
Busher funnel　布氏漏斗
centrifuge tube　离心试管
clamp holder　持夹器
cold trap　冷阱
condenser　冷凝管
crucible　坩埚
crucible tongs　坩埚钳
desiccator　干燥器
distilling head　蒸馏头
distilling tube　蒸馏管
Erlenmeyer flask　锥形瓶，三角烧瓶
evaporating dish　蒸发皿
extension clamp　万能夹
filter flask　吸滤瓶，过滤瓶，抽滤瓶
Florence flask　平底烧瓶
fractionating column　分馏柱
funnel　漏斗
gas measuring tube　量气筒
Geiser burette　酸式滴定管
gas-jar　集气瓶
glass filter crucible　玻璃过滤坩埚
graduated cylinder　量筒
Griffin beaker　烧杯，格里芬烧杯
ground joint　磨口接头
ground-in round flask　磨口圆底烧瓶
hair brush　毛刷
Hirsch funnel　赫氏漏斗
Iodine flask　碘量瓶
iron support　铁架台
long-stem funnel　长颈（柄）漏斗
magnetic stirrer　磁力搅拌器
medicine dropper　医用滴管
medicine spoon　药匙
Mohr burette　莫尔滴定管，碱滴定管
Mohr measuring pipette　量液管
mortar　研钵
muffle furnace　马孚炉
pestle　（捣研用的）杵，碾槌
Petri dish　培养皿
pinch clamp, pinchcock　弹簧夹
pipeclay triangle　泥三角
pipette　吸液管，移液管
plastic squeeze bottle　塑料洗瓶
reagent bottle　试剂瓶
ring clamp　铁环夹
rubber suction bulb, rubber pipette bulb　吸耳球
screw clamp　螺旋夹，螺丝钳
separatory funnel/separating funnel　分液漏斗
syringe　注射器
stemless funnel　无颈漏斗
stirring rod　搅拌棒
stopcock　水龙头，活塞
stopper　塞子
test tube holder　试管夹
three-neck flask　三口烧瓶
thistle tube　长颈漏斗
transfer pipette　移液管
tripod　三脚架
tweezer　镊子
vacuum pump　真空泵
volumetric flask　容量瓶
watch glass　表面皿
weighing bottle　称量瓶

References

[1] Shriver D. F., Atkins P. W. Inorganic Chemistry. Oxford: Oxford University Press, 1999.
[2] Solomons T. W. G., Fryhle C. B. Organic Chemistry. 8th Edition. New York: John Whiley & Sons Inc., 2004.
[3] Wade L. G. Organic Chemistry. 5th Edition. New York: Pearson Education Inc., 2003.
[4] Harris D. C. Quantitative Chemical Analysis. New York: W. H. Freeman & Co. Ltd., 2003.
[5] Holum J. R. Organic & Biological Chemistry. New York: John Whiley & Sons Inc., 1996.
[6] Ball D. W. Physical Chemistry. Boston: Thomson Learning Inc., 2003.
[7] Maizell R. E. How to Find Chemical Information. New York: John Wiley & Sons Inc,. 1979.
[8] Klabunde K. J. Nanoscale Materials in Chemistry. New York: John Wiley & Sons Inc., 2001.
[9] Robards K., Haddad P. R., Jackson P. E. Principles and Practice of Modern Chromatographic Methods. London: Academic Press Inc., 1994.
[10] Fifield F. W., Kealey D. Principle and Practice of Analytical Chemistry. 5th Edition. Blackwell Science Inc., 2000.
[11] Roussak O., Gesser H. D. Applied Chemistry—A Textbook for Engineers and Technologists. 2nd Edition. Springer US, 2013.
[12] Fahlman B. D. Materials Chemistry. Springer, Dordrecht, 2007.
[13] Mendricks L., Vanroeyen J. and Wang H. The future of pharmaceutical engineering. J. Pharm. Sci., 2004, 93: 235-238.
[14] 胡鸣等. 化学工程与工艺专业英语. 第2版. 北京: 化学工业出版社, 2000.
[15] 马永祥等. 化学专业英语. 第5版. 兰州: 兰州大学出版社, 2003.
[16] 魏高原等. 化学专业基础英语. 第7版. 北京: 北京大学出版社, 2011.
[17] 朱红军等. 应用化学专业英语教程. 第2版. 北京: 化学工业出版社, 2005.
[18] 万有志等. 应用化学专业英语. 第2版. 北京: 化学工业出版社, 2008.
[19] 荣国斌等. 化学专业英语基础. 第2版. 上海: 上海外语教育出版社, 2001.
[20] 叶永昌等. 化学英语文选和翻译技巧. 第2版. 北京: 化学工业出版社, 1985.